SMALLWOOD

FROM EILEN & KEN
CHRISTMAS 2002

Smallwood

The Unlikely Revolutionary

Richard Gwyn

Canadian Cataloguing in Publication Data

Gwyn, Richard, 1934-
    Smallwood, the unlikely revolutionary

Includes index.
ISBN 0-7710-3708-2

1. Smallwood, Joseph R., 1900-1991.   2. Newfoundland – Politics and government – 1949-   .   3. Prime ministers – Newfoundland – Biography.
I. Title.

FC2175.1.S63G89 1999   971.'04'092   C98-932936-4
F1123.S62G89 1999

We acknowledge the financial support of the Government of Canada through
the Book Publishing Industry Development Program for our publishing
activities. We further acknowledge the support of the Canada Council
for the Arts and the Ontario Arts Council for our publishing program.

Typeset in Bembo by M&S, Toronto
Printed and bound in Canada

McClelland & Stewart Inc.
The Canadian Publishers
481 University Avenue
Toronto, Ontario
M5G 2E9

1 2 3 4 5   03 02 01 00 99

Contents

Introduction

In life as in art, a clown is the most complex of characters: a buffoon who laughs to keep from crying, a political propagandist who cloaks his message with humour, a freak who has turned a physical defect into a livelihood.

Joseph Roberts Smallwood is a deadly serious clown. His natural talent for mimicry, his studied command of repartee, and his uninhibited zest for living have made him Joey, the Canadian folk hero, part rustic savant, part licensed national jester. Behind the wit, the quick passion, and the easy emotion is Joe Smallwood, the lonely visionary who has spent almost seventy years pursuing a dream: a revolution that would give his island the material and intellectual benefits the rest of North America takes for granted.

As a clown, Smallwood is in many ways typical of his race. Newfoundlanders have suffered more and for far longer than any other white people in North America. By turns sentimental and cynical, they have endured their lot by laughing at it. Their humour is antic and unselfconscious, and they have a Celtic gift for expressing it.

Smallwood the visionary is unique in Newfoundland. Although life there, at once cosy and cruel, has been a breeding ground of character, during four hundred years of recorded history the colony and province has produced few exceptional men. The struggle for survival exhausted ambition and creativity; the handful whose talent endured, such as the poet E. J. Pratt and the painter Maurice Cullen, lived their lives and made their names elsewhere. Smallwood is the exception. He chose to stay in

Newfoundland. It was there that he became an exceptional man. He is the only Newfoundlander to have done so.

Smallwood's love for Newfoundland has always been total and uncritical. For nearly thirty years in the political wilderness, he endlessly wrote and talked about Newfoundland; for more than twenty years as Premier he bluffed, bullied and cajoled his people into sharing his quixotic belief in a brighter future; in old age he has become a living museum of Newfoundland history.

For those born there, "this poor bald rock," as Smallwood once described his island, is easy to love. It is a hard land. Since the coming of the white man, one species of human beings, the Beothuk Indians, and one animal species, the Great Auks of the Funk Islands, have been wiped out. Perhaps by coincidence, the national flower is the carnivorous pitcher plant. The winters are long and fog-bound; the summers are chilly and brief.

Yet Newfoundland has a rare beauty. The rolling hills of the West Coast evoke the highlands of Scotland; the long dark clefts in the South Coast and the Northern Peninsula are as dramatic as the fjords of Scandinavia; the barren lands of the east, lightly covered with moss and sprinkled with free-standing, pink-grey boulders, are a northern mirror of the harsh, pure hills of Greece. The precious summer sun turns the sea translucent blue and aquamarine and, above the patches of kelp, to a royal purple. In winter, slate grey seas tear at slate grey rock; in spring, the hulks of icebergs bump along the shore like polar cathedrals.

The magic of this faery land forlorn, however, lies not in its landscape or its seascape, but in its people. "The best-tempered, best-mannered people walking," wrote A. P. Herbert, who fell in love with Newfoundland during a wartime visit there, "gay, good-hearted and generous; tolerant, temperate, tough, God-fearing." The novelist Paul West has called them "a community of Irish mystics cut adrift on the Atlantic." With fewer divorces, fewer suicides, and less crime than any other region of the country, Newfoundland rightly calls herself "The Happy Province."

Gentle mystics are poor politicians. Too small to attract the attention of the outside world, and too poor to be able to buy it, Newfoundland struggled alone for four centuries. It won independence at the price of bankruptcy, until failure and poverty conditioned Newfoundlanders to accept hardship as their immutable national heritage. Smallwood taught them to hope again, first by his words and later by his deeds.

Simple ambition inspired his decision to remain in Newfoundland instead of emigrating to the mainland as thousands of his countrymen have done. Only in that singular society could he, with his background and unco-ordinated array of talents, hope to rise to the top.

That pursuit of personal power and glory was given shape and substance by Smallwood's revolutionary purpose. He has expressed his purpose in different ways at different times, and always in heightened prose: "We can be one of the great small nations of the earth"; "We are going to be either a glorified poorhouse or else a self-supporting province, independent and proud"; "This is *our* land, this is *our* river, this is *our* waterfall. Newfoundland first. Quebec second. The rest of the world last."

Smallwood's ambitions for Newfoundland have been as extravagant as his ambitions for himself. This book is an attempt to describe his successes and his failures. It is a personal and political study of the author and architect of Newfoundland's union with Canada, and its Premier for nearly a quarter of a century. More than this, it is a study of a Canadian revolutionary.

Author's Note

Joseph Roberts Smallwood made this book possible by granting me his full co-operation. He was unstinting with his time and with his hospitality, and for both I am deeply grateful. He bears no responsibility for my judgments, nor had he any say in shaping them.

In the Author's Note to *The Shape of Scandal*, I wrote: "To use a phrase which is a cliché but which happens to be entirely accurate, this book could not, and would not, have been written but for my wife, Sandra." *Smallwood* also belongs to Sandra. She began as researcher and finished as editor during a final tortuous two months in which we slimmed and reshaped a sodden mass of two hundred thousand words to its present, bearable length. Not least, because she is a Newfoundlander, her insights inspired many of my own.

Because of the political nature of this book, some of those who helped me cannot be named. Most of them can. Among those whose help extended beyond a single incident or chapter, I would like to thank Edward Roberts, Albert Perlin, Dean Leslie Harris, Donald Snowden, Douglas Fullerton, and Cliff Scotton. I am indebted to Premier Smallwood and to the late Robert Winters for allowing me to quote extracts from their diaries, and to the Honourable J. W. Pickersgill who checked certain incidents for me in the diaries of Mackenzie King.

The staffs of a number of libraries made my work not only easier but a delight. I would like to thank in particular: Miss Agnes O'Dea of the Centre for Newfoundland Studies at Memorial University for her kindness, for her efficiency, and for many helpful suggestions on historical research; Erik Spicer of the Parliamentary Library, Ottawa, who placed the facilities of that institution at my disposal; the staff of the Gosling Memorial Library in St. John's, and in particular Mrs. Grace Butt, to whom Sandra and I became incessant and importunate visitors; George Baker of the Legislative Library, St. John's, for his help in transcribing unpublished *Hansards*; Mrs. V. Halpert of Memorial University, for access to unpublished "Barrelman" scripts and related material; and the staff of the Tamiment Institute Library (formerly the Rand School Library), New York, who treated us as comrades.

Among other individuals who gave me invaluable assistance, I would like to single out: Dale Thomson of the University of Montreal, for making available to me research collected for his own biography of Louis St. Laurent; Leo Moakler, St. John's, for access to his personal files of the "Barrelman" and the "Newfoundlander"; A. J. Mullowney, St. John's, for allowing me to quote from the only existing copies of speeches written by Smallwood for his 1946 campaign; and the management of CBC St. John's for permission to use transcripts of the original "Barrelman" and National Convention recordings.

At several points in the book I have given the historical background to recent and contemporary political events in Newfoundland. None of this historical detail is original. Since the amount of published material on Newfoundland history is not large and is well-known, a bibliography is unnecessary. I have quoted my sources in the text, but beyond this I acknowledge my debt to *A History of Newfoundland* (1895) by D. W. Prowse and *The Story of Newfoundland* (1959) by A. B. Perlin. For the brief biographical sketch of William Coaker, I relied heavily, and almost exclusively, since it is the only such study available, on the excellent Memorial University M.A. thesis, "Coaker and the Rise of the F.P.U.," by J. G. Feltham. By far the best sociological studies of outport Newfoundland are to be found in the series published by Memorial's Institute for Social and Economic Research.

Many circumstantial details of events described in the book were drawn, inevitably, from daily and weekly newspapers. From my experience, I would like to express two personal opinions: My disappointment with the *Toronto Star*'s policy of charging authors and researchers deliberately prohibitive rates for the privilege of access to its library of clippings; my deep concern that, for lack of funds, so many early Newfoundland newspapers, of which only single copies exist, have not as yet been microfilmed for safekeeping.

Last, but far from least, I would like to thank the Canada Council for a research grant which made my task, if not possible, then immeasurably easier.

Author's Note to the Second Edition

This second edition carries Smallwood's story forward from early 1968 to his retirement four years later. Six chapters, containing some 30,000 words, have been added. I have also corrected certain factual errors in the original text and brought several passages up to date.

Several developments since the first edition was published are of interest to contemporary history. For the first time a number of scholarly studies of Newfoundland's politics and economy have begun to appear; those upon which I have drawn include works by Parzival Copes, George Perlin, Peter Neary, Sidney Noel and Gordon Rothney.

Another development, a sad one, is that a number of individuals who played important roles in Smallwood's life have since died: Nimshi Crewe, Ewart Young, Alfred Valdmanis, Bill Keough, Robert Winters and Donald Gordon.

This edition has been produced by the same methods as the first: my sources of information have been many; my judgments are my own. The Canada Council has once again immeasurably eased my task by its generous assistance. My own Newfoundlander has been even more generous with her time and talent as researcher and editor.

For my own Newfoundlander

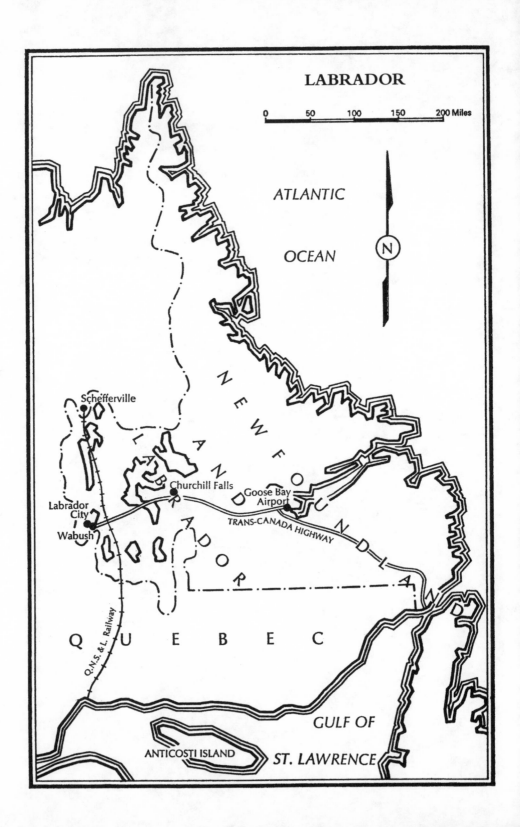

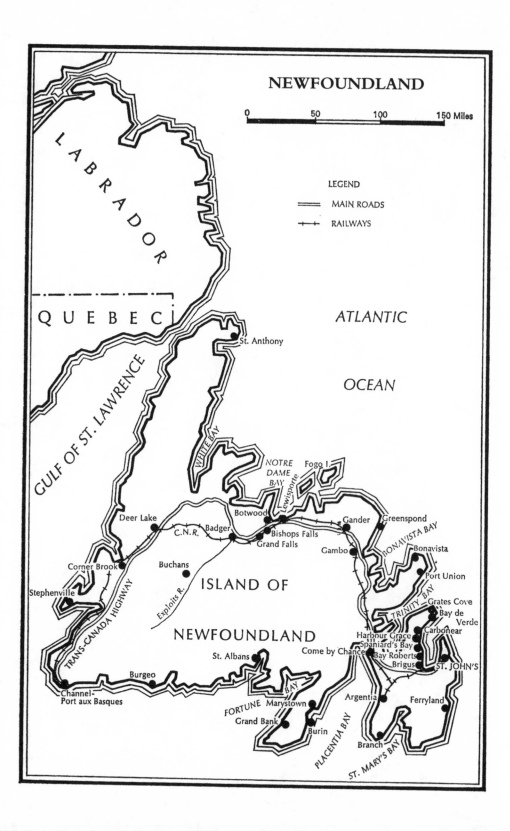

NEWFOUNDLAND

0   50   100   150 Miles

LEGEND

═══ MAIN ROADS

┼┼┼ RAILWAYS

LABRADOR

QUEBEC

GULF OF ST. LAWRENCE

ATLANTIC

OCEAN

St. Anthony

WHITE BAY

NOTRE DAME BAY

Fogo I.

Lewisporte

Deer Lake

C.N.R.

Badger

Botwood

Bishops Falls

Grand Falls

Gander

Greenspond

Gambo

BONAVISTA BAY

Bonavista

Corner Brook

Buchans

ISLAND OF

NEWFOUNDLAND

Exploits R.

Port Union

Stephenville

TRANS-CANADA HIGHWAY

TRINITY BAY

Grates Cove

Bay de Verde

Carbonear

Harbour Grace

Spaniard's Bay

Bay Roberts

Brigus

St. Albans

Come by Chance

ST. JOHN'S

Burgeo

FORTUNE BAY

Marystown

Argentia

Ferryland

Channel-
Port aux Basques

Grand Bank

Burin

PLACENTIA BAY

Branch

ST. MARY'S BAY

I

David's Grandson

Joe Smallwood's childhood was unhappy enough to give him a head start towards becoming an exceptional man. He came from that traditional source of revolutionaries, the lower middle class. And he was lucky enough to be born in Newfoundland, and not in a more ordered and affluent society which had no need of a saviour.

The first Smallwoods to come to North America left Chester in Northern England sometime in the 1770s, for reasons no longer remembered. They settled in Prince Edward Island, and David Smallwood was born there in 1838, on a small farm near Charlottetown. He was Joe's grandfather, and the only other member of the Smallwood family to make his mark on the community.

When he was fifteen, David was apprenticed to a carpenter; six years later he had learned his trade, collected a set of carpenter's tools, and was ready to make his way in the world. He sailed from Prince Edward Island for Newfoundland in 1861. The attraction was a building boom in St. John's. There was not much else to recommend the colony; after the scrubbed white paint of Charlottetown, the rickety fish flakes and randy wooden tenements of St. John's must have seemed bleak indeed.

Yet in 1861, and no less so today, the city had an uninhibited, untidy vitality not to be found within the prim Loyalist purlieus of Halifax and Saint John and Charlottetown. For St. John's was a seamen's town, snug in the lee of iron-grey cliffs, adrift with grog shops, and awash in the sweet heavy odour of dried and drying cod. More than just the capital, St. John's *was* Newfoundland; in and out the harbour narrows thronged schooners and coastal steamers, ice-scarred sealers, and sickle-shaped dories, carrying supplies for the whole island, nearly all of its produce, and at one time or another, most of its population. It was an improbable city-state of thirty thousand, ruled by bluff mercantile adventurers from Devon and Cornwall, peopled by blunt mariners from the West Country and mercurial Irishmen from Cork and Kerry and Donegal.

Landsman though he was, David Smallwood liked what he saw. He became founding father of the Newfoundland Smallwoods, and the formative influence on his grandson. From David, Joe inherited a lively and original imagination, a genius for promotion, and simple physical courage. The outstanding difference between them was Joe's single-minded ambition.

For this, Smallwood is indebted to his paternal grandmother, Julia Cooper. David met her on the day he landed in St. John's when, strolling along Water Street, the town's one shopping thoroughfare, he spotted an attractive girl behind the counter of a millinery shop. As recorded in family legend, she asked him: "What do you want, sir?" He replied, "I want you – if I can get you." And he did.

Julia's family clung to memories of quality. Her grandfather had arrived in the 1780s with an introduction to the governor, and even when he moved on to the outports he imported delicacies from England and regularly dressed for dinner. Once married, Julia Smallwood was determined to drag her husband, their twelve children, and herself back into the upper reaches of society. Since the merchants smoked cigars, so also must "Smallwood" – as she invariably addressed him. Instead, he took to a pipe, and filled it with foul-smelling tobacco. Their worst battles were about money; he viewed it with amusement, and she with the love of a miser. In the end, Julia won. With the connivance of her eldest son, she won control of the business David Smallwood had started, and he finished his days a pensioner from his own firm.

Even so, David Smallwood on his own climbed several rungs up the ladder of respectability. Within two years he became an independent contractor, and in the late 1860s he moved on to the north-east coast islet of Greenspond to set up as a "planter," or outport merchant. He quickly became one of the largest planters on his section of the coast; besides a grocery store, fish-drying and storage rooms, he owned three schooners and outfitted up to a dozen more.

David made his mark also as a man of courage. In 1869, Newfoundland was torn apart by the most dramatic issue in her history. On the mainland, that unlikely visionary, Sir John A. Macdonald, had inveigled four fractious colonies into forming a nation called Canada. Two Newfoundland delegates attended the 1864 conference in Charlottetown and returned to preach the gospel of Confederation. The patriotic response was an anti-Confederate movement that marched to the war song composed in Bonavista Bay:

Hurrah for our own native isle, Newfoundland,
No stranger shall hold one inch of her strand;
Her face turned towards Britain, her back to the gulf,
Come near at your peril, Canadian wolf.

David Smallwood came from the mainland, and to emphasize his sympathies he raised a staff in his dooryard and from it hung the Confederate banner. The next day, a mob, anti-Confederate to a man and their courage laced with rum, descended on Smallwood's house to tear down the alien flag. He met them with an axe in his hand and the mob dispersed, though its members helped to elect the three anti-Confederate candidates running in Bonavista. (Eighty years later, when David's grandson launched his own campaign for Confederation in Bonavista, he was careful not to mention that his grandfather had been there before him.)

Greensponders were quick to anger, and quicker still to forgive. Before he left, bankrupted by the "Years of Meal and Molasses" – a succession of disastrous fishing seasons named after the foodstuffs provided by the government as dole – Smallwood had become the outport's best-regarded citizen. He even survived installing in his house a Methodist preacher, as tutor to his children, although every other family on the island was Church of England. To do so took courage, for religion was the only other subject that could stir Newfoundlanders to so quick a fury as Confederation.

Back in St. John's, Smallwood branched into a new line of business and opened a boot and shoe factory with a shop attached. Inside he greeted customers, a small bright-eyed man in a tailcoat, his ornate fob watch-chain almost hidden by his flowing patriarchal beard. His principal contribution to the enterprise was his talent for advertising. Together with an itinerant Frenchman who had acquired, somewhere in mid-Atlantic, the title of Count de Courcy, he churned out doggerel for coloured cards and handbills:

> Smallwood's boots for lads and lasses,
> Smallwood's boots they suit all classes,
> Smallwood's boots they are so grand,
> They are the best in Newfoundland.

Since few fishermen could read, Smallwood hit on an even more ingenious way of catching their attention. Into the base of the cliffs at the entrance to the Narrows, he bored an iron bar which protruded twelve feet over the water and from it hung a giant black boot. Painted on both sides in luminous letters was the message: "Buy Smallwood's Boots."

As he grew older and until he died in 1928, David Smallwood spent most of his time with his grandchildren. They gathered round the kitchen fire to hear his marvellous soft voice spinning tales, of the great-great aunt who had danced the Irish jig on her 103rd birthday, of the Smallwood forbear who had never died at all, but grew older and older until at last he shrivelled up and the wind blew him away.

Among the crowd of eager, incredulous faces, none listened with more fascinated attention than young Joe. Together the old man and the boy worked in the vegetable garden or hiked across the fields. "No man influenced me more," David's grandson has said.

Indeed, it was David Smallwood who chose his grandson's Christian names. In a burst of Imperialist fervour, the old man picked, as suitable namesakes for the first child of his third son, Joseph Chamberlain, the Colonial Secretary, and Lord Roberts, Commander of the British forces in South Africa.

Joseph Roberts Smallwood was born in the small outport of Gambo. The date was Christmas Eve, 1900 – which made him exactly one year younger than the century – a handy reference point for one who, though he is gifted with an exceptional memory, has a blind spot for dates. He was in Gambo for less than six months. That, and another three years spent trying to start co-operatives in Bonavista Bay during the Depression, was all the time Joe Smallwood ever spent in the outports. The champion of the outharbour "baymen" was himself a St. John's "townie." But in St. John's, Joe was an outsider looking in at the charmed circle of name and inheritance.

The most surprising fact about Smallwood's childhood is that he was more than two years old before he spoke a word, so that his parents feared he was a deaf mute. Perhaps the most significant fact is that his immediate family were almost strangers to one another. He was close to none of his dozen brothers and sisters, which would have been unusual anywhere; but in Newfoundland, where families were invariably close-knit and affectionate, it made him an oddity from the start. As unusual was the family's lack of formal religion; although they were nominally Methodists, the Smallwoods rarely went to church. The absence of touchstones, familiar and defined, that other boys took for granted, turned Joe in towards himself. So did the rootlessness and insecurity bred by endless moving from house to house, and from school to school.

The circumstances of Joe's upbringing were established by his father.

Charles Smallwood was educated at Methodist College, the colony's equivalent to a high school, and worked for a time in the family bootstore. Like thousands of Newfoundlanders, he went to Boston to seek his fortune; like hundreds of them, he came home penniless. Back in St. John's, he used a natural aptitude for mental arithmetic to win a licence as a lumber surveyor, a job which required him to assess the quality and quantity of shiploads of rough, sawn lumber.

With his background and education, Charles Smallwood should have done better. Instead, he destroyed himself with drink. It was the curse of the colony; cheap West Indies rum imported in exchange for cheap cod, and rich and poor alike turned to it to blot out the narrowness and hardness of their lives. Careers of promise were destroyed and families destituted as inevitably as in a Victorian melodrama. To Joe, a bright and observant youngster, his father was a distant and terrifying figure, a solitary drinker who ran away from the bottle for weeks at a time and then went on savage benders that continued for days. The memories of watching his mother trying to sober up a sodden, helpless husband burned deep into the boy; for most of his life Smallwood was a rabid teetotaller and prohibitionist.

That vivid experience of trying to cope with an adult's ugly world brought Joe close to his mother, and perhaps to her alone in his life did he give total and unquestioned love. Her death in 1963 left him shaken as no other event has done.

Minnie May Smallwood was born Minnie May DeVannah, of mixed Irish and Huguenot stock, the daughter of an army sergeant from Halifax who settled in St. John's. She was a small bustling woman who possessed inexhaustible energy and a steel will, and passed both traits on to her eldest son. She bore and raised thirteen children: Joe, Marie, David, Ida, Isabel, Sadie, Charlie, Alex, Gus, Reg, Dorothy, Alice, and Maxine. They spanned an entire generation: Between Joe and Maxine there was a gap of twenty-five years to the day.[*]

---

[*] In 1972, all but one, Sadie, of Smallwood's brothers and sisters were living. Longevity is a family trait, as he liked to point out to his political opponents.

To them all, Minnie May was protector against the outside world, inflexible in her own standards of right and wrong, though she criticized only by silence. The others knew Joe was her favourite, yet she showed it with no word or gesture.

The Smallwoods were often wretchedly poor. There were weeks when fuel was short, and meals were a dreary succession of bread and potatoes and tea. Every year or so the family shifted from one small shabby wooden house to another that was smaller and shabbier, so that Joe had barely time to make friends with one set of classmates before he was faced with another. In four years he went to as many schools, all establishments where a teacher with a high-school education was a rarity.

Unchanged, this pattern would have educated him to be perhaps a stevedore. The break from the treadmill, which came when he was ten, was one of the turning points of Smallwood's life.

He went home one afternoon to electrifying news. Next term he was to go to boarding school, to Bishop Feild College, where the headmaster was a B.A. (Cantab.) and where the St. John's merchants sent their sons, or at least those sons they could not afford to send to public schools in England. Uncle Fred, now manager of the boot and shoe factory, had decided that his errant brother's eldest boy ought to have a decent education. The $37.50 a year for board and lodging, $3.00 for laundry, and 50¢ for a seat in church was a small investment in a bright lad who might work out well in the family business.

For all his delight, Joe's first days at Bishop Feild were difficult. It was odd for a "townie" to be a boarder, and his classmates wondered why. But it was hard for a ten-year-old to explain to boys whose parents had maids and fine silver and summer places at Topsail what life was like at the Charles Smallwoods. Because he was scrawny and undersized, and because of his name, the other boys nicknamed him "Splits" – the Newfoundland colloquialism for kindling. A classmate remembers: "He was different from the rest of us, a kind of nomad. I felt very sorry for him. He never had any pocket money, and tried to pretend it didn't matter." His poor grounding was another disadvantage: At the end of his first year he stood eighteenth out of nineteen in the Lower Third.

Still, Smallwood soon found his feet. The next year he was sixth out of sixteen, and by 1914 he was fifth in the Lower Fourth, had won an island-wide contest for an essay on his namesake, Lord Roberts, and was first runner-up for the Knowling Scholarship for best all-rounder. In this competition, he scored 117 out of 200 for academics, 65 out of 300 for athletics, and 45 out of 500 for character.

The poor mark for character was unsurprising: "Splits" Smallwood was already a natural enemy of authority. He became a school hero when he organized a strike against the food, lifting a campaign slogan – "More Treacle – Less Pudding" – from a British schoolboy comic book. He won his point: Subsequent Bishop Feild puddings came with larger dollops of molasses. His grandfather's enterprise was beginning to show too. Though there was no troop on the island, he wrote directly to Lord Baden-Powell asking to become a Boy Scout. The answer was yes, provided he could outfit himself with full regalia. Unhappily his scant resources only stretched to the scarf. Instead he became a bugler in the Church Lads' Brigade, the St. John's cadet corps.

Yet Smallwood never really belonged to the mock-Gothic, pseudo-public-school atmosphere of Bishop Feild where the masters, mostly itinerant Englishmen, must have found the thin, intense boy both a puzzle and a source of amusement. When he applied himself, he did well academically, but often he daydreamed, filling scribblers with the names and titles of Newfoundland Prime Ministers and then, with a flourish, adding his own: "The Rt. Hon. Sir Joseph Smallwood, K.C.G.M., P.C., M.H.A."

Like many bright but lonely children, Joe turned to books. Almost a recluse, he read on the edge of playing fields, at meals, or late at night in the dormitory, by the light of a naked bulb hidden beneath the bed-clothes, compounding a natural myopia so that he wore glasses by the time he entered his teens. He began with the British comics, *Gem* and *Magnet*, with their tales of Tom Merry and Harry Wharton, and graduated to Henty and Alger and R. M. Ballantyne, James Fenimore Cooper, and Robert Louis Stevenson.

Smallwood left Bishop Feild in the spring of 1916, when he was in the Lower Fifth (Commercial), a stream for those with no hope, financial or academic, of going on to university. Roughly equivalent to Grade Nine, this was the sum total of his formal education. He had acquired a lust for books, the bare bones of history and geography, basic arithmetic, and he could write a fair hand and a clear sentence. But the disciplines of formal logic were never to penetrate a mind already formed and set. Nor did he learn, as is the common benefit of formal education, how to compare alternatives or how to select the greys between the extremes of black and white. These deficiencies of scholastic training Smallwood has exhibited throughout his career. He has also demonstrated the advantages of a mind untrammelled by academic baggage: originality, imagination, a refusal to admit the existence of the impossible. In his own words: "I regret, of course, not having had more education, but it might have made me more a trained seal, less sure of myself. Action might have been lost in the pale cast of thought."

He left school for the most trivial of reasons, but, showing what was to become one of his principal characteristics, once his mind was made up he refused to change it. Because of a disturbance in class, he was gated – unfairly he was convinced. Rather than accept the punishment, he stalked out of class and then piled iniquity on iniquity by staying out the entire night, sleeping on a bag of wood chips in the manual-training annex. The next day he called at Uncle Fred's. Everyone agreed it was time for him to leave school. It was also obvious that he was not cut out to work in the family boot and shoe plant.

At fifteen, Joe Smallwood was on his own.

2

"The Best Job in the World"

A political adversary once taunted Smallwood: "Where were you in 1914?" The accomplished debater promptly replied: "I was four-teen."

He was lucky. Newfoundland suffered as heavily in the Great War as Britain herself. The tiny colony raised and equipped an entire regiment, and saw it all but wiped out in a single engagement at Beaumont-Hamel on July 1, 1916, the first day of the Battle of the Somme. Except that no poet recorded the slaughter of the baymen and the townies, Beaumont-Hamel rivalled Balaclava in blood, bravery, and British military stupidity. The best of a generation was buried in France, and the island left poorer for decades.

Smallwood at first was as eager as the rest of the Lower Fifth to fight for King and Country. With them he went to watch the Newfoundland Regiment drilling, and when the first contingent marched down to the troopships he marched alongside, proudly carrying the kitbag of one of his former masters. Before the war was over, he had become a convinced pacifist. Woodrow Wilson's speeches fired his innate idealism, and from there he went on to the works of Norman Angell and E. D. Morell. Later, in New York, he went regularly to hear the noted pacifist preacher, John

Haynes Holmes. In character, Joe spouted out these unconventional opinions and fiercely argued the merits of the Versailles Treaty with the editor of the ultra-jingoist *Evening Telegram*.

The war's immediate effect upon Smallwood was that, for once in Newfoundland, work was easy to find. His first job, a menial chore for a Bishop Feild boy, was as printer's devil for the weekly *Plaindealer*, at a salary of $1.50 a week. When the paper folded six months later, he moved on to another weekly, and when this too ceased publication he found work at the *Daily News*, first on the embossing machine and then in the back office as a circulation clerk.

For an energetic and imaginative youth, such work was childishly easy. It left him ample time to read, weightier works now, such as H. G. Wells's *Outline of History*, Buckley's *History of Civilization*, and earnest, turgid socialist pamphlets. He read at home, far into the night, through meals, on the streetcars, and at work. The rest of the time he talked and argued about everything under the sun: religion, politics, economics, and history. Contemporaries cannot recall seeing him without a book or, when he was not reading, with his mouth closed. Inevitably, all the knowledge poured in so haphazardly started to pour out again. He began to write.

His first published articles appeared in the *Fishermen's Advocate*, a daily put out by the Fishermen's Protective Union, a populist movement led by William Coaker, a strange rough-hewn demagogue. Under the penname "Avalond," Smallwood unreservedly embraced Coaker's cause, as in this article from the *Fishermen's Advocate* of January 18, 1918:

> The fisherman has at last come into his own — but we must not forget who put us where we are. We must not forget the man behind the gun, the super-genius, the man who directed the fishermen's efforts. The man who put the fishermen of Newfoundland where they are today is Mr. William F. Coaker. I admire him. He is a man among men. He is a noble man is Mr. Coaker and I say it expecting nothing for saying it.

Smallwood's command of the language was to broaden immeasurably over the years until he could draw upon a bottomless reservoir of analogies, synonyms, and allusions. But the two cardinal principles of his style – repetition and vigorous, direct statement – never changed.

Though Smallwood had nailed his radical colours to the *Advocate's* masthead, he was still young enough, and unsure enough, to be embarrassed by it. One day, hurrying out of the *Daily News* office, he dropped a freshly typed "Avalond" article on the floor. Before he could retrieve them, a fellow-worker snatched the pages away. Horrified, Smallwood stood waiting to have a strip torn off him, or, since the *News* was staunchly Conservative, perhaps even for the sack. Instead, and far worse, his piece was read aloud by his colleagues amid shouts of derisive laughter.

Nevertheless, he had found his *métier*. "I romanticized reporting as if it were the best job in the world," he recalls. "When I became a reporter, I was absolutely on top of the world. I just lived and breathed and ate my job."

The chance to enter the promised land came in October 1918. An advertisement "Reporter Wanted" appeared in the *Evening Telegram*, and Smallwood applied in a painstakingly handwritten letter, in which he admitted that he could do no shorthand but that he was a fast writer and an eager learner. He got the job; the pay was twelve dollars a week.

Except for silent movies at the Popular Star and the Majestic Theatres, St. John's in 1918 was untouched by the electronic age. The town was a tribal village where news travelled fastest by word of mouth. Its six dailies and innumerable weeklies existed less as mediums of communication than as propaganda sheets, and though it styled itself "The People's Paper – a live daily in a busy centre" and had the novelty of being printed on pink paper, the *Evening Telegram* was no exception. Local reporting consisted mostly of a listing of names of citizens lucky enough to be invited to tea parties and to Government House receptions, or unlucky enough to be dragged before the courts. "The Foreign Message" was relegated to a single column on an inside page where the dateline Canada appeared about as often as did Egypt. (Even so, a protest by the President of the

Women's Patriotic League of Toronto that too many of the Canadian boys overseas were marrying English girls found its way there.) Though the "Hymeneal" and "Necrology" notices were eagerly studied, most readers in search of hard news turned to the front-page advertising columns. There they could learn at a glance who was going bankrupt, who had a schooner to sell, which skippers were signing on for the seal hunt, which merchants had the newest shipments of prime, salt-beef navels and fresh oranges. In the "Help Wanted" columns, provided they could read, "good general girls with a knowledge of plain cooking" could always find a wide choice of openings, and middle-class matrons could determine which of their number had trouble keeping household help. There were constant pleas for outport teachers – at salaries up to two hundred dollars a year. For those in search of lurid detail, there was plenty to be found on the editorial page. One *Telegram* leader accused the Government "of a plot more sinister and deadly than any conspiracy ever entered into for the enslavement of a free people."

All this the seventeen-year-old Smallwood set out to change. Single-handed if need be, he would give Newfoundlanders a taste of the journalism of Hearst and Pulitzer. A contemporary remembers him as "in a class by himself. He put in sixteen hours a day without a thought. Mind you, he would also spend sixteen hours a day talking and arguing, also without a thought." His first major assignment was to cover the Armistice Day parade. To keep up with the procession Smallwood borrowed his father's horse, and trotted from one vantage point to another, a diminutive figure clutching reins, notebook, and pencil. The system worked:

> As the procession moved out of the Barrack grounds, the Church Lads' Brigade struck up "We'll Never Let the Old Flag Fall" and the spirited manner in which they played pleased everyone. . . . A soldier had a large bag of straw with the Kaiser painted on it, and as they moved on once more this was set on fire and the Kaiser was burned in effigy.

Within the year, his pay jumped to a princely eighteen dollars a week, more than enough for a contribution to the family's income and for pocket money. He haunted Sammy Garland's cavernous bookstore on Water Street, and acquired a sudden passion for music and that marvellous new invention – phonograph records.

The principal musical attraction in St. John's was Dot Vincent, a pretty dark-haired clerk in the Record Parlour of the Royal Stores, across the street from the *Evening Telegram*. She was Smallwood's first crush. To Dot, four years older, he was an odd, gentle, and engaging fellow with a pronounced weakness for addressing girls as if they were a political meeting. To Joe, Dot was "wonderfully pretty and very bright and intelligent." She was a good listener.

Smallwood's mightiest attempt to impress Dot failed by a hair's breadth. As press agent for the Majestic movie house, he conceived the idea of borrowing a recording of *I Pagliacci* from the Record Parlour and then playing it behind the screen during a silent movie of Caruso singing, or at least mouthing, the same aria. As Dot listened eagerly in the audience, Smallwood placed the needle on the disc a fraction too late, so that the Caruso on wax never caught up with the Caruso on screen.

On Joe's side, though never on Dot's, the romance was serious. One day he took courage on the wing and wrote a letter of proposal. The offer was gently declined. Soon afterwards, Dot left Newfoundland for Montreal, and later married an engineer.

It was not in Joe Smallwood to brood. He regarded self-pity or introspection, in himself or in others, as evidence of weakness. And as a balm to love lost, there was journalism. In an honour rare in that era of Newfoundland reporting, he was given by-lines and a free hand to write on almost any subject he chose. Such a mandate was all he needed. Early on the morning of June 30, 1919, he was the only reporter in town to notice that there were two ships of the Royal Navy anchored in the harbour. The presence of one ship of the Atlantic Squadron was normal; but there, in addition, large as life and unannounced, was the light cruiser *Cornwall*.

The *Cornwall* had hastened full steam from the Caribbean to execute one of the lesser-known epics of gunboat diplomacy: her dark and secret mission was to subdue the two-hundred-odd fishermen of Flat Island, a rocky speck in Bonavista Bay who were, so rumour had it, manufacturing moonshine. Thanks to Smallwood's reportorial instincts, this bizarre instance of the influence of sea power survives as a footnote to Royal Naval history.

The trouble had started a few weeks earlier, when two policemen arrived at Flat Island in search of illicit liquor, only to be chased away before they so much as set foot ashore. A second attempt by a magistrate and a squad of constables was met by a battery of sealing guns and the threat, as Smallwood wrote later, "to leave the island immediately or they would sink the boat and blow the policemen to hell." The magistrate attempted to reason with the crowd, but provoked only "curses and swears, while the women and children, lining the rocks overhead, added to the din and noise."

To quell such insurrection, the Government's only recourse was to appeal to British naval might. Smallwood guessed this, and in true Richard Harding Davis style dashed round and persuaded the Attorney General to let him go along. Within three hours of Smallwood's having seen her, the *Cornwall* slipped out of St. John's. He was aboard, disguised as the private secretary of the Inspector General of the Newfoundland Constabulary. As the cruiser turned into Bonavista Bay, the captain announced his presence in a manner calculated to impress the Flat Islanders:

At 6:55 the following morning, she went on, stopping off Grate's Point where a large iceberg of 300 feet in length and 50 feet in height was situated. The *Cornwall* was equipped with eight six-inch guns and the firing that followed was certainly the loudest ever heard by me. In all, 72 rounds were fired – hitting being 75%. One of the officer's cabins was almost completely demolished by the vibration, the door being torn from its hinges, beds, mirrors, bureaus and chairs smashed to atoms.

Still, the volleys had their effect. The landing, by a party of a hundred marines, sailors, policemen, and Smallwood, was unopposed: "A Maxim quick-firing gun, capable of firing 600 shots a minute, was mounted in the bow of the cutter with the gun team ready. The run to Flat Island was most impressive. It was very foggy and still and nobody spoke much above a whisper." The arrival, though, was something of an anti-climax. There were only women and children at the wharf. "This did not deceive the landing party, however, as it was felt that such an innocent-looking scene might easily have been a trap, and that behind the boulders and rocks lay dozens of desperate men armed with sealing guns and fowling pieces."

The men, however, proved to have been more circumspect than desperate: Most of them had left to fish on the Labrador. Only seven were captured but, Smallwood warned, "upon their return to their homes, the ringleaders will be arrested. Justice will be done – though the heavens fall."* In the course of the hunt, the fledgling revolutionary met his own reflection: "The schoolmaster of the place. He is a tall, thin man continually smoking cigarettes and bore all the marks of one who would be passionate and heedless at such a time."

To the surprise of the ship's company, for Smallwood had worn his disguise well, a full-page account of the sortie appeared on July 7. Next day the *Evening Telegram* reported proudly: "600 copies of the *Evening Telegram* were bought yesterday by officers and marines of H.M.S. *Cornwall.*"

Earlier that summer, the *Evening Telegram's* star correspondent had sold hundreds more extra copies of the paper by being streets ahead of his rivals in covering the most exciting news story to take place in Newfoundland – the first attempt to fly a heavier-than-air machine across the Atlantic. It was the most important story Smallwood covered in his career as a reporter and, until Lindbergh, it was the biggest bonanza in aviation journalism.

The war to end all wars was over, and the young men of the Royal Flying Corps and the Royal Naval Air Service were searching for new worlds to

---

* All the *Cornwall's* captives were subsequently acquitted.

conquer. By happy coincidence, Lord Northcliffe's *Daily Mail* was searching for extra circulation, and so renewed its offer, first made in 1913, of a ten-thousand-pound prize for the first flight between North America and Britain. Ten teams entered the race; four of them made it to Newfoundland. The island was a natural jumping-off spot, since prevailing winds blew from west to east, and Ireland was only 1,890 miles away.

Yet Newfoundlanders, by and large, were far less stirred by the news than were the *Daily Mail's* subscribers. Their lives were ruled by nature and not by technology. Since they had never seen a plane, they had no touchstones by which to judge the daring and ingenuity required to fly a frail and gawky machine across a limitless ocean. But Joe Smallwood was as excited as Northcliffe himself: "To be first across the Atlantic," he wrote, "will place the aviator's name alongside those of Columbus, Peary, and Scott." Again on March 22, 1919, he tried to communicate his extravagant enthusiasm: "The men who have given England her supremacy on the Western Front will not be found wanting in the exceptional genius, courage, and organizing abilities requisite for this venture."

The first plane to arrive came by sea at the end of the month "in two crated parts, of iron-bound flatcar boxes." She was the *Atlantic*, a two-seater Sopwith. The pilot was Harry Hawker, a slim handsome Australian with a flashing smile and the navigator was Lieutenant Commander Mackenzie-Grieve, a doughty Scottish sailor. Within a fortnight, competition appeared in the form of the *Martynside*, a tiny two-seater, manned by Captain Frederick Raynham and Major C. W. F. Morgan, which arrived aboard the Furness Withy steamer, S.S. *Sachem*, to be met on the jetty by Smallwood, armed with a box camera as well as his notebook.

For many Newfoundlanders, the two planes were two too many. One angry farmer protested in a letter to the *Evening Telegram*: "These infernal machines buzzing around are preventing my hens from laying." On the opposite page, Smallwood's accounts of the test flights were more lyrical: "It was a beautiful rise, even more graceful than that of a bird. The noise of the engine – sounding like 500 brass drums going full blast – could be clearly heard by the people gazing skywards."

Day after day the four aviators groomed their machines and put them through their paces, waiting through the gloomy Newfoundland spring for reports of favourable weather over the Atlantic. As April turned into May, even Smallwood became depressed at "the apparent enmity of the weather god to the Birdmen."

By now more birdmen were arriving, and of a different breed. On May 6, the United States Fleet sailed into the tiny southern shore outport of Trepassey and there disgorged thousands of sailors to set up machine shops, hangars, wireless and meteorological stations. Waiting to greet them was Smallwood. As he cabled St. John's, the Americans found the hamlet something less than an ideal liberty port: "The one and only shop was besieged and raided, and every stick of gum, every cigarette, and every drink that was in the place was absorbed." The planes arrived a few days later: four Navy-Curtis, five-seater amphibians known as "Nancies."

Far from foreshadowing the flight of the Lone Eagle, the United States's approach to the challenge of 1919 was a harbinger of the Teutonic thoroughness by which the United States four decades later sent capsules into space. Instead of blazing a lonely trail across the sky, the "Nancies" were to be nursed to the Azores, and then on to Lisbon, by twenty American warships stationed along the route. The *New York Times* deplored the lackadaisical approach of the British "on the principle that a British airman is always ready to do or die – an unnecessarily fatuous point of view." In reply, the general manager of the Handley-Page Company snapped that the American attempt did not count anyway since they were using seaplanes "which can always come down in the sea and hop their way across."

Hell or high wind, the Britishers were determined now to take off as soon as they could. Unhappily for Smallwood, they did it on a day when he was in Trepassey. On the afternoon of May 18, Hawker and Grieve's *Atlantic* bounced down a bumpy runway and vanished eastward. By dawn she was halfway across. The engine, though, was dangerously overheated, and the team could go no farther. After two hours of anxious flying over the shipping lanes, they spotted the Danish freighter *Mary* and brought their plane down alongside. When their rescue was made known a week later, Hawker and Grieve became public heroes: Each was awarded the Air Force Cross and a £2,500 consolation prize from the *Daily Mail*.

Their rivals, Raynham and Morgan, never left Newfoundland. Two hours after the *Atlantic* took off, they rushed the *Martynside* into the air. She rose thirty feet, was caught by a sudden cross-current, and smashed down onto the rocky field.

Determined not to miss any more of the action, Smallwood was back in St. John's in time to cover the two new entrants. Both were more substantial ventures. Two former R.N.A.S. officers, Captain Jack Alcock, the pilot, and Lieutenant Arthur Whitten "Teddy" Brown, the navigator, brought with them a modified Vickers *Vimy* bomber. As Smallwood reported: "They set up near St. John's on a large, moderately level field at the Ropewalk near Lester's Field [which] has been rented from Mr. Charles Lester. Some thirty men have set to rolling and otherwise preparing it."

Grander still was the huge Handley-Page brought out by Vice Admiral Mark Kerr. For once, words failed even Smallwood. "It is simply wonderful," he wrote of the sixty-three-foot-long plane, which had originally been designed to bomb Berlin. For his base, Admiral Kerr chose Harbour Grace on the far side of Conception Bay, sixty miles from St. John's.

Smallwood now had to decide which team to follow. Of the two, the Handley-Page looked by far the more promising. Early in June he set off for Harbour Grace to find "a busy scene with twelve mechanics working a full seven days a week getting the big plane ready for the trans-Atlantic flight." On June 10, he hurried back to St. John's to cover Alcock and Brown who had just made their first trial flight: "It is exceedingly likely," he wrote, "they will make the hop off without any previous announcement." That risk he had to accept. He returned to Harbour Grace to cover the favourite. "On getting out of the machine, the aviators posed for a cinematograph picture. They were very courteous to your correspondent to whom Admiral Kerr stated that the trip was highly successful and entirely satisfactory." Thanks to Smallwood, the fame of the Handley-Page had spread so far that "a young lady from Bell Island made application for a position on the flying staff, offering her services to do washing and scrubbing."

The days ticked by until, on June 14, watching a team of engineers feverishly overhauling the Handley-Page, Smallwood heard the news he dreaded: Alcock and Brown had taken off. The next day, sixteen hours and twenty-eight minutes later, after surviving a lightning storm and severe icing, the *Vimy* landed in an Irish bog.

For Alcock and Brown, the triumph meant knighthoods and the *Daily Mail* prize. For Joe Smallwood, it was an unlucky roll of journalism's dice. He was resilient enough to find consolation in other topics. Two days later, he wrote of his hero, Admiral Kerr: "He is a brilliant conversationalist, being conversant with all the great questions of the day, and is particularly fond of discussing the labour problem."

With the main prize won, Kerr attempted a flight to Long Island and then across to England, non-stop. He made it as far as Parrsboro, Nova Scotia, where he crash-landed, and abandoned the attempt. Of the four "Nancies," only one eventually reached Lisbon.

After such drama, the daily routine of small-town reporting began to pall. For Smallwood to get ahead, he would have to go away, like thousands of other Newfoundlanders. For Smallwood though, the journey would not be forever. As he recalls: "I left about two years too late for that. I had stayed long enough to get interested in Newfoundland and in Newfoundland politics. I carried a torch for Newfoundland." Everywhere he went, Smallwood took with him as a talisman an oilcloth schoolroom map of the island.

Though his goal was New York, he made his way south by short jumps. The first was to Halifax, where he won a job on the *Herald*. In his letter of application, he wrote: "My object in leaving Newfoundland is purely to receive a REAL newspaper training . . . I am a hard worker (this sounds like a matrimonial advertisement) and am, if anything, a little TOO enthusiastic." While there, Smallwood discovered his talent as an interviewer. Though he was a poor judge of character and had little finesse, even hard-fisted Bluenose businessmen were charmed by his naïve inquisitiveness, and his total unself-consciousness in asking for them won him interviews others missed.

From Halifax, Smallwood went to Boston to work on the *Sunday Herald*. Two months later, in October 1920, he took down his map of Newfoundland from the wall of his boarding house room just off Scollay Square in Boston. In his pocket was a ticket for New York.

3

The Call and the Cause

Joe Smallwood arrived in New York in October 1920, one among thousands of impatient young men who had fled the shibboleths of Main Street to seek fame and fortune in Manhattan. Most of them, as they got off the train at Grand Central, dreamed of supping at the Plaza with the god Fitzgerald, or of burning the candle at both ends in Greenwich Village with the goddess Millay. Since he had never heard of either of them, and since anyway he was never a conformist, Smallwood followed a different star. For four years he worshipped at the unfashionable altars of socialism and left-wing journalism, a pilgrimage so important to him that half a century later he can recall it in almost photographic detail. Only once again in his life, when he was fighting the climactic battle of Confederation, would he be as fulfilled and as totally contented as he was in New York. And it was in New York that he learned the skills that won him Confederation.

He looked in those days like the nineteen-year-old fledgling revolutionary he was. With the advance of years and the appurtenances of statesmanship, Smallwood has come to have the mien of a thoughtful but aggressive owl; when he was in his twenties, and for a good many years afterwards, he resembled an inquisitive but aggressive grasshopper. He was small, five foot six, and thin to the point of emaciation. (Though he once attempted to gain weight by drinking 120 bottles of Pabst Blue Ribbon yeast beer at the rate of one a day, the experiment left him as gaunt as ever.) Save for a nose which, while eloquently curved, was too large, he was good-looking, with dark brown hair parted on the side, a firm chin, and startlingly blue eyes which peered out through thick, horn-rimmed glasses. He owned a single suit of dark brown Harris tweed with a Norfolk jacket and trousers which hung in limp heavy folds, and he wore it summer and winter, weekday and weekend. He was desperately poor, and never noticed it except when there was not enough in his wallet to buy books or to pay the admission fees for socialist lectures.

He lived amid a crowd of fellow Newfoundlanders and young Scottish immigrants in a dingy but spartanly tidy boarding house on West Fifteenth Street, a block or so off Fifth Avenue, and five minutes walk from Union Square, the nerve centre of New York socialism, where Eugene Debs and Morris Hillquit and Norman Thomas came to sketch the golden vision, and garment-workers and waiters and plasterers and shopgirls, some of whom barely spoke English and all of whom worked more than sixty hours a week, gathered to hear them. Though they have gone long ago, their corner of Manhattan has changed little in fifty years; it remains a gloomy limbo of narrow streets shadowed by warehouses and grimy office buildings, suspended between the raucous caverns of Greenwich Village and the glamorous reaches of upper Fifth Avenue.

For Smallwood, it was Mecca. Though he had come to New York to better himself as a journalist, within a year what had once seemed "the best job in the world" had become little more than a convenient means of earning enough money to eat. Instead, he found a new cause on which to focus all his buoyant idealism. Convinced that socialism could cure the misery and poverty of Newfoundland, he embraced it with the uncritical passion of a convert.

He had first seen the light of the left four years before he came to New York. In a dentist's waiting room in St. John's, he fell talking with a fellow patient, George Grimes, a member of the Newfoundland House of Assembly, who told the talkative fifteen-year-old that he was a Socialist. Not to be outdone, Joe brashly announced that he was a Socialist too. Pressed to define his terms, however, he could think of nothing to say except that socialism meant doing good. Grimes set out to educate his young disciple, and the next day gave Smallwood two books, which soon became the most dog-eared in his little library. Each in its day was a landmark of protest literature.

What's So and What Isn't, by John M. Work, was an American publication, and pocket-sized, so that it could fit into a working man's overalls. It read like a question-and-answer catechism: "Who corrupted the Senate? The Capitalists. Who fixes Congressmen? The Capitalists. Who purchased the Illinois State Legislature? The Capitalists. Who bought the St. Louis aldermen? The Capitalists." The conclusion to be drawn from this was, "Capitalism is essentially anarchic. Socialism is not anarchy. The Capitalist system is planless, chaotic, and anarchic. Remove capitalism, and presto, the anarchists are gone." Then, in a peroration guaranteed to send a romantic teenager to the barricades: "A Socialist is a man of destiny. He is the only man who has read the signs of the time. He is therefore invulnerable. He draws his shining lance and challenges the champions of every other economic thought to meet him in the arena of debate. And they slink away like whipped curs."

From this Smallwood progressed to that epic of socialist propaganda, Robert Blatchford's *Merrie England, or a Plain Exposition of Socialism*, which won for Blatchford the title "The People's Plato." His argument was developed by means of taut dialectical analogies: "If 100 men had 100 loaves of bread, and if they piled them in a heap and fought for them so that some got more than they could eat, and some starved, and if some were trampled to death in the brutal struggle, that would be capitalism." Blatchford also knew how to rouse his reader's blood: "On the one side are ranged all the sages, all the saints, all the martyrs, all the noble manhood and womanhood of this world. On the other side are the tyrants, the robbers, the man-slayers, the libertines, the usurers, the slave-drivers, the drunkards, and the sweaters. Choose your party then my friend and let us to the fighting." To the young Smallwood there could be no choice at all.

"These books influenced me supremely, in my beliefs and in my style of life," he recalls. Closer to home, he was influenced decisively by William Ford Coaker, a man who in many ways was his direct forerunner. Until Smallwood came along, Coaker was the only populist leader Newfoundland had produced. Perhaps Coaker in truth is still the only one, for, unlike the middle-class townie Smallwood, he was a true man of the people. Coaker's failure is a tragedy of North American populism unknown outside Newfoundland, yet the reasons for his failure go far towards explaining the intractable problems Smallwood faced when, forty years later, he set out to fulfil Coaker's mission and which, indeed, he has not yet fully solved.

When Smallwood began his newspaper career in St. John's, Coaker was in his forties and at the height of his power – a strange magnetic individual, strong as an ox, with a great mane of ginger hair and a face that might have been carved from granite. He had spent most of his youth as a recluse, farming on a small northern islet in Notre Dame Bay, where, with the help of socialist pamphlets brought by schooner from St. John's, he sought, as he later wrote, "the answer for the toiler's life and its hardships while so many live lives of ease and luxury." Coaker's solution was an elementary form of co-operative, based on the experiment of the Rochdale pioneers, which he called the Fishermen's Protective Union. In November 1908, he strode into the tiny outport of Herring Neck to launch the movement. Clustered round the fishing flakes, his audience listened as they had never listened before, for, as Smallwood later described it, Coaker's rhetoric "was a thing of elemental power and passion. It stirred those phlegmatic fishermen as they had never been stirred before, even at revival meetings. In every sentence, there was the tang of the sea, the pungent flavour of fish. . . . It was hammer, hit, pound. The aroused discontent and indignation of thousands of fishermen poured from his lips."

The prophet, it seemed, had come. Within two years, Coaker's movement swept the island, except for the merchant stronghold of St. John's and the east coast Catholic districts where clerical conservatism proved more powerful than material populism.

With his Fishermen's Protective Union, Coaker aimed at nothing less than a transformation of the Newfoundland economy, which since earliest times had been founded on the semi-feudal credit or "truck" system. Instead of receiving cash for his catch, each fisherman lived on credit. He depended on a local merchant to supply him through the winter with flour, molasses, and tea, and to outfit him for the fishing season. These debts he paid off with the summer's harvest of fish. Because he could never square his account, the fisherman was bound in virtual serfdom to the local merchant, who constituted the only market for his produce and the only source for the necessities of his life. In turn, each outport merchant was bound to one of the dozen or so big trading houses of St. John's. Only the St. John's merchants, who actually sold the fish for cash in the export markets, possessed bargaining power. "The merchant is really no merchant here," observed Lieutenant-Colonel R. B. McCrear after his stay in the St. John's garrison in 1862. "He is simply a great commercial gambler. He must charge awful profits to remunerate himself against awful risks. Accordingly, while he sells a barrel of flour to the cash-customer (when he gets one) for 30s, he books it to the fisherman (who may or may not pay him) for £3.10s."

The system was not without merit. In an industry where six months or more elapsed between the time the fish was caught and salted and the time it was actually sold, some form of credit was essential. It was true as well that the small outport merchants – like Smallwood's own grandfather – lived among their clients, knew them as individuals, and could be counted on to carry them through a bad season. Nevertheless, the credit system sapped individual initiative and enterprise. As the historian A. H. McLintock wrote: It "enslaves its victims and makes them love their chains." As indentured peasants, Newfoundland fishermen were bred to accept their position at the bottom rung of society; since they could never accumulate the savings to better their lot, they did not try, and created instead a fiercely egalitarian society in which no man was better than his fellows, nor dared aspire to be.

All this Coaker hoped to change. His co-operatives would put cash in the fishermen's pockets; instead of serfdom he offered them dignity. Codfishing, he told them, was the honourable trade of free men. His union members wore distinctive dark-blue Guernsey pullovers and an enamelled blue and gold badge bearing the emblem of a codfish as a mark of honour. Through the outports his supporters marched with banners and flags, and sang, with the uninhibited poetry of a people who lived by the word:

> We are coming, Mr. Coaker, men from Green Bay's rocky shore,
> Men who stand the snow-white billows down on stormy Labrador.
> They are ready and awaiting, strong and solid, firm and bold,
> To be led by you like Moses led the Israelites of old.
> They are ready for to sever from the merchants servile throng.
> We are coming, Mr. Coaker, and we're forty thousand strong.

This was the battle hymn of the baymen. Though Coaker would fail them, and break their hearts, there are even today old men on the northeast coast who remember his magic, who recall the idol, and not the feet of clay.

At first, all went well enough. Coaker's Union opened a wholesale company in St. John's to market members' fish overseas and, for the first time in history, forty retail stores appeared in the outports. For his own headquarters, Coaker built a new model town, Port Union, and installed the island's first system of rural electricity. To speed the pace of progress, he turned the Union into a political party, and in 1913 eight of its nine candidates won office, himself as leader. For that election, which took place six years before Mackenzie King published *Industry and Humanity* and launched Canada on its elliptical slide towards a welfare state, Coaker drew up a platform which promised minimum wage laws and pensions at seventy. In the Assembly, the Coakerite members wore the heavy clothes and thick accents of baymen. They set earnestly to work, dug out evidence of government corruption, and proposed a stream of legislation to improve the lot, not only of fishermen, but of sealers, loggers, and stevedores.

Through the Great War, when Smallwood first began to haunt the legislative chamber to hang on his hero's words, and as "Avalond" eulogized him in the Union's organ, *The Fishermen's Advocate*, the Coakerites wielded real power. Even then, however, the movement's fatal flaw was evident. One contemporary politician noted that, after their maiden speeches, the Union members "lapsed into an abject dependence on Coaker." The truth was that while Coaker offered the fishermen democracy, they, in return, demanded dictatorship. Whatever he proposed at Union meetings was resolutely accepted; in the outports he was treated as a god, and when he arrived rugs bearing the message "Sink or Swim with Coaker" were placed in his path. As J. G. Feltham has written: "The fishermen were offered the opportunity to express their wishes, but centuries of economic peonage and political subservience had made them incapable of taking advantage of it."

Increasingly disillusioned, Coaker drew apart from his followers. "The country knows little," he later wrote sadly, "of the methods practised by unprincipled men to lead clean men into pitfalls and political corruption." He was beguiled into the charmed circle of St. John's society, given a knighthood, and shown how to earn himself a fortune, by turning the Union's cash stores into credit outlets.

By the 1930s, Coaker had become the largest creditor in Newfoundland. He defrauded his own companies openly and spent most of his time on a newly acquired estate in Jamaica. Shortly before his death in 1938, Coaker left a last bitter legacy to maritime Newfoundland – his blessing to the credit system he had once tried to overthrow: "Never take it [cod] if you have to pay cash for it."

Many Newfoundland politicians have been as corrupt; Coaker alone corrupted the trust of the people. Largely because of him co-operatives have repeatedly failed in the island, and when during the 1930s Smallwood tried to establish them on the northeast coast, Coaker, with a wisdom born of cynicism, commented: "He'll talk and he'll talk, and he'll

work and he'll work – but he'll never get a cent of dues out of them."
Coaker was right. Trust given and violated would not be given again in
the outports until Smallwood, in the late 1940s, found another way to
reach the baymen.

"On every occasion when I heard him," Smallwood wrote in *Coaker
of Newfoundland*, a brief and uncritical but moving biography of his hero,
"tears welled in my eyes and little shivers went down my back." Though
for many years he was an impressionable seeker of idols to emulate, no
subsequent hero ever replaced Coaker in Smallwood's affections. And in
the 1920s, as far as Smallwood was concerned, Coaker could do no
wrong. He returned home often during his New York years to report
Union conventions for the local papers. He wrote of a meeting in
December 1921: "Here was a little kingdom within the borders of
Newfoundland. Here before my eyes was a Parliament of fishermen." All
the time he was in New York, he trained himself to be a missionary for
Coaker, and regaled everyone who would listen with tales of his idol.
When New York friends questioned him about his future, he would say:
"It depends on what Coaker wants me to do."

Confident that Coaker would approve, on the day after he arrived in
New York, Smallwood marched down to West Fourth Street unannounced and found himself a job on the New York *Call*, the city's only
English-language socialist daily. It was a paper with considerable *élan*. The
John Reed of *Ten Days That Shook the World* – already a Smallwood hero
– had worked there; so had Dorothy Day who recalled in *The Long
Loneliness*: "Our function as journalists seemed to be to build up a
tremendous indictment against the present system, a daily tale of horror
which would have a cumulative effect of forcing the workers to rise in
revolution." Suitably alarmed by this philosophy, at the height of the
Great Red Scare on May Day 1919, a mob of veterans made a wild foray
into the offices, burnt all the literature they could find, and sent seven staff
members to the hospital.

By the time Smallwood arrived, the *Call*'s days of glory were over.

Between them, the Red Scare and the rise of Communism which split the left had winnowed its subscribers down from a wartime peak of close to a million to some thirty thousand. Yet it was still intellectually lively, and to a nineteen-year-old from a faraway colony, its staff seemed the most fascinating men in the world. Charles Erwin, the Executive Editor, solemnly addressed everyone as "Comrade"; Harry Rachmill, a Talmudic scholar who was head of the copy desk, gave his orders in sing-song verse. Before long, Smallwood had made friends with the reporters closest to his own age, a floating group of young intellectuals each certain the *Call* would produce in him another John Reed. Among them were Eddie Levinson, later Labour Editor of the New York *Post*; Philip Hochstein, who became an Executive Editor of Newhouse Publications; and Richard Rohman, a promising playwright who had already realized every American reporter's dream by working for a year on the Paris *Herald-Tribune*.

The group treated the *Call*'s shabby loft building as a second home. Amid the clatter of typewriters there was good talk and arguments about everything under the sun. Nights when they were not working, the crowd lingered at cheap eating places: The Three Steps Down cafeteria in Greenwich Village; the Russian Bear Tearoom; the Fourteenth Street Automat where they carried in their own sandwiches, bought a five-cent cup of coffee, and carried it up to the second floor balcony; and, when they were flush, at the Cafe Royal, close by the Yiddish Art Theatre and a hangout for Bohemian actors, writers, and painters. Friday was payday, and they celebrated by leaving the office at six to head for Child's Restaurant on Twelfth Street, where accompanied by wives and sweethearts they splurged on a full, four-course meal, for sixty-five cents.

Smallwood was accepted by these young Jewish intellectuals almost as a mascot, an eager young squirrel of a boy with a completely different set of references from their own. "He was not as speculative as some of us were, and terribly earnest and factual," one member of the group recalls. "On the one hand, he was rather quiet and retiring, and when art and literature were being discussed he hardly spoke at all. But when he got warmed up and started off about Newfoundland and Coaker, he could be quite aggressive."

Under their tutelage, Smallwood's interests broadened. Though he was never in any sense swept away by the city's artistic and intellectual ferment, he came to enjoy going to the theatre, and told a friend that *Rain* "was the finest play I have ever seen." Occasionally, he reviewed for the *Call* plays his more cultured colleagues spurned. Of a musical revue called *Moonlight*, he wrote: "We could appreciate, perhaps, more than the average reviewer, the humour of the union electrician who was continually about to deliver a speech or a lecture even while lovemaking because he had been delivering them at union meetings and had got into the habit. We have been that way ourselves." He met Ernest Shipman, producer of the epic *Cameron of the Royal Mounted*, and tried to promote the idea of a film on Newfoundland, "to smash down that miserable old misconception of Newfoundland as ice, fog, and Eskimo," as he reported to the St. John's *Star* in July 1922.

For all his veneer of sophistication, he remained as much a raw colonial as ever, agog at the flappers with their short skirts, rouged knees, and bobbed hair. "The girls in New York are perhaps the most interesting sight of all," he wrote home to the St. John's *Star*. "They have borrowed the Chinese ladies' custom of binding the feet – so that just about the same amount of the foot forward of the heel as the heel itself touches the ground. This gives them the appearance of a hen on a hot stove."

As a reporter, however, he took New York in his stride. Anyone who could talk his way aboard a British man-of-war had little to learn from New Yorkers about initiative. "Had he stayed, he could have done well in New York," one colleague remembers. Besides enterprise, he possessed boundless energy, insatiable curiosity, and a vigorous style. What he lacked, conspicuously, was any vestige of discipline, nor much concern for the facts – other than those that proved the point he wanted to make. All his qualities and deficiencies are evident in the first major story he wrote for the *Call*, which appeared on its front page on November 9, 1920, under the headline, "VANDERLIP'S AESTHETICS EVICTS WHOLE TOWNSHIP."

The day before, on the basis of a brief note in the papers, he had journeyed thirty miles upstate to call at the country mansion of Frank A. Vanderlip, "late President of the National City Bank, great financier and millionaire." By the simple expedient of banging on the front door, he

won himself an interview. As Smallwood saw the story, Vanderlip, determined to turn his estate into a latter-day Sans Souci, was evicting scores
of "horny-handed sons of toil" who lived in the nearby village of "poor
innocent harmless little Sparta," and demolishing their houses which,
according to Smallwood, spoiled the banker's view and offended his aes-
thetic sensibilities. Though Vanderlip was in fact replacing the toilers'
houses with new ones, Smallwood nonetheless reported the villagers as
outraged. However, he quoted none by name.

Unsurprisingly, Vanderlip interpreted events somewhat differently.
"My motives were the kindliest," he said, "I wanted to improve and beau-
tify the village and make it harmonize with the rest of the country." When
Smallwood asked if he intended to return the village to its original inhab-
itants once the improvements were completed, "Mr. Vanderlip appeared
not to understand the suggestion."

Most of Smallwood's early reporting for the *Call* was more routine. All
through October, while the Presidential campaign was at its height, he
covered socialist rallies and recounted an uninterrupted string of successes
under such headlines as "HUGE CROWDS HEAR STEADMAN. SOCIALISM
GROWING." On November 4, Warren Harding was elected and normalcy
returned to America; the Socialist Party polled fewer than one million
votes. Smallwood found consolation with his major political story – he
covered the first speech by Big Bill Haywood, Secretary of the I.W.W.
"Wobblies," after his release from jail. Haywood seemed most concerned
with getting the Socialist Party leader, Eugene Victor Debs, out of Atlanta
Penitentiary where he had languished since 1917, on account of his
wartime pacifism:

> "My greatest desire is to see the doors of the penitentiary open,"
> Haywood told the cheering workers present at the meeting, "and
> release Gene Debs a free man.
>
> "Jail is no place for any human being and it is certainly no place for
> such men as the government is now committing to the penitentiary."

He continued, "If I were not a political prisoner myself I should like to go out to the workers and urge that 10,000,000 men and women lay down their tools and refuse to do a stitch of work till Debs is freed," he declared.

Cheers and shouts filled the auditorium when Haywood declared, "If the workers really love Debs, they will set him free." Many of the audience were moved to tears by his description of the cruel and systematic tortures of political prisoners, and the anguish which resulted in insanity and suicide of many.

"And this is free America," he shouted.

Two days later, Haywood chose his own version of freedom. He slipped aboard a freighter and made his way to Russia to live his life in exile. As one of the last Western journalists to see the Wobbly leader alive, Smallwood, when he was in Moscow in April 1965 with former Vice President Richard Nixon, asked their guide to show them the plaque in the Kremlin Wall marking Haywood's burial place.

Yet for Smallwood journalism soon became a time-wasting drudgery that stood in the way of what had by now become his absorbing passion – the pursuit of knowledge. From 1921 to 1924, he turned himself into a college of one. He haunted the New York Public Library, filling notebooks with scribbled research for a projected book on the great liberal leaders, Mazzini, Garibaldi, Cavour, and Kossuth; he joined a West Side local of the Socialist Party and the Civic Club, a debating society that counted Lincoln Steffens among its members. He went to countless orgies of open-air oratory, and listened to Socialists, Communists, Wobblies, anarchists, atheists, one-worlders, and single-taxers.

He turned also to religion, though out of oratorical rather than spiritual need. Each week, for a year, he bought a copy of the Sunday *New York Times*, studied the double-page spread of church advertisements, and selected a service to attend. He judged the quality of the faith by the quality of the preacher and sat in innumerable churches, halls, chapels, and synagogues, listening to endless variations on the Christian theme, with side excursions to Judaism and Islam.

By way of more formal education, Smallwood enrolled in the Rand School of Social Science on East Fifteenth Street, a few blocks away from his boarding house. This institution had been founded in 1906 "to offer to the general public facilities for studying the principles, purposes, methods, and problems of Socialism."

Inside its dingy, redbrick walls, in classrooms which had once housed a Y.W.C.A. for genteel young ladies, Smallwood heard Norman Thomas discuss "Social Forces after the War," listened rapt as August Claessens outlined "The gathering and arrangement of material, verification of the facts and weighing of arguments and the psychology of persuasive speaking," and absorbed Will Durant's lectures on "Types of Philosophy," later published as *The Story of Philosophy*.

Of the School's fifteen hundred students, about half were trade unionists, and the rest radicals of every stripe. They were serious and dedicated. In the library, which housed one of the largest collections of protest literature in the world, they shivered in overcoats and mittens because the School, perennially short of funds, was behind in its payments of the fuel bill. In the evenings, they gathered in the basement Rendezvous Cafeteria which billed itself as "A Centre for Radicals, Liberals, and Those Who Enjoy Good Eating." (Smallwood went there often for coffee, but seldom for a meal since, because the School paid union wages, the prices were too high.) A staff member remembers him "as a sort of nightowl. He struck me as a pragmatic sort of socialist – not a theoretical one. He loved politics." To another, "He was not interested in socialism as an end in itself, but as something that might be good for Newfoundland."

When he was not at the Rand School, or at the Public Library, or at open-air meetings, or in church, Smallwood went to lectures at the Labour Temple on Fourteenth Street or at the Cooper Union Institute. Somehow he found time also to fall in love.

In May 1923, Smallwood went with a group of Rand School students on an outing to the New Jersey farm of one of the professors. Among the party, he noticed a pretty dark-haired, dark-eyed girl and snapped her photograph. Three days later he sent her the snapshot, and with it a carefully worded letter proposing that they meet the next day. She agreed, and they dined at Child's Union Square Restaurant and went to see Helen Menken in *Seventh Heaven*. The girl was Lillian Zahn, then eighteen and a student at New York University. A daughter of Jewish refugees from Galicia, she was vivacious and romantic, and in full rebellion against the strict orthodoxy of her home.

For some four months, all through the hot summer of 1923, the summer that Harding died and Pancho Villa was shot, Joe Smallwood and Lillian were inseparable. Together they went to plays, listened to concerts at Lewisohn Stadium or the Goldman Band in Central Park. Weekends they rode the Ferris Wheel at Coney Island or hiked hand in hand through Van Cortlandt Park. Even as it flowered the romance died.

One reason was Smallwood's return to Newfoundland late that summer when, amid the excitement of politics, he proved to be a poor correspondent. The real reason was that she was Jewish, and he gentile. Lillian did get as far as converting Smallwood to Zionism, a belief he held for years afterwards. She set out to teach him Yiddish, hoping that with his physical appearance he might pass for an English Jew who had unhappily lost the language and so be presented to her parents. On the day chosen for the confrontation, Joe waited for Lillian and her mother in the Lower East Side ghetto. As the two approached, dodging in and out between the pushcarts of Delancey Street, Smallwood, for once in his life, forgot his lines. Stagestruck, he stood bowing, and smiling – and saying nothing. Back home, Mrs. Zahn turned on her daughter: "I know he's a *goy*. You can't fool me. He's a *goy*."

The affair ended that autumn, and although Smallwood remained in New York for more than a year, they did not meet again. Lillian Zahn went on to become a successful Yiddish folksinger.

Alone once more, Smallwood was thrown back on his own resources – and still further so when the *Call*, floundering into bankruptcy, laid him off. As a stopgap, he found hackwork with Gilliam's Editorial Syndicate, and the *American Hatter* magazine, of which "I was ashamed to be there." It was not until early in 1924 that he found his reportorial footing again, as a low-paid but regular contributor to the *Call*'s successor, the weekly *New Leader*. By this time he was sufficiently well thought of that the paper sometimes ran the teaser: "Next week Mr. J. R. Smallwood writes on...."

His first effort for the *New Leader*, which appeared on February 23, 1924, analyzed a trade-union convention in Toronto, and he commented exuberantly: "It's all aboard with Labour in Canada – there are big doings across the border lines. They're in the process of organizing a great Dominion-wide Labour party." He interviewed a series of left-wing notables, among them, through an interpreter, General Plutarcho Elias Calles, President-Elect of Mexico, who said of his election victory, "For the first time the middle class of Mexico voted with the workers and agrarians," and Senator Burton K. Wheeler, Vice-Presidential candidate for the newly formed Progressive Party, who predicted that a "definite, organic third party" would emerge from the autumn's presidential election. His most memorable interview appeared on June 7. It began: "Interviewing a great and world-renowned philosopher, statesman, economist, and Socialist while he is getting out of bed, removing his pyjamas, and hauling on his socks and underclothing, is an entertaining piece of business."

His subject was Bertrand Russell, and "for the interest of historical accuracy and for the benefit of future students of human personality," Smallwood reported one idiosyncrasy Russell did not reveal in his own *Autobiography*:

The Hon. Bertrand Russell, M.A., F.R.S., grandson of Lord John Russell, twice Prime Minister of Great Britain, brother of an earl and heir to an earldom, wears no undershirt. His outside shirt, the one to which his stiff linen collar is attached, is his only shirt, and is worn next to his body. And furthermore, when Mr. Russell removed this shirt the evening before, he left the collar still attached by the collar button to the back of the collar band, just as a fireman would do, if a fireman were in the habit of wearing linen collars.

His last article for the *New Leader* was published on February 14, 1925. Its subject was the Canadian National Railways, which, he reported, had "given the quietus to lying statements that have been insidiously and industriously spread by the not over-scrupulous apologists for the purpose of damaging the cause of nationalization of industry." He went on to damn those who "range themselves about the institution of the Sacred Cow, Private Property."

Most of his writing was similarly naïve, in content and in expression. Every now and then, however, he used his pen to express the personal philosophy which lay behind his love of socialism. On June 14, 1924, in a *New Leader* article titled "Defining Socialism," he wrote:

> Socialism will automatically emancipate mankind from his present degrading and devitalizing need of using himself up in the scramble to get enough material things by which to live physically. And this, mind you, is the Frankenstein which we must attack and lay low. So long as most of the time and energy and ability and enthusiasm of most of the people are caught up and absorbed in the mere attempt to get enough food, clothing, and shelter to enable them to continue existing on this planet, so long, obviously, will people be quite unable to think of, much less achieve, human excellence.

His chance to put theory into practice came with the 1924 presidential campaign. By this time, Smallwood's application and sheer enthusiasm had won him a considerable standing in the ranks of the Socialist Party. A year later, the *American Labour Who's Who* listed him among fewer than two hundred non-American socialists.

Circumstances had also conspired to help Smallwood make his mark. Through the 1920s, American socialism, so powerful a force in the early years of the century, had run adrift in a sea of normalcy, becalmed between the Great Red Scare following World War I and the Depression. To make matters worse, the dedicated disciples of Marx and Lenin converted scores of the old faithful. Although the party could still count on a modicum of support from trade unions, particularly the militant International Ladies Garment Workers, for spokesmen it relied almost solely on a cadre of Jewish intellectuals, who spoke with the thick accents of European ghettoes and whose academic turn of phrase scarcely appealed to the average working man. Though Smallwood was not, in fact, a working man, with his garb and his Irish-tanged accent he could pass for one, and as a gentile to boot, he was a doubly valuable recruit. Above all he could talk.

For the election, the Socialist Party rallied behind Robert LaFollette to form the Progressive Party. In New York State, Norman Thomas ran for Governor. And all through August, September, and October, Joe Smallwood spoke for them on windy street corners and in small dingy halls. Billed as "a specialist in racial groups," he spoke most often in Harlem or in the East Side ghetto, exhibiting that total lack of racial prejudice common to Newfoundlanders.

It was a heaven-sent opportunity to learn at first hand the art of mob oratory and the elements of practical politics. Years later, Smallwood attributed much of his success as a politician to the fact that "I listened to and spoke at hundreds of meetings, handled every kind of heckler from Communists to drunken rowdies – learned how to handle them, that is. After that experience, there's not much that can frighten you."

He learned his trade hard and well. After two months campaigning in and around Manhattan, he was sent as a lead speaker on a three-week swing through New York State. In Buffalo, after the Ku Klux Klan broke up the meeting, Smallwood and his co-speaker, Frank R. Crosswaithe, known as the "Negro Debs," had to be hustled out of the hall and driven to their hotels through backstreets. The two sat up all night, talking of politics and racial discrimination.*

---

* Thirty years later, Smallwood, in New York on business, spotted Crosswaithe's name in the telephone book and dialled his number. There was a pause, and then a booming reply, "Comrade Smallwood." They spent the evening together, reminiscing of the old hard days until Crosswaithe, then a Manhattan Commissioner for Housing, returned Smallwood to his hotel in his own chauffeur-driven Cadillac.

Even when there was no violence, Smallwood found it hard to hold his audiences. The truth was that no one was much interested in socialism. On October 16, he was in Albany, and found himself competing with the Secretary of State, Charles Evans Hughes. The *Knickerbocker Press* compared the two performances the next day:

> About nine o'clock last night, two men in Albany were discussing publicly the constitution of the United States. . . . In the Chancellor's Hall in Washington Street, Charles Evans Hughes was speaking on "Our Constitutional Heritage." By the curb in Lower State Street, a young man stood behind a red and white LaFollette-Wheeler banner and also talked on the Constitution. His audience consisted of two men in a doorway, one assistant, and a small boy who stood gaping in the middle of the sidewalk, unheeding the pedestrians who stopped briefly – then went their way.

At Poughkeepsie, Smallwood set up his platform in the public square to find himself upstaged by two patrician Democratic ladies who had arrived in a car fitted with an enormous, teapot-shaped metal top – to make capital of the Teapot Dome scandal. From the car, surrounded by cheering Vassar girls, stepped Nancy Smith, daughter of the Governor of New York State, and Eleanor Roosevelt, wife of the former Secretary of the Navy. Years later, Premier Smallwood, using his old friend Philip Hochstein as intermediary, invited Mrs. Roosevelt to open the new Memorial University campus in St. John's. After the ceremonies, they talked of the 1924 campaign. Mrs. Roosevelt remembered the rally in Poughkeepsie, though not the competition from the Progressive Party spokesman.

On October 11, the *New Leader* reported: "The upstate campaign is booming. Meetings addressed by the state candidates . . . and by Comrades Still, Smallwood, Esther Friedman, and others are breaking all records." Three weeks later, Calvin Coolidge was returned to the White House. The Progressive Party was smashed beyond recall.

Smallwood was ready to leave New York. He had absorbed all he ever would of big city life, and he had learned everything the Socialist Party could teach him of politics. For four years he had pursued knowledge as if truth, total and inviolate, were just around the corner. In fact, he had never penetrated beyond the outer reaches of elementary socialist theory, and even to this point his understanding of it was largely superficial, and hopelessly disorganized. For all his passionate attachment to the cause, Smallwood was never a socialist in the theoretical sense, but a populist and an idealist by instinct, and a pragmatic politician and propagandist by nature.

Yet socialist ideals shaped his thinking for years to come, and even now, after two decades of absolute power, he likes to call himself a socialist, by which he means essentially a man of the people. The old memories lingered so that he would sometimes deliberately undertake policies that could be described as radical, simply to show that power had not changed the essential Smallwood. Nor was this just self-indulgent showmanship. From socialism Smallwood extracted its moral core: the conviction that a better life was possible for everyone, whatever his rank or origin. He best expressed this conviction during a radio interview in March 1967 when he was asked the question, "Are you still a socialist?" His reply was not one whit changed from the definition of socialism he had written in the *New Leader* forty-three years before:

> I still believe in the socialist ideal – more perhaps than I ever did, and I think I will go to my grave with that belief. I have changed, however, in the amount of faith I have in the state. I don't think that nationalizing an industry is necessarily the best system.
>
> We have a problem – to put an end for all time to the main problem of getting enough to eat, the problem of getting enough to wear, the problem of getting enough shelter from the elements.
>
> If that becomes almost automatic, as it can be, then that great part of man's time and energy and talent and ability and skill and ingenuity, inventiveness, creativeness, absorbed like a great blotter just in the task of living, then could be devoted to matters of the mind and the

spirit, and we could have a civilization of which even the poets have not been able to do more than dream.

Smallwood has spent his life trying to lift the people of Newfoundland to this level of comfort and security, so that their creativity, expressed in hundreds of stories and verses and song, but never in great art or visible monument, can soar. That, in truth, is Joey Smallwood's brand of socialism.

4

Publishing and Politics

In 1925, Joe Smallwood came home for good, bursting with eagerness to start a political career that would amaze all Newfoundland. Twenty years later, as he entered middle age, he had amassed a record of continuous failures: in politics, in business, in publishing, and in farming. He was on the brink of becoming one of those threadbare dreamers who haunt public libraries, scribbling notes for the great book they will someday write, and expounding visions to a dwindling group of believers.

His failure is a mystery only in the light of his later success. To his contemporaries his disasters came as no surprise. For all his talent and energy, Smallwood was almost unbelievably gauche, entirely without perception and understanding of other people, administratively inept, and financially irresponsible. People liked him because he was naïve, trusting, and generous to a fault. He lost friends by addressing them like a public meeting, endlessly arguing with them, and losing their money. Though he had a way with words and a gift for debate, he seldom really convinced. One who crossed swords with him at the Methodist College Literary Institute, a weekly debating society, remembers: "He could argue either side of almost any subject and win. To an audience that had never heard him before, he was terribly impressive. But if you had heard him the week before arguing the exact opposite of what he was now saying, he was a bore."

Newfoundland society itself was also to blame. The merchants had always ruled the island, and it was taken for granted, as much by the public as by the merchants, that they always would. There was scant room in the handsome drawing rooms of St. John's East for a visionary of any sort, least of all for one who was loud-mouthed, scruffily dressed, and patently not a gentleman. For two decades, Smallwood was dismissed as "that crazy radical."

Nor was Newfoundland society in any condition to experiment with Smallwood's brand of utopian populism. In the rest of North America, the great depression began on the day in 1929 when twelve million shares were traded in five panic-stricken hours; but in Newfoundland it had started as soon as the Great War ended and the market for salt cod collapsed. Newfoundlanders who grew up during the twenties and thirties were a true lost generation. Men were unemployed, on the average, one year in three, and earned an average of $150 a year. Women were old at forty from relentless drudgery and from endless child-bearing. Children grew up under-clothed, underfed, and ravaged by rickets and beri-beri. Tuberculosis scourged whole families and entire settlements. A 1936 government report noted that children sometimes fainted in class from hunger. Since education was not compulsory, many of them never went to school at all.

Under Coaker, the fishermen had made their one attempt to break out of social and economic servitude. Now they turned in upon themselves and accepted a natural order which trapped them at the lowest level of subsistence. In rock-bound outports they built their square, flat-roofed clapboard houses and grew "garden fruit" in tiny plots scratched from thin acidic soil. In summer, they picked berries, caught lobster, salmon, and cod, and always they lived off credit. Thousands of outharbourmen never handled a dollar bill from one year's end to the next, only nickels and dimes for the Sunday collection plate.

As the rest of the world rushed forward, the old ways and the old virtues held firm. Unrelenting hardship never reduced Newfoundlanders to a race of cap-doffers and forelock-tuggers. They lived too close to nature to be impressed by pomp or title, and they never lost their dignity as proud and independent human beings. Each outport was essentially a large family, which cloaked its members in shared warmth, humour, and security. Children were cheerfully spoiled; the old were never allowed to feel useless. Religion anchored their lives: It brought them into the world, and gave meaning to their deaths.

Yet the price of endemic poverty was fearful. Unending unemployment bred mute resignation; bright minds withered for lack of opportunity. For young men without name or means, the only escape was into the church or the chartered banks. Those who left in those days look back at Newfoundland now not with fond nostalgia but with bitterness at the waste. Smallwood should have been one of them. Ever a maverick, he came back. More profoundly, he never lost faith, in himself or in Newfoundland. His lost years parallel those of his country.

Smallwood originally intended, after he left New York, to go on to London and then, as he put it in a letter to Lillian Zahn, "to vagabond the earth" before going home. Instead, he was persuaded by a New York acquaintance, John P. Burke, Secretary Treasurer of the International Brotherhood of Pulp, Sulphite, and Paper Mill Workers of America, to become a Newfoundland organizer for the Brotherhood. In February 1925, he reached Grand Falls, the inland paper-mill town, and within two months had doubled the Brotherhood's local's membership to some seven hundred. This done, he launched a new project, and formed Newfoundland's first Federation of Labour. By early summer, he had enrolled six unions, in Grand Falls, in St. John's, and in the Bell Island iron mines; and he had become the Federation's first president.

In June he was off again, to Corner Brook, where a new mill was transforming a sleepy fishing village into a boom town. When Smallwood arrived the community was already substantial enough to boast a motor car, the only one in Western Newfoundland. He found lodgings at Curling, twenty minutes walk along the railway track from the mill, where he boarded at the home of Mrs. Serena Baggs, a widow with two young daughters. The Baggs children found Smallwood likeable enough, but different. While the other boarders, mostly schoolteachers and bank clerks, took occasional quick swigs of beer in the kitchen and played roughhouse games with the little children, Smallwood spent his time reading alone in his room.

Before long the loner found himself a companion. She was Clara Oates, the daughter of a fishing captain in the Conception Bay outport of Carbonear, who was spending a summer holiday with her cousin, Mrs. Baggs. Then twenty-three, Clara was a shy and gentle girl, with sparkling blue eyes and long luxuriant hair which she pinned up in Dutch-style buns on either side of her head. Like many a bright outport girl, Clara possessed little formal education, yet was filled with interests far beyond her narrow world. She had a fine singing voice, was an excellent pianist, and had studied music in Nova Scotia. She was an omnivorous reader with an astonishing knowledge of the kings and queens of England and of their multiple disasters and glories, which she could recount with the accuracy of a walking encyclopaedia.

Together, Joe and Clara talked of books and music. Between the hesitant girl and the voluble visionary, friendship flowered into love. Within six weeks they were engaged and that same year, on November 23, they were married. Clara wore a veil of handmade lace which had belonged to her great-great-grandmother.

Their first child was born the next year, and christened Ramsay Coaker after Britain's Prime Minister and Smallwood's current hero.* Their second son, William, was born in Corner Brook in 1928, and their daughter, Clara, in St. John's in 1930. Bill Smallwood became a lawyer and a member of the provincial legislature; Ramsay, who suffered severe first-degree burns in a tragic helicopter crash in 1957 that took the life of his first wife, manages Smallwood's farm outside St. John's. Clara married a farmer, Ed Russell, and together they run a riding school at the Smallwood farm. Between them, his three children have made

---

* He even dedicated his book on Coaker "To Ramsay Coaker Smallwood, by the author of both."

Smallwood the patriarchal grandfather of eleven. The eldest is Josephine, a pretty twenty-two-year-old; the youngest is six-year-old Douglas. The grandchildren call Smallwood 'Poppy Joe'; they gather round to hear his tall stories and to ignore his advice, much as he once sat before David.

By his own admission, Smallwood was a forgetful father and a negligent husband: "From the time I got married," he has said, "until I went to work as the Barrelman in 1937, I earned precious little and lived from hand to mouth. And I must say quite candidly that I had very little sense of parental responsibility or husbandly responsibility. I was married, but still carefree and footloose and quite impractical in money and material matters." Like many political missionaries, Smallwood's idealism embraced the mass rather than the individual.

Upon Clara Smallwood, a woman of great kindness and personal dignity, fell the full burden of building a home during those years. As Premier, Smallwood was able to shower upon his family the material comforts and affection lost during more than twenty years in a political and financial wilderness.

Though he ultimately came to cherish his role as patriarch, Smallwood's family played little part in his career.

The pattern of restiveness, which reflected his own intellectual and emotional rootlessness, soon became evident. After he left Grand Falls, the Federation of Labour, so promisingly begun, collapsed for lack of a leader. And he was hardly in Corner Brook before he left again, in pursuit of a new crusade.

That summer, in an attempt to economize, the Government had announced that salaries of section men on the publicly owned railway would be reduced, from 25¢ an hour to 22½¢. Each day, as he walked along the track to Curling, Smallwood met the section men; they told him of their plight and pleaded with him to organize all the men between Port-aux-Basques and St. John's against the cut. Such a task was virtually impossible, since no funds existed to pay the organizer's expenses. But, fired by the challenge, Smallwood announced that he would walk the six-hundred-mile length of railway, enrolling members as he went.

He set off in late August and "walked myself down to skin and grief." The nightmare journey cost him thirty pounds and three pairs of boots. Sun, rain, or fog, he walked as much as thirty miles a day, until even in darkness his feet could hit the ties, one after another, by instinct. He slept in sectionmen's shacks, on narrow cots, on chairs strung together, and sometimes on the floor. One evening, exhausted, and miles from the next hut, he rested for a few moments between the rails, and woke up two hours later, cold with fear.

As the days passed, and the first frosts began to bite, word of what he was doing ran ahead. Sectionmen waited with their fifty-cent dues; their wives shyly handed him packets of sandwiches and sometimes washed his clothes. Often he was offered rides on hand-pumped trolleys but found it more tiring than walking. By mid-November he had reached Avondale, thirty miles from St. John's. As Smallwood walked into the station a train pulled in from the opposite direction. Aboard was the general manager of the railway. Inside the station house, management and labour met. From his shabby coat Smallwood pulled a grimy notebook, its pages crammed with the names of every sectionman but one of the more than seven hundred he had passed. When the argument was ended, the pay cut had been rescinded. Smallwood caught the express train back to St. John's, and less than a fortnight later he had his first newspaper on the stands.

The *Labour Outlook* lasted three months. The first issue was sent free to the seven hundred sectionmen and the rest offered to the public at five cents a copy. There were few buyers and still fewer advertisers, and by February 1926, Smallwood had found himself more substantial employment, as editor of the daily *Globe*. Six months later he had left Newfoundland for London.

When Smallwood went to New York, he had gone convinced "that the United States was the great land of democracy and the greatest country in the world." He left persuaded "that the whole system was wrong" and, seeing it through the dark glasses of a socialist, "that the workers were being ground down while a few capitalists got rich." All his infinite capacity for hero worship he now transferred to Britain.

In London, where he stayed for little more than six months, Smallwood never achieved one-quarter his success in New York. Yet he returned with a burning and undying admiration for all things British. The explanation may be simple: that the British, with their presumption of superiority, were able to convince even Smallwood that they were superior to him. And Bloomsbury, if somewhat effete by the unsubtle and vigorous standards of New York, was exactly what would appeal to a raw colonial.

On his first day in London, Smallwood bought copies of the *Times* and *Herald* and then set out for the meeting he had chosen: a rally of the Fulham Labour Party Association. When the time for questions came round, Smallwood put up his hand and told the surprised audience: "I landed in England for the first time in my life today, and I came straight round to this meeting."

But entry to the Labour Party, then ensconced in power, could not be achieved in the free-and-easy manner of New York. The most Smallwood managed was to be one of a cadre of speakers on behalf of the Labour candidate in a by-election at North Southwick. Nor did he find a regular newspaper job; instead he eked out a living contributing articles to struggling socialist magazines, principally the *London Weekly*.

As Smallwood recalls: "I went to London to learn." He came close to starving doing it. He lived at a lodging house close by the British Museum and ate in restaurants until a fellow lodger taught him to cook for himself over a gas ring. On Christmas Day he dined by himself in a Lyons Corner House. "It was the first time in my life I ever felt lonely."

There were happier moments. On March 1, 1927, the evening papers reported that the Privy Council had awarded Labrador to Newfoundland over the competing claims of Canada. He wrote *Coaker of Newfoundland*, a passionate eulogy of his hero, in a non-stop, three-day fury of creation. He attended countless meetings, from Marble Arch to dingy Clapham basements, and once stumbled into a rally called to organize an English branch of Trotsky's Fourth Internationale. He haunted the British Museum and scrabbled through the cut-price stacks in second-hand bookstores on Charing Cross Road. (One of these was Marks and Sons, a firm with which Smallwood for years maintained a standing order for

Newfoundland books. It was his first stop, immediately before or after official business, whenever he was in London.)

In the summer of 1927, Smallwood returned to Newfoundland, determined to practise what he had so long learned. To break into politics, he decided to start a newspaper in Corner Brook, which had been newly established as an electoral district.

His weekly tabloid, the *Humber Herald*, was impossibly ambitious and finally collapsed in 1930 amid a welter of debts. During its life, Smallwood managed to cause a small local stir. He agitated for the unheard-of luxury of a children's playground, and organized a campaign to have a public telephone installed in a squatter's shanty settlement beyond the boundary of the tidy company town.

The financial troubles inconvenienced Smallwood, but they did not halt his pursuit of a political career. In his small apartment, he pored over well-thumbed books brought back from England; *Hansard*s from Westminster and St. John's; and the stream of British periodicals to which he subscribed: *The Tribune, John O'London's Weekly, Forward* – a Scottish socialist weekly – *Times Literary Supplement, Catholic Herald, Methodist Guardian*, and, rounding out his indiscriminate eclecticism, the Communist *Labour Monthly* and Oswald Mosley's *Blackshirt*.

The next summer, 1928, with the announcement of an election, the chance came for Smallwood to use all this knowledge he had so assiduously hoarded.

Newfoundland politics of the day were a merry, anarchic muddle. Parties and factions tumbled into and out of power, with some of their members getting richer along the way. The leader was all; and where he went in pursuit of policy or personal fortune, his supporters followed in an undisciplined phalanx. To the dismay of the colonial office, Newfoundland political customs bore only a glancing resemblance to British practices. Even the distinction between Government and Opposition was sometimes lost: In 1919, a government fell when the Finance Minister moved a non-confidence motion against it. Defeat was hastened by the fact that the Prime Minister seconded the motion.

Smallwood's new hero, Sir Richard Squires, moved easily amid this maelstrom. Newfoundlanders have always loved or hated their political leaders to enthusiastic excess. For none has folk memory reserved such cordial hatred as for Squires, an aloof, angular, self-made aristocrat, whose most considerable political quality was his speed of foot. He was a Cabinet Minister from 1913 to 1918 and Prime Minister from 1919 to 1923, when he resigned amid cries of bribery and corruption, to re-emerge as Prime Minister from 1928 to 1932.

As Coaker's star fell, Smallwood hitched himself to Squires's battered bandwagon. Through him, Smallwood, in the words of a colleague, "traces his line of Liberal legitimacy," for Squires's party called itself Liberal. Once Premier, for much of his term Smallwood measured his achievements against those of Squires. Because Squires got Newfoundland its second pulp-and-paper mill, Smallwood has striven for years to attract a third.

Smallwood revered Squires. In the days when the quality alone ruled Newfoundland, there was one home of distinction where doors were opened, occasionally, to him. In gratitude for the odd dinner or cigar in the study, Smallwood gave Squires total and uncritical loyalty. In return, Squires treated him as an expendable wardheeler.

The election was called for September. Smallwood had prepared for it by nurturing the new Corner Brook constituency in a way few Newfoundland politicians had ever attempted. He had visited every settlement, walked the roadless shore round Bay of Islands in mid-winter, and gone by train to inland communities. All he needed to become the Liberal candidate was Squires's formal appointment. The message came by telegraph from St. John's, a week before nomination day. The wireless operator at the telegraph office handed Smallwood the precious scrap of paper: "I HAVE CONSIDERED THE POSITION OF THE HUMBER CONSTITUENCY CAREFULLY AND HAVE COME TO THE CONCLUSION THAT AS THE LIBERAL PARTY HAS VIRTUALLY CREATED THIS DISTRICT IT IS MY DUTY TO OFFER MYSELF AS THE LIBERAL CANDIDATE STOP SQUIRES."

No copy of that telegram exists; Smallwood never forgot its words. He folded it carefully, walked out of the office, through the town, into the woods beyond. In the evening he went back to the cable office and wrote out a reply: "NOT FOR ANYONE ELSE WOULD I DO THIS BUT I WILL FOR YOU." There was nothing else Smallwood could do. No other party would have him.

Dutifully, he managed Squires's campaign in Corner Brook. He chaired each meeting, led the applause, and scraped his shoe on the floor to let Squires know when he had talked too long. Squires won in Corner Brook and in the colony by a landslide. As a reward, Smallwood was made a justice of the peace.

His admiration for Squires never wavered, and in 1930, when Squires "lifted his little finger, I came running" – to run the weekly *Watchman* for the Liberals in St. John's. When Squires died in 1940, his personal papers passed on to Smallwood, who has accepted the legacy as a fiat to defend Squires's scandal-wracked reputation against all detractors.

While still in Corner Brook, he wrote his second book, *The New Newfoundland*, which described Squires "as the most versatile and able statesman yet produced in Newfoundland." The island, he wrote, "has entered upon a new march that is destined to place her, within the next dozen years, in the front rank of the great small nations of the world." The *New York Times Book Review* of August 2, 1931, commented: "Mr. Smallwood speaks with justifiable pride and pronounced hopefulness of the evidences of progress."

In fact, the small nation was floundering into bankruptcy. A government of geniuses could not have prevented it; small minds in a small colony merely hastened the inevitable, though Newfoundland politicians were not markedly less perceptive about the forces of modern economics than Herbert Hoover or R. B. Bennett. By 1930, interest charges on the accumulated public debt equalled *half* the entire annual revenue of the Government. Of that $100 million debt, $40 million was accounted for by the unpaid bills of sending Newfoundlanders to fight in France.

By 1933, unemployment had soared to 65,000 – more than half the entire labour force. For these wretched men, there was dole at six cents a day given in the form of vouchers redeemable in kind. For stores to honour these was often an act of charity, since the Government ran six to nine months behind in refunding them, and sometimes payment came not at all. As Smallwood remembered those terrible years: "It was ghastly. We were already living on a low standard. Now that standard was more than cut in half."

The explosion, from a people stoic beyond belief, but destitute beyond parallel in North America, came in April 1932. It was ignited by yet one more political scandal. The anti-Squires *Daily News* wrung its editorial hands: "Young people are beginning to believe that Truth and Honour and Justice and Integrity are merely myths, and that life is nothing but a scramble to get what you can." Not only the young, the middle-aged and elderly were prepared to believe it. The Opposition staged a monster rally at the Majestic Theatre in St. John's and one thousand people attended, all howling for Squires's blood. All except one. Standing in the middle of the hall was Smallwood.

Courage to the point of insanity had brought him to the meeting. To get himself noticed, he stood up on a chair and shouted "Question." He was greeted with shouts of "Throw him out." Instead, one of the platform speakers, a merchant with a dash of *noblesse oblige*, invited him up to the platform. There Smallwood launched into a tirade which included a bite at the hand which had just fed him. "Beware of the Greeks when they come bearing gifts," he said. "And I say, beware of Water Street when they come giving advice in politics."

It was a good sally. As Smallwood warmed to his subject, he began, as always, to pace back and forth until he made the mistake of walking too close to the wings. Two hands reached out in the manner of a vaudeville hook and whisked Smallwood off the stage. Burly anti-government supporters surrounded him, and, with a few well-aimed punches, hurled him through a side door onto the street. A few minutes later Smallwood was back at the front door, trying once more to push his way towards the stage. A friend spotted him and dragged him, protesting, to safety.

For its organizers, the rally had been a riotous success. The following day they staged a protest march to carry the people's complaints to the government. Preceded by ex-servicemen wearing their medals, a crowd set off for the Colonial Building. By the time they reached the House of Assembly, the mob had swelled to ten thousand, many made bold with drink. At the foot of the steps the parade halted, unfurled a Union Jack to a volley of cheers, and sent in a delegation.

An hour passed without any sign of action from the legislators. Outside in a drizzling rain, angry mutters changed to shouts, and shouts to curses. Suddenly the crowd was out of control and rocks crashed against the sturdy building. Order was momentarily restored when the Guards Band struck up "God Save the King." Every man in the crowd stood rigidly to attention. As soon as the music died away, the riot resumed. The front doors held, but the crowd smashed open a side door that led into the basement and there ransacked everything in sight. Missing though was Squires, who waited behind the barred and bolted door of the Speaker's Chamber. With him were Lady Squires, a handful of ministers and, loyal if need be to the last, Joe Smallwood.

Suddenly there was a loud hammering at the door. Smallwood picked up a long iron poker from the fireplace and whispered that if he were going down he would, by God, take six with him. The pounding started again, and through the heavy door they recognized the voice of an Opposition member. He had come, he said, to take Lady Squires to safety. Half an hour later a group of members arrived to rescue the Prime Minister. With a cap pulled low over his face, Squires made it as far as a side gate that led out of the Colonial Building's grounds when he was spotted. In an instant the cry was up, and with a handful of his escorts Squires raced down the street. Behind him tumbled the mob, shouting, among other things, "Lynch him!" "Thief!" "Drown the Bastard!" A fluke saved him. Squires got far enough ahead of his pursuers to duck into the open door of a house while the mob, mistaking another man for him, roared on past.

Behind, in the Speaker's Chamber, Smallwood and the remaining Cabinet ministers waited a few minutes, and then made their own escape unnoticed. That night, gangs broke into the liquor stores and ranged the streets brawling and looting. Unable to stay away from the action, Smallwood sortied out with a hammer up his coat-sleeve, accompanied by two burly brothers-in-law each carrying a club. He was at least discreet enough to wear an outsized cap pulled low over his face. The trio was not accosted.

Within the month, Squires was forced to call the general election he was certain to lose. Now that it no longer mattered, Smallwood was given his chance. He chose the outport riding of Bonavista South. Of the twenty-seven Liberals who ran, all but two were defeated. Among the losers was Smallwood – by 812 votes to 3,528. It was the only personal defeat of his career.

5

Bayman and Barrelman

The short campaign of 1932 was Smallwood's first real journey through outport country. He found the experience traumatic. "It was desperate, absolutely desperate. Everywhere I went, destitution stared me in the face," he recalls. "The first time I saw a fisherman literally staggering from hunger, my ordinary political instincts collapsed." Instead of making speeches, he listened. And he learned.

Out of that experience it began to dawn on Smallwood that the independence of which Newfoundland was so proud was a cruel fantasy, sustained only by the unremitting poverty of ninety per cent of her population. Not even a revolutionary could save a country without an economy. In retrospect, the 1932 campaign was Smallwood's first step on the road to Confederation.

Certainly the election itself could solve nothing. By 1932, the government was forced to raise loans to pay the interest on previous loans. Faced with complete collapse, Newfoundland turned to Britain, to ask for what amounted to repayment for Beaumont-Hamel. In reply to the request for a formal inquiry into the island's financial disorder, Whitehall sent out Sir

William Warrender Mackenzie, first Baron Amulree. His report recommended – commanded is closer but too strong a word – that Newfoundland dissolve her legislature to make way for a six-man commission of British-appointed civil servants. In return, Britain would advance immediate grants and assume responsibility for servicing the island's debt.

On February 16, 1934, the seventy-eight-year-old, self-governing colony, and three-year-old Dominion (by the 1931 Statute of Westminster), voluntarily surrendered her independence. She became the second colony of the British Empire to relinquish self-government.* For the next sixteen years, Newfoundlanders reverted to a condition of political adolescence, comparable to the condition of Canada in the early nineteenth century, or to pre-Revolutionary America. Though three of the Commissioners were Newfoundlanders, islanders had no say in their appointment. A British governor with the right of veto presided over the Commission. The only elected body left in the colony was the St. John's Municipal Council.

The Commission of Government meant the end of Joe Smallwood's political career. In the long run, it proved a blessing in disguise. When the time came for the British oligarchy to depart, most of the old politicians had died, leaving Smallwood as plausible a leader as any of his rivals. As useful, Amulree's Report, which diagnosed Newfoundland's financial ills as the result of "a continuous process of graft and corruption which has left few classes of the community untouched by its insidious influence," left Newfoundlanders with a deep mistrust of their old-style politicians and prepared to listen even to the visionary outpourings of a "crazy radical."

Amulree's conclusion was, in fact, absurd. Corruption existed, certainly; but it was scarcely the cause of bankruptcy by a poverty-stricken colony in the midst of a worldwide Depression. As R. A. MacKay wrote in his 1944 study of Newfoundland: "The basic reasons for Newfoundland's collapse were economic, not political or even financial." Perhaps

---

* In 1932, the British Government assumed control of Malta, after that island had elected a government favouring union with Mussolini's Italy.

Amulree could be excused. Newfoundlanders are born story-tellers and exaggerators equally of disaster and triumph. Amulree was a prim bankerly Scot, and into his satisfyingly shocked ears were poured horrific tales of graft and malignant malfeasance which he then identified as the source of financial Armageddon.

Of the Commission's performance, Maxwell Cohen wrote that it was "honest, reasonably efficient, dull and penurious." There were some accomplishments. The Commissioners overhauled the civil service; launched an imaginative scheme of cottage hospitals; made schooling compulsory to the age of fourteen, and each year increased teachers' salaries, to an average of $981 just before Confederation. Yet the bureaucratic ambiance of its rule was established early. With a stunning disregard for Newfoundland sensitivities, the handsome old legislative chamber was partitioned to make room for Commission offices; the Newfoundland Museum was dismantled and its exhibits scattered, many to be permanently lost.*

Though at the start Newfoundlanders enthusiastically supported the Commission, their sentiments changed as economic conditions failed to improve. After dropping, slightly, from its 1933 peak, unemployment surged back to 58,000 in 1938. When the war came, the island was again on the brink of social collapse. The Americans came with their bases just in time.

Such prosperity was artificial and patently would not last beyond the war's end. Rule by the British had failed as miserably as rule by Newfoundlanders, and the island was caught in a vise from which there seemed no escape.

Throughout the 1930s, Smallwood sought constantly for a solution. His search is reflected most strongly in an article he wrote for his *Book of Newfoundland*, published in 1937:

The economic blizzard has strewed Newfoundland with considerable wreckage but the spirit of the people is still invincible. The wreckage

---

* The procedure was repeated in 1953, when the Federal Department of Transport demolished the 190-year-old Fort Amherst at the mouth of St. John's harbour.

will be cleared away. Newfoundlanders are the most tenaciously nationalistic and patriotic people in the world, and it takes more than a storm to destroy their pride.

Then he added: "Just a little bit ridiculous is their pride perhaps. Their country is small; their numbers are few."

If Smallwood, still a decade away from becoming a Confederate, had yet to reach the right answers, he had found the right questions. Thus, in that article he injected a note of realism into his earlier utopian populism:

It would be unmanly and untruthful, however, to place all the blame for our backwardness upon others. We ourselves have failed to use many of the qualities necessary to make a success of our country. Perhaps the very nature of our struggle, of our methods of wresting a living from nature, has helped to unfit us for constructive and creative effort.

It is a fact that for centuries we have lived by *killing* cod and other fish; by *killing* seals in the water and on the ice, and animals on land; by *cutting down* trees. Has all this developed in us a trait of destructiveness, or narcotized what ought naturally to be an instinct for creativeness? Is it not true that we have been intensely, bitterly individualistic, each of us preferring to paddle his own canoe and turn his back upon the other fellow? Have we not failed almost completely in the one virtue that the modern world has made an absolute essential, the ability and the desire to achieve a commonly desired end?

This remarkable analysis of the dark side of the cherished individualism of Newfoundlanders has rarely been equalled. Bitter experience had taught Smallwood the destructiveness of that individualism; he had just wasted three years trying to organize co-operatives on the northeast coast.

Smallwood could not forget the sunken grey faces he had seen in Bonavista during the 1932 campaign. The following spring the city-bred radical, who had never in his life set a cod trap or culled a catch, sailed off on a new crusade. He would go back to Bonavista to live among the fishermen and try to help them to help themselves.

Even the manner of his going marked Smallwood for a townie. He almost drowned. With $800 cajoled from a friend, he bought the *Margaret P*, a thirty-eight-foot schooner of uncertain age, driven or sporadically moved by a venerable eight-horsepower Atlantic. In her he chugged out of St. John's. The *Margaret P*'s former owner apparently was as good a salesman as Smallwood. After ten slow miles northward, the engine sputtered into permanent silence. He made the rest of the journey, by way of Baccalieu Tickle and Old Perlican, under sail. On the way, a sudden storm overtook the schooner and she nearly foundered, since neither Smallwood nor his one-man crew was seaman enough to know how to lower the sails. When she finally reached port, the *Margaret P* almost rammed the shore at full speed; Smallwood had neglected to find out how to drop anchor.

Undaunted, he hired a skipper and plunged heedlessly into what was to be the grimmest period of his life. For three years he sailed the Bonavista Peninsula or tramped from cove to cove along its roadless shoreline, trying to convince fishermen that their enemy was the credit system and their salvation the co-operative movement.

His immediate aim was to establish "fish pools," an embryonic form of a producers' co-operative. He told the fishermen they could improve their returns if they sold their catch in bulk to independent merchants who would pay for it in cash and not in credit.

In theory this was sound. Smallwood set himself up as secretary, manager, and president of what he called the Fishermens' Co-operative Union and signed up four thousand members. A Bonavista store owner was talked into renting a shed to store the fish, and another into lending his weighing scale so that the cod could be culled, or graded. In fact, the co-operative was doomed from the start. Baymen preferred the devil they knew; in Bonavista a barrel of weevily flour meant more than the promise of a dollar bill. As Coaker had predicted, Smallwood got scarcely a cent of dues for his co-operative and collected barely six per cent of the annual Bonavista catch. As he recorded sadly in the *Book of Newfoundland*: "The whole thing was approached by some of them, I fear, more in the spirit of employing the Society as a means of forcing up the fish merchants' prices than that of making a success of the Society itself."

Smallwood's lack of administrative talent did the rest. He forgot that any savings earned by bulk selling could be eaten up by the venture's overhead. There was money to be spent on a fortnightly, *The Co-operative News,* and on his own pitiful salary – which was, at least in theory, $500 a year. Even if everything had gone well, "We were trying to squeeze a little more from an economy that was already weak as water."

He was never poorer. If anything, he was worse off than the fishermen, for unlike them he had no vegetable plot and had to rely on co-operative members for sporadic round-ups of turnips and potatoes and cabbages. A friend remembers visiting the Smallwoods and being served tea without milk, and fish. (In a country where fresh fish could be had for the taking, tinned baloney was proper outport fare; only the poorest of families would be so impolite as to serve a visitor fresh lobster or salmon.) His house was large and rambling, and the rent was only eight dollars a month, but it was almost barren of furniture, and the only heat came from a woodstove in the kitchen.

Yet for all his disillusionment, love never died between him and the baymen. In Bonavista, Joe Smallwood found what he had never had before: an understanding of the essential Newfoundland, the sea-torn country where cod was king and life was cruel, but where shy and soft-voiced men were comrades in a way the earnest revolutionary had never known.

Some of that fellowship comes through in a passage Smallwood wrote in his *Book of Newfoundland*:

There the two or three other fishermen fishing in your boat join you. You launch your small rodney or dory and row out to your motorboat, which is moored at the collar a few gun-shots from shore. You climb in her; the chap who looks after the engine tinkers about with her until he gets her going; you cast off and head for the fishing grounds three or five or eight miles out from land on the bosom of the Atlantic Ocean. It is a fine time now to fill your pipe for a comfortable smoke, and you have reached the fishing grounds and commenced fishing an hour or two maybe before the first faint streaks of dawn begin to lighten the sky.

Early in 1936, Smallwood was back in St. John's, penniless and jobless. The past three years had been gruelling for his wife and children, and he began at last to think of providing some security for them. His first attempt to do so was as feckless as it was ambitious.

As if to make amends for its destruction of the Museum, the Commission of Government had just opened Newfoundland's first public library. Smallwood quickly became its most constant patron. One day he took down from the shelves a volume titled *The Book of Puerto Rico*. Before the day was out, he had decided to bring out an equivalent encyclopaedia himself. His would be called *The Book of Newfoundland*.

This book is Smallwood's most considerable literary achievement. Credit for it is due as well to a remarkable pair of contemporaries, Nimshi Crewe and Chesley Crosbie. Crewe, indirectly, provided the inspiration. He was a tall, craggy Bonavista man with a brilliant mind who, like most gifted Newfoundlanders of his generation, never found a true outlet for his talents. A Fabian socialist, he made a living as an accountant for the arch-conservative Commission and turned his intellectual energy towards local Newfoundland history, relentlessly mining those inexhaustible lodes of anecdotes, family and folklore, that, rather than any recital of dates and Prime Ministers, are the real story of Newfoundland. Crewe and Smallwood recognized each other as soulmates, and Smallwood was soon as keen an amateur anthropologist as his mentor. In character, Smallwood saw his new passion as a publishing venture.

For capital, Smallwood turned to Chesley Crosbie, a hard-driving, hard-living mercantile freebooter who had inherited a fortune and lost and remade it several times before he died. In the timid business community of depression St. John's, Crosbie was a throwback to earlier, bolder times. Without difficulty, Smallwood was able to persuade him that the venture could be profitable.

Besides cash, Crosbie provided an office in his office building. To give the undertaking proper tone, Smallwood created a board of editors made up of the island's leading citizens. It never met. He then lined up more than 120 contributors, at commissions ranging from $500, for a book-length account of Newfoundland's part in the Great War, to the three guineas demanded and received by Lord Winterton for his contribution, "A Trip to Newfoundland."

The task took the best part of a year, during which its scope grew steadily broader and more expensive so that Crosbie's stake leaped from an intended $5,000 to $25,000. When completed, the work filled two volumes of seven hundred pages, crammed with more than a thousand photographs, articles on history, geography, the history of flight, communications, radio and forestry, descriptions of cod and salmon fishing and of seal hunting, tales of disasters and shipwrecks and battles long ago. It was printed in England and Smallwood went over to supervise typesetting. He took his family with him and worked round the clock for ten days without shaving or sleeping to complete the manuscript before the S.S. *Nova Scotia* sailed.

He himself contributed an introductory chapter, "Newfoundland Today," and a short article on co-operatives which amounted to an apologia for his failure in Bonavista. His longest effort was entitled "Life in Newfoundland Today," a twelve-thousand-word study of a typical outport, Brig Cove. His eye was fond, but as an experienced reporter he missed little:

> The grasslands have not been ploughed under these fifty years and you could count the four or five-inch blades of grass growing on them. Their owners, if they have enough stable manure left after the potato-gardens have been cultivated, will sprinkle some manure on them. Otherwise they will wait until the caplin strike into the shore, and then haul a few "box-cart" loads, or push a few wheel-barrow loads of caplin to the scene and spread them sparsely over the surface.

Aside from Smallwood's own contributions, the quality of Newfoundland came across most strongly in the poems and ballads, many of which were printed for the first time. "Bound for Canada" went:

Oh love I'm bound for Canada
Dear Sally we must part
I'm forced to leave my blue-eyed girl
All with an aching heart
To face cold-hearted strangers too
All in a foreign land.

Among the many accounts of tragedies, where pain was sublimated in song, was the "Petty Harbour Skiff."

Your heart would ache for all their sake if you were standing by
To see them drowning one by one and no relief was nigh
Struggling with the boisterous waves all in their youth and bloom
But at last they sank to rise no more, all on the eighth of June.

Ten thousand sets were printed, bound in ox-blood alligator leather, with the title stamped in gold. Fewer than four thousand sets were sold at six dollars each, by salesmen ranging door to door across the island. The rest were stored in towering stacks in Crosbie's warehouse until World War II when hundreds were bought by American servicemen as souvenirs of their stay in Newfoundland. Today the original *Book of Newfoundland* is a collector's item, fetching from $100 to $150. It bears the flaws of most of Smallwood's undertakings: over-ambitious, executed too hastily, and filled with glaring omissions and inconsistencies; still, it exists, and in style, content, and mood, it is Newfoundland in the 1930s captured for posterity.

Like any adept journalist, Smallwood recognized that the material he had collected for *The Book of Newfoundland* could be reused and resold. Early in 1937, and for lack of any other means of making a living, he started rewriting much of it in a column for the *Daily News* called "From the Barrelman," after the masthead lookout on a sailing ship. The column quickly acquired a substantial audience. Encouraged, he persuaded a local importer and wholesaler, Frank O'Leary, to sponsor him in a daily

fifteen-minute radio program of local history and anecdote. He had
found his true bent, and his political platform. "The Barrelman" became
the most successful local program on Newfoundland radio. It also made
him one of the best-known men on the island.

The first show was broadcast in October 1937, over the government-
owned station, VONF. A ship's bell chimed six times, and Smallwood's
voice, harsh and unmodulated but powerful, announced that he was there
to make "Newfoundland better known to Newfoundlanders." For the
next six years he broadcast Monday to Friday at 6:45 P.M., clanging the
bell at the start and close of the program, and giving a single chime before
and after each commercial for O'Leary's products: among them
Pepsodent toothpaste, Palmolive soap, and Pet Milk.

In hundreds of outports, people crowded around the single battery-
operated set in the community, usually in the house of the minister or
local merchant. Listening to "The Barrelman" became almost as much a
part of outport life as going to church.

With the instinct of a born communicator, Smallwood made his
audience part of the program. "Send me stories, true stories," he said in
June 1938, "showing how brave Newfoundlanders are; how hardy they
are; how strong they are; what hardships they endure." He appealed
to prickly Newfoundland pride. "There are some people, you know,
who don't think much of Newfoundlanders. Let us prove to them that
Newfoundlanders have courage, brains, strength, great powers of
endurance. Let us show them that Newfoundlanders are witty and smart."

Written on the pages of school scribblers, wrapping paper, and precious stationery, letters poured into VONF. They included tales of terrible
disasters, feats of bravery, flights of verse, and songs:

"Dear Barrelman I send to you," wrote Mrs. Nat Brien in February
1939:

This letter that you see
To say we like your broadcasts
We hear just after tea
They are so very grand indeed
To us who like to hear

Of Terra Nova's heroes
Come floating through the air.

Though the early broadcasts were almost exclusively local history, Smallwood expanded his territory to include reports on Newfoundlanders who had made a name for themselves abroad; such as Sir Cyprian Bridge, the only native Newfoundlander to become an Admiral in the Royal Navy, and John Murray Anderson, the theatrical producer who succeeded the Great Ziegfeld as producer of the "Ziegfeld Follies." He spent the day gathering material, and late in the afternoon rushed into his office at O'Leary's warehouse overlooking the harbour to pound out a script, double-spaced, over five quarto pages. This he stuffed into his pocket without a second glance and dashed off to the broadcasting studio on the top floor of the Newfoundland Hotel. He usually arrived less than five minutes before air time, and at least once improvised an entire show, explaining *ad lib* how it was that he had nothing prepared.

As "Barrelman," Smallwood was essentially a populist teacher. "Baby talk but not baby thoughts" is his own analysis. Many in St. John's who knew their history far better than he were appalled at his insouciant refusal to let facts stand in the way of a predetermined conclusion and refused to take Smallwood seriously. To the baymen, he was the man at the top of the mast who took them seriously enough to tell them about themselves in their own language. When material ran short, he set off on new tacks. He tracked down the colony's oldest citizen, Mrs. Helen Carroll of North River, and recorded a program at her bedside every year on her birthday. When she turned 114, on October 11, 1942, he arrived with a hamper of presents which included a candlewick bedspread and a large turkey, and with messages of goodwill from King George VI, Pope Pius XII, and the Governor General of Canada. These Smallwood obtained simply by writing to ask for them.

At last Joe Smallwood was earning a respectable living. From the program and from editing a monthly paper, the *Newfoundlander*, in which his radio scripts now appeared, he made seventy-five dollars a week. He bought his first house, a plain but comfortable brown clapboard building on LeMarchant Road. Under Crewe's guidance, he acquired a taste for antiques and, as the proud possessor of a second-hand Dodge, roamed the outports in search of lustreware. His family was growing up, and in some ways he was becoming a person of at least some small substance. He was as interested in and as argumentative about politics as ever, but his only attempt to express his ideas was an unsuccessful weekly, *The Express*, which ran for six issues in 1942.

Politics rarely intruded into "The Barrelman," though in October 1940 he gave a wildly optimistic forecast of what Newfoundland would be like in 1990. In fifty years, he predicted, the railway would be abandoned and all transportation carried on over paved roads (there were then thirty-three paved miles on the island).

> And we'll have a large university. Education will be free and compulsory. Illiteracy will simply not exist and we'll be producing a Newfoundland literature full of creativeness and significance. Maybe you think my picture is too optimistic . . . just you wait and see.

Later that year, sparked by a speech by Senator William Duff, who proposed that Canada take over Newfoundland as "a wartime aid to Britain," and fed by approving editorials in mainland papers, rumours swept the island of a Canadian plot for instant Confederation. In a broadcast in December 1940, Smallwood hotly replied:

> There is no pretext, no excuse, no justification for putting Newfoundland into Confederation except by the free and ready will of the Newfoundland people, duly and regularly expressed by a secret ballot. Putting us into Confederation without our complete consent in writing would be illegal and unconstitutional. It would be more – it would be just as bad a piece of brutal aggression, just as callous a piece of dictatorial brutality, as any that has yet been committed by Germany herself.

Whatever brutality Canada might have in mind, as long as the Commission of Government ruled Newfoundland, there was nothing Smallwood could do about it. Chafing at his long surcease from politics, bored with "The Barrelman," and itching for a new cause, halfway through the war Smallwood abruptly abandoned all his hard-won security and flung himself into one of the most offbeat of Newfoundland's contributions to the war effort. He became a pig farmer at the Royal Air Force base in Gander.

Gander, in those days, was a latter-day Dawson City, a bizarre *fin-de-siècle* civilization in the bush. From a fuelling stop for fledgling trans-Atlantic airliners, it became, as soon as the war began, the biggest and busiest airport in the world. Scores of Ferry Command pilots touched down every day; the RCAF, RAF, and USAF maintained sizeable establishments. The Big Dipper bar stayed open twenty-four hours a day; fortunes were won and lost in all-night poker games; men fought for the privilege of a dance with one of the town's few women; Texas bush pilots swaggered in ten-gallon hats; RAF officers with handlebar moustaches drank champagne in toothglasses and bragged of prangs and pieces of cake.

The RAF was also practical when needs must. To give the King value for his shilling, the base commander decided to set up a "perpetual motion piggery." Swill from the messrooms would be fed to pigs which, in turn, would be slaughtered, cooked, and served to the officers and other ranks.

On the face of it, Smallwood was an unpromising swineherd. But he had developed a latent and unwise passion for farming, and in 1939, as a sideline, he had launched a small piggery of his own outside St. John's. Though it failed miserably – the herd was decimated by an epidemic of necrotic enteritis – he was, when the chance came, ready and eager to start again. He arrived in Gander in 1943 and, with capital rounded up from Chesley Crosbie, and the RAF Welfare fund, set up in business.

The first batch of breeding sows arrived from Prince Edward Island, in the blister of an RAF plane, and in time multiplied to three hundred.

They were housed in a long narrow wooden shed built from lumber liberated from the RCAF stockpile, and heated by a boiler removed from an
abandoned railway car. The establishment was less than a model of sanitation. The produce of the piggery was regarded with mixed feelings by
its consumers.

Since Smallwood neither drank nor gambled, he spent most of his spare
time arguing in the cafeteria and organizing impromptu debates. A
Canadian friend remembers, "He wasn't invited into many Newfoundland
homes." Instead, Smallwood won friends among Newfoundlanders of a
different sort. Standing in the queue outside the base theatre one night, he
realized that American servicemen were going in without waiting. "Why
should all the Yanks be going in?" he suddenly shouted. "What's wrong
with Newfoundlanders? This is our country." When an attendant came
out to remonstrate, a burly logger in the line decided that for once he too
would stand up and be counted. "You tell 'em, Joe," he shouted. All down
the line, Newfoundlanders took up the cry, and a riot threatened until the
manager emerged to restore order. He pointed out that the Americans had
built the theatre.

With the war's end, the foreign troops began to pull out. Smallwood prepared to sell his piggery while he could still get a good price for it. But he
had no thought of picking up his career as a reporter or broadcaster.
"Journalism's a losing, poorly paid game," he told a friend. Instead he
planned to start a cattle ranch, and had his eye on some suitable pasture
land in Bonavista Bay.

Even his best friends were beginning to believe that Joe Smallwood
had already had his future. He was now nearly forty-five, and for all his
outward cockiness the optimism of his youth was beginning to turn sour.
"It's very hard for a certain class of Newfoundlander to get any respect in
Newfoundland," he told a Canadian friend. "One day I'm going to make
them pay for some of the things they've done."

He was never more unconscious of his appearance, nor more unkempt.
When a visitor dropped round to the piggery to ask for him, a bystander
pointed to the animal barn and said: "Joe's the one with the hat on."

Most men, at Smallwood's age, and with his record of unbroken failure, would have been crushed by such contempt. Self-doubt never penetrated Smallwood's self-protective shell of egotism, and an iron will kept him going. Above all, he was still capable of thought, of speculation, and of hope.

Unending poverty and the heavy-handed rule of British civil servants had traumatized an entire generation of Newfoundlanders, robbing them of confidence in themselves and in their country. When, soon after the war, Britain offered Newfoundlanders the chance to decide their own future, only one man on the island was ready to rise to the challenge and seize the opportunity for himself and for his people.

6

A Cause Is Born

Late in 1945, his future uncertain, Smallwood travelled to Guelph, Ontario, to discuss the possibility of writing a manual on pig-farming. On the way home he stopped off in Montreal. The date was December 11. He checked into the Ford Hotel, stopped at the newsstand to buy a copy of the *Montreal Star*, for three cents, and went into the coffee shop. There he ordered a meal and idly picked up the paper. Above a Reuter's despatch from London, the headline leapt at him: "OLD COLONY TO REGAIN SELF–RULE. NEWFOUNDLAND PROGRAM GIVEN IN BRITISH HOUSE."

After twelve years of rule by an oligarchy of British civil servants, politics would be returned to Newfoundland, and to Smallwood. Whitehall, the story explained, was prepared to restore independence and self-government to the island if that indeed was what Newfoundlanders wanted. As a first step, they would elect a National Convention to discuss the future. Instantly, Smallwood decided that he would be a candidate. What he lacked, for the moment, was a platform.

Looking back on what ultimately happened, the linked fates of Smallwood and of Newfoundland had begun to crystallize the previous July, when British voters thanked Winston Churchill for leading them in war, and elected Clement Attlee to lead them in peace. Gone from Westminster were the flag-wavers, doggedly clinging to every tangle of jungle, every field of sand, and every outcrop of rock painted red on the map. In their places sat the earnest graduates of trade unions and the London School of Economics, determined to administer good in the name of the people, and should the people fail to recognize the good, to do it for them.

So far as the Labour Government was concerned, the good for Newfoundland lay in union with Canada. Attlee himself had visited the island in 1942 and had returned appalled by the conditions there. (One reform he initiated was the creation of municipal councils.) On the surface the colony enjoyed unprecedented prosperity. The American and Canadian bases provided jobs, and there was a surplus of some $25 million in the national accounts, accumulated by the Commission of Government's preference for debt retirement over human welfare. But Newfoundland's true economic equation was set out by R. A. MacKay in his comprehensive study for the Royal Institute of International Affairs:

> Newfoundland cannot, in normal times, provide the revenues to supply the island with the public services demanded by a Western people . . . without continuous and massive outside aid, the people of Newfoundland [will have to be] content to accept indefinitely much lower standards of public services than the present or probable standards of other English-speaking peoples.

Her standards were roughly comparable to those of rural Portugal. During the war, however, Newfoundlanders had discovered from the free-spending Canadian, American, and British servicemen how the other 99.9% of the Anglo-Saxon world lived, and had themselves been discovered by the outside world. Unstated in its policy, but implicit in its every act, the Labour Government was determined to allow

Newfoundlanders a chance to live as other Anglo-Saxons did. That they could do only through union with Canada was for Britain a happy conflux of beneficence and self-interest since, exhausted by the war, she could clearly no longer afford colonial liabilities.

The first hint of British intent was the decision to set up the National Convention. This was a violation of the spirit, if not the letter, of the 1933 agreement by which Newfoundland had given up self-rule. As voiced by the Newfoundland Prime Minister of the day, and repeated by Colonial Office officials, the understanding was that "a full measure of Responsible Government will be restored to the Island when we have again been placed upon a self-supporting basis." But instead of handing back independence immediately (as was done in the case of Malta), Whitehall ruled that Newfoundlanders should first elect forty-five delegates to a National Convention which in turn would debate and then recommend the future forms of government to be voted on by the public at a national referendum. This procedure not only delayed the restoration of independence but meant that Confederation, provided it found a champion, might win the referendum.

As broad an indication of Westminster opinion was its choice of Gordon Macdonald, a crusty former Lancashire coal miner, to be Newfoundland's sixty-third and ultimately its last Governor. At every turn, Macdonald was to aid the cause of Confederation; when he returned to England in 1949, his task completed, he was rewarded with a life peerage as Lord Gwaenysgor.*

---

* When Macdonald left Newfoundland, a poem of praise appeared in the St. John's *Evening Telegram*. Only later did an anguished editor discover that the poem was an acrostic; the first letter of each line spelled out THE BASTARD. The anonymous versifier's inspiration may have been Macdonald's role in bringing about Confederation; it may also have been his passionate advocacy, demonstrated at dry Government House receptions and over the radio, of the virtues of total abstinence – a proclivity that set him apart from most Confederates as well as most anti-Confederates.

As he read the *Montreal Star*, Smallwood of course knew nothing of this. All he recognized was that his moment had come. Leaving his food untouched, he got up from the table and went outside into the bright cold day. Though the temperature for the first time that winter hovered near zero, he paced the streets for hours, excitedly examining the possibilities before him.

In most of Smallwood's later recountings of the genesis of Confederation, the story ends at this point. The inspiration for his conversion came to him, as it were, from the wintry Montreal sky. At the same time, to rationalize their eventual defeat, anti-Confederates concocted the theory of a vast Anglo-Canadian plot to ensnare their blessed island, in which Smallwood was a willing and well-paid pawn. What happened is neither as dramatic as Smallwood prefers to remember nor as sinister as his opponents preferred to believe.

In twenty years of pondering, it had never occurred to Smallwood that Confederation might be the making of Newfoundland and of himself. Save in the lone "Barrelman" program, when he poured scorn on the suggestion that Canada annex the island, he had never even discussed the possibility in public, and only in the most academic of terms in private. Yet all his years in the wilderness had not changed his essential political motivations: a passionate love for his island; a sense of common cause with the common man; and, dating from his days in Bonavista, an acute awareness of the spiritual degradation of poverty, as well as personal experience of its physical pain. It was inevitable that he would someday realize that Confederation was the only logical answer to his solitary utopian speculation.

But in his abrupt attachment to the cause of Confederation, which he took up within twelve hours of reading the *Montreal Star* article, Smallwood, like most revolutionaries (though unlike most in his lack of hypocrisy about it), was motivated as much by personal ambition as by public good. Late in the afternoon of December 11, he encountered the agent who would spark his self-interest and Newfoundland's interest into an incredible, unstoppable drive that would carry Newfoundland into Canada's uncertain arms, and Joe Smallwood into the Premier's office.

The catalyst was a friend and fellow Newfoundland journalist, Ewart

Young, who had emigrated to Montreal where he earned a living free-lancing and by publishing a small monthly, the *Atlantic Guardian*. Young had spent most of the day on the telephone, talking to other exiled Newfoundlanders eager to discuss the momentous news. He also received a call from Boston, from the foreign editor of the *Christian Science Monitor*, who commissioned him to write a fifteen-hundred-word interpretive article by midnight.

The next ring was Smallwood's. "Have you seen it? Have you seen the news?"

"Yes," said Young, he had seen it.

"This is tremendous, fantastic. I have to talk to you."

Wearily, Young explained that he had to write a story for the *Monitor*. He suggested that Smallwood, fresh from Newfoundland, should write it for him, and this way leave them time to talk.

Barely fifteen minutes later, Smallwood was at the door of Young's apartment at 1625 Lincoln Avenue. He sat down at the typewriter and pounded away. As each take was finished, Young dashed to the telegraph office. Unbylined, the story appeared on the front page of the *Monitor* the next day, December 12.

London's decision to restore responsible government in Britain's oldest colony has delighted most Newfoundlanders but finds them almost totally unprepared to meet its implications.

Newfoundland must therefore start from scratch by organizing political parties and little evidence has been seen that any Newfoundlanders are interested in starting a party.

In the recent municipal elections in St. John's, a newly organized Labour party sponsored by some members of the trade unions nominated three candidates but they were defeated by the other candidates who ran as individuals without any party affiliations. Among the possibilities of the immediate future is the organization of a broadened Newfoundland Labour Party to contest the country as a whole.

The chore accomplished, and his conversion to Confederation still ahead of him, Smallwood and Young ate a hasty supper, cleared the table, and sat down to talk. At least, Young sat; until 3:00 A.M., Smallwood stalked up and down the tiny room, one hand tucked into his trouser belt, the other waving a cigarette holder that was never empty.

At first, both took it for granted that, whatever the constitutional procedures and delays, Newfoundland would shortly regain her independence, a circumstance that would return the old politicians to power. But Young had lived in Montreal long enough to be aware of the wider Canadian whole, and of its burgeoning system of social security. Newfoundlanders could share in all this through Confederation, he argued. Smallwood accepted the economic benefits without question; his point of disbelief was that Confederation was politically practicable. It was Young who sketched the golden vision and thereby clinched the argument. The man who brought about Confederation, he said, "will be the hero of the hour and of Newfoundland history." It was the answer to the question Smallwood had so often asked, and to so little avail.

From then on, Smallwood and Young no longer talked of issues, but only of ways and means. As he left the apartment, Smallwood's last words were: "I can't wait to get back to start preaching the gospel."

As an apostle of Confederation, the least of Smallwood's problems would be to convince Newfoundlanders of the material benefits of union. Even the farthest-flung outharbourman knew that Canada was an incomparably richer country. Instead, his most dangerous opponent was the Newfoundland mystique.

That mystique drew its strength from the Newfoundland character, forged in turn out of heredity and environment. Newfoundlanders, most of them, were Celts, their forebears from Ireland and the West Country. They were proud and sentimental, tough and impractical. Because they had rejected the dynamism and the tyranny of the Protestant Ethic for a humanism which placed people above things and the spiritual above the material, they had little in common with the sober Scots who had made Canada. A. P. Herbert, who visited the island in 1943, called Newfoundlanders "the best-tempered, best-mannered people walking."

To a later observer, the novelist Paul West, they were "a community of Irish mystics cut adrift in the Atlantic."

Isolation and hardship bred an overpowering sense of place. Newfoundlanders belonged to a series of widening circles; to their family; to their parish; to their faith; to their hamlet, bay, and stretch of coastline, and, above all, to their island. "Who are you *one of?*" they would ask of one another, and say of the outsider, "He comes from away." Without knowing what the word meant, Newfoundlanders had a *patrie*. With a passion only a Quebecker among Canadians could understand, they clung to the chimera of independence, even though independence amounted, as one Prime Minister put it, "to the trappings of an elephant on the back of a mouse." Like Quebeckers, their national ethic was endurance. Smallwood himself eloquently described its power when, at a dinner marking the tenth anniversary of Confederation, he compared his countrymen "to the mother of a crippled child, proud of hardship, misery, and privation, but still holding up our heads, still bearing the burden of our sorrows against the difficulty of living, or finding a substitute in pride for all we had not otherwise."

Yet if Newfoundland pride – and the songs, stories, and wit it produced – represented a triumph over adversity, it represented also a triumph over reality. Confronted by a stranger who questioned, Newfoundlanders hid behind a prickly sensitivity. A fastidious nomenclature board changed the name Famish Gut to Fairhaven; Sir Wilfred Grenfell, the great medical missionary of Labrador, was cheered in Boston, where he collected most of his funds, but was scarcely mentioned in Newfoundland where his work carried with it overtones of ministering to the natives. Articulate Newfoundlanders retreated into sentimental rhetoric about the arcadian virtues of simple, God-fearing fisherfolk; or, like the local magazine, the *Monitor*, they approvingly quoted Oliver Goldsmith:

Ill fares the land, to hastening ills a prey
Where wealth accumulates and men decay.[*]

---

[*] Smallwood quoted this same couplet at the Confederation for Tomorrow Conference held in Toronto in November 1967.

Such fierce, if doomed, patriotism boded ill for Smallwood's chances of success; so with equal force did the unhappy precedent of Newfoundland's previous relations with Canada.

From earliest times, Newfoundland, like Iceland and Greenland, has been a westward extension of the old world rather than an eastern extension of the new. Even in geographical terms, the two landmasses of British North America were farther apart than they appeared to be on the map. Until Trans-Canada Airlines inaugurated air travel to the island in 1942, the journey from St. John's to Ottawa via the "Foreign Express," by dilapidated ferry, and on CN coach took as long and was markedly less pleasant than the voyage to Liverpool by the Furness Withy "home boats." Merchants sent their sons and daughters to England to be schooled, the Catholic Church sent its seminarians to Ireland, and the only Newfoundlanders who had continuous ties with the Dominion to the west were the scattered few who worked in the Cape Breton coal mines or on Nova Scotia draggers.

Even so, Confederation had been an issue for nearly a century. "By the exercise of commonsense and a limited amount of that patriotism which goes by the name of self-interest, I have no doubt that Union will be good for the common weal," Sir John A. Macdonald wrote to the leading Newfoundland confederate, Ambrose Shea, in June 1867. Macdonald's vision of a new sub-continental nation was large enough to encompass Newfoundland, and his personality was substantial enough to breach the island's parochialism. At his invitation, Shea and Frederick Carter attended the Charlottetown Conference of 1864, and returned con-vinced, as Carter put it, that Newfoundlanders would be "besotted and insane" to reject a union "whose future it is impossible for the wildest imagination to over-estimate."

Britain, as she would do again eighty years later, did what she could to propel Newfoundlanders along the path of enlightenment. "Minor objections on the part of detached colonies," said Governor Anthony Musgrave, "must of necessity give way to the pressure of weighty motives of National Interest." He appealed to the legislature to approach the subject "in a spirit of calm examination."

It was as difficult for Newfoundlanders to observe this latter injunction as it was for them to define National Interest. They could already
look back on nearly four hundred years of independent history.

Their island was discovered, or may have been, by John Cabot in 1497,
though whether in fact Cabot spotted Cape Bonavista or part of the
mainland little matters, since he hoped it was Cathay. From then on,
before Jacques Cartier set foot in Gaspé, and long before Champlain
founded Quebec, European fishermen plied the Grand Banks in pursuit
of what Giovanni Casanova, a connoisseur of this and other delicacies,
called "the good sweet sticky salt cod of Newfoundland." Its status as a
formal British dominion, and the island's tenuous claim to be Britain's
oldest colony, dates from 1583, when Sir Humphrey Gilbert claimed the
island for Elizabeth. In fact, far from encouraging a westward daughter of
empire, Britain did everything she could to discourage settlement and
treated Newfoundland, as the historian A. H. McLintock has written, as
"her greatest experiment in retarded colonization." Though less assiduously applied, Britain's policies towards the island can be compared to her
oppression of the Irish and to her clearance of the Highlands.

For two centuries, Newfoundland was treated as "a great ship moored
near the banks for the convenience of English fishermen" and as a nursery
for training seamen for the Royal Navy. The West Country merchants
commanded a monopoly of the fisheries and a licence to seal the island
off to settlers who might provide competition. Ships were forbidden to
carry passengers or to allow their crews to remain ashore. The few that did
slipped into hundreds of tiny, untravelled coves; they owned no land by
formal title, and were forbidden to put chimneys in their houses, or to cut
wood within six miles of the shoreline.

There was no formal government of any kind, and such justice as
existed was administered by the brutal Fishing Admirals (the skipper of
the first ship in any harbour). An eighteenth-century naval governor
described his charges as "mere savages, without marrying or christening."
Sir Joseph Banks, the great naturalist, found St. John's in 1766 "the most

disagreeable town I ever met with" and its social standards so deplorable that for the Garrison Ball "the want of ladies was so great that my washerwoman and her sister were there by formal invitation." Ravaged by repeated French raids, harassed by the West Country merchants, and living in squalor, Newfoundlanders were driven to drink. One eighteenth-century estimate of the importation of rum to serve a population of perhaps 20,000 was 250,000 gallons a year.

Yet, by 1867, the colony's fortunes had dramatically improved. At the end of the Napoleonic wars, the ban against settlement was lifted, and land titles were granted. Through the nineteenth century, Newfoundland's population and wealth, based on her abundant fishery, increased rapidly. Representative Government was granted in 1832, a stage Nova Scotia had reached seventy years earlier, and twenty-three years later Newfoundland achieved full internal self-government – and so was raised to a par with the mainland colonies.

Within the larger union proposed by Macdonald, Newfoundland could presume to progress more rapidly than on her own. Yet independent, she could fare better in the fishing trade, and her *per capita* debt at that time was only $7.28 compared to Canada's $30.13. Newfoundland had no need of the railway that was so important to the mainland colonies, nor did she fear the Fenians whose cross-border raids had so powerful an effect on opinion in New Brunswick and Nova Scotia. The trans-Atlantic cable to Hearts Content in 1866 made London seem closer than Bytown.

The loquacious waywardness of Newfoundland legislators delayed matters long enough that no representatives were sent to the 1866 conference in London. On July 1, 1867, Canada became a nation; excluded from her territory in the east were Newfoundland and Prince Edward Island. The following year a delegation – "three attorneys and a speculator," according to a Colonial Office account – travelled to Ottawa and negotiated separate terms of union. In a concession to democracy taken by no other province on entering Confederation, these were put to the public at a general election.

The changed mood within the colony was soon apparent. A brilliant demagogue, Charles Fox Bennett, a merchant who feared the competition that union would bring, emerged to lead the anti-Confederate cause. Into the outports marched Bennett's men, singing the anti-Confederation song, with its famous line, "Come near at your peril, Canadian wolf." Fishermen were told that Confederation would bring a horde of Canadian tax-gatherers and that their sons would be recruited "to bleach their bones on the desert sands of Canada." Irish Catholics feared a sinister British plot. On a cresting wave of patriotism, the anti-Confederates won nineteen of the twenty-seven seats. "Firm in their adhesion to the fortunes of the mother country," declared the new Government, "the people of Newfoundland shrink from the idea of linking their destinies to a Dominion in the future of which they can at present see nothing to inspire hope, but much to create apprehension."

There was substance to that rhetoric. Though Smallwood has said of Confederation, "The only thing wrong with it is that we didn't join in 1867," the point is open to some question. The neighbouring Maritimes scarcely prospered in the new union; even in 1949 – the year of Newfoundland's actual entry – they were only just beginning to benefit from it. Family allowances were then only five years old; unemployment insurance had been in effect only nine years. The policy of equalizing have and have-not regions across the country was still nearly a decade away. The credits and debits to Newfoundland of joining Confederation in 1867 are hypothetical; if Newfoundland squandered her opportunities then, subsequent events made union inconceivable.

Of the outcome of the Newfoundland election of 1869, Macdonald commented, "The acquisition of the island itself is of no importance to Canada . . . we can wait with all patience for the inevitable reaction that must take place." The reaction came in 1894 when Newfoundland sank to the lowest point of her fortunes in history; two years earlier St. John's had been virtually destroyed by a fire; in that year, struggling with an economic depression and unemployment, the government was shattered by the collapse of the colony's savings banks. Bankrupt and with thousands of her people close to starvation, Newfoundland turned to Canada for help through union.

But Macdonald was dead, and buried with him was the vision of a nation from sea to sea. To his dour successor, Mackenzie Bowell, the offshore island was an unpromising addition to the Dominion. A Newfoundland delegation to Ottawa was received coolly and returned to report complete failure. The miserliness of Canada's terms moved even the British Government to comment that Canada was offering "a much smaller allowance to Newfoundland than was given to the other provinces."

To round out the image of Canadian indifference, the Canadian chartered banks rejected appeals for loans by the one remaining local financial institution, the Newfoundland Savings Bank, then suffering an acute run on its deposits, or to advance a loan to the Newfoundland Government. Bankruptcy was averted only when Newfoundland's Colonial Secretary, Sir Robert Bond, pledged $100,000 of his own money to the Savings Bank and raised a short-term loan for the Government in London.

Between Bond and Canada, no love was lost. Four years earlier he had travelled secretly to Washington to engineer a diplomatic coup which, had Canada not blocked it, might have transformed Newfoundland's fragile economy. This episode, a footnote to Canadian history, is one of the most important chapters in the chronicle of Newfoundland.

Bond's aim was to secure a reciprocity treaty that would encompass Newfoundland fish and American manufactured goods. A patrician and a man of parts, he quickly developed a close friendship with the United States Secretary of State, James G. Blaine, and within a month, at a diplomatic pace unheard of then, still less nowadays, the two had drafted a full-fledged treaty agreement.

At Ottawa this news was received with disbelief and with dismay. An official note was sent to London to protest that Canada was to be "placed at a disadvantage with a neighbouring colony." St. John's answered with a protest at "the interference of Canada and of our interests being made subservient to hers." From the Canadian Governor General came the ill-concealed threat that British ratification of the Bond-Blaine treaty "would perhaps be the most effectual method of impressing on the minds of the Canadian people that they cannot be British subjects and enjoy American markets." Invited to choose between a dominion of nearly five million and a colony of two hundred thousand, Britain had little difficulty in selecting the path of rectitude. The Bond–Blaine treaty was cancelled.

Out of this display of nineteenth-century brinkmanship, a minor trade war blossomed. Nova Scotia fishermen who bought their bait in Newfoundland were refused supplies. In retaliation, Ottawa imposed a special surcharge on fish imported from Newfoundland; as a counter-move, Newfoundland slapped a tax on all Canadian goods coming into the colony. Not until 1910, when Laurier's Government gave tacit approval to a second and ultimately unsuccessful attempt by Newfoundland to negotiate a reciprocity treaty, did relations between the two countries return to normal.

In fact, there were sound reasons for Canada to block the trade agree-ment. Macdonald's reaction to the Bond–Blaine treaty was dictated by reasons of high policy. Blaine was an annexationist, and as Donald Creighton has written, Macdonald aimed at "the maintenance of a united front by Great Britain and the whole of British North America against the United States." As for Bowell's parsimony on the terms of union, his grip on the Commons was weak, and the country at the time was suffering an economic recession.

No matter the reasons, Newfoundlanders neither forgave nor forgot. Canada had effectively killed Confederation for another half century. Until the 1940s, the idea was never again considered seriously, and the worst insult one Newfoundland politician could hurl at another was "Confederate."

Newfoundland and Canada continued diplomatic opponents. From 1902 to 1927 the two countries disputed sovereignty over Labrador. The issue was settled, until it broke out again amid the verbal thunder of Quebec's Quiet Revolution, on March 1, 1927, when the Judicial Committee of the Privy Council ruled: "The claim of the colony of Newfoundland is in substance made out."

Not until World War II did Newfoundland and Canada again find common cause. The great land ship moored near the Grand Banks could serve as aircraft carrier and guardian of the gulf. In June 1940, Canadian troops moved in to guard Gander air base. That fall, a Canada-Britain agreement proclaimed Newfoundland "an integral part of the Canadian scheme of defence." Canadian airmen moved to Torbay, to Gander, and later to Goose Bay in Labrador; St. John's harbour became safe haven on the long run to Londonderry.

On July 12, 1943, Mackenzie King enunciated in the Commons his Government's policy towards Newfoundland: "Canadians like and admire the people of Newfoundland. They will be happy if in any way they can contribute to the solution of their problems, many of which are common to both countries. If the people of Newfoundland should ever decide to enter Confederation, and should make that decision clear beyond all possibility of misunderstanding, Canada would give most sympathetic consideration to the proposal."

Yet few Newfoundlanders could see much evidence of Canadian admiration and sympathy. In contrast to the generous, gregarious Americans, Canadian servicemen tended to be aloof and patronizing; they poked fun at the island accent and coined the hated nickname, "Newfies." When the war ended, Canada remained an unknown country. For all his sudden devotion, it was equally unknown to Joe Smallwood.

7

Lighting the Flame

It took Smallwood about as long to win his first convert to the cause of Confederation as it had taken him to convince himself. He was no sooner off the plane and back in Gander than he rushed round to win over his friend, Tony Mullowney, civilian superintendent of works at the RAF base. Other disciples, though, would not come as easily; and since Smallwood knew almost nothing of Canada, not even the names of the five provincial capitals west of Quebec, he would be hard put to answer their questions, or those of the voters in the June election for the National Convention. He immediately plunged, "body, bones, and blood," into a marathon study of the body politic of the Dominion.

"Dear Sir," began Smallwood's letter to the Prime Minister and to the nine provincial premiers, "I wish to make a study of the Canadian Confederation, especially with a view to what effect union would have on Newfoundland. I would be very grateful for any material you could send me."

Within a fortnight the replies began arriving, a random harvest of thick brown paper parcels stuffed with yearbooks, departmental reports, budget speeches, surveys, statistical summaries, and all the other effluvia of government. Sternly warning his family not to interrupt him, Smallwood shut himself in his room and abandoned himself to the mountain of material. For two months, he pored over it, filling notebook after notebook, reading all night, catching up on his sleep during the day, and eating hasty meals off trays with a book propped in front of him. Besides his exceptional powers of concentration and of stamina, Smallwood brought into service his capacious memory, so that months later he would be able to quote key documents almost word for word. Nothing else in the world existed for him; when a friend asked how he intended to dispose of the piggery which still represented a considerable investment, he received a blank stare and the reply: "Piggery? What piggery?"*

In mid-February, by now as confident as any Ottawa mandarin of the complexities of the Canadian system, Smallwood travelled to St. John's to take part in a Methodist College Literary Institute debate on Newfoundland's future. He tailored his argument to the sensitivities of his audience. "Just as we are now Newfoundlanders under British rule, so we should be Newfoundlanders still, but under Canadian rule."

This opening shot aroused little response. Smallwood did better the next month when he pounded out a series of eleven articles outlining the benefits of Confederation for the St. John's *Daily News*. Anxious not to appear partial to the unpopular cause, the publishers ran them as letters-to-the-editor, in small type.

Smallwood began each letter with a terse opening paragraph to introduce its substance, and then in crisp, confident prose led his readers through the complexities of finance, trade, economics, and dominion-provincial relations, all the way down to such minutiae as: "Newfoundland would derive benefits from the Dominion Division of Child and Maternal Hygiene . . . Newfoundland would derive benefits from the Department of Nutrition. Newfoundland would be represented on the Physical Fitness Council. . . ."

Some passages were ingenuous: "As part of our deal with Canada," he wrote, "we should offer to allow the Dominion to take over title to Labrador, always reserving our fishing rights." Payment, he estimated,

---

* During an expansion of Gander Airport in 1955, Smallwood's piggery buildings were sold to the Department of Transport for $15,000.

would come in fifty annual instalments of four million dollars each. There were occasional rhetorical flourishes: "Under Confederation, we would be better off in pocket, in stomach, and in health. . . . For the first time in Newfoundland's history, Newfoundland's people would get a chance to live." The dominant tone though was didactic rather than hortatory. He aimed less to convert than to inform.

The letters stirred up a hornet's nest of protest, and Smallwood had to write three additional pieces to answer readers' objections. Yet for him the newspaper campaign was no more than a start. At best the *Daily News* reached ten thousand Newfoundlanders and most of these were in St. John's, the hotbed of anti-Confederate feeling. Few of the voters in Smallwood's own district of Bonavista Centre read any newspapers at all.

Time and again in Smallwood's checkered destiny, apparent misfortune turned into good luck. Thus, in the spring of 1946, what a close friend has called "Joe's pig lunacy" proved to have been a remarkable stroke of pre-science. As a gesture towards grass-roots democracy, and to prevent the St. John's merchants from dominating the National Convention, Whitehall stipulated that candidates must live in the districts they represented. Had Smallwood clung to his security as "Barrelman" and remained in St. John's, he could never have been elected.

In his bleak northeast coast riding, Smallwood's problem was to get his message across in a way that could be grasped by people accustomed to looking on politicians as something of a cross between public entertainers and snake-oil salesmen. Fired by this cause as he had been by no other, and summoning up all the skills learned on Harlem sidewalks and St. John's broadcasting studios, the revolutionary stormed into the murky Bonavista spring. Since his family was now in St. John's, his friends the Mullowneys left a light in their window, ready at any hour of the night with a meal, a clean shirt, and most important of all, a supply of fresh lemons to recharge Smallwood's most precious asset – his voice.

If a spark of political genius burned in this unlikely saviour in this odd corner of the world, its source was his mastery of the art of communication. Newfoundland in the 1940s, and only slightly less so today, was an oral society. People admired good gossips, good storytellers, and good stump orators less for what they said than for how they said it. It was a sound standard of judgment, for few events in the outside world made much difference to a fishing village, and the promises of politicians were rarely kept. Smallwood, the idealist, aimed much higher; he wanted to communicate, and to affect. To do this, he built his own oratorical style. The best description of it is his own:

> One. Nothing but nothing can take the place of an enormous amount of practice, an enormous amount of reading, and an enormous amount of argument. The more you talk, the better you become at talking. Two. Reading is absolutely vital – anything under the sun, including Eaton's catalogue, so that you can reach out for analogies and parallels to give your speech colour and life. Without massive reading, your speeches will be narrow and limited and arid. Three. To convince others, you must first convince yourself. Sheer sincerity can carry an audience.

Smallwood applies these rules to two types of speeches: "Shorthand" for literate audiences and "the full treatment" for the ordinary public. Of the second, and more common, category, he says: "If I haven't made myself fully understood to the least-educated man in the audience – fully understood to the last syllable – I feel I have wasted my time. In the process, I may say, I drive educated listeners in the audience to distraction."

The keystone of Smallwood's style is repetition, presented in a pre-ordered pattern. He first tells his audience what he is going to say; then he says it; then tells them what he has said. Sometimes he does this with a battery of rapid-fire, one-word synonyms for a single idea: "In spite of criticism, in spite of scepticism, in spite of jeering when we miscalculate or fail." Or he will hammer home his point with a string of synonymous phrases:

Newfoundland will fail because her people will not be able to earn a living. Thousands of our young men pour out of the schools each year; and either Newfoundland will get them or Ontario will. They will either stay in Newfoundland or they will leave. And whether they stay or go makes the difference between Newfoundland successful and Newfoundland a miserable failure.

His actual prose is hard and lean, uncluttered by adjectives and adverbs, but full of descriptive imagery. Instead of saying: "I was dragged in," he will say, "I was dragged in from the other side of the world with ox-chains." On the platform and over radio or television Smallwood emphasizes not words and sentences, but clauses and phrases, the true bone and muscle of the English language. His speeches acquire a powerful natural rhythm that is felt rather than heard. With the instinct of a born communicator, he involves his audiences in the process of speechmaking: Pretending to be at a loss for the right word, he will say "all the king's . . ." and suddenly stop to ask, "What's the word I need?" Delightedly, the audience shouts, "subjects," "horses," "men." Then Smallwood says, "Of course, all the king's *men*," and congratulates the audience for being better educated than he.

It was by a variant of this technique of contrived but effective audience participation that Smallwood acquired his famous nickname, "Joey." Conscious of the political value of an easily remembered diminutive, he set out to create one. During one outport rally, where the children, as always, were clustered close round the foot of the dais, he stopped in mid-speech and declared, with an air of irritation: "Ladies and gentlemen, I am going to have to stop. I cannot continue. I cannot go on. That boy down there, in front of me, has just called me Joe Smallwood. My name is not Joe Smallwood." The audience listened in horror to this apparent *lèse-majesté* and suffered for the poor boy who in fact felt no pain since he did not exist. "I will not be called Joe Smallwood. I will not allow it. My name is not Joe Smallwood. It is not Mr. Smallwood." He kept the crowd in suspense a second longer. "My name is *Joey* Smallwood." There was an instant of incomprehension, and then cheers and laughter. Joey

Smallwood repeated this performance at meeting after meeting until he no longer needed to: The legend was feeding off itself.

No examples remain of Smallwood's earliest speeches as a candidate for the National Convention. In fact, the only records of any of his speeches are tape recordings, *Hansard*, and newspaper accounts, for in all his long career he has written out the full text for only two addresses: a major statement of government policy on industrialization delivered in March 1953, and his remarks to the 1957 federal-provincial conference, of which an initial draft was prepared by his great federal ally, John W. Pickersgill. Neither was among his best efforts. As a corollary, Smallwood is justifiably proud that he has never used a speech-writer. Nor, since he knows Newfoundland so intimately, has he ever needed a research assistant. Smallwood's speeches may be, and not infrequently are, one-sided and demagogic. They are also entirely his own.

All that is left to posterity of Smallwood on the hustings in 1946 are the speeches he wrote out for Tony Mullowney, who planned to run as a Confederate candidate but because of illness was forced to withdraw. These are gems of single-minded propaganda, structured from strong ideas and simple words.

"In all the Western Hemisphere, in all the Western World, Newfoundland has the lowest standard of living of all. Our people eat less food, and eat worse food and wear less clothing and have poorer homes and poorer medical services and poorer education than any country this side of the Atlantic." Only Confederation could end destitution because, "Now here in [he left a space blank for the name of the hamlet] you have about [a space for the number of children] under the age of sixteen. Every one of these children will receive the family allowance, five dollars, six dollars, or seven dollars, according to the child's age. That will bring $ . . . into this settlement every month of the year, or about $ . . . for the whole year." (Mullowney was supposed to fill in the blanks with the appropriate figures.)

Into these speeches, as in his letters-to-the-editor, Smallwood packed a vast amount of basic information. He was then, as he has been through-out his political career, simultaneously preacher and teacher, self-serving politician and populist professor. Thus the electors of Bonavista were told: "In the past when you elected a man, you always had the feeling that he would be able to get jobs for you sometimes; that he would be able to get a bed in the hospital for you . . . things are different this time . . . the man you elect will not be in the government, he will not have any money to spend . . . he and the other delegates will put their heads together to try to figure out what would be the best form of government for Newfoundland, for Newfoundland's people."

Smallwood succeeded where his grandfather before him had failed. His candour and his concern for their well-being convinced the people of Bonavista that the bouncy little man with the big glasses and the loud voice would represent them well. On June 21, they elected him, by 2,129 votes to 277. It was the largest majority in Newfoundland. Elsewhere on the island, voters were indifferent. The over-all turnout was a scant forty-six per cent – an accurate reflection of the public's attitude towards so academic an idea as a discussion of possible forms of government by which the colony might possibly be governed at some unspecified date in the future; and perhaps, as well, an indication of public disquiet at the novelty of being asked to elect politicians who could return the favour with neither jobs nor hospital beds.

Smallwood had lit the Confederate flame in Newfoundland. It was time for him now to poke the embers at Ottawa.

8

―――

"We Are Not a Nation"

Taking a day-coach on the "Newfie Bullet" to save money, Joe Smallwood set out for Ottawa in August 1946. When he arrived, he found the cheapest room he could, in an attic of the Chateau Laurier. By now, with the piggery turned over to a brother, his scant resources were all but exhausted; he was able to make the trip only because Tony Mullowney contributed his share of a lucky war-surplus profit the two had made when they bought a load of army blankets for one dollar each, and sold them to a logging company the next day at double the price. Supremely unaware of the impression he created by his shiny suit and scuffed shoes, the Confederate set out to conquer the capital.

In the first summer of the peace, Ottawa was awash in the wake of Igor Gouzenko and absorbed in the first problems of the postwar era. Despite Mackenzie King's warm words three years before, the official attitude towards Newfoundland was best summed up by a chance remark the Under Secretary of State for External Affairs, Norman Robertson, made at a meeting called to discuss the possibility of the island's joining Canada. "There are collected here," said Robertson glancing round the room,

"just about everyone in Ottawa who is interested in Newfoundland."
There were four others present.

As much as Canadian indifference, Smallwood had to battle against his
own reputation. Word of his coming had preceded him, passed along by
the Canadian High Commissioner in St. John's, Scott Macdonald.
Smallwood, he reported, was of slight consequence and without political
following.

Since the Canadian Government had no intention of backing a loser,
this advice was acted upon, and R. A. MacKay, an External Affairs official
familiar with Newfoundland, was detailed to chaperon Smallwood while
he was in Ottawa. In particular, MacKay was enjoined to keep Smallwood
from bothering cabinet ministers and important officials.

The two met on Smallwood's first day in the capital and lunched
together in the Chateau's basement cafeteria. For MacKay, it was an
uncomfortable meal. He found Smallwood likeable, enthusiastic, and
unabashedly naïve. Smallwood, for example, peppered him with requests
to meet cabinet ministers, heedless of MacKay's grave explanations that
they were all extremely busy and utterly unable to find time for strangers
happening by at short notice. Three days later they met for lunch again.
"Well," reported Smallwood, "I've seen the Prime Minister." Smallwood
had managed this, as he has always done, by the simple expedient of
knocking on doors and asking.*

He had some help. Senator Neil McLean, owner of a fish plant at
Black's Harbour, New Brunswick, and squire of the company-owned
town there, who was a long-time supporter of Confederation, introduced him to another New Brunswicker, Fisheries Minister Frank
Bridges, and between them they opened several doors.

Smallwood, though, made most of the openings for himself.
Ministers and members of all parties, grudgingly persuaded to grant an

---

* As Premier, he no longer knocked on doors but dialled. With little modesty
and some exaggeration, he once claimed: "I can get anybody in England on
the telephone except the Queen and the Prime Minister. On second
thoughts, I could probably get the Prime Minister as well."

interview, sat spellbound as the pint-sized visionary expounded his beliefs. A freshman M.P., Robert Winters, set fifteen minutes aside but insisted Smallwood stay for over an hour. With the CCF leader, M. J. Coldwell, he discussed his background as a socialist, and said encouragingly, "Newfoundland will be a first-rate stamping ground for the CCF, the best in Canada."★

He called as well on John Bracken, the Conservative Leader, and Solon Low of Social Credit and, buoyant with success, dropped in on the Acting Prime Minister, Louis St. Laurent. (King himself was away at the Paris Peace Conference.)

By carefully scrutinizing the leader's movements, Smallwood determined that St. Laurent usually left the Commons shortly after Question Period and retired to a small private office beside the Speaker's Chamber. Unannounced, Smallwood arrived there one afternoon to be greeted by King's private secretary, who crisply asked his business and then posed a series of sharp, probing questions. Persistence had brought Smallwood a double reward. In John Whitney Pickersgill, he had encountered Ottawa's most ardent advocate of union with Newfoundland, and certainly the most influential among those who supported the idea. Within an administration that equated good government with sound business, Pickersgill was a rare bird – an emotional nationalist. He was convinced that if Newfoundland and Labrador joined Alaska as another northern arm of U.S. expansion, Canada would be "strangled, not physically, but spiritually."

Smallwood and Pickersgill talked for the best part of an hour. When St. Laurent came into the office, Pickersgill introduced him to the Newfoundlander, and they chatted briefly before St. Laurent went on to more pressing business.

★ Though they became political opponents, Coldwell remained an admirer of Smallwood. They met in person only once more, when Coldwell travelled to St. John's as a member of a federal committee studying election expenses. In the middle of the discussion, Smallwood broke off to tell Coldwell, "You know, I'm just as good a socialist as I ever was."

By the time Smallwood left Ottawa, the question of Newfoundland had begun to make its way up the ladder of government priorities. For the first time, union was judged a practical possibility.

Along with Confederation, Smallwood had sold himself. When Winters asked him if, in view of the unhappy history of relations between Newfoundland and Canada, union was really feasible, Smallwood answered, "You'll just have to take my word for it. If Canada wants us, I can do it."

The categorical "I" was significant. At home, Smallwood was still a prophet without honour. In the Newfoundland of the 1940s, he could be no more than the Confederate movement's principal lieutenant. For the position of public leader, a man of means and family was required. In the spring of 1946, Smallwood had found himself such a man – Frederick Gordon Bradley.

Then fifty-eight, Bradley was the son of a cabinet maker and was himself a former cabinet minister, a graduate of Dalhousie University, K.C., and a successful businessman in Bonavista, where he ran a restaurant, a movie theatre, and a fish plant. He was also one of the few left in the colony who had actual parliamentary experience, having been one of the two Liberals to survive the debacle of 1932. Of those days he recalled: "My partner didn't always keep close track of what was going on. But he knew that when I kicked him it was time to get up and second my motion."

Tall, and of imposing mien, with rimless glasses and heavy dewlaps under his eyes, Bradley resembled an irritable but well-informed pedagogue. Unlike Smallwood, he cut the kind of figure Newfoundlanders expected of their political leaders. He was also a long-time and convinced Confederate. Smallwood wrote to Bradley to suggest a meeting and then called on him at Bonavista. They talked all through one day, and through the night until breakfast next morning. By then, they had found common cause and, perhaps more important, they had agreed on a division of the spoils: Bradley would become Newfoundland's first federal cabinet minister, and Smallwood its first premier.

Along with his name, Bradley brought to the movement intellectual gifts in his own right. He had a quick and agile mind, and a flair for a well-turned phrase. He once accused the anti-Confederates of "being chained to the chariot wheel of a single idea." But his talents were dulled by indolence of truly monumental proportions, which he attributed to the fact that, ill as a child with scarlet fever, he had been swaddled for days in hot blankets, and so robbed of his energy. Lazy though he was, Bradley's contribution was nonetheless invaluable. He gave the Confederates respectability. Without it, Smallwood could not have won.

Other recruits were less respectable and less tractable. The most important and, certainly, the most interesting were Greg Power and Harold Horwood. Like Smallwood, both were outsiders and socialists; unlike him, both were true intellectuals. Horwood, then in his early twenties, was a fierce and lonely youth who wore a bright red beard as a banner. He was intolerant of others, yet nursed a rare and precious sensitivity which showed up years later when he discovered his true bent as a novelist (*Tomorrow Will Be Sunday*) and as a naturalist (*The Foxes of Beachy Cove*). Power, in his late thirties, was lean, saturnine, and handsome, a once-champion athlete crippled by an attack of tuberculosis that had turned him into a jaundiced cynic who cut down others with a barbed-wire wit. Power was a man of unexpected and catholic talents: for a year he supported himself in some style as a poker player at the U.S. Naval Base at Argentia; he could also write lyrical and moving poetry, evocative of Robert Frost. Together, Smallwood, Power, and Horwood were nicknamed "The Three Bolsheviks."

Some became Confederates for more predictable reasons. Aboard the "Express" that transported most of the outport members of the Convention to St. John's, Smallwood lobbied from night to morning. By the time the train pulled into the city, at least three delegates disembarked convinced they were to be Finance Minister. There were also five potential chairmen of the Liquor Board, while would-be Senators were as common as spruce trees.

With proper attendant panoply, the National Convention was formally opened on September 11, 1946. To make room for the delegates, the Lower Chamber of the Colonial Building had to be cleared of civil service offices. This done, the delegates set about finding out what they were there for, and how to go about accomplishing it. Theirs was not an easy task: although Whitehall's residence qualifications had had the desired effect of restricting the merchant compact to an enclave in St. John's, none of the flock of newcomers had any legislative or parliamentary experience. (Despite the well-meant attempt to broaden the base of politics in the colony, not a single fisherman was elected; many of the new men were co-operative fieldworkers or teachers.) The Convention's most serious flaw, though, was its philosophy. While the notion that an elected debating society of political neophytes could objectively debate future forms of government might delight a Fabian, it was enough to horrify anyone familiar with Newfoundland politics. Except for Smallwood and a scattered few mavericks like him, Newfoundlanders are imbued with a Celtic love of argument as a happy end in itself. For the National Convention to get anywhere, somebody had to tell it what to do. With a bluntness that shocked the courtly politicians around him, this Smallwood shortly proceeded to do.

Within the Convention, the anti-Confederates held a commanding majority. From the opening day they expended it in pointless assaults upon the present and the past sins, mortal or venial, of the ruling Commission of Government. So reminiscent of the old, factious House of Assembly, such debates left the public massively indifferent. At tea parties and over bridge tables, Newfoundlanders talked of the Nuremberg trials and, almost as exciting, of the colony's imminent switch to driving on the right.

On October 27, Smallwood put an end forever to the Convention's cheerful composure. He did it by talking, not about politics, but about Newfoundland. Defying the rules of procedure, he brought down a motion that invited the Convention to send a delegation to Ottawa, where it would discuss terms of union with Canada. Delivered to a full

house, and to packed public galleries, it was the most eloquent speech he
has ever made.

> The history of this island is an unbroken history of struggle. . . . The
> war has widened our horizons and deepened our knowledge of the
> great gulf which separates what we have and what we are, from what
> we feel we should have and should be. We have become uncomfort-
> ably aware of the low standards of our country, and we are driven irre-
> sistibly to wonder whether our attempt to persist in isolation is the
> root cause of our condition.
>
> Our very manhood, our very creation by God, entitles us to stan-
> dards of life no lower than our brothers on the mainland. We are fifty,
> in some things one hundred, years behind the times. We live more
> poorly, more shabbily, more meanly. Our life is more a struggle. Our
> struggle is tougher, more naked, more hopeless.
>
> We all love this land. It has a charm, it warms our hearts, go where
> we will, a charm, a magic, a mystical tug on our emotions that never
> dies. With all her faults we love her. But a metamorphosis steals over us
> the moment we cross the border which separates us from other lands.
>
> We are so used [to our ways] that we do not even see their inade-
> quacy, their backwardness, their seaminess. We take for granted our
> lower standards, our poverty. We are not indignant about them, we
> save our indignation for those who publish such facts.
>
> Except for a few years of this war and a few of the last, our people's
> earnings never supported them on a scale comparable with North
> American standards, and never maintained a government on even the
> prewar scale of service.
>
> We might manage, precariously, to maintain independent national
> status. We can resolutely decide to be poor but proud. But if such a
> decision is made it must be made by the sixty thousand poor families,
> and not by the five thousand families who are confident of getting
> along pretty well in any case.
>
> Our danger, so it seems to me, is that of nursing delusions of
> grandeur. We are not a nation. We are a medium-sized municipality.
> There was a time indeed when tiny states lived gloriously. That time

is now ancient European history. We are trying to live in the mid-
twentieth century, post–Hitler New World.

   We can, of course, persist in isolation, a dot on the shore of North
America. Reminded continually by radio, visitors, and movies of the
incredibly higher standards of living across the Gulf, we can shrug
incredulously or dope ourselves into the hopeless belief that such
things are not for us. By our isolation from the throbbing vitality and
expansion of the continent, we have been left far behind in the march
of time, "the sport of historic misfortune," "the Cinderella of Empire."

Those paragraphs *précis* all that is essential in the sociology of
Newfoundland: the long history of struggle and the pride of having
endured; the inexplicable wayward charm of the land and of its people;
the pathetic, unending poverty to which all but a handful were condemned.

   That speech was not only the most eloquent Smallwood has delivered,
but the most courageous. Even in the seventies, Newfoundlanders are not
yet confident enough of their material progress to accept so blunt a catalogue of their handicaps. In context of the mid-forties, Smallwood was
guilty of public treason. He was called a "Judas" and a "traitor" who for
the sake of personal ambition had dragged Newfoundland's good name
in the mud for outsiders to jeer at.

   In the succeeding weeks Smallwood absorbed volleys of personal
abuse unequalled in Newfoundland's political history. At the same time,
by his undeviating advocacy of Confederation he forced the Convention
to face reality; he transformed an ineffectual debating society into a political cockpit in which, in keeping with the importance of the issue, no
holds were barred and no quarter given or asked. Within that cockpit
Smallwood was, of course, by far the ablest politician.

9

Summer of Decision

A cause was born and died today on the floor of the National
Convention." Thus Newfoundland's most popular broadcaster,
Don Jamieson, concluded his radio report on Smallwood's passionate
speech on behalf of Confederation on October 27, 1946. Jamieson's
judgment was shared by almost all Newfoundlanders, certainly by anyone
who had any experience in island politics. Smallwood, the perennial
loser, had championed yet another hopeless cause. A fortnight later his
motion, to send a delegation to Ottawa to discuss the terms of union, was
defeated by a vote of twenty-eight to eighteen.

That defeat Smallwood could, and should, have predicted. Within the
Convention, battle lines were already set, and a clear two-thirds of the
members, including the entire bloc from St. John's, were adamant anti-
Confederates. The Convention now returned to its routine work, principally of taking potshots at the Commission of Government, and
Smallwood, robbed of his platform, seemed stalemated. Instead, in his
first demonstration that a professional politician was at work, he abruptly
reversed his tactics and pushed the cause of Confederation from a new
direction. He proceeded to ignore the Convention delegates and set out
to appeal, over their heads, to the public at large.

The opportunity for Smallwood to do this was handed to him, in the first week of November, by the Commission of Government. In a rare flash of enterprise, the Commission decided to broadcast the debates of the Convention and so bring parliament to the people. For its day this was a unique experiment in the use of modern mass media as an instrument of grass-roots democracy. Each night from nine to midnight, the full day's proceedings as recorded on wax discs were replayed over the government-owned station, VONF. Nothing was edited, and some gems of uninhibited oratory wafted over the airwaves, including one delegate's aphorism on the disadvantages of Confederation: "Them as gets their arses burned will have to sit on their blisters," and another's passionate enjoinder: "I for me do not believe the ship of state is sinking and have no intention of sending out an S.O.S. for a Canadian tug."*

Smallwood instantly recognized the propaganda potential of the new medium and he exploited it superbly. In hundreds of outports, people gathered around their battery-operated sets to listen for the first time, to *their* politicians talking about *their* country. More often than not they heard the familiar rasp of their old idol, the Barrelman. He monopolized the airtime with a constant barrage of interjections, questions, set speeches, and points of order. (In fact, Smallwood shouted "Point of Order" so often that many of his listeners, thinking he was shouting "pint of water," feared their hero was about to collapse from thirst.) When his opponents, driven to distraction, tried to have the microphones removed, Smallwood crushed them with the retort, "To despise these microphones

---

* The lack of editing in the broadcasts precipitated one precedent-setting law case on the limits of parliamentary privilege. It arose when Peter Cashin, a flamboyant anti-Confederate, accused three members of the old Newfoundland Government of having accepted bribes in return for voting for the establishment of the Commission of Government. The three, since they were named and the accusation was widely believed, launched a libel suit on the grounds that the libellous statement, though made on the floor of the Convention, breached the bounds of privilege as soon as it was broadcast over the public airwaves. The trial ended in a hung jury, and Cashin was carried from the courtroom on the shoulders of his cheering supporters.

is to despise the people of Newfoundland." In one attempt to silence him, the anti-Confederates stalked out of the Convention in a body and thus robbed it of a quorum. Unruffled, Smallwood proceeded to give a running commentary into the microphone, "There goes another one..." and accused them of trying to prevent the public from learning what was going on. As he later observed: "When people think that facts are being kept from them, they become very keen to get facts that they wouldn't normally give a damn about."

If Smallwood toyed with the Convention delegates, he was deadly serious in his approach to the public. He structured his speeches to appeal to ordinary people, abandoning complicated statistics and constitutional arguments for simple, emotional phrases. He did what he could to improve his voice, which was far from pleasing, and which when he was excited soared to a high, nasal whine that carried with it disturbing undertones of fanaticism. To minimize this, he arranged for a Confederate among the radio technicians to signal, by removing his earphones, each time his voice climbed into the upper registers.

Within the chamber itself, events began to flow his way. Directly or indirectly, the passion and excitement generated by his initial Confederate motion had struck down two Convention members: the Chairman, Cyril Fox, died from a fatal heart attack; Ken Brown, one of the ablest anti-Confederates, was paralyzed by a stroke. Though these tragedies were promptly blamed on Smallwood, he was more than compensated, for in its choice of a replacement for Fox the long arm of British policy made itself felt. The new Chairman was Bradley, a questionable decision since, for all his parliamentary experience, Bradley was an open Confederate. With him as referee, Smallwood now enjoyed the benefit of the doubt in procedural disputes.

On February 27, 1947, Smallwood once again brought down a motion to send a delegation to Ottawa. Learning by hard experience, this time he had carefully prepared the ground in advance. He lobbied for support among a group of delegates who favoured some kind of economic union with the United States, and he persuaded them to vote for his motion in return for his support of their own motion to send a delegation to Washington "for general trade discussions and other relevant matters affecting the future economy of Newfoundland." The Washington motion was overwhelmingly accepted by the Convention, but was then disallowed by the Commission of Government, as Smallwood had guessed would happen, on the grounds that negotiations with a non-member of the Commonwealth could not be permitted.

Smallwood's motion now came up for debate, and too late the anti-Confederates realized they had been outmanoeuvred. To recoup, they brought down yet another motion, this one to send a delegation to London to determine the prospects for British aid to an independent Newfoundland.

The two resolutions came to a vote on March 1. The first to be decided, the London motion, went through unanimously in a gesture of conciliation Smallwood could well afford. His own motion, "To ascertain what fair and equitable base there may exist for federal union between Canada and Newfoundland," rolled through by a vote of twenty-four to sixteen. Canada, making haste by propitious caution, waited a month to reply. On April 1, word came from the Canadian High Commission in St. John's that the delegation would be "warmly welcomed" at Ottawa. On the same day, External Affairs Minister St. Laurent, displaying some of the verbal agility of the Prime Minister he was to replace, said, "It will be essential to have a complete and comprehensive exchange of information and a full and careful exploration by both parties of all the issues involved, so that an accurate appreciation of the position may be gained on each side."

The London delegation left first. It was composed of seven members, with Bradley as Chairman. Even the advance portents were disturbing. The delegates were asked to bring their own towels with them. The reception at Whitehall was little warmer. Lord Addison, the Dominion Secretary, painstakingly explained Britain's postwar financial problems to the visitors which, he said, left the Mother Country "not in a position, however kindly may be our disposition, to be generous in these matters." At the final meeting, Addison closed proceedings with the injunction: "God bless Newfoundland." One departing delegate shot back: "God help Newfoundland." Addison was unruffled: "God helps those who help themselves."

There were a few brighter moments. A. P. Herbert, author and Independent Member for Oxford who had fallen in love with Newfoundland while there on a goodwill mission during the war, passionately championed the anti-Confederate cause and suggested Newfoundland "nestle up to the United Kingdom" in a kind of associate-state status similar to Northern Ireland. Herbert gave the delegation tickets to his latest play. When their spirits were at their lowest, he took them to lunch at the Savoy and startled the other patrons by chivvying his guests into a boisterous chorus of "We'll Rant and We'll Roar like True Newfoundlanders."

Back in St. John's, Peter Cashin charged that Newfoundland was "an international pawn being used by the United Kingdom Government for the purpose of making international deals with the United States and Canada." Less emotionally, and more accurately, Smallwood pointed out that Britain had been "bled white by her magnificent war effort. She is kept going now by loans of Canadian and American dollars."

In sharp contrast, the official attitude at Ottawa was warm and friendly from the first. The delegation, again of seven members – with Bradley as Chairman and, this time, with Smallwood as Secretary – arrived in the capital on June 23, to be met at Union Station by Louis St. Laurent. In his welcoming speech, at a reception and dinner at the Ottawa Country Club, Prime Minister King struck the right note by saying that union "is of course for the people of Newfoundland themselves to decide. It is not a matter in which either the people of Canada or the Government of Canada would wish to interfere." The following day, a Canadian negotiating team was assembled. Headed by St. Laurent, it included Justice Minister James Ilsley, Finance Minister Douglas Abbott, Defence Minister Brooke Claxton, and Fisheries Minister Frank Bridges. The two teams exchanged background documents and recessed for a week.

The Ottawa talks were expected to last no more than a month; nor was it envisioned that anything more than a broad and appropriately vague statement of Canadian intent would emerge from them. At home in

St. John's, June 24, 1947 was celebrated as the four hundred and fiftieth anniversary of Cabot's disputed landfall. The *Evening Telegram* put out a twenty-four page supplement on Cabot's exploits that sold an unprecedented twenty thousand copies. There was scant news from Ottawa and what there was made union seem even more remote. The *Halifax Chronicle* was openly gloomy: "The gains the Old Colony might obtain are too vague and doubtful. The picture presented by the Maritimes under Confederation is too discouraging to evoke ready enthusiasm among Newfoundlanders to share their lot."

For Smallwood, the immediate source of discouragement was the attitude of his leader, Bradley, who had arrived in Ottawa wearing his standard Bonavista rig of Harris tweed suit and Stanfield's woollen long johns only to discover that the capital was in the midst of a heat wave that left him prostrate in his Chateau Laurier suite. Bradley openly pined to return as soon as possible to the cool breezes of Newfoundland. With some difficulty and unaccustomed tact, Smallwood persuaded him to buy a lightweight suit and summer underwear, and thus refreshed Bradley agreed to stay. Other members of the delegation found the heat equally distressing, but discovered other diversions until the federal officials charged with taking care of the visitors were bombarded by police complaints of official cars roaring around town at all hours of the night filled with men apparently wearing woollen undershirts and singing "Irish-sounding" ballads at the tops of their voices.

More disturbing, for someone as single-minded as Smallwood, was the vacillating attitude of the Canadians. The hot dusty summer of 1947 was a poor time for brave decisions at Ottawa. The Government was passing through an interregnum. The essential decision required of it was whether merely to pass the time with Newfoundlanders, in pleasant platitudes about the benefits of union, or to get down to the actual negotiation of possible terms of union, a step that would morally commit Canada to accept Newfoundland into Confederation. After two weeks of aimless if amiable discussion, this basic contradiction of purpose was brought out into the open by a civil servant, the Under Secretary of State for External Affairs, Lester Pearson. One of Pearson's regular background briefings for Ottawa newsmen resulted in a story in the St. John's *Daily*

News that quoted "authoritative Canadian sources" as saying that the Newfoundland delegation "has no power to agree to or promise anything . . . Canada would prefer to negotiate with an elected government, to forestall any possibility of future complaints by Newfoundlanders that they had no voice in the actual negotiation of terms."

Pearson's undiplomatic frankness gave Smallwood his worst moments of that summer. Bradley was outraged by Pearson's abrupt dismissal of the importance of the Newfoundland delegation. Well aware his leader would take this attitude, Smallwood hid the *Daily News* article from him for a week but, inevitably, Bradley came across it anyway in a batch of clippings sent to him from St. John's. He promptly exploded. The Canadians, he declared, were play-acting, just as they had in 1894, and he for one was going home. Had Bradley done so – the official Confederate leader quitting Ottawa to denounce the perfidious Canadians – the Confederate movement would have died stillborn. Frantic, pleading and arguing through successive late evenings in Bradley's hotel room, Smallwood persuaded him to hold on at least until the Canadians had made their final decision on how to treat the delegation.

That decision, and the debate leading up to it, had already split the Canadian cabinet. Ostensibly, the argument was about constitutional proprieties: whether union could be negotiated with any body other than an elected government. The root problem was political. Ilsley, in particular, as representative of the disaffected Maritimes, questioned the impact upon Canadian public opinion of the financial concessions that would have to be made to persuade Newfoundland to join. Against him were ranged C.D. Howe, Pickersgill, and, outstandingly, Louis St. Laurent. On July 18, St. Laurent impressed upon King, as the Prime Minister recorded in his diary, "of the value it would be to my name and to the future to have Newfoundland come into Confederation while I am still Prime Minister." This reminder of the opportunity for immortality inspired King to summon a special cabinet committee meeting, chaired by himself, to make the final decision whether to elevate the talks to the status of negotiations. Through Canada's High Commissioner to Newfoundland, Scott Macdonald, Smallwood knew all of these developments, and he sweated out the wait.

The cabinet committee held its meeting in the East Block in the last week of July. Outside on Wellington Street, Smallwood paced up and down, chain-smoking in an agony of impatience. Macdonald, who had promised to let Smallwood know the decision as soon as it had been taken, sat in on the cabinet meeting. Late in the morning, Macdonald emerged and came down the stone steps of the East Block. He was smiling. "Is it O.K.?" shouted Smallwood from across the road. "Yes, Joe," said Macdonald, "it's O.K."

Once again, the cause of Confederation lurched forward. To say that it sped forward would be to exaggerate, for there were still endless difficulties for Smallwood to overcome. Maurice Duplessis, in the midst of a provincial election, raised the touchy question of ownership of Labrador, and inspired Smallwood to a withering blast. He compared Duplessis to "Hitler marching on the Sudetenland." In Ottawa, the federal negotiating team reassured the Newfoundlanders that Labrador would remain theirs.

For tactical reasons, the chief of which was to avoid an uproar from the anti-Confederates back in St. John's, it was important to conceal so far as this was possible the fact that actual negotiations rather than exploratory discussions were going on in the capital. To keep the show going, Smallwood, on instructions from MacKay, invented a series of questions about the Canadian federal administration, and put these to the civil servants on the other side of the table, who usually took their time about replying and, indeed, had sometimes suggested the questions.

Every delay, including a trip by slow train to Niagara Falls, was welcomed by the King Government. For no sooner had the decision to negotiate been taken than a new and more obdurate difficulty had arisen. The sudden death of Frank Bridges, the cabinet minister from New Brunswick, left Ilsley, a preternaturally gloomy Nova Scotian, as the only Maritime cabinet representative. He would not, said Ilsley, put his name to any agreement on terms of union unless there were a second Maritime minister to help shoulder the possible burden of political blame.

King needed little persuasion of the virtues of caution. On August 14, he lectured the cabinet that if the Maritimes opposed Newfoundland's entry, "We would have utter chaos in Canada, the Government would be defeated, and we would be further away from Confederation with Newfoundland than ever." Once more, an intervention by St. Laurent, backed by Pickersgill, saved the day. As a compromise, St. Laurent proposed that Canada "continue discussions with the Newfoundland delegates, get to the point where they are agreed, and then ourselves decide whether we could offer them these particular terms." The terms would then be withheld from the public until the by-election to fill Bridges's seat was safely over. As the Liberal candidate in York-Sunbury, King named Milton Gregg, a V.C. and President of the University of New Brunswick.

For Smallwood these were glorious days. He revelled in the twin stimuli of action and of challenge. One afternoon, walking back to the Chateau Laurier with MacKay and Bradley, he stopped to stare up at the bronze statue of Sir Wilfrid Laurier on the grassy slope of the East Block. "Do you think," he asked the others, "they will one day put up a statue of me?"

Then there was trouble back in St. John's. With the Convention idled now for nearly three months by the absence of its Chairman, a group of anti-Confederates had called on the Governor to demand the delegation's immediate return. Smallwood jumped into the fray with a letter to the paper denouncing them for "unfounded, inaccurate, and highly-coloured guesses, speculations, inferences, and sheer mis-statements."

The real work was being done behind the closed doors of the Railway Committee Room in the Centre Block of the Parliament Buildings. There many broad but crucial points were agreed on with little debate. As a province, Newfoundland would be allowed to retain her unique denominational school system; in the absence of local divorce courts, Newfoundland divorces, like those of Quebec, would be granted only by the federal parliament; Canadian social welfare payments would automatically be extended to the citizens of the new province; the CNR would assume responsibility for the deficit-ridden railway and the coastal steamers.

The nub of the debate in the Railway Committee Room, and the nub of Confederation itself, was financial. Once a province, Newfoundland

would surrender customs and excise duties to the federal government, and
so lose sixty per cent of its pre-Confederation revenues. This loss, and the
deficiencies in existing public services, could only be made up by special
federal grants, and for these the ceiling was set by Maritime sensitivities,
the floor by Newfoundland needs. At the same time, the paucity of economic data on the colony made it impossible to forecast financial needs for
more than a few years ahead. Thus the terms would have to contain a
clause to take care of future contingencies. The task of drafting it was
given to MacKay and Smallwood. For four days they worked together in a
small office in the East Block, Smallwood stripped to the waist because of
the oppressive heat. At the end of each day, they collected all their working
papers and scrupulously tore them to shreds. At last the draft resolution
was completed and accepted at a plenary session. A decade later, it would
become infamous, at least in Newfoundland, as Term 29.

The last meeting between the two teams was held on September 23,
and after ninety-nine days and eighty-four working meetings, the
Newfoundlanders left Ottawa. They carried with them a report on the
discussions which covered general topics like education and welfare. The
key report on the financial terms remained in Ottawa.

A month later, on October 25, Milton Gregg was elected to
Parliament by a record 4,118 votes. Insofar as their opinion had been
asked, Maritimers had spoken in favour of union with Newfoundland.
On November 6, Smallwood proudly tabled in the National Convention
two documents: a White Paper on the general agreement; and two black-
bound volumes on the financial proposals for union.

It was upon a platform fashioned from this financial offer that Smallwood
carried Newfoundland into Confederation. For him to have done so
required skill. The terms were by no means a bargain, and had they been
left unchanged would have bankrupted the new province within half a
dozen years. The 1947 terms (as they can be called to distinguish them
from the final terms renegotiated in 1948) even contained such elementary
errors as the failure to mention that Canadian veterans' allowances would

be extended to the ex-servicemen of Newfoundland, an omission that the anti-Confederates used to advantage in the succeeding campaigns.

Such minutiae provided small-arms fire for political wars. What mattered was that a serious offer had been made, and thereby constituted proof of Canada's serious intent. According to the 1947 terms, Newfoundland would pay Ottawa, in customs duties, income, and corporation taxes, $20 million a year and receive in return $35 million for a net annual gain of $15 million. In addition, Ottawa would absorb the bulk of Newfoundland's national debt.

The contrast with Britain's parsimony was obvious. Few needed be reminded of the difference, and any who did had it constantly pointed out to them by Smallwood. Overnight Confederation with Canada ceased to be an academic issue and became a practical and immediate one.

This much Smallwood had accomplished in little more than a year in a country where Confederation was a dirty word. By sheer persistence, he had got everyone talking about Confederation, even those who passionately opposed it. Every day Canada seemed to draw a step closer. All through the summer, the dateline "Ottawa" had appeared in the St. John's papers. Just two days before the Ottawa proposals were tabled, Trans-Canada Airlines inaugurated a new "time-saving" schedule that cut the Montreal–St. John's flying time to ten hours and fifty minutes. Later that month, Simpson's opened mail-order offices in three island centres.

Though a Responsible Government League had existed in name since 1945, the anti-Confederates were so confident of success that they had until now made no attempt to organize effectively. Belatedly they unfurled their banner: "Responsible Government is what our forefathers fought for and won nearly one hundred years ago," ran their full-page newspaper advertisement on July 21, 1947. "We feel that the present generation of Newfoundlanders has a duty and a trust to restore this temporarily lost heritage. . . ."

The first anti-Confederate counterattack was intended to be launched when the Ottawa delegation reached home. Confident of their majority within the Convention, the anti-Confederates decided to move a motion of censure against Bradley, for exceeding his mandate in Ottawa. Smallwood was told of this plan by Ewart Young who had picked up the rumour while in St. John's for the *Christian Science Monitor*. On the train journey home, he devised a strategy to parry the blow.

As the Convention reassembled, Bradley took the Chair. Hardly had the delegate who was going to move the non-confidence motion begun his speech than Bradley interrupted him. With persuasive outrage and injury, he denounced the delegate for his impudence and finished with a dramatic flourish: "Gentlemen, this Convention is without a Chairman." With that, Bradley stalked out of the chamber, leaving pandemonium in his wake. While the anti-Confederates sought frantically for some way of censuring a Chairman who no longer existed, Smallwood lit a cigarette to demonstrate the collapse of parliamentary procedure, and assiduously compounded the confusion by shouting: "What are we going to do? This is terrible. This is awful. We have no Chairman. What are we going to do?"

Another Chairman was found. By then, Ottawa had forwarded the financial terms, and the issue of the conduct of the Ottawa delegation had dwindled to a footnote in history. From this point on, thanks to Smallwood, the Convention debated almost nothing except the Canadian terms. He used every trick of the practised parliamentary debater to keep the spotlight on himself. Once he turned on a delegate and told him: "Does the honourable gentleman believe that because he has so much money he has the right to insult me?" The delegate denied he had intended to insult anybody. In the shouting match which ensued, the hapless delegate's original point was irretrievably lost and the issue became how much money he had, and why he should have tried to insult Smallwood. Smallwood firmly staked out the high ground for himself. He denounced his opponents for "dealing not in ideas but personalities, not politics but name-calling, not great political principles, but accusations of graft, bribery, treachery and all the rest of those old-time political ammunition dumps of trash and garbage."

It is a political truism that you cannot beat somebody with nobody. Smallwood was producer, director, stage-manager, stagehand, and star actor of the Confederation movement. He wrote some, drafted most, and advised on all of the speeches of his supporters. He devised strategy and nearly always had the final say. Above all, Smallwood always knew exactly where he was going, and how. As he wrote in his account of the Confederation battles in Volume Three of the *Book of Newfoundland*: "When you include the earlier motions and the debates on them ... there was a total of thirty-four days in the National Convention when the sole topic of discussion was Confederation with Canada. The opponents of Confederation must have been asleep."

Not entirely so. They tried to interrupt him, only to draw the unanswerable retort: "Why are you trying to hide the facts from the people? Let the people hear the facts." And the people, clustered around their radios in the outports, cheered. Only one anti-Confederate, Peter Cashin, was undaunted by Smallwood's oratorical ferocity, and since Cashin could shout a good deal louder, their battles were epic. At one committee meeting they came to blows and the two rolled on the floor until they were wrenched apart, when Smallwood added insult to injury by blowing smoke into Cashin's face.

As 1947 turned into 1948, and the Convention's work drew to a close, the anti-Confederates were left with one trump card. The Convention's last task was to recommend the forms of government to be put to the public in the upcoming referendum. The easiest way to defeat Confederation, Smallwood realized, was simply to vote against putting it on the referendum ballot paper. Overnight he became a staunch defender of political fair play. The Newfoundland public had the right to decide on Confederation for themselves. For the sake of democratic principle, he argued, it must go on the ballot paper. On the eve of the vote, during a session that continued until 5:00 A.M., Smallwood delivered his last speech to the Convention. His intended audience, however, was not the delegates who would vote, but the fishermen, the loggers, the labourers, the unemployed, the destitute old, and their wives, listening to the broadcast.

We are seeing people trying to scare and frighten us with a bogeyman they call Confederation. Ladies [all the delegates were men] and gentlemen, you and I are children no longer. Politicians and others might have been able to frighten and cow our people about Confederation in years gone by, but now we are grown up. . . . A new hope has arisen in the hearts of our people. They see in Confederation a new hope for the common man; they see in it a new hope for justice, for fair play, for a new day for Newfoundland. Let no man dare to crush that hope that has arisen in our people's hearts.

He closed by quoting a passage from William Blake's *Milton*, making one change in the wording:

I will not cease from mental fight,
    Nor shall my sword sleep in my hand,
Till we have built Jerusalem,
    In *our* green and pleasant land.

Elsewhere in his speech, Smallwood found support for the ideals of Confederation in Bunyan, Milton, Shakespeare, Longfellow, Tennyson, and extensive passages from the Bible. He spoke for over two hours.

On January 29, the Convention held its final sitting. Unanimously, delegates recommended that "Responsible Government, as it existed prior to 1933," should be placed on the referendum ballot paper. For the sake of propriety, although it was a certain loser, the Commission of Government was also added to the list. Smallwood's motion: "Confederation with Canada on the basis of the terms submitted to the National Convention, November 6, 1947, by the Prime Minister of Canada," was defeated, twenty-nine to sixteen. This was virtually the same margin, and indeed a shade wider, by which his original motion to send a delegation to Ottawa had been defeated fourteen months earlier. The Convention dissolved.

The defeat would have crushed many men. Smallwood, in one of the many displays of resilience that sapped the morale of his opponents, took all of twenty-four hours to recover.

He laid his plans the day the Convention dissolved, and two days later Bradley took to the radio to deliver a speech Smallwood had written for him. He damned as "the twenty-nine dictators" the delegates who had voted against Confederation, and thus thwarted the people's right to decide for themselves. The people could make their will known by a mass petition "and the more thousands the better."

The first wires of protest from distant outports had already come in to St. John's before Bradley spoke. Now they poured in, more than seventeen hundred telegrams and hundreds of letters covered with signatures. As the tally mounted. Smallwood spurred it on by a series of running bulletins to the press. The final total was 49,796. This Smallwood presented, with appropriate ceremony, to Governor Macdonald to be forwarded to London.*

London took its time about replying, and for Smallwood it was an agonizing wait. One reason for the delay was the need to make discreet inquiries to determine the Canadian attitude. The response was favourable. Whitehall also had to justify contradicting the stated purpose of the National Convention, which had been to recommend the wording of the ballot paper. At last, on March 10, the Commonwealth Relations Secretary, Philip Noel-Baker, announced that since "it would not be right to deprive the people of the opportunity of considering the issue," and "having regard to the number of members of the Convention who supported the inclusion of Confederation with Canada on the ballot paper," it would be so included. The date for the referendum was set for June 3. Smallwood called it "a victory for the people."

---

* Surprisingly, as Smallwood discovered later, Macdonald had never bothered to forward the actual petition to London, and had merely mentioned its existence and its numerical size in a despatch.

10

Confederate and Independent

In the spring of 1948, the cause of Confederation stood exactly where it had in 1869, dragged there by Smallwood's oratory, willpower, and effrontery. If history were not to repeat itself, he would have to demonstrate talents for stamina, organization, and attention to detail that no one had ever suspected in him. He rose to the challenge.

As the telegrams demanding that Confederation be put on the ballot paper flooded in, Smallwood stood over his family, his friends, and his supporters until they had copied down every name and address. When the mammoth task was completed, he could identify more than half his potential supporters.

Smallwood was as demanding of himself. Throughout his life, he had been used to getting eight or nine hours sleep, and had even been something of a layabed. He now began each day at eight o'clock and except for one or two catnaps, from which he awakened as refreshed as after a long sun-drenched holiday, he was on his feet until two or three in the morning. Though he was as oblivious to his surroundings as ever – he lived in a shabby, crowded apartment on Duckworth Street and worked in a tiny campaign office above a barbershop a few blocks away, cluttered with ancient typewriters, filing cabinets, maps of Newfoundland bright with drawing pins and calendars which showed June 3 circled in red ink – he paid more attention to his appearance, affecting double-breasted suits and gaudy floppy bow-ties as appropriate for a future premier. He was still "skin and grief"; because his hair was thinning too, and flecked with grey, he was beginning to look older than his forty-six years. His energy was that of a twenty-year-old.

Smallwood quite literally never stopped working. He could give every ounce of his attention to a particular problem, switch effortlessly to another subject, and then back again. Even with his closest associates, Power and Horwood, he abhorred small talk, and regarded unproductive leisure with contempt. Saturday, Sunday, or Monday were all the same to him. Smallwood's was not nervous energy, brittle and ultimately exhaustible, but the steamroller drive of a man of action who once seized of an idea allowed nothing to stand between him and its attainment. A more sensitive man might at times have flagged or indulged in the luxury of defeatism. Smallwood possessed only a brutal and hungry willpower, for which he had at last found a worthy goal.

Smallwood held the formal inaugural meeting of the Confederate Association, his campaign organization, on March 26, in the ballroom of the Newfoundland Hotel in St. John's. He was nominated – to use that term loosely – as campaign manager, and Bradley as president. The meeting also nominated 115 vice-presidents who were community leaders in towns and outports dotted strategically around the island. To many of these men, the honour came as a surprise, particularly to those who happened to be anti-Confederates and subsequently had to be dropped from the roster.

A fortnight later, the first issue of *The Confederate* was on the stands. Since Smallwood had long considered the weekly as the centrepiece of his campaign, he had prepared it well in advance. Each issue contained cartoons by Jack Boothe of the *Globe and Mail*, the ablest political cartoonist in Canada, whom Smallwood had hired on a side-trip to Toronto during the Ottawa negotiations. The paper's professional layout and snappy style reflected the work of the "Three Bolsheviks," who among them churned out all the copy. Power's principal contribution was "The Sacred Cow" column, a series of witty and caustic profiles depicting the

main anti-Confederate personalities and their policies. He was also a tal-
ented doggerelist, and sent some of his best efforts to the daily newspapers
under the *nom-de-plume* "Interested Housewife."

Because it was lively, and fun to read, *The Confederate* was welcome
even in anti-Confederate homes, for there is little Newfoundlanders like
better in their politicians than the ability to give and take repartee. But
Smallwood never forgot that, while people may applaud a well-delivered
speech, elections are won on bread-and-butter issues. Each edition contained columns outlining in detail the benefits specific outports would get
from Confederation, and articles which compared the cost of living in St.
John's to that in, for example, Sydney, Nova Scotia. "Beef Stew 19¢ vs.
45¢; Heinz Baby Food 20¢ vs. 32¢; Bologna 25¢ vs. 40¢." The paper was
exuberantly optimistic: "Confederation is very strong in 18 out of 24 districts"; "A great welcome was given J. R. Smallwood by the people of Bay
Roberts last Friday afternoon." The opposition was given no quarter.
One front page contained these headlines above different articles: "A
CHEAP LIE!" "ANOTHER ROTTEN LIE," "A FOUL INSULT," "BRIBERY," and
"THE WORST LIE OF ALL."

Next in importance to *The Confederate*, which reached fifty thousand
homes, were Smallwood's speeches, delivered either in person or through
Bradley's mouth over the radio. In all of them, Smallwood never deviated
from the unarguable thesis he had set out in Bonavista two years earlier:
Confederation meant hard cash in the pockets of the people, for many of
them for the first time in their lives.

In his own appearances, Smallwood was enough of a master of the art
of platform drama to embellish this simple theme with a grab-bag of
sprightly variations. Skilfully, he capitalized on the uninhibited enthusiasm of children, which contrasted strikingly with the deep-rooted
shyness in public of most Newfoundland adults. At meeting after
meeting, Smallwood cajoled children onto the stage beside him, and
made a great show of asking their names and ages. Then, holding one
child by the hand, he would turn to the audience and say: "Now, Peter.
You are eight, and you have two brothers and one sister, all under sixteen.
When Confederation comes, your mother, Mrs. X., will receive every

month, $22.00 to look after you, to buy your clothes, to buy your food." He then repeated this procedure with each child on the platform.

As he had done as Barrelman, Smallwood adopted also the mantle of teacher, knowing well that except for minister or priest it was the most respected position in outport communities. "Next week," he would say, "you will go to the polling station and vote for the kind of government you would like to see in Newfoundland. What you will decide by your vote is the kind of government you would like to see in Newfoundland. What you will decide by your vote is what form of government – not what party – but what *kind* of government we shall have. You will see three forms of government on the ballot paper." At this point, he produced a sample ballot sheet and acted out an animated and graphic demonstration of how to go inside a voting booth and mark it: "If you want Confederation, mark an X against it; if you want Commission of Government, which is what we now have, mark an X against that. And you'll see on the paper, Responsible Government as it was in 1933. Now most of you will remember our Government in 1933. You remember the dole of six cents a day, the unemployment. If you decide, I don't want family allowances, I don't want pensions, I don't want veterans' benefits, I don't want anything from Canada, then mark an X for Responsible Government."

To spread his message in a country with almost no roads, Smallwood took to the air. He campaigned in an ancient seaplane that took the best part of a mile to taxi into the air; when it was grounded for repairs, he used a Grumman Widgin. Bellowing down over twin loudspeakers, he flew above tiny, far-flung communities until the outharbourmen, many of whom had never seen a plane before and considered anyone connected with such machines faintly God-like, had taken to their boats and put out into the harbour. Smallwood would then land, one hand clutching a strut, the other a hand microphone. After the speech and the cheers and the shouts, he clambered back into the plane and took off – the people's champion who had cared enough to come.

In the eastern part of the island, where a network of roads existed, he campaigned in a car, with a sound truck following behind. At each stop, the loudspeakers were switched on for a medley of marching songs and Newfoundland ditties; once a crowd had gathered, Smallwood delivered his address standing on a boulder or an upturned dory. Other Confederate speakers went on the stump as well, using chartered schooners.

To pay for all this expensive transportation, and for the other election expenses, which included outlays for the traditional bottles of beer and shots of rum, and individual votes that could cost five dollars, the Confederates amassed a campaign fund of close to $150,000. Though at the time Smallwood skilfully portrayed himself as the underdog – a pose he is astute enough to adopt in every political contest he can – the anti-Confederates had in fact less than half that amount. Smallwood, as he has always done, simply worked harder at fund-raising than his opponents did.

As an opening shot, on a tip from Ewart Young, he flew off to Montreal to call on Lady Amy Roddick, a Redpath heiress and the widow of Sir Thomas Roddick, a noted surgeon from Newfoundland. Wearing a fresh white shirt, knife-sharp trousers, and highly polished shoes, he took tea in the garden of her stone mansion on Sherbrooke Street. Lady Roddick, who was of a romantic turn of mind and devoted to her husband's memory, heard out Smallwood's story and forwarded a cheque for $1,500.

Newfoundland itself was a second source. Although a public fund-raising campaign brought in less than $1,000, the advance sale of senatorships proved more lucrative. The going price was $10,000 and two were purchased, though unhappily one donor became involved in an income tax case and never reached the Red Chamber.*

The real money, of course, lay in Ottawa. Though Smallwood had yet to make a formal commitment, public or private, to join the Liberals, that he would do so was taken for granted by both sides. As a province,

---

* The highest price recorded since is $25,000 – an appropriate escalation to keep pace with rising Senate salaries. One senator died shortly after receiving the honour and his widow refused to honour his promissory notes. As one Liberal official commented ruefully: "We can hardly sue to collect."

Newfoundland would muster only seven federal seats; even so it would be a useful addition to Liberal ranks. Campaign funds were a small price to pay for them.

Smallwood made the first approach by calling on two key contacts: C. D. Howe and Senator Neil McLean, the party treasurer in the Maritimes. They in turn introduced him to Senator Gordon Fogo, the National Liberal Treasurer. Since from this point on discretion, which was never a Smallwood virtue, was an imperative, negotiations with Fogo were taken over by Ray Petten, later a Senator and Newfoundland Liberal fund-raiser, a mantle of delphic succession now descended on his son. From Fogo, Petten received that most sacrosanct of all political documents, a list of pliable Liberal donors, including, unsurprisingly, most of Canada's liquor, beer, and wine manufacturers and importers.

With all this wealth to draw on, the Confederates were never short of cash. Indeed, Smallwood frequently amazed his more cautious colleagues by flashing thick wads of bills and, with the panache of a cod culler, parcelling out payments to almost any comer, including several who were never seen again.

Although they were without mainland allies, the anti-Confederates should have been able to muster as much financial support. Their ranks included almost the entire business and professional class of St. John's. The two pulp-and-paper companies were also openly anti-Confederate, because union with Canada would mean an end to their exemption from corporation tax. In fact, the St. John's few were miserly donors whose parsimony hastened the end of their privileged position.

Yet these families were formidable opponents. Only once before, during Coaker's brief heyday, had their authority been directly challenged. Shortly before the campaign began, Smallwood declared proudly: "We don't expect the support of the merchant class, but we can do without them."

The Confederate habitually slammed Water Street and lampooned its occupants as bloated, top-hatted capitalists, a piece of undisguised playing to the gallery since there were more fishermen than merchants. But it was also a political risk. Newfoundlanders rarely questioned their leaders, whether these individuals were simply the natural leaders of their outport, where, as the saying went, "The harbour is as good as the best man in it," or the men at the top of the pyramid, the bearers of the proud old names: Ayre, Baird, Bowring, Crosbie, Cashin, Goodridge, Harvey, Hickman, Job, MacPherson, Monroe, Outerbridge, Winter, which bespoke inherited grandeur, and the irreproachable infallibility that is bestowed by even a quasi-British accent. If the merchants were born to privilege, they were also born to responsibility. They were the guardians of the Newfoundland mystique.

Luckily for Smallwood, only one man among the anti-Confederates, the persuasive rabble-rouser Peter Cashin, knew how to communicate such patriotism to the public. His powerful voice shook the wooden walls of outport meeting halls, and his speeches were eagerly awaited gala events. Short, stocky, and bull-headed, Cashin began by removing his jacket, rolled up his sleeves, took off his tie, and then smashed his fist on the table. Logic was scarcely Cashin's strong point. He continually charged that Confederation was an Anglo-Canadian-American plot hatched by King, Roosevelt, and Churchill during the 1941 Atlantic Charter Conference at Argentia on the South Coast. Once, asked to produce evidence of this, he triumphantly retorted: "You ask me to prove that this is so? I ask you to prove that it is not so." He denounced the baby bonus as an incitement to adultery and as "the most immoral and corrupt enactment that has ever stained the pages of the statutes of Canada." Smallwood he damned as "traitor" and "Iscariot" and added darkly: "Incidentally, Judas Iscariot at least had the decency to hang himself."

Only half-secretly, Smallwood admired Cashin's fire and verve. After Confederation, the Irishman lingered on in the legislature for a few years, refighting the lost battle of union. When he stepped down, Smallwood found him a sinecure as Director of Civil Defence and kept him in that post, despite Ottawa's protests, long past normal retirement age.

But Cashin was a political loner, mistrusted by his Responsible Government colleagues. Not without reason. His political record included the defeat, by his own hand, of two governments in which he had been a cabinet minister. Yet Cashin was the only political personality in the group. The others were decent, intelligent men, none of whom knew how to run a campaign. Compared to Smallwood, they were gentle amateurs. The anti-Confederates were also hopelessly divided among themselves. They knew what they were against, but they disagreed violently about what they were for: everything from union with the United States, through full independence, to union with Great Britain.

To counter *The Confederate*, the Responsible Government League put out its own tabloid weekly, *The Independent*. Issue after issue proclaimed that Confederation meant taxes, which would take back all the benefits of social welfare. A cartoon showed a pensioner cashing his family allowance cheque at the bank, while behind him a spectral figure labelled "Ottawa" reached out to seize his house. The dominant theme was negative: the *Independent* played on the generations-old fear of Confederation, and on an undercurrent of hostility toward French Canadians because of the past Labrador dispute. Typical of anti-Confederate placards were "Keep Newfoundland for Newfoundlanders" and "Canadians from Quebec will take jobs from Newfoundlanders when Labrador is developed by U.S. capital." Even the inevitable ballad, sung to the tune of "A Mother's Love," was more anti-French than pro-Newfoundland:

> Don't vote Confederation, and that's my prayer to you,
> We own the house we live in, we own the schooner too;
> But if you heed Joe Smallwood and his line of French patois,
> You'll be always paying taxes to the men at Ottawa.

These were the forces that had triumphed in 1869. Too much had happened to Newfoundland during the eighty years between for the old anti-Canadian shibboleths to succeed again by themselves. Help came from two quarters: The Roman Catholic Church and a group of young anti-Confederates who realized that the economic arguments for Confederation could be defeated only by as strong a positive attraction. These free-thinkers settled on the idea of economic union with the

United States, a revival of the old Bond–Blaine treaty, by which Newfoundland would sell its fish duty-free and in return import duty-free American consumer goods. Their leader was Smallwood's old friend Chesley Crosbie, a leading businessman who brought zest and status to the cause, but whose political potential was hampered by the fact that in public, though not in private, he was shy and inarticulate to the point of almost total incoherence.

This challenge was tailor-made for the talents of Crosbie's campaign managers, Geoffrey Stirling and Don Jamieson. Because of their skills, the campaign of the Economic Union movement presented Smallwood with his most serious threat of the campaign. Alone or together, Stirling and Jamieson were a remarkable pair of promoters to be found in so small a colony. After Confederation, they pushed on to build one of Canada's largest private radio and television empires. Jamieson, then in his early twenties, had to some extent followed in Smallwood's footsteps. He was self-educated and had turned his great energy and exceptional command of crisp colourful prose to journalism to become the island's best-known broadcaster. Gifted with a mellow persuasive voice, he could, as the political columnist Douglas Fisher once wrote, "be as brutally frank as any old robber baron and as piously high-minded as an archbishop." Stirling, who was twenty-six at the time, was tough, ambitious, and cocky. Born in St. John's, he was educated at the University of Tampa and then joined a college friend to run an alligator and snakeskin import-export business in Honduras, until one day he picked up the *Miami Herald* and hit on the idea of starting a similar tabloid in Newfoundland. In 1945, he bought up at bargain price sixty tons of newsprint left over from a defunct weekly, *The Express*. The paper's owner told him, "You won't last six weeks." Stirling ignored Joe Smallwood's advice and went ahead anyway. Within two years, on a diet of gossip, juicy court reports, and cheesecake photographs, Stirling's *Sunday Herald* had the largest circulation of any weekly on the island.

Stirling and Jamieson put that same brand of enthusiastic hokum to work on the campaign for Economic Union. They coined the upbeat slogan "For a Brighter Tomorrow," and dug up a mother of twelve who, suitably primed, declared on the air her passionate preference for honestly earned wages over Canadian handouts. In his best Billy Graham style, Jamieson made nightly broadcasts to report an avalanche of support, including a telegram from the Newfoundland Club of Brooklyn and a wire from a distant outport: "SPOUT COVE IS BOILING OVER FOR ECONOMIC UNION."

Economic Union was not, of course, on the ballot paper. Stirling and Jamieson could do nothing about that; nor could they do anything to extract an expression of serious intent from the United States Government. They could, however, bluff. Stirling wired every Senator in Washington asking for his views, and received a surprising number of favourable replies from such well-known figures as Robert Taft, Wayne Morse, and Leverett Saltonstall. One improbable ally was Colonel Robert "Bertie" McCormick, publisher of the *Chicago Tribune*, who had heard that the unspeakable British were trying to push Newfoundland into union with Canada. Deep in the Midwest, the isolationist *Tribune* blossomed with articles about brave Newfoundlanders in search of American succour.*

The notion of Economic Union was too far-fetched to be decisive. Yet it was effective, mostly because Newfoundland's ties with the United States were far stronger and far more affectionate than those with Canada. Thousands had emigrated to "the Boston States" and thousands of Newfoundland girls had married American servicemen. R. A. MacKay has said of the Confederation negotiations: "The Americans could have walked in at any time with an offer for duty-free fish and it would have been all over." Perhaps Economic Union's greatest value was to send shock-waves of alarm through Ottawa and so improve Newfoundland's chances of getting better terms the second time round.

---

* McCormick's enthusiasm for Newfoundland waned. In 1952, on a round-the-world tour in his private plane, he was held up for four hours at Gander, a mishap he attributed to "moronic customs officials" and "torpid baggage handlers." He absolved Newfoundlanders of blame, though, since "they are so inbred as to be half-witted."

At the time, Smallwood took the threat seriously enough to offer Crosbie the Premiership if he would change sides. Though this supreme sacrifice was declined, the offer was intended as genuine by Smallwood and accepted as such by Crosbie. Aware of it, the anti-Confederates took on new life and vigour, and slowly the tide of events began to turn in their favour. Smallwood was starting to repeat himself. Everything that could possibly be said about family allowances, pensions, and the cost of living had already been said.

Adversity separates political professionals from the lucky amateurs. In the pages of the *Confederate*, Smallwood, Power, and Horwood, skilled propagandists all, blasted at Economic Union with all their ammunition. Power coined the gag "Comic Union" which Smallwood used so often that many Newfoundlanders thought it was that move-ment's official name. If there was a decisive turning-point, it came when Smallwood spotted the fatal emotional weakness of Economic Union: union with the United States meant abandoning Britain and the flag. Overnight the Confederates became super-patriots and indulged in the luxury of being as sentimental and emotional as their opponents. More than fifty thousand hastily printed posters, emblazoned with the Union Jack and reading CONFEDERATION-BRITISH UNION, were fes-tooned on walls or in windows.

The last few days before voting saw a bitterness Newfoundland had not known since 1869. Families, life-long neighbours, small, tight-knit communities, split into hostile camps. Women, nurtured to a Victorian primness when in public, shouted and screamed at packed meetings; men cursed, booed, and resorted to fisticuffs. Threatening, anonymous phone calls were made to the leaders of all the parties and poison pen letters were stuffed into mailboxes. Beneath the surface, religious enmity smoul-dered, soon to flame into a vicious and destructive issue.

The feeling against Smallwood was ferocious. To protect him, the Confederates hired two bodyguards, a former paratrooper and an ex-wrestler, who walked beside him even on the shortest journey across the street. The front door of his apartment building was placarded with anti-Confederate posters. Smallwood himself carried a revolver, without a permit. On one occasion, a fisherman walked into Confederate head-quarters and demanded that Smallwood come down to his community. Told that this was impossible, the man persisted, and when asked why, answered: "Because we want to drown the bastard." Another time a crowd gathered outside the radio station where Smallwood was broad-casting, shouting that they had come to lynch him. Whether this in fact was likely, no chances were taken, and Smallwood was hustled to safety through a back entrance. His major rally in St. John's ended in a wild *mêlée* with Smallwood dodging fists as he was hustled out between supporters. He made his escape on top of a car that roared off through the crowd at high speed. Smallwood saw the bright side: "What we really need to be sure of winning," he said, "is a martyr."

Not for reasons of caution, but for reasons of strategy, so as to create an impression of an irresistible winning tide, Smallwood campaigned exclusively in districts where sentiment was known to be Confederate. In the last two and a half days he staged an incredible final rally by car over narrow, potholed roads. He visited more than thirty outports to deliver fifty-six speeches. He stopped only when his voice gave out.

On June 3, 1948, the weather was seasonable for Newfoundland in early summer – cool and cloudy. Off the coast, the white hulks of icebergs glided down the Labrador current. The campaign was over. The last issues of the *Confederate* and *Independent* had been read and discussed. For all the passion of the preceding months, the day itself was calm. There were no brawls or fist fights. Some 176,000 Newfoundlanders were eligible to vote, including by special dispensation from the Commission of Government women aged twenty-one. (The previous age minimum for females was twenty-five.)

The first districts to report were in St. John's. Smallwood and his family heard the returns as they crouched over a radio in the Confederate campaign office. The merchants had spoken and they had been heeded. Responsible Government took a commanding lead. Then the returns from the outports poured in. This was Smallwood's fiefdom. The gap

began to close. For two days, and into a third, until even far-off Labrador
was heard from, the votes were counted. The final tallies were checked,
rechecked, and published:

Responsible Government	69,400
Confederation	64,006
Commission of Government	22,311

No one had won. The rules required a clear majority. After so many
anguished months, it meant yet another battle. Commission of
Government would be dropped from the ballot and the principal con-
tenders would face each other alone.

The second referendum was set for July 22, seven long weeks away.

II

The Orange and the Green

Bitter as the first campaign had been, it was at least a fair and open fight. But the stalemate on June 3 stirred emotions too powerful to be contained within the consensus society Newfoundlanders had evolved for themselves to cope with the strains and tensions inherent in any people living isolated from the rest of the world, and too close to each other. During the second campaign, for lack of any other safety valve, repression and jealousy bared into an ugly and consuming religious war. Catholic was pitted against Protestant, and Irish puritanism against Orange fanaticism. In the process, Smallwood was almost defeated. He has never forgotten the experience. Rather than offend Pentecostalists and Catholics, who strongly opposed change, he was for years a staunch defender of the denominational schools system; in successive redistributions, Newfoundland electoral ridings were gerrymandered on religious rather than on political lines.

The roots of sectarianism are deep in Newfoundland's history, and owe more to race and politics than to religion. In contrast to both the

American melting pot and the Canadian mosaic, Newfoundlanders
spring from two scarcely adulterated racial stocks: West Country English
and Southern Irish. Since until 1782 the colony's official religion was
Anglican, conflict between the two groups was inevitable. In the early
years, Catholic priests were forbidden to come to the island, and Catholic
marriages and funerals were banned.

From the beginning, organized religion, whether Catholic or
Protestant, held not merely a dominant, but an irreplaceable position
within Newfoundland society. The church represented not only the good
life to come, but the better things of life today; it provided a code of
behaviour as well as schools and hospitals for a society that was without
civilian government, formal learning, or organized charity.

Over the years, commitment to good works hardened into possession.
One result was a rigidly denominational school system, perpetuated at
the cost of an extravagant use of scant resources, particularly of teachers.
Just before Confederation there were 1,300 settlements in the island and
1,165 schools. Some hamlets supported as many as three separate, one-
roomed schools. Six denominations – Anglican, United, Roman
Catholic, Salvation Army, Pentecostal, Seventh Day Adventist – operated
autonomous school boards and received a proportionate share of the
annual budget for education.

Each denomination thus remained a cohesive unit, and at the same
time, because of conflict with other denominations, a divisive force
within Newfoundland. Unsurprisingly, the divisions were exploited by
politicians. Through the nineteenth century, there were repeated if sporadic riots and brawls between Catholics and Protestants, the worst a *mêlée*
in St. John's in 1861 that left three dead and twenty wounded. Order was
restored only by the device of extending the denominational system to
every branch of government: cabinets, civil service positions from deputy
minister to night watchman, patronage contracts, judicial appointments,
knighthoods, and Rhodes Scholarships. With this went a scrupulously
observed agreement to keep religion out of political debate.

The agreement broke down on the issue of Confederation. The cause
was as much racial as religious. In a real sense, the Irish were the true

Newfoundlanders. To them the rocky island was home, a land of freedom compared to the country from which they had fled, and it was they who had agitated for and won Representative Government in 1832 and full Responsible Government in 1855. Confederation meant surrendering the nation they had made to the larger Canadian whole. That Britain advocated Confederation simply added fuel to the Celtic flame. Cashin stalked into the Catholic districts denouncing the conspiracy "to lure Newfoundland into the Canadian mousetrap." More powerful than Cashin's rhetoric was the persuasion of the Catholic hierarchy.

One of the enigmas of the Confederation battle was the motive for the unyielding opposition to union with Canada by the Catholic Archbishop of Newfoundland, Edward Patrick Roche. He was an aloof, ascetic prelate nicknamed by some Catholics, after the place of his birth, "The Placentia Machiavelli," the "Borgia from Branch." Then in his seventies, Roche had been Archbishop since 1917. Educated in Dublin, Roche, like all staunch Irish Catholics, held to a faith that came pure and unalloyed from Rome. Union with Canada meant union with the Catholics of French Canada, their faith stained by dark infusions of Jansenism. Perhaps a stronger motive was that, within Newfoundland, Roche answered only to Rome; within Canada, he would be one archbishop among several, and lesser than the two cardinals.

In common with many among his clergy, Roche deeply feared the effect upon a sweet and God-fearing people of the crude and irresistible impact of Confederation. Mainland ways were coarse and sceptical. During World War II, the outside world had come to Newfoundland's shores in the form of Allied servicemen with money in their pockets, who wanted to enjoy themselves before venturing out again to dodge torpedoes on the cold grey seas. And by its lights, the Catholic clergy was right: kept isolated, the faith of Newfoundlanders was secure.

While it was overwhelming, the Catholic vote against Confederation was never solid. On the West Coast, the island's third bishop was openly pro-Confederate. Within the Archdiocese, some, with wayward

Irish logic, supported Confederation simply because their Archbishop
was against it.

The attitude of the hierarchy was expressed in the pages of *The Monitor*,
a small parish organ that was turned in the summer of 1947 into a political vehicle and sent to every Catholic family on the island. There were
two themes: the virtues of independent self-reliance, and the purity of the
simple life:

June, 1947:

The fate of Newfoundland will be irrevocably determined by weal
or woe in the very near future. . . . It would surely be the supreme
tragedy of our history, if by apathy, indifference, lack of enlightened
leadership, or the influence of sinister propaganda we were to alienate irretrievably the inheritance which was won for us by our patriotic forbears.

November, 1947:

We must consider what is best for the country. . . . We do not necessarily mean best in the material sense, but rather wherein lies the best
chance of continuing to live decently and soberly and honestly, continuing to recognize that there has grown up with us during the past
four and a half centuries a simple God-fearing way of life which our
forebears have handed down to us and which we must pass on untar-
nished to posterity.

April, 1948:

We alone [in comparison to the quest for independence by such countries as India and Egypt] are measuring the issue solely in dollars and
cents. We alone are prepared to become a nation of shopkeepers,

bartering autonomy and self-competence for a political and economic mirage.

May, 1948:

In the decision which we make on polling day, we would do well to remember that apart from our obligations to this and to future generations, we owe a deep and lasting one to the past [to] those men who have added dignity and lustre to the story of our land. Could we but hear them . . . their voices seem to come to us with a note of appeal in this crisis in our country's history.

These editorials constitute the most eloquent expression of anti-Confederate philosophy that was mustered. Beside them, the promotion gimmicks of the Economic Unionists were tawdry, the rhetoric of Cashin inflammatory, and the pronouncements of the Responsible Government League dusty and academic. In the pages of *The Monitor*, the old Newfoundland fought the twentieth century. It nearly won.

Although through *The Monitor* the attitude of the Catholic hierarchy was widely known, during the first referendum campaign it was commented on only in private. Once the votes were counted, the political consequences of this attitude became apparent. Overwhelmingly the anti-Confederate victories were in the Catholic districts. Even so, the extent of the clergy's involvement was made public only by accident. In its first post-referendum issue, the *Sunday Herald* reported that, for the first time in Newfoundland's history, nuns and brothers had gone to the polls.

For the Confederates this was too tempting an issue to resist, particularly since Catholics accounted for only one-third of the population. They sallied out to drugstores and newsstands all over the city to buy up every available copy of the paper. These were sent to every Loyal Orange Lodge on the island, with the article about the nuns and brothers prominently blue-pencilled.

A few days later, on June 9, two local Orange Lodges met in special session and approved resolutions calling for a meeting of the National Lodge because "the Roman Catholic Church is attempting to dominate Newfoundland." The Convention was held at Grand Falls the week before the second ballot. At its close, letters were sent out to all Orange Lodges, signed by the Grand Master, requiring "your immediate consideration" of the fact that "the Roman Catholic Church ... the attitude of the clergy ... indicates clearly an attempt to influence the result of the said Referendum" and that therefore "this Grand Lodge, in regular session assembled, condemns such efforts at sectional domination [and] warns the Orangemen of Newfoundland and calls on them to use every effort to bring such attempts to naught."

This letter, which unlike *The Monitor* specifically attacked another religion, turned racial antagonism into sectarian war and the second referendum into a maelstrom of bitterness. Though sectarian conflict died away soon after the campaign ended, the Catholic hierarchy was slower to forgive. When Prime Minister St. Laurent visited St. John's in 1949, Archbishop Roche refused him an audience, and Health Minister Paul Martin, a Catholic like St. Laurent, was turned away from the door of several rectories on his visit the same year.

Smallwood himself was without a trace of religious bigotry. He was, though, the complete politician. In 1948, he was not a member of the Orange Lodge and did not attend the Grand Falls meeting. Bradley, a past Grand Master, was there, however, and he rarely acted except on Smallwood's instructions. Smallwood's direct contributions were more subtle. In *The Confederate*, he published maps which isolated anti-Confederate sentiment in the Catholic districts under the heading "The Tail that Wags the Dog," and on the radio he read off lists of anti-Confederate outports, all of them Catholic, followed by lists of pro-Confederate Protestant outports. The message was understood.

The most blatant attempt to exploit sectarian feelings was made on a Sunday morning in June, when the parishioners of the Gower Street

United Church and the Anglican Cathedral in St. John's arrived at early services to find that during the night someone had plastered the buildings and nearby telephone poles with crudely lettered signs: "CONFEDERATION MEANS BRITISH UNION WITH FRENCH CANADA." At the time each side blamed the other. Many years later, Horwood recounted that the signs were the work of anti-Confederates incited to do it by a Confederate *agent-provocateur* within their ranks. (Both sides had spies in the opposite camp; since Newfoundlanders are superb gossips, it was probably an unnecessary luxury.) From the final results, it is impossible to calculate how much difference sectarianism made. For all its reputation, the Orange Lodge was an ineffectual organization, and the famous Orange Letter was read mostly by the converted. At least as decisive was that the anti-Confederates, to use a word not then fashionable, had "peaked." Almost their only flash of originality in the second campaign was yet another stunt by the young Economic Unionists.

To breathe life back into the vision, Stirling flew down to Washington and there tried to persuade McCormick's protégé, Senator Charles Wayland Brooks, to record for broadcast a statement in support of Economic Union. He returned with what was in fact a statement written by Brooks, but recorded by a professional announcer. Back home, the message was aired, preceded by Jamieson explaining that listeners were about to hear "the words of Senator Brooks." The fine distinction was lost on most of the audience.

From the jaws of defeat Smallwood snatched a pack of new ideas. Probably his most effective was a full-page newspaper advertisement which listed prominent citizens, among them a Bowring, a Baird, and an Outerbridge, who had seen the light since the last referendum and were now committed Confederates. This breach in the thick Water Street line gave the sanction of social respectability to the Confederate cause. Smallwood also bid hard to woo the now homeless supporters of Commission of Government, mostly civil servants and their dependents. Thanks to the government's eager co-operation, two of three Newfoundland members of the Commission were allowed to deliver speeches over the government network in favour of Confederation.

Although the government's motive for thus acting as both referee and contender were undisclosed, those of the two Commissioners were less opaque: one became a Senator and the other a provincial cabinet minister.

In the closing days of the campaign, Smallwood put on a second grandstand spurt touring all the outports he had visited at the end of the first referendum. Again he talked until his voice gave out, and even his patent remedy of sucking on lemons failed him.

Through the night of July 22, the voting returns followed the same broad pattern as before. Once more St. John's and its environs gave the anti-Confederates a lead. Again the outports were massively pro-Confederate. The gap between the totals narrowed; slowly they shifted positions. The final result:

Confederation	78,323
Responsible Government	71,334

It could not have been closer: In votes, the margin was just under 7,000; in percentages, it was 52.24% to 47.76%. The turnout for this historic day of decision was an exceptional 84.89% – a performance that was helped by the fact that the official returns, showing the turnout among those eligible in each district, listed Ferryland at 104.59% and Labrador at 119.44%. To the end, Newfoundlanders were individualists.[*]

For the first time in nearly three years Smallwood allowed himself to relax and sniff the sweet smell of success. He and Mrs. Smallwood were driven by supporters to a day-long monster celebration held on a meadow outside the village of Spaniard's Bay, fifty miles from St. John's.

---

[*] Offshore fishermen cast their ballots in the Ferryland and Labrador districts and so pushed the number of votes cast above the number of voters registered.

Virtually single-handed, he had dragged Newfoundland into the twentieth century. The crazy radical had become, as Ewart Young had predicted, "The hero of the hour and of Newfoundland history." He had also become the most powerful man in the island. Those who had once laughed at Smallwood as a "crazy radical" would have to turn to him now for patronage, position, and prestige.

At anti-Confederate headquarters, when hope was gone, many of the grown men present broke down and wept. Jamieson stayed in the office until early sunrise; he then set off on a three-day drunk.

Far too late, the anti-Confederates organized a series of desperate attempts to stave off the inevitable. Six former members of the Newfoundland Parliament issued a writ against the Commission of Government charging that Confederation was unconstitutional. The case was dismissed by the Newfoundland Supreme Court and then lodged before the Imperial Privy Council before it was finally abandoned. In November 1948, Cashin and two other leading anti-Confederates sailed for London, with a petition signed by fifty thousand Newfoundlanders. Once again Sir Alan Herbert was their champion. He introduced them to the Commonwealth Affairs Secretary, Philip Noel-Baker – "not a very cordial encounter" – and arranged for them to address a private meeting of M.P.'s from all parties. The next day Herbert was told that his guests were "tough guys" and "typical Irish politicians," to which he smartly responded: "There was no reason to suppose that Confederation with Canada would refine and purify the personality of Newfoundlanders." On November 23, Sir Alan presented the anti-Confederate petition to the Commons. The House accepted the petition, and let it die.

In the referendum, Newfoundland had spoken. How Canada would answer was uncertain, and for Smallwood this meant one more agonizing wait. King had pledged himself to accept the colony, provided Newfoundlanders declared their affection for Canada "clearly and

beyond all possibility of misunderstanding." The margin of seven thousand votes hardly fulfilled King's conditions.

Into this delicate breach stepped Pickersgill. As amanuensis to King,
his most considerable talent was his ability to read his patron's mind. On
July 23, Pickersgill came early into the office and there proceeded to
compile statistics on all King's campaigns. When the Prime Minister
telephoned, at 10:00 A.M., Pickersgill was ready. "Mr. King, it is wonderful," he said in response to a request for his opinion. "Do you realize
that this is a larger majority than you received in any election except
1940?" There was a pause while King digested this. "I hadn't realized
that at all, Pickersgill," replied King. "That puts a different light on the
whole situation."

In fact, King was determined to mark his retirement with the grand
gesture of rounding out Confederation, the last star in his political crown,
and to refuse Newfoundland at this point would have damaged Canada's
international image. Pickersgill's argument was more useful in helping
King to convince doubting cabinet colleagues. Persuasive as well was
a flying visit to St. John's by MacKay, who reported back that anti-
Confederate feeling was fast subsiding.*

On July 30, 1948, King announced formally that Canada accepted the
outcome of the referendum. "A result," he added parenthetically,
"attained without any trace of influence or pressure from Canada." He
then invited the Commission of Government to send a delegation to
Ottawa to negotiate the final terms of union.

---

* Feeling remained high enough, though. When Smallwood later that year
attended the Liberal Convention in Toronto, the event was recorded for the
newsreels; going to St. John's movie houses to boo Smallwood whenever his
face appeared on the screen became a popular form of entertainment.

12

"I Never Thought I'd See the Day"

The delegation that had gone from St. John's to Ottawa in the summer of 1947 had been composed, as one of its members engagingly confided to a reporter: "Of two fish merchants, two lawyers, a journalist, an insurance salesman, and a minister of the Gospel. What do we know about the profile of the roadbed of the railway?"

The 1947 terms, however, were provisional and subject to amendment. Those which remained to be negotiated in the autumn of 1948 would be terms with which Newfoundland would have to live as a province, and Smallwood as its Premier. For this task, the Commission of Government mustered the best talent the island could provide. For chairman, it chose one of its own members, Albert Walsh, a leading lawyer and subsequently Chief Justice of the Newfoundland Supreme Court. The other members of the team, besides Smallwood, were Bradley, Chesley Crosbie, Gordon Winter, a prominent St. John's businessman, John McEvoy, who had succeeded Bradley as the third and last Chairman of the National Convention, and Philip Gruchy, general manager of the pulp-and-paper mill at Grand Falls. As financial and technical consultant, the government hired a prominent Montreal accountant, James Thompson.

The delegation was not, however, the Government of Newfoundland. The constitutional issue – whether union between two countries should be consummated except by two elected governments – was resolved by the expedient of ignoring it. The prospect and cost of a third campaign so close on the heels of the two referendums could not be countenanced. Thus an appointed delegation negotiated and signed the terms with the Government of Canada. These were then ratified by Westminster on behalf of Newfoundland.

This time Smallwood played little part in the negotiations. They began on October 11, 1948. The Canadian team was headed by St. Laurent and backed by such high-level advisers as James Coyne, later Governor of the Bank of Canada, and Mitchell Sharp, later to be Deputy Minister of Trade and Commerce and, later still, Minister of External Affairs. Against this galaxy of talent, the Newfoundlanders bargained with considerable skill, particularly Walsh, who used to the limit his single ace – the threat that without satisfactory concessions the delegation would quit the capital.

The principal sticking-point revolved around the "transitional grants" designed to guarantee self-sufficiency for the new province. After endless wrangling, a figure was agreed on in the classic Ottawa tradition, at a dinner meeting at Madame Burger's restaurant in Hull, organized by the non-political advisers on each side, including Sharp and Thompson. The total amount to be paid to Newfoundland would be almost tripled over the 1947 agreement – to $46.75 million. The payments, however, were still to end after twelve years. Beyond that, it was agreed that Term 29 of the terms of union would be applied. This term, which Smallwood and MacKay had sweated over during the 1947 negotiations, was redrafted into juristic form by St. Laurent.

Newfoundland secured other substantial concessions. Canadian veterans' benefits were specifically extended to Newfoundland ex-servicemen; Canada agreed to maintain freight and passenger steamship service; Newfoundland was allowed to retain for five years her unique system of marketing salt cod through a government-sponsored association of merchants – NAFEL – even though this system violated Canadian anti-combine laws. Perhaps the most distinctive agreement was Term 46, without which the Newfoundlanders made it clear they would refuse to sign. It provided that "oleo-margarine or margarine may be sold in the Province of Newfoundland," the only part of Canada where such a concession was then allowed in the face of the powerful dairy lobby.

With hindsight, it is clear that the 1948 terms of union were seriously inadequate. For example, the size of the transitional grants was based upon the assumption that provincial spending on education would reach a plateau of $4.7 million in 1951-52, when in fact the actual expenditure in that year was $5.7 million, and had almost doubled four years later. The most serious omission was that the Newfoundlanders failed to secure an all-weather, trans-island highway, which Canada could hardly have refused, since even the Maritime road systems were incomparably more advanced than those of Newfoundland. It took the island another seventeen years to achieve such a highway; the lack of it during those years was a crippling economic liability.

Even at the time there were serious doubts. Chesley Crosbie refused to sign the final Terms, saying, "I would not, and could not, take the responsibility of committing the people of Newfoundland to financial suicide." The night before the official signing ceremony, Walsh told a fellow delegate that he had agreed to the Terms only because there was no alternative. Nor was there; Newfoundland was committed to union whatever the consequences.

Her fate was formally sealed in the red-carpeted Senate chamber on the morning of December 11, 1948. To sign the Terms of Union, the six Newfoundlanders, St. Laurent, who had a month before succeeded King as Prime Minister, and Brooke Claxton (substituting for the newly appointed External Affairs Secretary, Lester Pearson, who was away negotiating a larger union, that of NATO), dipped their pens in turn into a massive glass inkstand last used in Charlottetown by the Fathers of Confederation. St. Laurent declared, "We the people of Canada look forward to the last great step of Confederation," and Walsh expressed his hope that "our people will find a prosperous and happy place in this great union." An RCAF band played "God Save the King," and "O Canada." They had intended to play, as well, the new province's anthem, "Ode to Newfoundland." Unhappily the music could not be found in Ottawa. St. Laurent closed the program by calling for three cheers and a tiger for Newfoundland.

During this time of transition, Smallwood moved at full speed along a different track. He could now take Confederation for granted, but not so his own political future. All his attention was turned to making sure that he would indeed become Premier. Any lingering doubts about his political affiliation were soon dispelled. Immediately after the second referendum he flew to Toronto, and on August 6 he and Bradley made a dramatic appearance at the National Liberal Convention. Smallwood's speech, and his peroration, "We Canadians," won him a standing ovation. It was Canada's first exposure to the oratorical style of the outport statesman, and delegates found it a refreshing contrast to the accustomed starchy monologues by Liberal patriarchs.

Smallwood discussed what he blithely called "the distribution of the spoils" and related that he had told Bradley, "Which do you want – the Premiership of the province or the Prime Ministership of Canada? He decided that since he had had a fling in local politics he would like to take over Canada, so I was happy, because I wanted Newfoundland." Afterwards a reporter discovered Smallwood's hastily scribbled notes on the back of a menu card: "1. – No vote. 2. – Wouldn't give it to us because afraid we'd run for leadership. 3. – Premier B.C. – Senator Robertson. 4. Great Nation – great British nation. 5. Happy Province. 6. 'We Canadians.'" Such cards – official menus, invitations, and programs – covered with similar brief subject-headings, were Smallwood's standard way of preparing for a speech. Usually he scrawled the notes in the last few minutes, while he was being introduced, before he spoke. As he explained: "I only really think about what I am going to say when I know I actually have to say it."

The division of the spoils, however, had been achieved less easily than

Smallwood claimed. Once victory was in sight, Bradley had begun to have doubts, not because he himself wanted the Premiership, but about Smallwood's suitability for what then seemed the junior post. During a stroll together early in the second campaign, Bradley had confided to Smallwood that once Confederation was achieved, the best plan would be for he himself to become Premier, with Smallwood one of his provincial cabinet ministers. Within a few months, said Bradley, he would resign and move on to Ottawa and then do what he could to work Smallwood in as Premier. When Smallwood angrily protested, Bradley remonstrated: "But Joe, you just don't understand your standing in Newfoundland." Furious, and by threatening to pull out of the Confederate campaign, Smallwood drew from Bradley a pledge to abide by their original agreement. The incident, though, he did not easily forget.

By the end of 1948, their positions were reversed. Smallwood had become a full-fledged political personality in his own right. That he would become Premier was no longer in much doubt. Bradley's own future was less certain. All along Smallwood had expected, and had said so in public, that Newfoundland's federal minister would have the Fisheries portfolio. He had much to learn, though, of Ottawa politics. The Liberals were prepared to placate their new tribal allies, but at a modest price. For one thing, neither British Columbia fishermen nor those of the Maritimes would take kindly to a minister from a brand-new province, and one with the most backward fishery in the Western World. For another, it was still an era when cabinet titles were considered as immutable as if carved in stone. The notion of simply creating fresh portfolios when they were needed to accommodate fresh personnel was unknown.

Over lunch at the University Club, Pickersgill explained some of the complexities of cabinet-shuffling to Smallwood. He went on to disclose that James MacKinnon, Minister of Mines and Resources, was soon due for elevation to the Senate, thus creating a convenient vacancy for Bradley. Both were readily agreed that Secretary of State would be a suitable portfolio for him.

Getting St. Laurent's approval for this redisposition of his cabinet was more delicate. The first attempt failed. Bradley called on the Prime Minister at his suite in the Roxborough Apartments and emerged an hour later seething with rage and frustration. "Minister be God-damned," he told Smallwood, "it wasn't even mentioned." What had happened was a conflict of cultures. Bradley came from a society where hypocrisy is a vice and to be evasive is to be effete. St. Laurent had meant to convey to his visitor that a cabinet post awaited him, but he had done so in the standard elliptical Ottawa style, where circumspection is a virtue and to be candid is to be a Philistine.

The next day Smallwood, himself no practitioner of the art of circumspection, was called to the Roxborough. When St. Laurent broached the subject of Bradley's future, Smallwood asked bluntly if he would join the federal cabinet and drew the reply, "That should be a pretty fair assumption." Smallwood then mentioned Secretary of State as a possible post, adding that it was a portfolio which required almost no ministerial activity and yet, because so many Newfoundlanders were familiar with the American cabinet system, would readily be assumed to rank with the Secretary of State in Washington. St. Laurent smiled, and the deal was made.

Smallwood himself had still to be formally taken care of, and because of St. Laurent's absorption as a constitutional expert in the procedural proprieties of turning colony into province, there was a brief contretemps. The Prime Minister argued that until the people had voted one into office there could be no Premier. Until such an election, the province should be administered either by the existing Commission of Government or by a Lieutenant Governor. Egged on by Smallwood, who was desperately anxious to be the man at the top of the pyramid as his country entered Confederation, Liberal pragmatists, notably Pickersgill, argued back that it would be improper for a British-appointed Commission of Government or Lieutenant Governor (St. Laurent had suggested Governor Macdonald) to rule a Canadian province. Instead, Ottawa should appoint a Lieutenant Governor who in turn would swear in a Premier and a cabinet committed to calling an election at the earliest possible moment.

This settled, the Lieutenant Governor remained to be nominated. Leonard Outerbridge, one of the island's most respected citizens, appeared to be the obvious man, and indeed he had been Smallwood and

Bradley's choice from the start. Assuming his house now in order, Smallwood returned to St. John's, and then toured the South Coast by steamer. In the meantime, however, a bizarre chain of events had been set in motion. To ensure that Outerbridge, once he was Lieutenant Governor would in fact call upon Smallwood to form a Government, Walter Harris, then Parliamentary Secretary to the Prime Minister, flew down to St. John's as a confidential emissary. Once again Canadians and Newfoundlanders spoke a different language. Harris, quite mistakenly, left the interview far from certain that Outerbridge would bestow the mantle of power on Smallwood. Back in Ottawa, Harris's report caused consternation and an immediate change of plan: the Lieutenant Governorship was offered to Albert Walsh, who, as a Catholic, would "make distinguished Catholics such as the Archbishop and Bishop O'Neill less apprehensive," as St. Laurent recorded in his diary. Walsh agreed, and was made both Lieutenant Governor and a Knight of the Bath. Sir Albert continued as Lieutenant Governor only until June 1949, when he moved to the Supreme Court and was succeeded at Government House by Outerbridge.

The legislative formalities to bring about union were quickly accomplished. Early in February 1949, Smallwood, muffled in a heavy double-breasted coat and white silk scarf, flew to Ottawa for the occasion. He listened from the Diplomatic Gallery and explained to a reporter: "The more I can learn about House of Commons routine now, the better."

The Newfoundland bill was St. Laurent's first important legislation as Prime Minister. It was also the first chance for the new Conservative Leader, George Drew, to show his parliamentary mettle. The bill was launched smoothly enough: St. Laurent called the union "a lesson to the whole world of what can be accomplished by men of good will," and rebutted an accusation, made by a Conservative backbencher, John Diefenbaker, by saying, "I wish to deny emphatically that any attempt was made by the Canadian Government to induce Newfoundland to become associated with us." After second reading, Drew suddenly counter-attacked with an amendment that before union was completed all the provincial governments should be consulted. Drew's point was that if the BNA Act could be amended unilaterally by the federal government in this instance, "it can amend any other clause in the same way." The final vote came on February 16, and the bill was passed seventy-four to fourteen, with Social Creditors and Conservatives opposed, and the CCF supporting the Government.

A week later, an act to amend the BNA Act "to confirm and give effect to Terms of Union agreed between Canada and Newfoundland" was brought before the Commons at Westminster. Sir Alan Herbert made his last stand: "I have done my best for these people, and I can do no more." The legislation was approved 217 to fifteen.

Newfoundland constituted the first addition of territory to the Dominion of Canada since Prince Edward Island entered Confederation in 1873. Perhaps because civil servants were unused to coping with history, Ottawa managed to manufacture one last hurdle for Smallwood to leap. April 1 was chosen as the official day of union, because it coincided with the start of the federal fiscal year. At Smallwood's outraged insistence, "I wasn't going to celebrate Confederation on April Fool's Day," Ottawa agreed to move the date ahead. Union would formally take place a few minutes before midnight on March 31, though the actual ceremonies would take place the following day, as already planned.

Canada had already intruded at a quickening pace. A Director of Family Allowances had opened an office in St. John's, and mailed out letters addressed "Dear Mum and Dad" to eligible parents. On February 21, a sale of Newfoundland stamps in London fetched $25,000, and far-sighted islanders began to hoard their national stamps and distinctive coins, including a tiny five-cent piece and a unique twenty-cent piece. On March 15, Ottawa issued a commemorative, four-cent stamp showing a fifteenth-century sailing ship inscribed "Cabot's *Matthew* – Newfoundland." On March 26, a special Newfoundland honours list was issued from Buckingham Palace; it comprised three knighthoods; three Commanders of the Order of St. Michael and St. George; three

Commanders of the Order of the British Empire; five Officers of the same order; and three M.B.E.'s.

During those last few days, there was a final, despairing remembrance of things past, and in that remembrance, an affecting sadness and nostalgia. "Today and tomorrow are all the time left to an independent Newfoundland," began the *Daily News* editorial on March 30. "If some people are waiting with an almost ghoulish glee for the demise of the Newfoundland we knew, others are watching with anxiety and with sorrow the hands of the clock move slowly round." When the External Affairs Department notified Newfoundlanders living abroad that they could turn in their passports and receive free Canadian passports in return, several of them immediately had their existing passports renewed for the maximum five years. In a technical sense, these individuals were the last Newfoundlanders.

For the nation, there were countless elegies and laments. Perhaps the best of these was written by Albert Perlin, and published on April 1:

> On this day of parting, sad nostalgic thoughts arise,
> Thoughts to bring the hot tears surging to the Newfoundlanders' eyes;
>
> Thoughts that bring to mind the story of the struggles of the past,
> Of the men who built our island, nailed its colours to the mast;
>
> Those who lost the fight for freedom have the greater pride this day,
> Though their country's independence lies the victim of the fray.
>
> They have kept *their* faith untarnished, they have held *their* honour high,
> They can face the course of history with a clear and steadfast eye;
>
> They will have their day of sorrow, but will ever take the stand,
> As the staunch and faithful servants of a well-loved Newfoundland.

In a less sentimental vein, Perlin on the same day wrote in his editorial: "What is done is done . . . we are now launched, to use a local metaphor, on a strange, new ship. How well we shall ride it will depend partly upon what the Canadian Government may do to launch us fairly and well, partly on how well the crew are prepared to work together for the success of the voyage."

April 1, 1949, dawned cold and dour. Fog hugged the coasts and curled through the Narrows into St. John's harbour. A light rain fell on the grey old city. At one-thirty-five that morning, the first native Newfoundland Canadian was born. She was christened Sharon Rose Healey.

There were no demonstrations or parades. Plans for St. Laurent and the federal cabinet to come to St. John's were cancelled. The anti-Confederates called off a march to Gibbet Hill, which was to have been headed by an open truck bearing a coffin. Above dozens of houses in St. John's and in nearby settlements hung black flags, many made from dyed flour sacks. Here and there the unofficial flag of Newfoundland, the pink, white, and green, flew at half mast. At the base of one pole was the placard, "We let the old flag fall." A few people wore black ties and armbands. Jack Higgins, an anti-Confederate leader, draped his house with black crêpe.

In Ottawa, the official ceremonies were short. Over the CBC's national radio network, St. Laurent welcomed Newfoundland to "a good country, a country of which you will become as proud as we are. . . . In becoming a province of Canada you will not lose the identity of which you are so proud." For his part, Bradley gave a demonstration of Newfoundland eloquence: "In fancy I see them now – Macdonald, Brown, Cartier in Canada, and Carter and Shea in Newfoundland bending over this scene in silent and profound approval. We are all Canadians now."

Then, standing on a wooden platform erected above the steps leading into the Centre Block of the Parliament Buildings, St. Laurent carved the first stroke of the Newfoundland coat of arms* into the stone archway at

---

* An elk above a crossed shield emblazoned with lions and unicorns and flanked by two Beothuk Indians, with below it the motto *Quaerite Prime Regnum Dei*, "Seek ye first the Kingdom of God."

the base of the Peace Tower. A space suitable for Newfoundland – or for the Yukon or the Northwest Territories – had been left when the tower was built in 1920. The ceremonies concluded with a peal of music from the carillon of the Peace Tower and a nineteen-gun salute.

At high noon, in the drawing room of Government House in St. John's, birch logs blazed in the white marble fireplace, and an ornate crystal chandelier sparkled above a long table covered with a blue and gold cloth. Filling the room – though they did not crowd it, for as the *Daily News* recorded, "Quite a number of prominent citizens were unable to attend" – were civil servants, businessmen, judges, clergy, and rising politicians. Also present were Smallwood and his incoming cabinet, the new Lieutenant Governor, Sir Albert Walsh, and, representing Canada, the Secretary of State, Colin Gibson.

Two movie cameras recorded the scene. It was reported by a newly designated radio station; at 1:35 P.M., VONF St. John's had signed off to re-emerge instantly as CBN, the newest member of the national network. Walsh took up the New Testament and was sworn in as Lieutenant Governor by Gibson, who then presented him with a certificate of Canadian citizenship framed in mahogany. Gibson welcomed the people of Newfoundland as "equal partners with Canada." The new Lieutenant Governor then swore in Smallwood and his first cabinet. At the back of the room, standing rigidly at attention, was the long-time Government House constable, Vincent Walsh. Tears streamed down his face.

At home that evening in his shabby apartment on Duckworth Street, Smallwood sat amid admiring supporters and pored over the hundreds of wires and letters of congratulation that had come in from all over the country. Among the telegrams Smallwood had sent out was one to Bradley: "WE SAID WE WOULD DIVIDE BRITISH NORTH AMERICA BETWEEN US AND WE DID." As the crowd thinned, Smallwood found time to savour the moment of triumph. His thoughts went back to his schooldays when ambition first had stirred. At Bishop Feild College he had filled notebooks with the names and titles of the colony's Prime

Ministers, and then added at the bottom of each list: "The Right
Honourable Sir Joseph R. Smallwood, K.C.M.G., P.C., M.H.A." He had
finally made it. "The Honourable J. R. Smallwood," he said delightedly
to the small group of close friends which remained, "I never thought I'd
see the day."

13

"His Majesty's Outport Government"

The Smallwood Government," said its first Minister of Fisheries and Co-operatives, Bill Keough, "has a mandate to proceed with a revolution." Confederation alone presaged a new order in the island. The accession of a man of Smallwood's background to the Premiership meant also that the power of what Hugh MacLennan has called "the last Family Compact in North America" had been shattered. For the first time in their history, rank-and-file Newfoundlanders felt themselves masters of their own destiny.

Upon Smallwood himself, hero to one half of Newfoundland and traitor to the other, the responsibility was awesome. That he recognized this was evident in the uncharacteristic caution of his first speech as Premier: "We are not archangels and we are not supermen. I think I can say we are a bunch of Newfoundlanders determined to do their best for the toiling masses of Newfoundland, to make Newfoundland fit for Newfoundlanders."

Confederation itself, he recognized, could do little more than "dull forever the sharp cutting edge of poverty." Within a month of the date of union, the three thousand pensioners who had been receiving the pre-Confederation pension of $18 a quarter increased to ten thousand who now received $30 a month. The average family allowance cheque for Newfoundland mothers was $16.38, the highest in the country. Otherwise, once the rhetoric and gesture of April 1 was past, Newfoundland was on its own.

Innocent of any experience in administration, and a neophyte even in politics, Smallwood had to govern a province which had the greatest liabilities and the least resources of any in the country. He had to contend also with a society that was archaic and ultimately decadent. What passed for commercial enterprise was controlled by a quasi-monopoly of timid and conservative businessmen, barely aware of the industrial revolution, let alone the atomic. Among the public at large, decades of paternalism had withered initiative and the willingness to accept responsibility. Newfoundland for practical purposes was without even such nurseries of democracy as municipal councils, co-operatives, and trade unions.

Single-handed, Smallwood had to transform his society. To recognize that this had to be done required intellect and imagination of a high order; to dare attempt it required courage that bordered on the foolhardy. As the architect of Confederation, Smallwood had already demonstrated his imagination; even his worst enemies had never faulted his courage. His attempt to bring about a new order, which encompassed his first five years in office, was the Smallwood Revolution that failed – if the term failure can be applied to an undertaking for which there was no hope of success.

The least of Smallwood's problems, though he was too astute to assume it, was the acquisition and retention of power. He called Newfoundland's first provincial election for May 27, 1949, and to prepare for it organized a mammoth convention in St. John's. Some fifteen hundred delegates brought in by chartered train were informed that they were "Liberals," the "party of the toiling masses." To guide the masses towards the light, the Public Works Department discovered a cache of unspent funds, and tobacco prices, a bellwether of outport opinion, were cut. Smallwood campaigned with his customary vigour. Behind the slogan, "Let Joe finish the job," he toured by motorboat, plane, train, and car; his campaign photograph, a glossy studio portrait by Yousuf Karsh, hung on thousands of kitchen walls. Health Minister Paul Martin flew down, to be introduced to awed audiences as "the Father of Family Allowances" – an honour Smallwood bestowed freely on visiting federal Liberals. He won twenty-one of twenty-eight seats and sixty-five per cent of the vote.

A month later, Smallwood emerged as campaign manager in Newfoundland for the federal Liberals. On June 27, he returned five of the island's seven M.P.'s. From then on, for the next generation, M.P.'s went to Ottawa by his grace, and Senators by his favour.

The federal Liberals also learned early that he was an unsettling as well as a valuable ally. By way of instructing the voters of the Ferryland district, Smallwood told them: "I don't need you. I've been elected. But you need me. I'm sitting on top of the public chest, and not one red cent will come out of it for Ferryland unless Greg Power is elected. Unless you vote for my man, you'll be out in the cold for the next five years.... Those settlements which vote against Greg Power will get nothing – absolutely nothing." The electors of Ferryland, overwhelmingly Catholic, gave their due to Church and not to State, and Power was defeated. He became instead Chairman of the Liquor Board.

Swamped by the "Uncle Louis" tide, the federal Conservatives made what they could of the issue. St. Laurent saw otherwise: "Those who are so generous in their accusations against us should not ask us to interfere with something which really relates to provincial autonomy." Nevertheless, Smallwood was struck from the list of speakers for the party's closing rally in Toronto, and asked to stay away from the meeting, which he did. At the same time, and in a rare flash of ingenuity, the Newfoundland Tories launched a lawsuit against Smallwood for violation of the Canada Elections Act, and collected eighteen affidavits from Ferryland constituents to use as evidence. The judge saw good reason for postponing the case until after the election, when it was dropped. The Globe and Mail accused Smallwood of offering "the most brazen bribe ever offered to Canadian voters." It was, certainly, the most brazen of the 1949 campaign.

The affair also shed light on the dark side of Smallwood's political style. He had learned his trade the hard way, on the streets of New York and from his pragmatic mentor, Squires, whose papers he studied assiduously during his first years in office and from which he extracted many of his techniques. On the local scene at least, he never learned to rise above the past that had produced him, nor to aim anywhere than at his opponent's jugular. Yet at the same time he was scrupulously loyal to his friends, a quality rare in Newfoundland's anarchic, faction-ridden politics. Even when the image of the party suffered for it, he never forgot those who had helped him when he was down and out. These men, and the comrades who had fought by his side for Confederation, could do no wrong. Many times over Smallwood repaid old debts by the time-worn devices of jobs and patronage. Often his gratitude was less obvious: he provided the funds for the child of one old friend to go to college; flags flew at half-mast above the Confederation Building to mark the death of Charles Garland, a close friend of the Confederation era, the only time a private citizen has been so honoured in the province.

In the subsequent provincial elections of 1951 and 1956, Smallwood won even larger majorities than in 1949. (In 1956, he scarcely bothered to campaign and still won thirty-two out of thirty-six seats.) The statistics in fact underscored the extent of his support: He was backed in election after election by an incredible seventy-five per cent of the electorate,[*] adulation unmatched by any contemporary politician in Canada.

Superficially, and to some degree in substance, these triumphs were those of a demagogue over an unsophisticated and uninformed electorate. As Smallwood himself said: "After Confederation, any fool could have become Premier and stayed for some time." The candour was well placed. In 1949, Ottawa's foresight had ensured that two month's supply of family allowances had reached voters before polling day. Smallwood had promised these benefits and they had arrived; he had promised there would be no taxes imposed to pay for them and none were. These

---

[*] Sometimes Smallwood allowed Opposition candidates to win unopposed, and in safe Liberal districts – which meant almost every riding outside the shadow of St. John's – the turnout was low.

fulfilled pledges, a novelty in Newfoundland, were enough to carry him through two subsequent elections.

He was also helped materially by the ineptitude of his opponents. The Conservatives fought their first election as unregenerate anti-Confederates, and after their crushing defeat lapsed into a sullen hatred of Smallwood the usurper, which bankrupted them of ideas or of viable policies. Even when they were not attacking the Premier, the Tories had no ear for the language of the people. As Malcolm Hollett, the party leader for six years, once told the legislature: "We laugh at, and make fun of sixteenth and seventeenth century minds and we look with contempt at the Middle Ages. Yet in what era will be found greater men than Duns Scotus, Bonaventure, Aquinas, Dante? Progress indeed, and here we are wondering and worrying whether a third world war is in the offing."

Smallwood was in a political class by himself. Within the legislature, he was soon untouchable. As in so many fields, he achieved his pre-eminence in large part through sheer hard work and concentration. Only Smallwood was single-minded enough to study the rules of procedure – or daring enough when need be to invent them. He alone bothered to spend his evenings poring over *Hansards* from Ottawa and Westminster. He read every new political biography, and his library grew to include most of the standard works on the theory of politics, parliament, and government. He scrupulously attended debates, and unlike his colleagues he listened intently to every word that was said.

When he was not talking about the toiling masses, he lovingly referred to "His Majesty's Outport Government." The merchants he damned as "waffle-iron salesmen" and "cocktail party butterflies" whose "delicate nostrils twitch at the honest smell of fish." Of his basic technique for rebuttal, he said: "I listen hard and jot down all the mistakes my opponent makes – a statistic here, an exaggeration there. Then I string them together and throw them back at him. It's an old lawyer's trick, but it nearly always works."

In sum, Smallwood was far too good for the little political cockpit in the hundred-year-old Colonial Building where, by readily given consent, members stopped in mid-speech for a four o'clock tea break, and where the only physical change within the chamber during the first ten post-Confederation years was the installation of Venetian blinds to prevent the afternoon sun blinding the Opposition. On one side, on the hard oaken seats, sat the tiny huddle of Conservatives; on the other, Smallwood and "this swollen lump of Government supporters."

On the hustings he was, of course, the master. His style softened: he began to temper his forceful and repetitive delivery with evocative imagery, as in his description of Prince Edward Island, "an itty-bitty province. You could drop it into the middle of Newfoundland and need a good guide to find it." He discovered a hidden talent for comedy, and began to delight in playing the role of clown. During one campaign in St. John's, he removed a shoe, wiggled his toes at the audience, and told them, "Despite what the Tories say, I don't have hooves and horns."

Such engaging buffoonery was scarcely the accepted style of a charismatic leader. Yet Smallwood's appeal went far beyond being simply the best available politician. The Karsh portrait, which showed him stern-faced, intent and faintly glossy, became part of the furnishing of thousands of kitchens and bedrooms. Mrs. Mary Brown, ninety-three, of Northwest Brook, announced she would be buried with it in her coffin. One fisherman on the South Coast proposed that when Smallwood died "they should put him in a 'frigerator so everyone can see him, for he led us into the promised land." As ordinary Newfoundlanders explained such adulation, "He's the only one that ever did anything; he's the only time we ever had anything worthwhile; he makes mistakes but he tries; he's the only one that ever tried."

He became the only genuine national leader Newfoundland has produced. Those before him gained power, or lost it, by shifting alliances of class, region, and religion. Smallwood's dominion encompassed the entire province. Superficially, this was an unremarkable achievement. Newfoundlanders all sprang from the same two racial stocks; one outport looked much like another. Religion was strong everywhere, and family ties sacrosanct. In fact, to an extent only a sociologist could explain, Newfoundland was a bewilderingly complex society. Character eccentricities were encouraged and cherished. As much as its people, the island's communities were individuals. Two hamlets alike in every external might differ as much as if they existed in separate countries. In one, fishermen uninhibitedly experimented with new techniques, and in another they clung to seventeenth century ways. From one community men emigrated in search of work to Labrador, Nova Scotia, and Toronto; in another, dole was accepted without shame. One outport would unconcernedly pass an entire winter without a schoolteacher; another would produce generations of outstanding citizens. (The nine families of Green's Island produced in one generation – and this before universal education and television – twenty-seven schoolteachers, all but eight with university degrees.)

By the power of his personality and because he understood his people in a way that no one had before, Smallwood breached the barriers of physical isolation and parochialism. By doing so, he became more than just the sum total of Newfoundland's fragmented needs and wants; he came to embody Newfoundland.

In the beginning, Smallwood set out to achieve his revolution through socialism. His was not a variety that would be recognized at Transport House, but it was still far enough to the left to give Newfoundland the most progressive administration in the country (with the exception of the CCF in Saskatchewan, which operated in a region incomparably more sophisticated in industrial and political terms).

"We are going to be either a glorified poorhouse or else a self-supporting province, independent and proud," he said at the opening session of the first post-Confederation legislature. "Confederation brings automatically with it solutions to a number of problems that would otherwise be almost insoluble. It does not automatically solve some of our problems of a basic and fundamental nature."

The unprecedented volume of legislation proposed in the Throne Speech was his start towards solving them. There would be new Departments of Economic Development and of Co-operatives; loan banks for the co-operatives and for the fisheries; a Public Utilities Commission; a Resources and Conservation Commission; a Hydro-Electric Commission; a Housing Corporation. Memorial College was to be raised to the status of a degree-granting institution. The next year there was more of the same: Smallwood's Workmen's Compensation Act brought Newfoundland standards to those of Ontario; his slum clearance bill was rated, at Ottawa, among the most advanced in the country; his Fisheries Accident Insurance Bill was the first of its kind in Newfoundland history.

A second wave of reform legislation was set in motion after a disastrous attempt at crash industrialization had run its course. In 1954, a bill was passed to provide for regional amalgamated schools, tied in with a scheme of high-school bursaries. Most ambitious of all was his medical program of January 1957, through which children under sixteen received free hospital and medical coverage. Since the province already had a system of cottage hospitals in remote areas, where doctors were paid by the government, Newfoundland thus had an elemental system of medicare five years before Saskatchewan.

Smallwood's pride in his progressive legislation was the expansive joy of a preacher finally able to practise. "We, in the past twelve months," he said on March 3, 1950, "have done more than all the Newfoundland Parliaments in history in conceiving and enacting social welfare legislation for the toiling masses." But he was realistic enough to recognize that his margin to reform for reform's sake was limited. Of his amendments to the Labour Code, brought down in March 1950, he said, "Personally, consulting my own feelings, I would like to be associated with labour legislation that would be a model for the world [but] we must temper that desire with our urgent desire to attract capital to Newfoundland."

Yet the St. John's businessmen who feared Smallwood as a dangerous radical did not misjudge their opponent. Through him spoke the authentic voice of the other Newfoundland: "The day is past," he said, "when people believed, if they ever did believe, that the old mercantile system was ordained by God, or that it is outrageously sacrilegious to question the right of the merchant to have the sole and exclusive monopoly of trade or industry." In April 1954, he delivered his most devastating indictment of the old order: "Down through history, ever since there were fishermen in Newfoundland, they have been crucified. That crucifixion was not always the crucifixion of cruelty. Today I accuse the fish merchants of Water Street, not of showing cruelty to the fishermen. I would almost prefer they did that. I accuse them of showing stupidity, of ignorance, of laziness, of which the fishermen are the victims."

Reform legislation, however ambitious, could only scratch the surface of events. The society itself had to be changed. For this to happen, other than by dictatorship, Newfoundlanders would have to involve themselves in government through organizations and mass movements through which they could express their will, and learn to manage their own affairs. The only model, in Newfoundland, was Coaker's old F.P.U. This Smallwood set out to duplicate. He made the same mistakes as Coaker and was defeated by the same forces; as the only alternative to stagnation, he created the movements himself, and thereby robbed them of initiative and self-reliance; once created, the organizations themselves reached out to grasp the heavy hand of paternalism.

Smallwood's chosen instruments for social revolution were the Newfoundland Co-operative Union, the first island-wide body of its kind, and the Newfoundland Federation of Fishermen which was, in effect, a fishermen's trade union. To create the Co-operative Union, Smallwood staged a mass meeting at Grand Falls on November 22-3, 1949. "What we need is a real people's movement," he told the delegates and, in an echo of Coaker, "You can take over the province if you want to." With a backward eye towards his own experiences in Bonavista, he set up a joint Department of Fisheries and Co-operatives to provide cash and counsel for new co-operatives. In fact, both the Department and the Union spent all their money and energy trying to save existing co-operatives from foundering. (To save the St. John's Consumers Co-operative, Smallwood himself signed a personal note for $3,000.) Spoon-fed by Government so that it never acquired a sense of true responsibility, and debilitated by its own financial ineptitude, the Co-operative Union withered. Its epitaph was written by Donald Snowden in his 1965 report for the Co-operative Union of Canada: "Government has made repeated and obviously sincere gestures to the co-operative movement to stand on its own feet; the movement has been incapable of responding."

The Fisheries Federation was yet another hostage to the past. Conceived as a direct revival of Coaker's F.P.U., Smallwood launched it with an extravagant flourish. From all over the island, 240 delegates representing more than seven hundred settlements were brought into St. John's at government expense for the founding convention, held from April 2 to 7, 1951. The legislature recessed for the week, and the Lieutenant Governor watched from a reviewing stand as the fishermen marched through the streets in ragged file to the convention hall at the Gaiety Theatre, its entrance transformed into a triumphal arch of fish casks. The keynote speaker, Monsignor Coady, founder of the co-operative movement at St. Francis Xavier University, told them: "You must kick off the old feudalism, the kind of feudalism when you were serfs under some overlord who did your thinking for you." Smallwood's own address was as moving: "The men of the South are not different from the men of the North," he cried. "The West is the same as the East," and then called on the delegates from each coast to stand and cheer the men of the other coasts. "In the past, the fishermen have always wondered what *they* were going to do about the problems of the fisheries. That day is dying tonight," Smallwood told the delegates.

Yet the Federation's flaw was already apparent. The *Daily News* reported: "During discussions, the Premier rebuked a number of delegates who were continually leaving the chamber without asking permission from the chair. 'Are you not interested in the Union, or is it that you just don't give a damn?' he said." Impatient for quick results, Smallwood never allowed the Federation to stand on its own feet, or the dignity of making and learning from its own mistakes. In 1956, he kicked away the last pretence that the Federation was an independent body when he broke the rules he had himself helped draft, to run and elect the Federation's Secretary General as a Liberal candidate. Thereafter the Federation was reduced to a pale shadow of the Smallwood Government.

Like most populists, who love the mass rather than the individual, it was always in Smallwood's nature to become a dictator. That he had won Confederation all but single-handed confirmed his conviction that he alone knew what was best for Newfoundland. Yet the Co-operative Union and the Fisheries Federation began as honest attempts at participatory democracy. When Newfoundlanders proved incapable of responding to the challenge he had set for them, Smallwood became more and more the autocrat supreme. The inevitable was hastened also by the vacuum that existed around him. In Smallwood's case, the truism that a leader's stature can be measured by the height of his subordinates must be qualified by the shortage of available talent he had to draw on, and by the social irresponsibility of those who refused to join him at all.

His first cabinet lacked so much as a single representative of the St. John's business community. It contained only one lawyer – the Attorney General – because no others could be found. To strike a religious balance, Smallwood approached in turn five of the most prominent Catholics in the province; he was rejected in turn by each of them. To plug the religious gap, Smallwood appointed Michael Sinnott, a citizen so advanced in years that he never dared ask his age. (Sinnott was seventy-eight.)

There was a handful of able ministers. Leslie Curtis, tough, shrewd, pragmatic, was the lawyer who came in at the start; over the years Smallwood added Fred Rowe, a serious, high-principled former university lecturer, James McGrath, an urbane, Dublin-educated doctor, who viewed the unruly scene around him with amused detachment, and Alain Frecker, a gentle scholar born in St. Pierre.

Yet right down to 1966, the cabinet remained woefully weak. Smallwood himself regarded his ministers with a disdain he often made no effort to conceal. From the start it was preponderantly made up of two types: political hangers-on who added nothing but took much, and schoolteachers and co-operative organizers whose intentions were admirable but who could neither administer nor execute. One such idealist was Ted Russell, a one-time co-operative fieldworker who resigned in March 1951 because "the Provincial Government is heading for financial ruin." While his opinion was broadly sound, Russell's reason for holding it was not. He had misread the government's proposed initial spending plans for the coming fiscal year as the final official estimates, and by adding up the totals concluded that bankruptcy was certain.

In part because of Smallwood's increasing arrogance, even Power and

Horwood, his close friends and fellow "Bolsheviks," who matched him in intellect and who had once shared his ideals, contributed little. Horwood preferred the emotional excitement of perpetual revolution to the dreary grind of trying to implement it. "It would be all very well for us to make our peace with the merchant princes," he said in the legislature in February 1950. "I am afraid that is what Coaker did. I am afraid this is what Squires did. I want to make it clear to the people of this province, who have been robbed wholesale and retail, that we have not made peace with the gang of entrepreneurs who have looted their heritage: a corrupt and decadent aristocracy of wealth."

This was fine stuff for the barricades – but they had already been stormed. As Premier, Smallwood could ill afford to add to the number of enemies he already possessed. Of Horwood's outburst he said soothingly: "If in the course of his speech, he indulged in a sentence, perhaps in a sentence or two that were a bit radical, what else would you expect from a man in his twenties?" Too proud to make allowances and embittered by such patronizing, Horwood broke with Smallwood in 1951. In the manner of many ex-believers, he developed a near-hatred for the man he had once followed. As political columnist for the *Evening Telegram*, he fearlessly slashed into the government, writing of "millions poured out in graft and corruption," and into Smallwood, whom he damned as a "mountebank" with an "inferiority complex the size of Signal Hill."

Horwood attacked with a rapier; in reply Smallwood used a bludgeon. In the legislature on June 17, 1954, he unleashed a stream of barrack-room vitriol against the columnist: "This dastardly clown, this loath-some literary scavenger, this cut-throat, this rat who has been using the columns of the *Telegram* to carry on his own personal vendetta. He hates me like the devil hates Holy Water." Horwood, he added darkly, had been investigated "on the score that he was possibly a Communist or had Communist connections or affiliations." (The day before, under routine Opposition attack, Smallwood had accused the Conservatives of "McCarthy-ist smear tactics.")

Power, who joined the Government as a minister in 1951, understood Smallwood better. He was a cat among the cabinet's pigeons, a brooding, Pinteresque figure with a mordant wit and a malevolent view of life. He alone was never in the least in awe of the Premier, and with him alone Smallwood let down his guard of iron self-sufficiency. On the night of the 1949 election, when Smallwood by his "not one red cent" speech had cost Power his seat, a fellow minister chanced to come into the room just as the news of the defeat came over the radio; he was about to say something when he noticed that Smallwood's eyes were filled with tears. On a Jamaica beach in 1953, Smallwood turned casually to Power and said: "Greg, if you don't stop drinking it will kill you." Power, who was then a bottle-a-day man, replied: "Joe, if you stop smoking, I'll stop drinking." They shook hands and each kept the bargain.

Power's wit lightened Smallwood's long days, and sometimes pricked the thickening bubble of vanity with which he was beginning to surround himself. After one speech, of which Smallwood was inordinately proud, Power told him: "I've never heard so much nonsense in so short a time in my life." Smallwood was unfazed: "I know that, but it's tough to make a good speech when you don't know what you're talking about." (The subject was economic development.)*

For a decade, Smallwood allowed Power to exercise authority second only to his own, and it was Power who decided who would or would not get in to see the Premier. The trust went unreciprocated; Power was too uninvolved to put his formidable intellect to work on any problems other than his own, and his interest in public affairs lapsed as soon as Confederation was won.

For such singular men, their friendship was too close to last. It ended when Smallwood, often without realizing, began increasingly to demand sycophancy as a condition of employment. Power was too free a spirit to accept such pretention. He simply walked out of the government and out of Smallwood's life. When he first resigned, late in 1958, Smallwood,

---

* Years later, Smallwood resurrected what was probably Power's deftest verbal shaft. After they had called on the Pope at Castel Gandolfo, Power reported to a colleague: "After dealing with Archbishop Roche, I can only say I deeply appreciate the humility of Pope Pius XII." In 1967, Smallwood commented to columnist Peter Newman: "After six years of dealing with Jean Lesage, I have learned to deeply respect the humility of Charles de Gaulle."

anguished at the loss, managed to talk him back. Then in January 1959, Power simply stopped going to the office. Smallwood waited for three months and finally asked for his resignation. It came by the next mail. "He has always been a tower of strength to me personally," Smallwood told the House of Assembly. "I will miss him acutely. It is going to be more difficult for me than ever before." Smallwood did not tell the legislature that before he accepted Power's resignation he had driven to his house and rung the bell three times. When no one answered, he turned and walked away.

Today, Power, a bitter and lonely man, talks of Smallwood with unconcealed contempt. Smallwood speaks of him with regret and of their estrangement with bewilderment. Though they continue to live in the same small community, they have not spoken to each other nor even met for more than ten years.

Many of those whom Smallwood attracted to him came with the conviction that government would be as it had always been in Newfoundland, a spare-time pursuit and an open sesame for spoils. Early cabinet meetings were like a Restoration play: ministers came in and got up to leave as soon as their own department had been discussed – until Smallwood irritatedly explained the purpose of cabinet was to consider the affairs of the entire government. If amateurish, graft was rampant. Of the conduct of some ministers, one ex-minister has said: "We were like children from the bottom of the hill given the keys to the squire's mansion at the top." Within a month of taking office, one minister proposed to a prominent St. John's lawyer that they jointly buy up the privately owned printing firm which held the government accounts and make a killing on assured government contracts. One Minister of Supply was universally known as "the Minister of Ten Percent," although, as one colleague commented, "It was sometimes fifteen per cent."

Often corruption came right out into the open. One minister had to be fired after he requisitioned the government hospital ship for a week-long fling in St. Pierre and then steamed back to his own constituency.

Among a welter of minor scandals, the Opposition discovered that government supplies were being purchased, at retail prices, from a store owned by the brother of the Minister of Supply; three Liberal members had to be hastily scuttled in the midst of a campaign when word got out that they were employed by companies the Government was in the midst of negotiating with. O. L. Vardy, a long-time crony of Smallwood's who, as Director of Tourism and Chairman of the St. John's Housing Corporation, was an excellent tuna fisherman, was named by a newspaper, the *Newfoundlander*, as being part-owner of a firm from which the Corporation was buying its supplies. Two cabinet ministers were confidential shareholders in Radio Station CJON, co-owned by Stirling and Jamieson, which got its licence through good Liberal offices.

Smallwood knew of everything that happened and was supremely unconcerned. It is worth standing back to take a look at a man who could condone such practices and yet stoutly declare in the legislature: "I have smashed the spoils system . . . there never was a cleaner government in the history of Newfoundland."

His personality and actions were an interlocking series of contradictions. As he himself has said: "I have never been in the least bothered when somebody says to me that something I did today completely contradicts something I did before. I haven't had time – in trying to build Newfoundland – to think about such things." This approach amounted to a sensible divorce of tactics from long-term strategy. To an onlooker, the interim result was baffling.

Thus, while not in the least disturbed by the behaviour of some of his colleagues who, not to put too fine a point on it, were virtually plundering the public treasury, Smallwood himself was that oddity in Newfoundland – a Puritan. He was totally uninterested in material comforts and possessions. His suits, dark blue or dark grey, which he eventually discarded in favour of pure black, hung as limply over his slight, 130-pound frame as they had when he worked on the *Call*. His one sartorial affectation was a bow-tie, a political symbol he fostered with the same far-sightedness as the nickname "Joey." When he ate, he scarcely noticed the food before him, and save for the occasional glass of port, he drank neither wine nor spirits. His regular midnight snack was the bayman's treat: home-made bread, covered first with molasses, "which should be allowed to sink in," and then with butter. (In later years, forced for the first time to think of dieting, he switched to Florida oranges.) He lived in Canada House, a rambling thirty-two room, white frame Victorian mansion on Circular Road, which had formerly been the residence of Canadian High Commissioners. This relative splendour, and an official car which his more status-minded colleagues persuaded him to buy, were the only outward changes in his style.

At first, Smallwood refused even the car, "because people will say I've sold out," and accepted it only on the condition he drove it himself. The cabinet accepted the compromise reluctantly. Smallwood's driving inadequacies were locally famous, so that aspirant successors invited to drive with him nervously weighed the honour against the prospects of extinction. A diminutive figure crouched over the wheel of a vast, custom-built Cadillac or Chrysler Imperial, Smallwood can commonly be sighted hurtling through fog at seventy miles an hour, two wheels across the centre line, or smartly overtaking round a corner. According to St. John's legend, he was once spotted doing this by an RCMP patrol car, which gave chase and finally overtook him. As the officer approached, notebook in hand, a familiar face peered out the window. "My God," the officer said. "Yes," replied the Premier, "and don't you forget it." With cars, as with cameras, tape-recorders, intercoms, and hi-fi sets, all of which he delights in but quickly demolishes, Smallwood is a mechanical illiterate. Only quick reflexes have saved him from worse accidents than a moose decapitated on a New Brunswick highway, a carload of provincial cabinet ministers overturned on a back road, and a night spent in reading official documents in the back of his car, in the midst of a snow-covered field, after a skid off the highway.

At home, Smallwood answered his own telephone, whether the caller was a plumber or the Prime Minister of Canada. Anyone could see him at any hour of the day or night. An interview with the Premier was a happening. Visitors crowded into the corridor outside his ground-floor office at Canada House. If the wait happened to be too long, as it usually was, they were welcome to drop into the kitchen and brew a pot of tea. Once inside, knee-booted fishermen and double-breasted corporate presidents picked their way around untidy mountains of papers, books, and documents in search of the Premier. Often they found him crouched on the floor, excitedly examining a set of blueprints spread out in front of him. Or he might be behind his desk holding a telephone receiver to each ear. As the visitor stated his business, he would call a brief halt to the telephone conversations and then ask what the newcomer thought about the matter under discussion. Federal civil servants, in particular, were astounded to find themselves giving advice on local and not necessarily democratic politics.

Smallwood's intellectual zest and enthusiasm, and his total lack of pretence or side, won him friends as disparate as Robert Winters, by now a federal cabinet minister, and Beland Honderich, then financial editor and later editor and publisher of the *Toronto Star*. Smallwood met Honderich when he was covering the Confederation campaigns; they got on so famously that Smallwood offered him the post of Director of Tourism, at $10,000 a year. Honderich declined, preferring to try his luck in metropolitan journalism.*

If Smallwood's enthusiasm – for politics, for power, for ideas, and above all for action – was often childlike, it was never childish. His vocabulary excluded the word "impossible." While this led him into several monumental blunders, it produced also ideas far ahead of their time. In July 1949, he proposed that the four eastern provinces unite into a Maritime Union to increase their bargaining power at Ottawa. In November 1950, he proposed an Atlantic Provinces Crown Corporation to develop industry, an idea which the Maritime Board of Trade dismissed as "socialist."

---

* Their friendship broke up, however, over the 1959 loggers strike, when the *Star* severely criticized Smallwood. When Honderich asked one of his reporters what Smallwood thought of his editorials, he was informed, "He called you a son of a bitch."

Though he was rising fifty, his energy was as prodigious as ever, and he held to the pace he had set for himself during the Confederation campaigns. His day began at 9:00 A.M., and rarely ended until past midnight, interrupted only by a twenty-minute, post-lunch nap in his office, and another hour-long sleep in the early evening. During his first year in office, he claimed to have received a daily total of one hundred letters, fifteen telegrams, one hundred phone calls and fifty visitors.

Whatever interested him at the moment absorbed him totally, and had to be acted upon immediately. Unaware that the metabolisms of others responded to different time clocks, Smallwood telephoned ministers and civil servants at all hours of the night to demand their instant appearances. Dishevelled and bleary-eyed, the wretched men would stumble into Canada House to be confronted with an inhumanly wide-awake Smallwood excitedly expounding some complex and costly project. To argue with him at any time was next to impossible; at four in the morning, sheer exhaustion muffled the mildest pleas for caution.

Smallwood made no secret of the source of his energy: "I love this job. I love it to death. I love every waking minute of it, from the time I get up to the time I go to bed."

In Smallwood, as in many men, this open lust for power was a far more potent motivating force than the conventional lust for the flesh. Such an admission said much about Smallwood's lack of hypocrisy. Even in the 1970s, when so few pruderies concerning sex remain, few individuals are willing to acknowledge lust for power as the mainspring of their actions.

Yet, for all his passion for power, Smallwood displayed few of the usual characteristics of men so motivated. He drew no pleasure in the exercise of authority for its own sake, nor in having others bow down before him. He despised pomp and pretence. Instead Smallwood loved power because it gave him the chance to act, and above all to build. Of his role in Confederation, he has said: "What was I? A catalyst, a propagandist – no more," and added, "but I do fancy myself as a father of new industry, new roads, schools, and hospitals. I hope I'll be remembered for these." At heart, Smallwood is an engineer who has used the opportunities political power has given him to build the foundation of the new Newfoundland he dreamed of. The weakness of an engineer is to be concerned with structures rather than the people who will use them. It is a weakness that characterized Smallwood's record as Premier.

Smallwood articulated his philosophy of building early in office. He was convinced that social welfare could be no more than a palliative, and that only industrialization could propel Newfoundland forward. "Newfoundland," he said on August 2, 1949, "must develop or perish."

During the winter of 1949-50, Smallwood discovered anew how close Newfoundland was to perishing. The long postwar boom collapsed, and with it the last illusion of the island's self-sufficiency. By the autumn, thirty thousand were unemployed, one-third of them ineligible for unemployment insurance and destitute.

In similar crises, past Newfoundland governments had resorted to the dole. "Dole is degradation," declared Smallwood, "a thing of the past." Instead, he formed a Public Relief Administration that would, he promised, employ some nine thousand men, at fifty-five cents an hour to build roads, and to clear slums. Six months later the scheme was abandoned; it had cost $3.4 million. "A little too rich for our blood," Smallwood sadly admitted.

His attention shifted to the goal of new industries, and for the next four years remained there. When the bill to create a new Department of Economic Development was being debated, Smallwood had said, "We ought to have, and please God we will have, as outstanding an economist as money can get in the Dominion of Canada." The legislature closed on December 3, 1949. Smallwood set off to find his economist. Together they would engineer Newfoundland's industrial revolution.

14

Valdmanis: The Welkin Ring

W e have been in our thinking in the cabinet deadly afraid that the months and years would pass by, and that in the absence of a plan the money would be going this way and that and the other, and that in a year or two or three, the legislature here and the public outside might wake up to discover that six, eight, ten, twenty millions had gone without having made any basic change, any fundamental change, in the Province's over-all economy." Thus Smallwood, on October 21, 1949, outlined the premise behind his policy of economic development. He would spend money to earn money.

The sums Smallwood referred to were the cash surplus Newfoundland had carried with her into Confederation. This surplus was at once real and a mirage. In amount it was real enough: $45.5 million. This was larger than the government's total annual revenue. "*Forty* million dollars," Smallwood would expound to his colleagues. "My God, can you believe it, *forty* million dollars." The substance of the surplus, however, was an illusion. It existed only because the old Commission of Government had put book-keeping and debt-retirement ahead of human welfare. The demands on the surplus were incessant and insistent: everything from roads, schools and hospitals, to higher pay for teachers, nurses, doctors, civil servants, policemen.

"Are we going on year after year, with things getting worse, using up our surplus on destitution, building hospitals and schools?" said Smallwood on March 30, 1950. "For what purpose? As I see more and more destitution come among us, I would not be human, I would have no bowels of compassion at all, if I didn't regret every day that passes without development coming to a head. If this present trend continues, nothing faces us but slow attrition."

Already that attrition was apparent. In the two immediate pre-Confederation years, 1947 and 1948, an estimated 4,900 Newfoundlanders had left. "There was," recalls Smallwood, now that customs and immigration barriers to the mainland had ended, "a real danger that we would be denuded of our population." To prevent it, "I felt I had to make the welkin ring. From that moment to this, I've never ceased to make the welkin ring. I've never for one moment allowed a feeling to develop in people's minds that the future here was dull or uninspiring, or that this was a place to leave, or that this was a sinking ship."

He proposed to make the welkin ring with the sound of new industries, of factories and full-time, high-wage jobs. Smallwood's choice – for secondary manufacturing rather than a reformed fishery – was significant. It appealed to his own instincts as an engineer, and to his love as a promoter for wheeling and dealing with industrialists. It appealed also to a deep instinct within Newfoundlanders. If the sea has given much to Newfoundland, it has taken more, in poverty, human misery, and human lives.

Nor was Smallwood's enthusiasm so far out of line with the economic insights of the day. This was the era when Britain planted groundnuts in Africa; when the United States gave Afghanistan a jet airport, and the Soviet Union built a four-lane highway in the same country. A few years later, Canada glimpsed a Northern Vision.

Among the influences that triggered Smallwood into going outside the province to hire an economic expert was a four-page memorandum Albert Perlin of the *Daily News* had written him on November 10, 1949. "The initial requirement," Perlin suggested, "is for a first-class man, young enough to have plenty of drive, equipped with a technical knowledge of the kind obtainable in an industrial engineering outfit which has experience in rehabilitating the economics of under-developed countries." Smallwood forwarded Perlin's letter to C. D. Howe at Ottawa, adding the scribbled postscript, "Do you know anyone like this?"

Four months later, Smallwood hired Dr. Alfred Valdmanis, a Latvian economist and politician of inscrutable heritage. Four years later, Valdmanis, of whom Smallwood in one of countless eulogies had said, "He is worth his weight in gold to Newfoundland," pleaded guilty before the Newfoundland Supreme Court to defrauding the provincial government of $200,000. Only Smallwood could have survived such a debacle. He handled the crisis in demagogic style; he survived it because the public, with keen memories of past fiascos, would not condemn him, as he put it, "as long as they can feel in their hearts that the Government is trying to do something; that this is not a do-nothing government." Even before Valdmanis's appearance on stage, Smallwood had suffered one painful lesson in the complexities of economic development. On Christmas Eve, 1949, four men emerged from a blizzard to knock at the door of Canada House. They were, they explained, Icelandic herring fishermen, and had come because "Iceland is going down and Newfoundland is coming up." Newfoundland could go way up, they suggested, if Smallwood bought herring boats for them and inaugurated a new industry. The quartet left with the Christmas present of a contract in their pockets. They returned the following spring with four purse seiners, ranging from fifty to 290 tons. To practised Newfoundland eyes, the vessels seemed uncommonly aged and their gear composed of antique oddities. Nine months and $412,000 in government funds later, the Icelanders had caught six barrels of herring. They were never seen again. The boats remained unsold for three years. A buyer was finally found; he paid $55,000 for them – a sum he was able to afford by way of a government loan of $55,000.

The saga of the Icelandic boats has become a minor Newfoundland classic, requiring only a "come all ye" to be enshrined forever. Smallwood today can laugh about it. At the time he did much the same. To the dismay of his colleagues, Smallwood flung himself into the task of public confession with the same gusto he applied to any other project: "We have made mistakes, of course," he contritely told the legislature in March 1951. "Look at the Icelandic boats. An awful mistake. A blunder. It cost us a lot of money." The Conservatives could add little by way of condemnation, but Smallwood continued, "And we have made other mistakes. I have made more than one mistake. The only man who makes no mistakes is a man who does nothing, and that is a mistake. Therefore he makes one. I have made mistakes. They have been, perhaps, mistakes of the heart."

After Valdmanis's star had disappeared, Smallwood usually allocated the credit for his appointment to C. D. Howe. The honour was unappreciated – and inaccurate. In the spring of 1950, Valdmanis was scratching out a living as an "advisor" to the Department of Immigration, and as a part-time consultant to the Department of Trade and Commerce. This was the extent of his contact with Howe.

Instead, Valdmanis came to Smallwood's attention by accident and by his own persistence. In search of full-time employment he called regularly on cabinet ministers and got to know Robbins Elliott, Executive Assistant to Robert Winters, by now Minister of Resources and Development. Elliott took a liking to Valdmanis and mentioned to him that the Premier of Newfoundland was looking for an economist. Smallwood was next in Ottawa on May 18, 1950 (after a cross-country tour that included a stop in Edmonton to be made an honorary chief of the Blood Indian tribe, *So-ee-na*, Chief Big Water). Valdmanis telephoned him and was invited to lunch at the Chateau Laurier.

Premier and economist met in the basement restaurant and continued their discussion in Smallwood's suite until 3:00 A.M. By then,

Valdmanis had accepted the job, at $10,000 a year – "Smallwood proposed and I was willing" – and the title of Director General of Economic Development which he himself suggested, "because it will impress the Europeans."

There are two versions of Valdmanis's career: the account which all Newfoundland soon heard about, and the account dragged into the open once the Latvian became the centre of controversy. These begin to diverge with Valdmanis's childhood.

He was born in 1908, he told Smallwood, in the village of Zeimipe in the Baltic backwater of Latvia, then a province of Tsarist Russia. His father, a university professor who was killed by the Russians when Valdmanis was still a boy, taught his son to read and write by the age of four, but never to play or to enjoy himself.

As a schoolboy, Valdmanis was selected for a special education course designed to produce a future governing élite. Of the more than one hundred who started the spartan system, he was among the dozen who finished. He went on to study at Riga and at universities in France and Germany until, by the time he was twenty-four, he had earned degrees in economics and philosophy and was a Doctor of Jurisprudence at the University of Frankfurt. He spoke fluent English, German, French, Russian, Italian, and Latvian. For a time, at the Reichsbank, he was a student of Hjalmar Schacht, the mastermind of Germany's war-preparedness. When Valdmanis was twenty-nine, he was appointed Minister of Economics, Finance and Trade, the youngest such minister in all Europe. Simultaneously, he was President of the Latvian Iron and Steel industry, head of the social welfare board, and a director of the state insurance system. His country's economy flowered.

All this promise and achievement was destroyed by war. In 1940, the Russians moved west; Valdmanis was arrested, imprisoned, and tortured until he escaped to hide in the woods. In 1941, the Germans rolled east: as a leader of his country's resistance movement, Valdmanis was jailed. He was spared execution only by the personal intervention of Hermann Goering, like Valdmanis a Grand Commander of the Swedish order of

Stella Polaris, "the highest decoration that the Swedish government could give to anyone."

After the fall of Germany, Valdmanis joined the civilian staff of the British Army of Occupation, served at the headquarters of General Eisenhower, and finally became a senior staff member of the International Relief Organization in Geneva. In 1948, he was discovered by the Lady Davis Foundation of Montreal, a privately sponsored organization which specialized in helping displaced scholars and scientists to emigrate to Canada. He arrived on October 14, 1948, aboard the *Empress of Canada*. He brought with him his wife, three daughters, a son, and a seven-year-old boy adopted after his parents had been transported to Siberia by the Russians. "I know I will not be as rich a man as I once was," Valdmanis told reporters on the Montreal dockside, "but money is no longer important to me."

The second, later account of his career was less flattering, but no less dramatic. His father was only a schoolteacher. He was never a Doctor of Jurisprudence at the University of Frankfurt, nor an apprentice to Schacht. He served as Finance Minister to Latvia for only nine months before being fired, though for political rather than for administrative reasons. According to Latvian refugees, he had worked for the Russians, and when the Germans arrived he was reported seen fleeing eastward in a commissar's car. Again, according to Latvian refugees, Valdmanis mysteriously returned, served the Germans as a Director of Justice, and took part in efforts to raise a hundred-thousand-man Latvian Legion to join the crusade against Communism. Far from being jailed by the Germans, he spent the latter part of the war at Biebrich am Rhein where he was in charge of cement, limestone, and gypsum production. The Swedish *Stella Polaris*, North Star, was a third-grade decoration.

Obscured by the fog of wartime memories and personal vendettas, Valdmanis's past followed him to Newfoundland. A New York Jewish weekly, *Der Taag*, accused him of persecuting Jews in German-occupied Latvia. (The charge was later retracted.) In the House of Commons, a Conservative M.P., W. J. Browne, read out a 1943 pamphlet by the Latvian exile Gregory Miskins which called Valdmanis "the Quisling of Latvia and a Nazi collaborator."

Although one war refugee's memories are as unconvincing as another's, there was never any doubt of Valdmanis's talent for survival. In occupied Europe, survival was the highest virtue, achieved by alternately grovelling before Allies and Axis. On cue, Valdmanis told the Canadian immigration authorities what they wanted to hear. He had survived the war; he had put distance between himself and old enemies. When his chance came, he took it. He told his wife, as she later wrote to Smallwood, "If I ever get in a position to make a large amount of money, I'll make it, no matter how I do it."

Until he was summoned to the Chateau Laurier, Valdmanis's Canadian career had been mixed. He held and lost jobs with the Nova Scotia government and a lectureship at Carleton College in Ottawa. He appeared as an advisor before a session of a Senate Committee on Immigration on April 27, 1949, to argue that Canada should accept as citizens former members of the Baltic Waffen S.S. who, he said, "wore German uniforms much like the Germans and who fought the Russians, but not any other allied country." No action was taken on his suggestion.

The characteristic that most attracted Smallwood was Valdmanis's capacity for work. This was as considerable as his own and was applied with the same intense concentration. Then forty-two, Valdmanis was trim and athletic, just below medium height. His jet black hair was brushed precisely back; his mouth was tight and hard; his eyes, green and penetrating, glared out with a disturbing intensity. Though accented, his English was fluent; he danced impeccably and was an excellent pianist; he played tennis superbly and lost fewer than half a dozen sets while in St. John's; he was a connoisseur of wines, ordering them by vineyard rather than vintner. As useful, Valdmanis was a skilled flatterer. He never addressed Smallwood as anything but "My Premier," a possessive familiarity which irked other ministers but delighted Smallwood who in turn always called him "Doctor Valdmanis." Of one policy concoction he told Smallwood: "My Premier, you have invented a new thing. You have created a new idea in the realm of economic thought."

Confident that he could always dominate Smallwood's affections, Valdmanis made no attempt to make friends among Newfoundlanders. In St. John's, he lived alone, while his wife and family remained in Montreal; his only personal confidante was a secretary in the Economic Development Department, Olga Leikus, twenty-three, an elegant honey blonde who as a schoolgirl had known Valdmanis in Latvia, and who reminded the other girls in the office of Ingrid Bergman. As a $4,000 a year civil servant, her administrative duties were restricted to typing out Valdmanis's occasional letters in Latvian, and sometimes acting as a travelling secretary.

While Smallwood was well aware of Valdmanis's defects of personality, particularly of his arrogance and pomposity, he chose to ignore them. His partnership with Valdmanis went far beyond business and government: He had found a soulmate. "I loved him as I loved no brother or sister of my own," he once said.

Though Smallwood rarely indulged in introspection, he could not help but be aware of the fearful responsibility on his shoulders for committing the province's slender resources to so imponderable an attempt at crash industrialization. In Valdmanis, Smallwood believed he had found someone to share and lighten his load. "Watch out when we start to dream," he told the legislature on February 15, 1950, "our dreams come true. Watch us, we always win." By late May, Valdmanis was by his side, and the time had come to give shape to those dreams.

Their first project, in what was to be the most ambitious program of industrialization attempted by any province in proportion to its size, took shape as early as the first meeting at the Chateau Laurier. There Valdmanis had impressed Smallwood by arguing that the Newfoundland market was large enough to support a cement plant. The raw materials for Portland cement – limestone and shale – existed on the island, and could be mixed with slag from the Sydney steel mills. On August 2, 1950, Smallwood announced plans for a cement mill at Corner Brook; it would employ three hundred men and manufacture 150,000 tons of cement a year.

To find a builder, Smallwood and Valdmanis in mid-September flew to

New York to negotiate with the Cement and General Development Corporation. The company's estimate was $5 million. This, Valdmanis argued, was too high. He suggested instead Miag Machinenbau Gesellschaft, a giant engineering firm which had its plant at Brunswick and its head office at Geneva. Valdmanis knew Miag from the war years (when the firm had manufactured parts for Tiger tanks). Miag's price was $3.5 million.

Soon two other new industries were unveiled: a hardboard plant using local birch which would employ 150 in a factory near St. John's, and a gypsum plant to employ three hundred. These two plants were to be built by another German firm recommended by Valdmanis, Benno-Schilde Machinenbau Gesellschaft. The three plants combined, declared Smallwood, would earn "a clean, net operating profit of $1.25 million a year." All three were to be built entirely out of government funds and subsequently sold, and the money then used to start new industries in an endless cycle.

By now, the total sum allocated to new industries was $6 million. The Opposition expressed alarm and demanded details of the contract prices, and of the collateral used for the government loans. "It is not in the public interest to do so at this time," replied Smallwood. "At the right moment, the facts and figures will come out, and he who laughs last, laughs best."

To confound his critics further, Smallwood evolved a system of budgeting that would have baffled a Social Crediter, let alone the attenuated Conservative opposition. There were two spending accounts, "Capital" and "Current," and the distinctions between them blurred. The pre-Confederation cash surplus was maintained as an entirely separate account. To this, Smallwood each year added a surplus on the "Capital" account, subtracted a deficit on the "Current" account, added the sale of any special assets, and struck an inscrutable balance. According to the budget for 1951, the cash surplus would stand at $14.2 million by the end of March 1952. Smallwood had continually to beat back accusations that the heavy spending covered large-scale graft and corruption. "The Government," he declared hotly, "was honest, hard-working, perhaps wrong, perhaps blundering, perhaps incompetent, but at least honest and trying to do its best." Yet the difficulties could not be hidden. Construction fell behind schedule, design changes increased costs, and the estimate for the three plants climbed to $9 million.

It was Valdmanis who came up with an imaginative scheme for doubling the value of the government's capital. Instead of building complete factories itself, he suggested that the government loan fifty per cent of the cost to private investors who would then make up the balance with machinery and technical know-how. The most abundant source of such investors, he advised Smallwood, was Europe, particularly Germany, where businessmen looked anxiously over their shoulders at the Russian border.

To test this theory, Smallwood, accompanied by Valdmanis and two cabinet ministers, flew off to Europe on October 14, 1950. He would, he said, "turn myself into a flying saucer" in the cause of industrial development. "Our target is ten thousand new jobs in the next two to three years."

The two-week tour through the length and breadth of Germany was an astonishing success. Smallwood's group dined with Ludwig Erhard, inspected the massive plants of I. G. Farben and Krupp, where Smallwood, angling for a steel mill, negotiated with Alfred Krupp, still jailed by the Allies, by means of messages carried by Valdmanis between hotel and prison. Everywhere, the visitors were fêted, accommodated in the best hotels, transported in gleaming Mercedes, and toasted at a succession of banquets with Hocks and Moselles, an experience that gave Smallwood his first taste for wine.*

The credit for the triumph was due to Valdmanis. Everywhere he was known and respected. At the dinner table he was scintillating; around the bargaining table he negotiated in fluent German, translating appropriate passages for Smallwood and his ministers.

Everywhere, the industrialists were intensely respectful of the bow-tied Premier and his briefcase full of North American dollars. Partnership offers flowed in from German manufacturers of textiles and leather goods, fashion furs, automobile tires, and heavy machinery. To show his

---

* He subsequently became a late-blooming connoisseur of red wines, with Chateau Latour his favourite.

appreciation, Smallwood increased Valdmanis's salary to $25,000 – compared to the $17,000 earned by the Deputy Minister of Finance at Ottawa, and the $7,000 by Smallwood himself. In the legislature, Peter Cashin protested: "I would not trust him with a hot stove. He will go out of here wealthier than any of you fellows when you leave the government."

Opposition to the new industries program, which became more and more vocal throughout the 1951 session, only stiffened Smallwood's determination. A leather tannery was announced on July 6, 1951; fur-dressing, dyeing, and leather goods plants on July 8; a textile plant on August 10; a heavy machinery plant on September 21. Even more ambitious was Smallwood's announcement, in June, of an agreement with Dr. Arthur Seigheim, president of the Swiss-based Latuco Company. In return for a grant of land around Lake Melville in Labrador, Dr. Seigheim undertook to cut two hundred thousand cords of wood a year, to provide employment for fifteen hundred loggers, and to settle them at two new townsites complete with schools, churches, and market gardens. (In October, Smallwood had to announce sadly that Dr. Seigheim had apparently failed to raise his share of the finances and the deal was off.)

The legislature adjourned on June 18 and was called back into session on October 24. In between those dates, Smallwood had carried his program to new heights. On August 24, accompanied once more by Valdmanis, and by Attorney General Curtis, Smallwood boarded the *Empress of France* for a six-week European tour "to fish in troubled waters." He returned to announce new industries for everything from machine tools to steel that would "create fifteen thousand new jobs before the end of the next two years."

Once again, the pilgrimage had become a triumphal procession. It covered four thousand miles from Sweden to Switzerland via Denmark, Holland, Belgium, and Germany. There were multi-course dinners, tours of vast factories, evenings at opera houses. At one *schloss* in Bavaria, the trio were entranced by a tableau of ballet dancers upon the lawn, which culminated in a fireworks display, while an offstage choir sang "Ode to Newfoundland."

One of their hosts, Smallwood reported to the legislature, "lives in a house which has one of the most famous art galleries of Europe, two-quarters of a million dollars worth of famous paintings in that house alone. . . . He is a very great figure in industry, has manufactured cars and tractors and aircraft machinery of all kinds." There was, unhappily, a catch. "He has no money in dollars." Don Jamieson, sent on a mission to check the credentials of a film company that wanted to come to Newfoundland, discovered that though the company occupied superb modern studios in Amsterdam, these were open for his inspection only at late-evening hours or on weekends. Jamieson reached the conclusion the firm was simply renting someone else's studio. (The company was still awarded the contract.)

Smallwood harboured no doubts. "We'll dot Conception Bay with factories," he told a press conference at the Savoy Hotel in London on his way home. "People are beginning to catch on. After all, you don't say no to Santa Claus."

For Curtis and Valdmanis, perhaps the most memorable event of the trip occurred during breakfast in the Grand Hotel in Stockholm. The Director General and the Attorney General had just begun their meal when the Premier joined them. Smallwood sat down, picked up the menu, looked at it, and put it down. "I'm going to call an election," he said. "I decided it in bed last night." As the pair gaped, Smallwood explained his reasons: the Conservatives were unprepared; victory would give the government four clear years to nurse the new industries through their teething troubles. There was a third reason: the cash surplus was down near the $10 million minimum which, it had been agreed at Confederation, would remain inviolate in the vaults of the Bank of Canada.[*]

The Throne Speech for the new session was as brief as it was remarkable. "In all her long history," intoned the Lieutenant Governor,

---

[*] When the time came, Smallwood negotiated that obstacle by the obvious route. He used the "reserve" cash surplus at Ottawa as collateral for further loans.

"Newfoundland has never known such a high degree of prosperity." He went on to heap praise upon the government. By the coming spring, the Speech promised "more than twenty new industries." The Conservative leader scoffed: "I can see the glare of Pittsburgh in our eyes," and Russell, from his vantage-point as an Independent, contributed a scrap of doggerel:

> Thou too drive on O truck of state
> Drive on O Government strong and great
> Thy driving power has what it takes
> But where O where thy brakes.

A week later, Smallwood slipped into high gear. He dissolved the legislature because "the people of Newfoundland have not given the Government a specific mandate to go ahead with this great program of economic development."

Before the campaign began, there was time for a few more examples of the Smallwood-Valdmanis style of industrial development. The tannery was to be operated by a Czech, William Dorn, who would ship out an entire plant from Hamburg. Beside it would be a boot-and-shoe plant and a glove factory, the latter using only the skins of gazelles. Another industry would be United Cotton Mills, turning out shirts, women's dresses, aprons, and sugar, salt, and flour sacks from the raw material imported from the United States, Haiti, Turkey, and Egypt. The parent company, Smallwood explained, employed fifteen hundred men and women operating sixty thousand spindles. It was, unfortunately, without any dollars of its own to invest. "How," demanded Cashin, "do they get their equipment across?" "That," answered the Premier, "is none of my business."

The campaign was short, vicious, and a foregone conclusion. Smallwood won twenty-four of the twenty-eight seats. It was perhaps the most frustrating campaign the Conservatives endured. Their arguments about financial waste and economic insanity were a spit in the wind against the apathy of the electorate and the political skill of Smallwood. The only success the Conservatives scored was in a smear attack upon Valdmanis, as a foreigner and an ex-Nazi.

The mudslinging alarmed Smallwood sufficiently that he called Ottawa to check on Valdmanis's past. The RCMP gave the Latvian a clean bill of health. Smallwood also called Sir William Stephenson, the "Quiet Canadian" of British wartime intelligence in Washington. Sir William checked his sources in London and Washington, and once again Valdmanis was cleared. "One day the people of Newfoundland will erect a monument to Dr. Valdmanis," said Smallwood in an exuberant counterattack. "No government of the eleven is better served, nor with greater effect and efficiency."

The Conservatives had one last card to play. With less than two weeks to go, the party announced that a Dr. Luther Sennewald had wired the Conservative campaign manager to promise "ALL DOCUMENTS REVEALING SURPRISING MANIPULATIONS IN BOTH ST. JOHN'S AND GERMANY BEHIND ALL NEW INDUSTRIES STOP READY TO COME IMMEDIATELY IF YOU PAY EXPENSES." The expenses were forwarded, and Sennewald crossed the Atlantic. When the moment of truth came, though, he issued a statement to explain "a serious misunderstanding," and flew back to Germany. Four months later, Sennewald was awarded a $110,000 government contract to start an optical instruments factory.

In justifying that loan to the legislature, Smallwood sketched in Sennewald's qualifications. He had studied at Dresden, Vienna, Berlin, and London, and had once been nominated "for the Nobel Prize in Physics, but Hitler's government would not permit him to accept it, so he never was a Nobel Prize winner." This Nobelist *manqué* had heard of Newfoundland in 1950, and bombarded Smallwood with letters demanding a loan to set up a factory based upon a secret optical process that would manufacture 300,000 eye-glass frames and 450,000 lenses a year, since as Smallwood explained, "one person in five of all the population of Canada wears glasses." In 1950, this proposal had been too much even for Smallwood. The project was rejected. In revenge, Sennewald intruded upon the 1951 election.

When Sennewald reached Gander, he was met by one of the most exotic personalities the new industrial program had brought to the

province, Max Braun-Wogan, founder of the Neue (New) Technique
Corporation and a member of Valdmanis's staff. Braun-Wogan made it
to Gander aboard an RCAF Canso that was made suddenly available, after
Smallwood put through a call to the Prime Minister's office in Ottawa. At
the foot of the ramp, Braun-Wogan greeted Sennewald, took him for a
walk and an earnest talk in the terminal building, and flew with him to
St. John's aboard the Canso. There they drove to Canada House, where,
explained Smallwood, there had been a most unfortunate breakdown in
communications. On reflection, Sennewald's proposition deserved reconsideration, yet such reconsideration could clearly not be given if he were
to spread false and unfounded stories about the new industries program.

Unhappily, once the campaign was over, Sennewald failed to justify
the faith thus placed in him. Early in 1952, Finance Minister Power
received a call from an official at the Bank of Montreal in St. John's.
Sennewald, for reasons which the official chose not to speculate, was
removing the government payments from his account as fast as they
were made and transferring them to Montreal. A hurried check disclosed that Sennewald himself had moved to Montreal. A second check,
this one on the cases of optical manufacturing equipment Sennewald
had imported, revealed their contents were largely scrap metal, stones,
and waste packing.

Smallwood sent his executive assistant, Gordon Pushie, to intercept
Sennewald a second time. Armed with a warrant for his arrest, Pushie
arrived in Montreal to find that Sennewald had purchased three airline
tickets, one to South America, two to European countries. Since a court
case might be widely misinterpreted in Newfoundland, Pushie persuaded
Sennewald to return to St. John's, carrying $110,000 in a suitcase. All of it
was returned. It was the only one hundred per cent loan refund on the
new industries program.

With victory, Smallwood was freed of all restraints. All along he had
aimed at much more than simply seeing manufacturing plants. The
Throne Speech at the start of the first session of the new legislature, on

March 2, 1952, forecast "the greatest drive for mineral resources ever experienced in this province." To bring off his resources program, Smallwood would have to sell Newfoundland's wares to the investors of Toronto, Montreal, New York, and London. How well he would succeed depended partly upon his skills as a salesman. It depended far more on what Newfoundland had to offer.

15

Valdmanis: The Carpetbagger

arly in office, Smallwood gambled that Newfoundland might find mineral fortune the easy way. On a tip from Beland Honderich, he flew to New York late in 1949 to negotiate with the International Basic Economy Corporation, a Rockefeller-owned company which specialized in the development of backward economies. IBEC readily signed a $240,000 contract to survey the prospects for a third pulp-and-paper mill. A few months later IBEC reported that the outlook for a third mill was bleak; the company was never heard from again. Smallwood then hired Aero-Magnetic Surveys Ltd. of Toronto to survey potential mineral deposits on the northeast coast, and the Power Corporation of Montreal to assess the hydro potential at Baie d'Espoir on the South Coast. The cost of these surveys was $750,000. They aroused no commercial interest.

"I must play in Ottawa the part of a poor struggling province, and I do," Smallwood confided to the legislature in March 1951. "But I also, when I deal with the bankers, financial houses, industrial firms, paint Newfoundland in bright colours as a land of vast untapped wealth." But words could not put minerals and metals beneath the ground, nor make Newfoundland's stunted forest grow more quickly, nor transport

Labrador with its iron ore and hydro resources close to the market. There were in Newfoundland no pat economic hands to mould a golden image for a lacklustre government, no Midas touches like the oil of Alberta or the timber and minerals of British Columbia. Smallwood had to stack the cards himself.

In July 1950, he and Valdmanis boarded the Newfoundland Express to visit the site of the proposed cement mill, named North Star Cement after Valdmanis's Swedish decoration. By the time the train reached the West Coast, eighteen hours later, they had concocted a new and visionary scheme for economic development, which drew for inspiration on the Hudson's Bay Company and the East India Company.

Their brainchild, the Newfoundland and Labrador Corporation (NALCO), constituted a government-industry partnership visionary for its day. It would, hopefully, develop Newfoundland's resources and, at the same time, keep control of them in Newfoundland hands. In concept, it anticipated Quebec's *Société Générale de Financement* and the Canada Development Corporation by more than a decade. The corporation was ninety per cent owned by the government, and ten per cent by private investors, principally Harriman, Ripley, and Company of New York and Wood Gundy of Montreal. As assets, the corporation held exploration and development rights for an area the size of New Brunswick, including timber, minerals, and the Churchill Falls power site.

When the NALCO bill came before the legislature in June 1951, it met with an avalanche of criticism. The *Evening Telegram* protested that it "virtually dispossesses the province of all its remaining natural resources." Opposition criticism "of pure gamble and speculation" centred around the Government's commitment to buy shares back at par if the corporation failed. When Smallwood refused to back down, the Opposition stalked out of the chamber in protest.

The criticisms were well aimed; the terms were extravagant. They were also the best Newfoundland could secure. NALCO was Smallwood's bid to reverse the melancholy history of Newfoundland's struggle to escape its heritage of a one-crop economy of fish. Each time in the past that government and people had tried to develop Newfoundland, they had done so at a cost that almost ruined the colony.

The process had begun half a century before with the narrow gauge, trans-island railway, Newfoundland's dream of catching up to the industrial progress of Canada. To get the railway, the government granted Robert Reid, a Scottish-born engineer, perpetual rights to two and a half million acres of land on either side of the track; a monopoly on rail, mail, telegraph, and steamship services; exemption from all taxes; a sum of $15,000 for each mile built; and an outright grant of $3.5 million to maintain and operate the service. "It seems that the Ministry are going to sell the colony to a contractor – a rather novel proceeding," commented the Colonial Secretary, Joseph Chamberlain. "We cannot prevent them, but we might at least wash our hands of the affair." Unlike the CPR, Newfoundland's railway opened up neither agricultural lands nor mineral deposits. By 1921, the company was bankrupt. The railway and its annual deficits were taken over by the government.

Each subsequent industry was acquired in the same way. The first pulp-and-paper mill, at Grand Falls, was secured at the cost of signing away forever the best timber stands on the island. The second mill, at Corner Brook, came higher. The government had to guarantee a $10 million bond issue, and accept a payment of $150,000 a year in lieu of taxes. (In the first year of Confederation, this company, Bowater's Ltd., paid $3.5 million in Canadian corporation tax.)

In Smallwood's words, NALCO was to be the "instrument through which the Newfoundland Government can develop for the benefit of the people natural resources which have gone so long undeveloped." To do this, NALCO had to attract investment capital. In a memorandum to Smallwood in December 1950, Valdmanis wrote: "What we need is American interest, American names – the bigger politically or economically the better and their even if only token participation, because once we have their names, then for the sake of their own names they cannot let us down." Among those on Valdmanis's shopping list were Herbert Hoover, Harold Stassen, and Robert Taft. He did almost as well. On December 11 to 13, 1951, the eleven NALCO directors (including Smallwood and Valdmanis) held their first board meeting. As chairman they elected Sir William Stephenson.

Though he had yet to reach the heights of fame brought him by Montgomery Hyde's *The Quiet Canadian*, Stephenson was one of the most exotic and impressive figures of the day. Born in Winnipeg, he had served in the Royal Flying Corps during World War I and in the second became Director of Security Co-ordination in Washington and a confidante of OSS Chief General William "Wild Bill" Donovan, services which won him a knighthood and the honour of being the model for Ian Fleming's "M." After the war Stephenson settled in Montego Bay, Jamaica, to run a chain of companies, among them the Cement and General Development Corporation.

Stephenson began his work with NALCO in March 1952. His aims, he said, were "an extra bottle of milk for every kid in Newfoundland," and "to get the Government of Newfoundland out of business." To accomplish the latter objective, Stephenson proposed to raise a $10 million bond issue and buy up the government-owned cement, birch, and gypsum plants.

Seven months later, on October 27, 1952, Smallwood dictated a letter to Stephenson: "It is with some reluctance and great regret that I agree to the acceptance by the Board of Directors of the Newfoundland and Labrador Corporation of your resignation as their chairman." In the preceding months Stephenson had spent thirteen days in Newfoundland. The $10 million bond issue aroused not a single sale. "The first time Sir William was given the ball," said Conservative Gordon Higgins, "he dropped it."

Smallwood rushed forward to pick it up. All the new industries were now in serious trouble. None had repaid their loans, and with the failure of the bond issue all hope of recouping the government's outlays was gone. At the same time, Opposition criticism grew more insistent. They noted that machinery imported for the hardboard plant had been paid for by an initial loan of $60,000 (in theory equivalent to the machinery's value) made to Moaser and Sons of Hamburg, but sent to an address in Liechtenstein. "Who," demanded Conservative Malcolm Hollett, "values the machinery?" "I do," answered Smallwood. "You have someone else do it, surely?" "Yes," said Smallwood, "I cannot tell you who though."

Yet economics was the lesser of Smallwood's problems. His partnership with Valdmanis was foundering. Valdmanis was too intelligent an economist not to recognize the chaos around him. Early in 1952, he proposed a one-year moratorium on the creation of new industries. This Smallwood angrily rejected.

The two had become jealous of each other. The nerve was first touched, unwittingly, by the Conservatives. Their 1951 campaign slogan had been: "Defeat the Smallwood-Valdmanis dictatorship." Smallwood's objection was less to the epithet than to the assumption that the dictatorship was dual. A *Financial Post* report, which heaped praise on Valdmanis and Stephenson but dismissed Smallwood in a single sentence, sent him into a towering rage. He had shown himself a better politician than the merchants; he would now prove himself a better economist than Valdmanis.

In the autumn of 1952, Smallwood and Valdmanis made their last journey together. Along with Greg Power, they travelled through Germany, Switzerland, Holland, Belgium, and Italy. Using his old diplomatic contacts, Valdmanis won for Smallwood and Power a private audience with Pope Pius XII at Castel Gandolfo. The trio called on the pontiff carrying a supply of rosaries and religious articles to be blessed and distributed back home. This was the Latvian's last major service for Smallwood. At the end of the trip, Smallwood went on to London and Valdmanis flew home alone.

Back in St. John's, on December 24, 1952, Smallwood declared that Newfoundland was on the verge of "the biggest real estate deal on this continent in this century." It involved, he told the legislature, a British consortium headed by N. M. Rothschild and Sons, representing "the biggest combination of industrial and financial interests ever brought together in the world's history for prospecting and developing natural resources."

The coming of the British Newfoundland Development Corporation opened the door of history once more. Newfoundland's assets were signed over to foreign capital. Leased to Brinco were most of NALCO's prime holdings, including Churchill Falls.

As an instrument to keep control of natural resources in Newfoundland's hands, NALCO survived another six months. On April 5, 1953, Smallwood brought down a bill to "uncrown the corporation" and to end the government's majority ownership. A campaign to attract private capital by the sale of NALCO shares closed in September. Of 80,172 shares sold, 67,672 had been bought by a little-known and strangely titled company: Canadian Javelin Foundries and Machine Works Ltd. of Joliette, Quebec. Its president was John Christopher Doyle.

"I would make a deal with the devil himself," Smallwood once said in public, "if it were for the good of Newfoundland." He added that he was speaking figuratively.

Doyle's rising star passed Valdmanis's in descent. Early in June 1953, the Latvian resigned his post as Director General of Economic Development and moved to the vacant Chairmanship of NALCO, picking up a salary increase to $30,000. He presided over a dissolving empire. Doyle's initial bid to win control of NALCO was pre-empted when, in October, Javelin shares were delisted by the Montreal and Toronto stock exchanges after they had mysteriously soared from $2.25 to $10.75 and had fallen back, equally mysteriously, to $5.75. Instead, in March 1954, Smallwood gave Doyle exploration and development rights to NALCO's last prime holding – 2,400 square miles of Labrador territory, containing known iron ore deposits.

Clearly, there was no longer room within the emerging order for the Latvian economist. Valdmanis's performance reflected his changed status. It turned out that there was, after all, a human being behind the cold efficient machine who terrorized civil servants and cabinet ministers. He was arrested on a drunk-driving charge, an astonishing lapse in self-control. Always an insomniac, he took larger and larger doses of sleeping pills, and one minister who on a trip slept in the same room with him reported that he seemed tortured by nightmares during which he shouted out streams of German. Valdmanis could no longer sustain Smallwood's work pace, and late at night, as they laboured together, would burst out, with histrionic, arm-waving gestures: "My Premier, I cannot go on. The pace is killing me."

Many in St. John's preferred the new, humbled Valdmanis. His personal staff at NALCO, Newfoundlanders as well as German and Latvian immigrants, found him genial and easy-going. To compensate for such quirks as a ban on cigarettes because the smoke irritated his eyes, he took his staff out for late-evening dinners at Frost's Restaurant graced with expertly chosen white wines from a copious supply stored in the office closet. He was a great hand at office parties, and at his last, on Christmas Eve, 1953, he danced with all the girls and was given a sealskin paperweight as a Christmas present from the staff.

Although Valdmanis was now removed from the new industries program, its costs continued to soar, largely because of Smallwood's extravagance and Valdmanis's shortcomings as an administrator. The fifty-fifty contract they had negotiated with one of the new plants, Atlantic Gloves Ltd., was a standard example. This operation, owned by G. Hohlbrock of Hamelin, was designed to employ 150 people and to turn out 114,000 pairs of gloves a year. To accomplish this, Hohlbrock, a latter-day Pied Piper, was loaned $350,000 which he matched with $350,000 worth of machinery, its value estimated by himself. By way of guarantees, the contract enjoined that "the company will repay any bank loan guaranteed by the Government as soon as it is able to." To make the repayment, "the company will use its best endeavours to raise the sum of $350,000 from a commercial bank or by the sale of its bonds." Should the company fail to raise the money (and none even attempted to), "the government agrees to guarantee such loans or bonds both as to principal and interest." In other words, the Government would guarantee a bond issue, raised to repay a loan the Government had itself made.

By mid-1953, the Government had loaned a total of $20.2 million. Five plants were in operation (cement, gypsum, birch, machinery, and a tannery); four were under construction (rubber, textile, pressboard, and a battery plant); and four on the way (furs, gloves, boots and shoes, and ceramics). Among the proprietors was a Herr Grube of Hamburg, manager of Superior Rubber Ltd., which planned to import natural rubber from the Far East and turn it into rubber boots and seamen's all-weather clothing. Grube, explained Smallwood, "is dogged and rugged and blunt, and has very little polish. But he is a man of dynamism, energy, push, and ability." Herr Grube also spoke no English. He lasted a year in Newfoundland, to be replaced by Max Braun-Wogan.

Mercifully a projected steel mill was cancelled. But the so-called machinery plant was almost as ambitious. This, said Smallwood, would "grow to twenty-three acres of buildings." The Germans in charge, he explained, were bringing with them "58,000 blueprints, micro-filmed prints." In the hope that he would channel defence orders into it, the plant was opened by C. D. Howe in September 1952. But German equipment, much of it antiquated, and the exorbitant cost brought on by unskilled labour and absentee management were too much even for Ottawa's then flexible system of public tendering. Instead, the plant ground out rust-prone bumpers for St. John's buses and school desks for the government. Of the fifty men employed, a dozen were Germans.

By the spring of 1954, when there were fifteen new industries, the Auditor General's report disclosed that one of the government-owned plants had at last been sold. The cement mill, said the report, "has been sold to North Star Cement Ltd., for $4.3 million. Funds to purchase the cement mill were advanced by the Government to North Star Cement Ltd."

Faced with imminent debacle, Valdmanis cut and ran. Late in 1953, he proposed that the NALCO office be moved from St. John's to Montreal, to be within easy reach of mining investors and promoters. Reluctantly

Smallwood agreed. It had always irked him that Valdmanis had never brought his family to settle in the province. Now, as a crisis loomed, he was convinced his trusted colleague was deserting him. For this defection, Valdmanis paid dearly.

On February 7, 1954, Valdmanis flew in from Montreal on one of his occasional visits to Newfoundland. He telephoned the Premier, and was told abruptly, "Come right over." Cheerfully, he walked into Smallwood's office, hand outstretched in greeting. Smallwood looked away. Puzzled, Valdmanis turned towards Power, standing by the window. Power also looked away. Valdmanis's hand fell to his side.

"I want," said Smallwood in a cold, hard voice, "your resignation and I want it right away." There was a minute of dead silence. A clock ticked. Slowly, Valdmanis sank to a couch, looking, in Power's words, "like a rabbit in a trap." Valdmanis finally spoke, in a voice that seemed to come from miles away, "Yes, my Premier. Certainly. I understand."

Smallwood looked hard at him. "Good," he said, and picked up a piece of paper to signal that the interview was over. Valdmanis rose slowly and walked out.

A master storyteller, Alfred Valdmanis had just delivered his finest performance. He had said nothing at all. Back at the NALCO office he dictated a brief letter of resignation. He was leaving, he wrote, because of the pressure of private work in Montreal. (To soften the shock to the public, Valdmanis remained a NALCO director, at $7,500 a year.) "With all my heart," his letter ended, "I wish to thank you and Newfoundland for these difficult but proud years of co-operation while pursuing your policy of economic development. By the same token, pray forgive me where I have failed."

Mrs. Valdmanis came down to help him pack. At the airport, on February 10, only a handful of Germans and Latvians came to say good-bye to their patron. "I didn't expect you to come," Valdmanis told them. "People have seemed more afraid of me than anything else." No cabinet minister or civil servant was present. Smallwood confined himself to a single enigmatic comment: "Newfoundland will not soon again see so remarkable a man as Alfred Valdmanis."

The economist left without knowing why he had been dismissed. The reason, or pretext, could hardly have been more mundane. Valdmanis had padded his expense accounts. Power unearthed the first lead. Valdmanis for three months had collected double salary, both as NALCO chairman and as Director General of Economic Development. Provoked into a wider search, Smallwood discovered that among other outlays Valdmanis had debited NALCO for the cost of a brand-new green Chevrolet, four extra tires, a private suite at the Mount Royal Hotel. He had also charged purchases from Morgan's and Birks, including a complete set of custom-built furniture and a $500 antique clock.

This was the sum total of Smallwood's knowledge, though Power also passed on to him a fresh batch of gossip about Valdmanis's wartime exploits. Beyond that, the pair were as much in the dark as Smallwood had been when he hired the Latvian.

When a titan is about to fall, small men become brave. Within the German and Latvian community of about a hundred, some had long opposed Valdmanis – particularly those convinced they had received less than their share of the Government's seemingly bottomless treasury. Twice, late in 1952, a Latvian engineer approached Smallwood to ask him puzzling questions about the nature of Valdmanis's non-administrative duties for the government. Each time Smallwood brushed him aside, and the man retreated, assuming that the Premier knew what was afoot and approved of it.

A month after Valdmanis had left the province, this man made a third approach to the Premier. "My Premier," he said, "would it be asking too much if we could get into your car and talk?" Smallwood drove his companion into the countryside. Had Valdmanis, asked the Latvian, ever made campaign contributions to the Liberal Party? No, answered Smallwood. Had any of the new industries contributed? Again Smallwood answered no. Was then the Premier unaware that Valdmanis had collected commissions supposedly for the Liberal Party on the contracts negotiated with German companies? From this point on Smallwood took charge of the conversation. He bombarded his passenger with questions and extracted from him names, places, dates, and amounts.

Back in St. John's, Smallwood called Power and ordered him over. The informer repeated his story. He was thanked and ushered out. It was just after midnight. Smallwood quickly made his decision. He called Superintendent D. A. MacKinnon, Head of the RCMP's "B" Division in St. John's, and asked him over. He told MacKinnon the story and asked him to launch a full investigation. Smallwood also asked for one favour. "Find that money. Nothing in the world will wash me clean if you don't find out what happened to that money. Valdmanis will say that he got it for me and that he gave it to me. That exculpates him, but where does it leave me? What does it do to me?"

Of that decision Smallwood has said: "It was one of the hardest I have ever had to make . . . I was taking my political life in my hands."

Whatever the risk, it had to be taken. Once one immigrant knew the story they all soon would, and if Smallwood took no action he would be ripe for blackmail. The local Conservatives also showed signs of being uncomfortably well informed. On April 4, 1954, one Opposition member asked if Valdmanis was a director of the Douay Export Company of New York, which in turn owned a fish plant in St. Andrew's, New Brunswick. "It can be proved," he said, "that not only the Director but other people in this country invested largely in this plant." Valdmanis himself had shown signs of uncommon affluence. Besides the New Brunswick fish plant, he owned a Latvian newspaper in Toronto and once mailed, from St. John's, a brown paper parcel of $25,000 to his wife in Montreal.

Smallwood also sought personal revenge. Like all salesmen, at least by legend, Smallwood himself was the softest of targets for other salesmen. Compared to Valdmanis, Smallwood was an apprentice, full of potential, but still gauche and rough at the edges. Valdmanis had treated him as a babe in the woods of financial intrigue. To have thus pricked Smallwood's vanity was perhaps the most grievous of his offences.

At 5:10 A.M., on April 24, 1954, the Canadian Press reporter in St. John's was awakened by a telephone call. "Get dressed, I've got a big story for you," said a familiar voice. By the time Stewart MacLeod reached the street, Smallwood was waiting outside in his car. At the Canadian National Telegraph office, MacLeod typed out the story Smallwood had given him as they drove down. He showed a copy to Smallwood who said, "Good. That's just right." Smallwood drove the reporter home. Back at Canada House, he rang Albert Perlin to tell him what had happened.

"The RCMP arrested Dr. Alfred Valdmanis in New Brunswick early today," ran the Canadian Press story and Smallwood's official statement, "on a warrant issued on my request by Magistrate O'Neill of St. John's. He is being brought to St. John's by the RCMP to stand trial on charges preferred against him by me that he extorted very large sums of money from various firms with whom he dealt on behalf of the Government of Newfoundland. It will always be for me a matter of intense regret that one with his great talents should have to face such charges."

The circumstances of Valdmanis's arrest must have reminded him of the worst moments of the war. Two days earlier he had driven from Montreal to the New Brunswick village of Chamcook where his brother, Osvald, was manager of the St. Andrew's fish plant, its main product cat food. Shortly before 3:00 A.M., two RCMP cars drove up to the Valdmanis house. Three officers emerged, banged on the door until Mrs. Osvald Valdmanis flung open on upstairs window, and told her that they had come to deliver a message to Alfred Valdmanis. Inside, the officers went straight upstairs to Valdmanis's room. "I don't know," he said, when Osvald and his wife asked him where he was going, "probably to Newfoundland."

Bad weather grounded the plane in Saint John, and it was not until 3:55 P.M. the following day that he reached St. John's. The airport was jammed as though for a royal visit. Few, though, spotted Valdmanis during his short walk down to an RCMP car drawn up on the tarmac. One hour later he appeared in court, to be charged with a violation of Section 44 of the Criminal Code.

For Smallwood, Valdmanis was already a figure of the past. When Perlin, a day later, chanced on Smallwood at his farm, he was taken on an extensive tour of the buildings and cleared land. Not a word was said of Valdmanis. It was a striking illustration of Smallwood's ability to distinguish between what might have been and what is. He wastes no time worrying over his mistakes or in refighting old battles; once a project fails, he instantly applies his prodigious energy and concentration on the most pressing new problem at hand.

In character, he chose at this juncture to unfurl "a great fisheries development plan" which would involve the expenditure of $100 million over ten years. "I don't care what other benefits Confederation might have brought," he said, "they will all be a hollow mockery without a prosperous fishery. This is a problem which has licked every government which ever had anything to do with it, and it may lick this government. We may not be brainy enough, we may not be courageous enough. Time will tell. But if we go down we will go down fighting for the fishermen of Newfoundland, for their wives and children."

The Conservatives, hardly opposed to the fishermen or to their wives and children, did what they could to down Smallwood. They demanded his resignation, and when that showed no sign of happening, called for a Royal Commission to investigate the new industries. "When there is need of a Royal Commission, I will see that there is a Royal Commission," answered Smallwood. "And when you don't?" asked a Conservative. "I am leader of the Administration until the people fire me out," came the reply.

He set out also to wrest honour from the jaws of humiliation: "I am the man who called in the RCMP . . . I could have buried the whole matter . . . had I done so nothing would have been heard of this whole business, nothing. . . . This was the choice I had to make – to drop the whole matter, to bury it, or to force it out into the light of truth." He even managed to work up a fine rage because the Conservative Leader had credited the source of the charge against Valdmanis to the RCMP rather than to Smallwood. "This," he said, "was so unutterably false, so unutterably indecent, such a scandalously dishonest and unfair statement that words fail me to describe the viciousness of it." He spoke for another half-hour.

The revelations of Valdmanis's trial made it hard for Smallwood to sustain the pose of hero. The amount of the alleged fraud was raised by a second charge to $470,000. It had been amassed with a skill and despatch that defied belief.

The affair had begun during Valdmanis's trip to Germany with Smallwood in 1950. Because he alone understood the engineering technicalities and because he alone spoke German, the actual negotiations had been handled entirely by Valdmanis.* The most complete account of what happened during those discussions was given by Dr. Hubertus Hertz, President of Benno-Schilde, in his evidence to the St. John's court. Valdmanis, he recounted, had knocked down Benno-Schilde's initial price for the gypsum plant from $1.5 million to $1.3 million. This done, the economist had mentioned that there would, of course, be the standard ten per cent commission payable to the party on all government contracts. For the Germans, nothing could be more routine. Equally commonplace was Valdmanis's request that "Mr. Smallwood's name must not come into this, of course." Such delicacy the Germans well understood.

In all, Valdmanis received $200,000 from Benno-Schilde, and from Miag, constructors of the cement plant, he allegedly received $270,000. In

---

* There is an enduring local legend, which it is a shame to bury, that Valdmanis negotiated his ten per cent commissions by talking in German, while Smallwood and his ministers were in the same room, so that whenever the name "Smallwood" was mentioned, the German industrialists bowed politely towards the Premier and he innocently smiled back. In fact, Valdmanis was far too intelligent to take so unnecessary a risk. Some of the Germans also spoke English. Once, however, in Geneva, he negotiated a commission while Smallwood and his companions were elsewhere in the same building.

each instance, there was a cash down payment of $50,000 with the balance paid in instalments to Valdmanis's account with the American Express in New York.

The final instalment from Miag was deposited in New York in October 1951; the final instalment from Benno-Schilde on February 24, 1954. It was this latter payment which blew the case wide open, for by then Valdmanis had been dismissed from his post and was in public disgrace. Only a man who was desperate, or completely contemptuous of Smallwood's ability to wreak retribution, would have taken such a risk. Valdmanis wired Benno-Schilde to say that $40,000 was "urgently" needed by the Premier. Since by now the company had paid off its commission, Hertz was sufficiently puzzled to fly over himself, carrying the money. He handed it over, but also made inquiries among the workers at the new industries. One of the men he talked with went on to ride in Smallwood's car.

Hertz's chronicle confirmed in detail what Smallwood already knew. He had still to learn what had happened to the money, and this was the RCMP's responsibility. Plainclothes police officers shadowed Valdmanis every day until his arrest. An RCMP sergeant who was a trained accountant and an FBI officer who was a lawyer went to the American Express Office in New York and, unknown to the staff, photographed the documents in Valdmanis's file after office hours. The actual account was held in the name of Katrina Mateus, his wife's sister. Date by date, and amount by amount, the two policemen added up the deposits, until all the Benno-Schilde and Miag payments were accounted for. The crucial withdrawals could also be traced. The bulk of the money had been paid out by Valdmanis to two refugees, a Latvian, and a Rumanian, living in New York.

"Thank God," said Smallwood, when told of the discovery. While it was conceivable that Liberal funds might have been deposited in New York, since St. John's was a small and gossipy town, it was inconceivable that the Liberal Party would have handed its money over to two war refugees.

Evidence was one thing, conviction quite another. Apart from genuine doubts about Valdmanis's culpability, the St. John's citizenry, and therefore any jury assembled there, was predominantly Conservative. As defence counsel, Valdmanis hired Gordon Higgins, a surprising choice since Higgins had managed the 1951 Conservative campaign with its smear attack upon the Director General. An able lawyer, Higgins's outstanding asset was to be a Newfoundlander. Whatever their political views, Newfoundlanders felt keenly that the Valdmanis affair was, in mainland eyes, one that "could only happen in Newfoundland." At George Drew's suggestion, the noted Toronto lawyer Joseph Sedgwick flew down to St. John's to help Higgins, but after forty-eight hours concluded "an outsider would do Valdmanis more harm than good."

Higgins's first aim was to secure Valdmanis's release on bail. Over the prosecution's protests, he succeeded in calling to the stand the consulting physician at the penitentiary. The doctor testified that had he not known of Valdmanis's history in wartime prison camps he would have judged him to be "acutely mentally ill." Under such circumstances "a trial would be a farce." Mutely, Valdmanis corroborated the medical evidence. His fingers played a ceaseless, nervous tattoo on the wooden prisoner's box; his eyes were ringed black from lack of sleep. The magistrate set bail at $50,000. A fortnight later it was raised through Higgins's good offices.

Valdmanis remained at liberty only three days before the police moved back to re-arrest him, this time on a new civil charge laid by the government for which bail was set at a prohibitive $270,000. "This is persecution, not prosecution," said Higgins.

Back in jail, Valdmanis gave an interview to the *Toronto Telegram*. "Dr. Valdmanis wept when he told me he felt a great hopelessness about his chances to defend himself," wrote Allan Kent. He spoke of Smallwood as "the one man I thought I could trust – my friend that I thought would help me out."

In the political exchanges, the Government came off worst. Olga Leikus was reported missing, and then turned up in St. John's, having flown down from Montreal for a long interview with her former patron. From Ottawa came reports of a federal income tax investigation into Valdmanis's accounts, forcing Smallwood to deny that he had acted only to forestall a trial at Ottawa that would be beyond his political jurisdiction.

By August, only the preliminary inquiry had been completed, held *in camera* while Smallwood and the German businessmen gave their evidence. At last, on September 15, the trial before the Newfoundland Supreme Court began. Flanked by two RCMP officers in full-dress uniform, Valdmanis entered the courtroom. He looked more like the Director General of old: his walk was stiff and erect, his hair was neatly brushed, his shoes gleamed, and his trousers were smartly pressed.

The clerk read out the first charge, that of a $270,000 fraud against Miag. A defence lawyer shook his head at Valdmanis. "Not guilty," the Latvian replied. The second charge was read, of a $200,000 fraud against Benno-Schilde. Valdmanis answered in a low voice: "My plea is guilty, Your Honour." Like a well-rehearsed script, the proceedings rolled on. In an appeal for clemency, Higgins recounted Valdmanis's service to the province, his state of health, and his ruined career. As character evidence, "for there is nobody I can quote who had more knowledge of him," Higgins recited passages from Smallwood's abundant eulogies: "I say thank God for the day I discovered Dr. Valdmanis . . . a man of honour, of remarkable ability . . . one of the most brilliant, most clean, and honest public servants."

At 11:10 A.M. the next day, Albert Walsh handed down his sentence: "Four years at hard labour in Her Majesty's Penitentiary." Valdmanis swayed and his head slumped forward. He left the courtroom looking neither to the left nor to the right, and was driven off to join fifty-two prisoners in the grey-walled prison.

Valdmanis ended his career in Newfoundland as much a man of mystery as he had begun it. For his abrupt decision to change his plea to guilty there was a ready explanation. The long weeks in jail had dulled his instinct for survival. Several times he tried to call Smallwood and each time the call was refused. Instead, in desperation, Valdmanis wrote a letter to a friend to get Benno-Schilde to say the money had been given as a commission for the Liberal Party. The letter was intercepted before it ever left the province, and the government received it like a prize. By asking his contact to say that the payments were a political commission,

Valdmanis had admitted implicitly that this had *not* been their purpose. Confronted with the letter, Valdmanis abandoned the struggle. In return for a promise of prosecution on only one of the two charges, and on the understanding that he would be allowed to keep a few possessions, including his house in Montreal, Valdmanis agreed to plead guilty.

One major riddle remained. Valdmanis's investments, which showed a book value of $509,759.80, had been taken over by the courts. On March 30, 1957, Leslie Curtis announced that the government had closed accounts on the sale of Valdmanis's assets. The amount recovered was $13,452.39.

What had happened to the balance, some $450,000, was unknown then and remains so today. Pressed to explain, Valdmanis answered, "Blackmail." But he refused to give the reason, or to name the black-mailers. For this explanation, there is the circumstantial evidence of Valdmanis's payments to the two New York Jewish refugees. (In return for the money, he was given by them the St. Andrew's fish plant, a virtual derelict.) Smallwood believes he may have met these men. During a visit to New York in 1951, Valdmanis introduced him to two seedily dressed foreigners, owners of the Douay Fish Export Company who said they wanted to move to Newfoundland. Smallwood never heard from them again. (The two men were contacted by police, but refused to come to St. John's to give evidence.)

For many years afterwards, it was almost taken for granted in Newfoundland that Valdmanis was allowed to keep the money as a payoff for pleading guilty. But there was only $850 in his American Express account at the time of his arrest. Nor was Smallwood forgiving towards his old comrade. When a federal parole officer called to get the Premier's signature for Valdmanis's release on parole, Smallwood refused to sign it. Curtis did so instead.

On New Year's Eve, 1956, Valdmanis walked out of Salmonier Jail carry-ing with him the same suitcase he had brought from Chamcook. It bore the label: "Atlantic Hotel, Hamburg." Fellow inmates were sorry to see him go. He had been, they reported, the best cook the institution had ever known.

If Valdmanis was blackmailed, and the obvious source for it was the war years in Latvia, he took the secret with him to his grave. After leaving Newfoundland, he eked out a living running a small import-export business in Montreal, and later as a "consultant" in Edmonton. In September 1969, he filed bankruptcy papers in an Edmonton court; his assets were $5,630, his earnings in the previous year had been $3,613. All that remained of a once-bright career was pride: he had never gone into hiding, and never changed his name. A year later, in August 1970, he died; the car in which he was driving alone crashed and he was killed instantly. The St. John's papers carried brief stories. Smallwood made no comment. A few days after leaving office, though, he listed, in the *Daily News*, the triumphs and tragedies of his reign. There were four of the latter, and the fourth was "The Valdmanis tragedy." (The others were deaths of close colleagues.) The new industries were less easily disposed of. Fifteen were started, manufacturing everything from ceramics and woollen goods to storage batteries. The last to arrive was A. Adler and Sons of London, which drew a loan of $500,000 in 1956 and the accolade from Smallwood: "It is the genuine thing. It is real English chocolate. You can be the most bigoted, the most prejudiced person alive on earth but if you eat Adler's chocolate you must say it is good." The company went out of business two years later.

To sustain the illusion of success and to avoid the embarrassment of boarded-up plants, each year more money was pumped into the new industries. Such expenses were a severe strain upon the provincial budget, and on an evening in May 1955, Welfare Minister Herbert Pottle who, a moment before he spoke, whispered to Smallwood, "I'm sorry but I have to leave the Government," announced his resignation and explained, "It is not too late to save much of what is left, but there should be a frank investigation by the Government."

Other reasons for such an inquiry kept emerging. On March 27, 1955, Conservative Bill Browne tabled an affidavit from an employee of the Superior Rubber Company which showed that the plant manager, Max Braun-Wogan, was drawing a salary of $600 a month and his wife $400 as secretary. Braun-Wogan shortly returned to Germany. Behind him he left a plant in which some of the machinery dated back to World War I, while one piece was clearly labelled: "MARSHALL AID."

In 1957, Smallwood at last called a halt. He engaged the Arthur D. Little Company of Boston to survey several of the new industries, and subsequently five plants, among them Superior Rubber and Adler's Chocolates, were closed. The other nine, all small, high-cost, low-wage operations, struggled on, and a few, notably the cement mill, finally emerged solvent.

The total cost of the program had been $30 million. Had Smallwood literally taken $10-15 million and burnt it in a bonfire atop Signal Hill, the end result, in terms of Newfoundland's progress, would not have been greatly different.*

Smallwood's first revolution was over. He had spent his province's single asset, the cash surplus, and replaced it with neither economic industries nor mines. His parallel attempt to revive the decaying fishery was as complete a failure. From the mid-fifties to the end of the decade, Newfoundland stagnated: the government had barely enough money for day-to-day expenses, let alone to plan for the future.

If its consequences had not been so serious, the Valdmanis affair could have been enjoyed as Marx Brothers comedy. Ignorant of economics, gullible about human motives, and incapable of accepting advice from anyone but his hero of the moment, Smallwood had more than justified the sceptics who questioned his competence to run a corner-store grocery, let alone a province.

"We go down the road," he told the legislature contritely, "and if it doesn't seem to be going anywhere, we abandon it, and try another." Setback and ridicule had neither demoralized him nor robbed him of his precious capacity for enthusiasm. He now set off to blaze two new trails: a short unhappy one to the sea in an attempt to revolutionize the fishery, and a long high path to Ottawa and to John Whitney Pickersgill.

---

* In 1967, the government finally dropped from its lists of accounts due $10 million worth of loans dating back to the early fifties.

16

Our Man in Ottawa

For all his outward cockiness, the Valdmanis affair left Smallwood
deeply shaken. Though it would be easy enough for him to fool his
public about the failure of the new industries, the investment houses to
which Newfoundland would now have to turn for money could not be
deceived. Nor, despite his awesome ability to believe that what he had
wanted to happen *had* happened, could Smallwood much longer fool
himself.

The financial consequences were one thing, the psychological effects
another. After the debacle, Smallwood trusted only himself. From now
on, he alone made the decisions on all matters of consequence within
Newfoundland. In his escalation to one-man rule, there was one other
major milestone. Besides Valdmanis, Smallwood had brought in one other
outside expert, Clive Planta, as Deputy Minister of Fisheries, and allowed
him in this domain as much authority as the Latvian. Planta's failure was
less spectacular than Valdmanis's, and far from all of his own – or
Smallwood's making – yet its long-term results were as disastrous to
Newfoundland.

It is one of the many paradoxes of Smallwood's character that his passion for his island has never encompassed the sea around it. The barren Grecian grandeur of Newfoundland's coastline holds little charm for him. Instead, he talks with longing of the lush green fields of England, and it was not by happenstance that when he came to build his dream-house he built it in a valley four miles out of sight of the Atlantic. Nor, unlike virtually every other Newfoundland male, is he so much as a sport fisherman. Throughout his life he has caught barely half a dozen salmon.

This lack of affection for things maritime is reflected in what is perhaps the largest puzzle of Smallwood's administration: its lack of attention to the fishery. Although the fishery supports one Newfoundlander in three, right down to the late 1960s it has been the most neglected industry in the province. For twenty years, Smallwood has sought to turn his people away from the sea.

There are more cogent reasons for Smallwood's personal distaste, and these explain much of his revolutionary thrust. Although cod created Newfoundland, cod has also compelled Newfoundlanders to live for centuries at the level of subsistence. To be close to the fishing grounds, the men who prosecuted the inshore fishery lived in tiny, isolated hamlets, beyond the reach of roads, doctors, high schools, and all but the meanest of public services. Moreover, archaic, inefficient, and low-paying as it was, any massive attempt to revamp the fishery, to scrap inshore dories and trap boats for deep-sea trawlers and draggers, would drastically reduce the number of men the fishery employed. Smallwood's revolution aimed, as he put it in one election campaign, "to take the boys out of the boats" and put them in year-round jobs in new industries rather than to improve the boats for the boys.

Early in power Smallwood made one convulsive – and courageous – attempt at fisheries reform. To help him do it, he sought out Planta, a forty-two-year-old economist from British Columbia.

The two met in September 1950 when they sat at either end of a head table at a dinner meeting of the Fisheries Council of Canada which Planta had founded, and of which he was then Secretary General.

Smallwood was impressed with the economist's address and after he had sat down, to be succeeded by a tedious speaker, Smallwood jumped up and scurried along, bent double, behind the head table to Planta's chair. In what he at least supposed was a whisper, Smallwood hissed: "I want you to be my deputy minister. I'll pay you more than whatever you're making." Smallwood's unorthodox tactics succeeded. Planta started work the following January, at a salary of $15,000.

Though he was so impractical that his own financial affairs resulted in personal bankruptcy, Planta was nonetheless an outstanding theoretician. He and Smallwood organized a joint federal-provincial study of the Newfoundland fishery that was chaired by Sir Albert Walsh. Its report, which appeared in 1952, recommended a $100 million development program jointly financed by Newfoundland and Ottawa. Specific proposals called for the centralization of uneconomic outports, and government loans to private companies to build fresh fish plants to complement the historic saltfish industry.

But Ottawa, in those days, had scant concern for a decaying fishery on an island two thousand miles away. Nor was there any love lost between Smallwood and the federal fisheries minister, James Sinclair, a Vancouverite preoccupied with the prosperous, efficient British Columbia industry. At the end of a federal cabinet committee meeting assembled to discuss Newfoundland's development program, Sinclair handed the minutes of the meeting to his Deputy Minister, Stewart Bates. Scribbled on the back of an envelope, they read: "(1) No capital aid; (2) no participation; (3) normal services only."

Smallwood and Planta gamely decided to go ahead on their own. Through the fifties, thirteen million dollars was paid out in loans to private fish plants. None of it was repaid, and though a few firms prospered, principally those on the ice-free South Coast, the failure of most of them was written in the Auditor General's report for 1957: "Fortune Bay Products, $211,595. The company has filed a voluntary assignment in bankruptcy. . . . The plant [was] offered for sale by public advertisement but to date no sale has been registered." One company evaded repaying its loan by forming a U.S. subsidiary into which all its profits were channelled.

Just as disheartening for Smallwood was the collapse of the centralization policy. Without help from Ottawa, the provincial government could afford to pay families initially only $150, and later $600, to cover the costs of moving. This left most families out of pocket and, much more serious, without any cash to resettle in their new communities. By 1960, only 534 families had taken advantage of the scheme. For lack of proper planning, many of them moved out of one dying community into another, to subsist on relief in what turned into some of the worst rural slums in North America. Still, even at its worst, centralization did bring some families into contact with the outside world, and ended for them what Smallwood has called "Newfoundland's curse of isolation."

In March 1954, in a last attempt to salvage the development program, Smallwood asked Ottawa to allow him to establish a provincial marketing board that would process, package, and market Newfoundland fish. Although Planta had patterned the board after the familiar agricultural marketing boards of British Columbia and Ontario, federal permission was required since the cod would be sold in export markets. Before Smallwood could press his case at Ottawa, Newfoundland's new federal cabinet representative, Jack Pickersgill, warned him that if he did so he would resign – a stand Pickersgill took on the grounds that the board was unconstitutional, though as heavy a reason was the certainty of political opposition from the Maritimes. Faced with such a choice, Smallwood dropped the marketing board to the bottom of his list of priorities, and Ottawa quietly vetoed the scheme. Five months later Planta resigned. His personal financial disorder (he left the province owing Smallwood money), as well as the disclosure he had accepted private loans from fish plant owners who had sought government loans, compelled it.

For a decade afterwards the Newfoundland fishery stagnated. The only innovation was the introduction of unemployment insurance for fishermen, an income subsidy that turned hundreds of outports into what Professor Parzival Copes has called "havens for the unemployed." From some twenty per cent in 1949, Newfoundland's share of the Northwest Atlantic fisheries had sunk by 1964 to 10.6%, as Russians, Norwegians, French, Portuguese, and Icelanders scooped up the harvest with large ships and modern gear. During this period, the average cash income of Newfoundland fishermen was $500.

Ottawa's indifference to the plight of Newfoundland fishermen had a profound effect on Smallwood. For the first time he began to question the benefits of Confederation itself. Superficially, these were obvious: by the mid-fifties, one family in four owned a car compared to one in sixteen in 1949; construction had quadrupled and power consumption had doubled.

Yet at the same time the province's benefits from Confederation grew progressively slimmer each year. Contrary to mainland myth, Newfoundland, through the 1950s, ranked second-lowest among provincial recipients of federal welfare, behind only Quebec.[*] Newfoundland won no defence contracts, a national pump-primer, from which Ontario and Quebec principally benefited. Because of a series of nation-wide freight increases, which hit Newfoundland hardest since it imported almost all its consumer and industrial goods, the cost of living increased faster than in any other province. From Ottawa, Smallwood received only advice – distant and uninvolved. There was no ARDA program, and no Area Development Agency to subsidize his new industries; not until 1961 did the Bank of Canada open a branch of its subsidiary – the Industrial Development Bank – in St. John's.

Smallwood could do nothing to change federal policies; he could, however, change personalities. In the early winter of 1953, he set out to find himself a man at Ottawa.

---

[*] Though children eligible for family allowances were numerous, there were proportionately few old people, and still fewer claimants for unemployment insurance until 1957, when this was extended to fishermen. And Newfoundland veterans, having served with British units, drew their basic pensions from Britain, with Canada paying only the difference needed to bring these up to Canadian standards.

Newfoundland's ostensible ambassador to the cabinet, and its emissary at the doors of the federal treasury, was Gordon Bradley, the Secretary of State. Bradley, though, interpreted his role differently. "I am not here," he told Smallwood, "to gouge money for Newfoundland. I'm here to represent Canada." To which Smallwood replied bluntly: "Don't kid me Gordon. You're here to hook what you can get for us."

Even as a pan-Canadian representative, Bradley was less than adequate. To the distress of his colleagues, he fell asleep at cabinet meetings. To their greater distress, since it blurred the image of businesslike Liberal efficiency, he fell asleep in the Commons. His seatmate, Lester Pearson, was once moved to complain of the difficulty of delivering a truly stirring speech while the man beside him slept soundly. In other surroundings, Bradley might have risen to the occasion; in Ottawa he was out of place, and he knew it. He had come to federal politics too old, at sixty-one, to learn his way through its political and bureaucratic maze.

Rarely warm even during the Confederation campaign, relations between Bradley and Smallwood froze into icy formality once he moved to Ottawa. Matters reached the point where Smallwood, when he visited Ottawa, would call on Howe, Winters, Sinclair, and Pickersgill as a matter of course, but often did not bother to see Bradley at all. The final, inevitable break came late in 1952 when Smallwood dropped by to watch the Commons from the public galleries. Below him, the Secretary of State was asleep. "I knew he fell asleep in the House," Smallwood later stormed to a federal minister. "My God, I never thought he'd do it while I was there."

As the elector of all the island's Liberal M.P.'s, and the selector of all its senators, it required only modest presumption for Smallwood to set about choosing its next federal cabinet minister. He approached the task with great thoroughness, and by the end of the year had considered, and rejected, every possible nominee within Newfoundland. He then turned to Ottawa for advice, and one afternoon late in January 1953 telephoned Pickersgill to announce that he was flying up to the capital that weekend.

When he got on the plane, Smallwood intended only to pick the brain of his closest Ottawa confidant. He met Pickersgill in his office on Saturday morning, January 31. The two adjourned to the Rideau Club for a dialectical lunch and, back at the office, the discussion continued for the rest of the afternoon.

Neither, in retrospect, can remember who first came up with the final solution. In the beginning, they discussed only Newfoundland candidates, and discarded these one by one. Halfway through lunch, Pickersgill speculated aloud whether a mainlander accustomed to Ottawa ways might not be able to serve the province well, much as C. D. Howe and Lester Pearson had each discovered interests in common with Northern Ontario. A few minutes later Smallwood seized the opening: "You know, if you hadn't taken on your new job, you would be just the man." Pickersgill had been appointed Clerk of the Privy Council seven months previously.

Through the rest of the meal, and all day, the conversation sped towards its seemingly predestined conclusion. The day's end left Smallwood in a state of willing suspension of disbelief. He was astounded at his good luck, and exhilarated at his triumph in pulling off what he already realized was one of the greatest single coups of his political career. For Pickersgill, in the early 1950s, was, as the newspapers liked to put it, "Canada's least known, most important man." He had made the Clerkship of the Privy Council into a civil service command post, and a supply depot for the Liberal Party. To his office, five doors down the hall from the Prime Minister's, flocked cabinet ministers, diplomats, and deputy ministers. No better cabinet representative for Newfoundland could be imagined.

In persuading so majestic a figure to migrate to a fog-bound island, Smallwood had played his cards brilliantly. He needed Pickersgill far more than Pickersgill needed him, and yet he could offer the one thing Pickersgill lacked – a constituency where he could hope to be elected. He made his offer at precisely the right time: Pickersgill was beleaguered by opposition criticism for using a civil service position to carry on unabashedly partisan activities on behalf of the Liberals, yet because he was a civil servant he could make no reply. Pickersgill was also deeply concerned about the ability of the aging St. Laurent, to whom he was devoted, to withstand the stresses of the coming campaign without him at his side. Above all, Pickersgill had been a backroom boy long enough; at forty-eight he wanted to execute as well as to advise.

Smallwood had quickly resolved all Pickersgill's doubts about the move. When Pickersgill wondered whether Newfoundland would accept an outsider, particularly since this would constitute a public admission that no native sons were fit for the job, Smallwood replied: "No worry at all. After I'm finished with you, you won't recognize yourself." Pickersgill then explained that since he intended to campaign with St. Laurent, he would have little time to visit the riding before the election. "That's no trouble," said Smallwood, and added as an afterthought: "But you will come down for a few days, won't you?" To this condition Pickersgill agreed.

As wise in the ways of Smallwood as he was in the ways of Ottawa, Pickersgill got to the office early on Monday morning, determined to break the news to St. Laurent, before the Prime Minister read about it in the papers and exploded into one of his legendary Irish rages. He scanned the *Globe* and *Gazette* and, reassured that Smallwood had so far managed to keep silent, went into the Prime Minister's office. He told St. Laurent of the scheme, and waited for the verdict. "Let's do it," said St. Laurent. "I can't wait to see George Drew's face when he hears the news."

The final arrangements were quickly made. Smallwood persuaded Bradley to accept an appointment to the Senate, and the two then tackled the task of explaining the switch to Newfoundlanders. Late in May, they flew to London to represent their province at the Coronation where, along with the Prime Ministerial party, they were booked at the Dorchester Hotel. A night or two after the Coronation, Smallwood and Bradley dropped round to Pickersgill's room and spent the evening in a fury of activity, composing Bradley's formal letter of resignation and Pickersgill's acceptance of the nomination, which would serve as opening salvos in the coming campaign. These drafted, debate switched to the merits and demerits of Coaker. Smallwood was pro, and Bradley con, and they argued on until 3:00 A.M., when an exhausted Pickersgill finally convinced them it was time to retire.

Smallwood quickly fulfilled his side of the bargain. He turned Pickersgill's first campaign into a baroque triumph. The electors of Bonavista-Twillingate — Bradley's old riding — first spotted their new member as a tweed-coated figure waving uncertainly to them from the deck of the *Glencoe*, an aged CNR coastal steamer. Beside him stood their Premier. At the first stop, Smallwood introduced the stranger as "one of the most important men in Ottawa who played a part in getting us Family Allowances." A few communities later this description had been elevated to, and thereafter remained, "the next Prime Minister and the Father of Family Allowances." Smallwood also set out to teach the voters how to pronounce their new candidate's name, of which, until then, the commonest pronunciation was "Skipperskill." At one stop, he called children on to the stage and got them to chant out "P–I–C–K–E–R–S–G–I–L–L: PICKERSGILL." In the larger harbours, the *Glencoe* tied up to the jetty; in smaller ones she moored in mid-stream while Pickersgill bellowed at his constituents through a loud-hailer. At Joe Batt's Arm, an armada of boats bearing lanterns put out to escort the two to shore, and circled the ship while they made their way down a rope ladder. At Twillingate, the pair were met on the dock by a Salvation Army band playing "Hold the Fort for I Am Coming," and at Fogo by a three-round salvo from a 240-year-old cannon.

The tour ended at Hare Bay, and from there Pickersgill was rushed off to catch a flight to Windsor, Ontario, for the start of the national campaign. To get to Gander, the Premier, the new minister, and a reporter and photographer from the *Toronto Star* leaped aboard a diesel-powered section trolley and sped westward along the railway track. They made it with twenty minutes to spare after an epic journey through the gathering dusk, passing curious moose and bears. As the trolley rounded one curve, the photographer's suitcase hurtled off into the bush and the four spent precious minutes groping in the underbrush for pyjamas and shirts and shaving gear. In the election of August 10, the Liberals won – and so did Pickersgill. He received eighty-seven per cent of the votes cast in the riding.

Never again did Pickersgill need Smallwood's help to win Bonavista-Twillingate. Indeed, Smallwood never again entered the riding during a federal election campaign. For Pickersgill's contributions to his electors went far beyond his own political need. He visited the constituency regularly, and inaugurated a style of political fence-mending unknown in the island. For a summer, he toured the coasts aboard his 125-ton schooner, the *Millie Ford*, until she fetched up on the rocks. After that, he spent the summers in his cottage at Traytown. More than just a convenient political foothold, Newfoundland became a second home for the Pickersgill family – his son Alan enrolled at Memorial University, his daughter Jane, a doctor, went into medical practice at Gander. As Smallwood once said: "I'd hate to run in Bonavista against Jack."

The Manitoba farm boy turned archetypal Ottawa man had become a Newfoundlander, an eccentric progression which was nonetheless an apt reflection of Pickersgill's own personality. Among contemporary Canadian politicians there are few more enigmatic figures. No one has been at the centre of power for longer, from 1937, when he joined Mackenzie King as a secretary, until 1967, when he retired to accept a $40,000-a-year post he had created for himself, as President of the Canadian Transport Commission. During those thirty years, he was successively right-hand man to King and St. Laurent, a senior cabinet minister from 1953 to 1957, and again from 1963 to 1967.

Yet Pickersgill's accomplishments, other than the exercise of power itself, can be counted on the fingers of one hand. He played a part in the establishment of Family Allowances and in Newfoundland's union with Canada; as House Leader in 1963-64, he sustained the Pearson Government through a difficult period; he revised and piloted through the Commons the epochal Transportation Act of 1967.

No one understood the means of power better than Pickersgill. He once explained his success as confidant to King: "I first tried to learn the bent of his mind, and then acted accordingly." Yet the long years he spent studying the minds of other men cost Pickersgill his own creativity. Though he was a conservative, opposed as much to big government as to big labour, he never articulated that philosophy; though a convinced nationalist, he never effected his ideals. Even his personal dream of closer ties between Canada and the West Indies came to nothing.

But the public mask of a political Machiavelli hid an emotional and sentimental man with, as former Secretary of State Judy LaMarsh aptly if inelegantly put it, "a heart of mush." In Newfoundland, Pickersgill the romantic found himself a cause, for if Newfoundland is not a haven for romantics, it is nothing but fog and cod and bog and rock. One Burns night in St. John's, an awestruck audience watched Pickersgill, tears in his eyes, turn to them and say, "You will never know how much I owe you." Pickersgill's greatest political accomplishment, judged in the only terms that matter – its impact upon human welfare – is his service to Newfoundland.

From the start, Pickersgill justified Smallwood's faith in him. Spending on federal works, from wharves to post offices, escalated immediately. His most considerable achievement in the early years was to lobby for the extension of unemployment insurance to fishermen which, in its first full year of operation, 1958-59, poured $3.5 million worth of new transfer payments into the province.

Until 1957, Smallwood was cast as supplicant for favours, and Pickersgill as senior partner. During the Diefenbaker Years, their roles were reversed, and remained so. Their true intimacy dates from this period, when only through Smallwood could Pickersgill remain in public life, and when Smallwood relied heavily on Pickersgill's counsel in his contest with Diefenbaker. By then, Pickersgill had hostaged his fortunes to Smallwood's. Had the Federal Liberals censured the Premier for his intervention in the 1959 loggers' strike, Pickersgill intended to lead the Newfoundland members out of the Liberal Party.

From 1963 onwards, with the Liberals back in power, Pickersgill really hit his stride. He made Newfoundland the most favoured province in the country. He won for the island a federal commitment to pay ninety per cent of the cost of completing the Trans-Canada Highway, a new fisheries aid scheme, some $30 million worth of new ferries and docks, a $7 million twenty-mile paved "access" road, which made it the longest ferry ramp in the world, and the $150 million Atlantic Development Fund. He put his priceless knowledge of Ottawa to work for his adopted province and searched tirelessly for loopholes which could be turned to Newfoundland's benefit. He trained Newfoundland political starlets in his office, and spotted promising recruits for the provincial civil service. A federal cabinet colleague remembers, "What made me so mad was that on everything else he was an arch-conservative, but whenever it came to Newfoundland and spending federal money, he tugged at our heart-strings. And it always worked!"

Although it would be difficult to think of two Canadian politicians who, in personality, differ more than Smallwood the emotional populist and Pickersgill the rational strategist, there have been none who worked more effectively as partners. Through his contact with Pickersgill, Smallwood's political horizons broadened immeasurably and he acquired a deeper and more sophisticated understanding of the sources and nature of political power. To some degree he learned also the art of restraint. Time and again he used Pickersgill as a court of sober second thought. As one of half a handful of people whose advice Smallwood was prepared to listen to, Pickersgill reckons he saved him from a hundred impulsive decisions or public pronouncements. On such occasions, Pickersgill would hear Smallwood out, and then comment coolly: "I'm glad you tried that out on the dog first, Joe, because if I were you, I wouldn't try it out on anybody else."

In return, Smallwood introduced Pickersgill to the human side of politics. With less success, he lectured the minister on the art of public speaking and continuously, but fruitlessly, enjoined him to "keep your hands in your pockets. You look ridiculous waving them around."

Their alliance was firmly secured by mutual admiration. Of Smallwood, Pickersgill has said, "I have known many politicians and statesmen, but only one political genius – Smallwood." Smallwood has said of Pickersgill, "He is the most brilliant and the most completely honest man I know in Canadian politics."

Inevitably, their relationship had its strained moments, all the more so since each was too proud to admit error. Although they usually talked on the telephone at least every other day, after a tiff as much as a week would pass without a call, while each man grew more and more irritable and his staff more and more unhappy. At last, whichever of the two was faced with the more pressing problem would pick up the receiver and, by unspoken consent, the original source of disagreement was carefully eliminated from the ensuing conversation. Their most frequent cause of argument was the mining promoter John Doyle, whom Pickersgill disliked and distrusted. Doyle was eventually dropped as a topic of discussion. In the early years of their partnership they disagreed over the fish marketing board and the regulations for the first federal national park in the province. More recently, their most spectacular difference was over the new flag in 1964. Had Smallwood persisted with his plan to introduce in the provincial legislature a motion of censure against the Pearson Government, Pickersgill would have resigned.

"Nobody can take his place," said Smallwood at the farewell dinner he staged for Pickersgill in September 1967. To honour him, the Newfoundland Government established a $4,000 scholarship for a graduate of Memorial University to study history or political science at any university. Mrs. Pickersgill was presented with a brooch bearing the Newfoundland coat of arms. To Pickersgill, Smallwood gave a silver bowl. Fixed to its base was a "Cabot" silver dollar issued in April 1949 to commemorate Confederation. "There's only me left," said Smallwood.

17

Premier Against Prime Minister

On March 31, 1959, Newfoundland was due to celebrate the tenth anniversary of her union with Canada. To mark the occasion, five hundred guests had been invited to a formal banquet at St. Patrick's School auditorium in St. John's, to hear speeches by Smallwood and Lieutenant Governor Campbell MacPherson. On March 29, however, the banquet's organizers announced a dramatic change in plan: Instead of celebrating Confederation, "because we have nothing to celebrate," the evening would honour Smallwood, "the true champion of our province." And when he spoke, the architect of Confederation instead of praising Canada damned its Prime Minister, John Diefenbaker.

The immediate reasons for Smallwood's – and all of Newfoundland's – anger were obvious enough. Six days earlier Diefenbaker had announced a settlement of Term 29, the financial escape clause of the Terms of Union, that gave Newfoundland far less than anyone had expected; a fortnight before that the Prime Minister had ignored a request by the Newfoundland Government to send RCMP reinforcements to police a long and bitter loggers' strike.

These incidents were no more than insults added to injury. Even if they had not taken place, and the banquet gone ahead as scheduled, the speeches would have lacked conviction. Newfoundland's tenth birthday as a province coincided with her worst misfortunes since the Depression. The island was in the depths of an economic recession; as seriously, Newfoundlanders had come to regard Confederation itself, if not as a snare and a delusion, as at best a questionable advantage. Because of this disappointment, tension, yearning to find release in a scapegoat, Smallwood faced the most serious political crisis of his term. He survived; by channelling those passions towards substitute scapegoats: Diefenbaker and the loggers.

As most Newfoundlanders then saw it, Confederation had brought them all the disquiet of change and few of its benefits. On the face of it, astonishingly little had happened to the island in ten years. The outports were almost as isolated as ever. In St. John's, society still revolved around Government House, and the grubby red brick establishments of the merchant princes still lined Water Street like so many faded dowagers. Life seemed as tranquil and as introverted as it had always been. Barricaded behind the denomination system, the churches tended and dominated their flocks; labour knew its place and trade unions were impotent.

In fact, the old order was in crisis. Because they had learned from television how the rest of Canada lived, the younger generation was no longer willing to mind its elders and submit cheerfully to hardship and privation. Even in the outports things were different. Each time a new dirt road ended a harbour's isolation, every man in that harbour wanted a car. As Smallwood lectured the legislature: "There is a sociological law – that much wants more."

The trouble was that, far from getting more each year from Confederation, Newfoundlanders were getting less. Smallwood himself was one of the first to realize this. "We are not resisting being Canadians," he told the Royal Commission on Coastal Trade back in July 1955, "but our right to prosper must not be abridged by our being Canadians. . . . I had something to do with persuading a stiff-necked people to enter Confederation. If anything goes wrong, I would be expected to make a great effort to reverse it, including disaffiliation with Canada."

Smallwood's rhetoric was excessive and his threat empty. Yet from his own limited but bitter experience he had diagnosed, ahead of conventional judgment, the fundamental weakness of Confederation itself. Although the St. Laurent-Howe policy of economic *laissez-faire* meant that each year the total wealth of the nation expanded, it was at the same time increasingly unevenly divided between have and have-not provinces and people.

As the least equal among the provinces, Newfoundland drew the least benefits. Between 1950 and 1957, direct federal grants to the island increased from $21.1 million to $23.6 million. This was an actual decline in dollar value, and an even steeper decline when the figures were related to population growth. Steadily, Newfoundland slipped further behind the rest of the country. Between 1949 and 1959, the gap in average per capita incomes between island and mainland widened, from $460 to $680.

From late 1957 onwards, as the post-Korean War boom finally petered out, Newfoundland's fortunes plummeted still further. With a speed that left Smallwood shaken, almost all the pitiful advances of a decade were virtually wiped out. By 1959, unemployment had soared to a staggering 19.2%; during the winter months, for the first time since the thirties, close to half the labour force lived on welfare. In another grim reminder of Depression days, "No Help Wanted" signs sprung up outside construction projects to keep away the crowds of job seekers. The final blow came on March 6, 1959, when Smallwood rose in the legislature to announce: "This is the saddest thing I have had to say since I have been in this House. The Crown-Zellerbach deal is off." He had now negotiated with six companies to try to secure a third pulp-and-paper mill; Crown-Zellerbach was the closest he had come to success.

Once again the brute art of endurance was demanded of Newfoundlanders. Ever since the twenties, employment in the inshore fishery had been dropping. Now, driven from the towns where they could no longer subsist, men flocked back to the bays. Between 1958 and 1963, the number of fishermen increased from 15,000 to 23,000. But they returned to an outport society that had changed beyond recall. Instead of the old proud self-reliance on home-grown vegetables, home-stitched clothes, and homemade fishing gear, there was only the disguised dole of unemployment insurance.

For ten years Smallwood had worked fourteen hours a day, seven days a week, to drag Newfoundland out of its historic cycle of subsistence or bust. And he had failed. Never had he been more frustrated. In the legislature, on May 9, 1957, he did his best to communicate his sense of urgency to his people:

> Newfoundland statesmanship is confronted by the greatest task that ever faced it. The task is to inspire our Newfoundland people with faith in Newfoundland, to persuade Newfoundland people that Newfoundland has a great future, not only as a place in which, if you are middle-aged, you can live yourself with some comfort and some little feeling of security, but a place in which you can feel that your children and grandchildren can live.
>
> Our fight is a fight against time. It is a fight that is uphill. It is a fight that may be doomed to failure, and I am not going to guarantee success. In the end we may have to close up shop and go off to live, the thousands of us who can't afford to go any further than Nova Scotia, and the thousands who can afford a little more and go to Ontario, and those of us who are really well fixed can go to Jamaica. But we may have to close up shop because the fight is unequal, uneven, too much for us, the centrifugal pull of Upper Canada with her magnificent universities, her magnificent schools, her magnificent super-highways, her movies and theatres and all the metropolitan life. The force and effect of that kind of life may be irresistible in the end, and our population may not always grow as it is now growing. So we are not in too big a hurry. We are not going too fast. We are not going fast enough. We are not seized by too much sense of urgency. We are not seized by enough of it.

A month after he made that speech, Smallwood thought he had found, if not a partner, at least an ally with a sense of urgency equal to his own: "The best thing that can happen to us," he told a cabinet colleague on the eve of the 1957 election, "is for this fellow Diefenbaker to be elected." Diefenbaker's National Development Policy, "One Canada, with equality of opportunity for every citizen and equality of opportunity for every province from the Atlantic to the Pacific," could have been drafted for Smallwood. Smallwood hoped for a heavy loss of seats which would frighten the St. Laurent Government into heeding the needs of underdeveloped provinces. To show how he felt, Smallwood sat out the 1957 campaign, except for a single speech delivered in Liverpool, Nova Scotia, on behalf of his friend Robert Winters. He even arranged for the Conservatives to win one of the St. John's seats, not to help Diefenbaker, however, but to rid himself of Bill Browne, his most effective Conservative opponent on the provincial scene.*

This pragmatic cordiality extended past Diefenbaker's victory until the end of 1957. At Diefenbaker's request, Smallwood delivered a speech of welcome to the new Prime Minister on behalf of the premiers at the November federal-provincial conference. He allowed a Newfoundland government doctor to act as *locum tenens* so that an Ontario Conservative M.P., who was a doctor, could attend the parliamentary sessions.

Nevertheless, a clash between the two was unavoidable. For one thing, Diefenbaker had won one more seat in Newfoundland than Smallwood had bargained for. Belatedly, he realized that the man from Prince Albert constituted the first threat to his own political domain. For another, although they were a world apart in background and in personality, Diefenbaker and Smallwood were too much alike to rest easy in one another's company. Both were proud and quick to interpret opposition as personal insult. They even used many of the same political techniques. Diefenbaker would often prove a point by quoting passages from his copious mail; Smallwood similarly resorted to unidentified sources and justified his intervention in the loggers' strike by quoting a distraught woman who had told him: "My home is torn up. My son Bill and my

---

* Smallwood's attitude during this election was governed even more by a tragic helicopter crash which took the life of his daughter-in-law and left his son Ramsay with severe, third-degree burns. Smallwood spent three weeks by his son's bedside while he was in hospital in Toronto.

husband Bill are fighting each other." Both men were adept at first sum-
marizing, in suitably emasculated form, their opponents' position on a
given subject, and then demolishing it.

Acutely aware that Diefenbaker, as Prime Minister, would be a far
more formidable opponent the second time round, Smallwood prepared
for the 1958 federal election as he had for no other. Long before the date
was set, he replaced two veteran M.P.'s with personable newcomers; he
organized 2,100 rallies and meetings, and ordered every provincial minister and member into the fray. At the start of the campaign itself, he
staged a gala rally in St. John's to launch a Liberal canvass of every home
in the city, and then boarded a train to spend three weeks crisscrossing
back and forth through the most vulnerable ridings. He collected every
moral debt a decade of family allowances had piled up. "The Tories are
still against Confederation," he told an audience packed into the Roxy
Theatre in Deer Lake. "They hate me, and they will hate my guts until
the day I die."

All the Tories wanted to do was to beat him. At last they had a leader
to whom Newfoundlanders responded. In St. John's, Diefenbaker drew
adoring crowds. In Grand Falls, he brought shy and undemonstrative mill
workers and loggers roaring to their feet with his message, "We'll build a
nation of fifty million people within the lifetime of many of you here."
And the Conservatives clasped at last the keys to the federal treasury.
Exuberantly, they promised a new ferry to Bell Island, a $12 million
harbour redevelopment for St. John's, and a major, low-cost housing
scheme. Since Smallwood responded in kind, for Newfoundlanders the
1958 election was the happiest ever. He promised a five-year education
program which included 1,200 high-school bursaries, a $56 million
highway program, and a vast fishery development scheme for the south-
west coast.

On March 31, Smallwood won. Five of Newfoundland's seven federal
seats remained Liberal. Yet it was the tightest election Newfoundland had
known as a province, and until the upset of 1968 the only real electoral
contest in the nineteen years since Confederation. Though Diefenbaker
added no seats to the two he had won the year before, he won 45.5 per cent

of the vote. By his extravagant standards of that year, this was meagre; in a one-party state it was a near miracle. Moreover, Diefenbaker had provided the hapless local Conservatives with a base on which to build.

A third, and this time decisive, round between Premier and Prime Minister was now inevitable. Smallwood sketched Diefenbaker's motive in memorable language:

> Every province of Canada, with one exception, went clean overboard for Mr. Diefenbaker. Nine provinces, three of them unanimous, and one dirty little cur had the brazen gall, the ingratitude, to turn a blind eye to the Vision. I have often felt that our Great Prime Minister has had many a sleepless night wondering what in the devil got into that crowd down there. We are the constant reminder to him that he is not infallible. I believe it has become an obsession to him, and we are now paying for it.

As for Smallwood, quite apart from political exigencies, he was spoiling for a fight for the sheer joy of it. By 1959, he had run out of worthwhile political opponents in Newfoundland, a frustrating circumstance for a man who could say after a gruelling campaign: "That's over, now I suppose I have to get back to work." In time-honoured political tradition, Smallwood also needed a political enemy abroad to distract attention from his difficulties at home. Had Diefenbaker not existed, Smallwood would very likely have been forced to invent him. Had he also been forced to invent an issue on which to fight Diefenbaker, it could scarcely have been more favourable than the one which presented itself: Term 29.

Although it sparked what was, until Quebec's Quiet Revolution, the most acrimonious federal-provincial dispute of the postwar era, Term 29 as written was something less than explosive. Smallwood liked to call it "the unfinished clause of the Terms of Union"; in reality, Term 29 was hardly more than a footnote. The actual clause over which so much passion was to be spent read:

Provision for Financial Review: In view of the difficulty of predicting
with sufficient accuracy the financial consequences to Newfoundland
of becoming a province of Canada, the Government of Canada will
appoint a Royal Commission within eight years of the date of Union,
to review the financial position of the Province of Newfoundland,
and to recommend the form and scale of additional financial assistance, if any, that may be required by the Government of the Province
of Newfoundland to enable it to continue the public services at the
levels and standards reached subsequent to the date of Union, without
resorting to taxation more burdensome, having regard to capacity to
pay, than that obtaining generally in the region comprising the
Maritime Provinces of Nova Scotia, New Brunswick, and Prince
Edward Island.

This prolix clause, which required Ottawa to set up a Royal Commission
but did not commit it to accept any of the ensuing recommendations, could
be interpreted to mean almost anything – or nothing. Even its spirit was
obscure. Newfoundland was plainly intended to receive supplementary aid,
yet the formula proposed to decide the amount of such aid was geared
to *maintain* and not to *improve* such public services as Newfoundland
had achieved eight years after union. Since Newfoundland had joined
Confederation with public services incomparably lower than those of
any other province, and could hardly have been expected to improve
them at any faster rate than mainland provinces, the formula condemned
Newfoundlanders to permanent second-class citizenship.

Ambiguous and legalistic as it was, Term 29 was all that Newfoundland had, and Smallwood was determined to make the most of it.
He had prepared for it with quite uncharacteristic thoroughness. As early
as 1953 he had appointed a five-man provincial royal commission, backed
by such advisers as labour lawyer Carl Goldenberg and McGill economist
Donald Armstrong to prepare the province's case on Term 29.

After more than four hundred meetings, the commission produced its
thousand-page report in April 1957. In massive detail, it recounted "tragic
deficiencies in Newfoundland's public services" compared to "the
minimum tolerable levels of services that ought to prevail in a Canadian

province." Ottawa should bridge the gap, it recommended, by an annual grant of $15 million.

Later that year, the necessary federal royal commission was established. Smallwood advised St. Laurent on the choice of Commissioners: John Babbitt McNair, Chief Justice of the New Brunswick Supreme Court, was Chairman, the other members were Albert Walsh and John Deutsch, then an economist at Queen's University, and later Chairman of the Economic Council of Canada.

Smallwood left no doubt as to the importance of their work: "I am very confident," he told the legislature, "we will soon be in a position to spend very large sums of money that we are not now in a position to spend." More lyrically, he reported in the 1957 budget speech: "Newfoundland faces the future with unwavering hope and confidence. She is part of the great Canadian nation and she will go up with that nation. Great Canada wanted Newfoundland, and Great Canada will treat her now with justice and generosity."

By the time the McNair Commission turned in its report, on July 25, 1958, the decision on what to do with it rested with a new government. The report itself criticized Smallwood for expending his funds on the new industries "at the expense of greater progress in the provision of basic facilities and services." As for these services, there had been "a fairly steady improvement," although, on a *per capita* basis, spending on education had actually declined. Newfoundland's road system was "abysmal," the proportion of houses with water and plumbing was "one-third that of the Canadian average," and the lack of municipal government "comparable with the Maritimes in 1867." To remedy all this, in "one of the most economically exposed and least self-sufficient areas in the world," the McNair Commission recommended a payment of $8 million a year until 1962 (in lieu of the existing so called "transitional grants") and "thereafter" $8 million.

Smallwood's initial comment was mild, at least for him. "Very disappointing," he said. He quickly hit his stride. "It's trash, a lot of it," he told the legislature on September 5. "The Commission was a dead loss. The Commissioners were a dead loss. God help me, I had something to do with choosing them." McNair was deeply hurt. "We tried to do the best we could for Newfoundland," he told a friend. They had in fact done so, and the fault lay not with the Commissioners but with the opaque wording of Term 29 itself.

In the hope, and need, of quick action, Smallwood secured an all-party resolution from the legislature, which asked Ottawa to make an interim payment pending a permanent settlement of Term 29. Diefenbaker declined to take action, and for the rest of the 1958–59 fiscal year, the Newfoundland Government was so severely strapped for funds that some accounts ran nine months and more behind payment.

This early, Term 29 had begun to take shape as the issue on which Smallwood and Diefenbaker would clash. In fact – and this was the ulti-mate irony of the Term 29 affair – it had already been overtaken by events. Although recession and unemployment obscured their effect at the time, the range of programs Diefenbaker inaugurated to fulfil his vision of a nation equal from sea to sea marked a decisive turning point in Confederation. Less evident than his achievements on the prairies and the Maritimes, Diefenbaker also laid the foundation of the new Newfoundland.

Rural electrification in the province dates from Diefenbaker's Atlantic Provinces Power Development Act; because of his Vocational Training Act, ten new vocational schools were built by 1962; highway construction expanded as a result of the Roads to Resources program. Above all, Diefenbaker's Atlantic Provinces Adjustment Grants brought New-foundland an extra $7.5 million a year, almost as large as the sum proposed by the McNair Commission.

Yet to a large extent, and this Smallwood never forgot, Newfoundland was the accidental beneficiary of programs drafted to help the Maritime Provinces, all then ruled by Conservative premiers. The Atlantic Adjustment Grants, which Smallwood praised as "one of the best pieces of legislation brought down by any government," originated as Maritime Provinces Adjustment Grants. (Newfoundland was to be taken care of separately by Term 29.) Smallwood learned of this at the 1957 federal-provincial conference and largely through the intervention of Premier

Robert Stanfield, managed to ensure that the program was broadened to include Newfoundland and the total amount increased from $22.5 million to $30 million.

In January 1959, Smallwood once again put on the mantle of supplicant: he called on Diefenbaker in Ottawa and pleaded with him to increase the Term 29 settlement to the original $15 million proposed by the provincial commission. Diefenbaker's reply was noncommittal. Two months later, at Smallwood's behest, Pickersgill made a personal call on Diefenbaker carrying with him a message from Pearson. If the McNair Commission award of $8 million a year in perpetuity was accepted without change, Pearson would rise in the Commons to praise Diefenbaker for his statesmanship. Again the Prime Minister's answer was inscrutable.

When the announcement was finally made, its timing caught Smallwood by surprise. It came on March 25, just six days before the tenth anniversary of Confederation. Diefenbaker's opening remarks made it clear that the coincidence would not be a happy one.

"Both governments," he said, "have entertained serious reservations concerning the basis of the conclusions reached by the Commission." He agreed to Newfoundland's request for periodic reviews, "since it would be quite inappropriate to endeavour to provide for a fixed amount payable annually over a period of unlimited duration." For that reason, the $8 million a year would be paid only until 1962 when "Newfoundland's position can be considered in the light of the general methods of providing financial assistance to the provinces." The payment of special amounts to Newfoundland up to 1962," Diefenbaker concluded, "will be in final and irrevocable settlement of . . . the contractual obligations of the union consummated in 1949."

Across the floor, Pickersgill leaned forward to listen. At first he was angry, then, as the phrase "final and irrevocable" rolled out, he hid a smile of delight. He leaned forward to whisper to Pearson, who rose to denounce Diefenbaker's declaration as "quite unwarranted." Pickersgill then hurried out of the Chamber to call Smallwood in St. John's. After a quick conference, each man set out to fire the first shots of a counter-barrage.

Mystifyingly, Diefenbaker had staked out all the low ground for himself. The most succinct comment on his performance came from the Toronto *Globe and Mail*, which called his statement a "classic example of how to do the right thing in the wrong way at the wrong time." The explanation for his first blunder – his use of so provocative a phrase as "final and irrevocable" – was simple, if incredible. Diefenbaker had never read the statement before he delivered it in the House. It had been drafted by the Finance Department, and handed to him by Finance Minister Donald Fleming just before he spoke. As the Prime Minister later ruefully told a cabinet minister: "I knew it was wrong the moment I said it." As for his unhappy choice of timing, Diefenbaker was so out of touch with Newfoundland sentiment, and cared so little for it, that neither of the two Newfoundland Conservative M.P.'s, Minister without Portfolio Bill Browne, and Jim McGrath, was consulted about the date, or even forewarned that the announcement would be made. Instead, they heard the news by chance, over a car radio while on their way to a meeting outside St. John's.

"I am only one among twenty-two members of the cabinet and I can't ram my opinions down their throats," said the hapless Browne when he was finally cornered by reporters. McGrath, younger and less equable, flew to Ottawa, demanded an interview with Diefenbaker, and was treated to a half hour of vintage, finger-stabbing Diefenbaker fury. It was directed at Smallwood, who by now had taken off in full, unstoppable flight.

In the spring of 1959, Diefenbaker stood at the height of his dominion over Commons and country. Two months earlier, a Gallup Poll had shown that fifty-seven per cent of Canadians were ready to vote for him at the next election. But even The Chief was powerless in a debate in which he was cast as Scrooge and Smallwood as Tiny Tim. Smallwood inflicted on Diefenbaker his first major setback since taking office. By August, when Smallwood had completed his work, only forty-seven per cent of voters considered themselves Diefenbaker supporters. For good measure, Smallwood also used the Term 29 issue to destroy the

Newfoundland Conservatives so thoroughly that the party took a decade to recover.

On the day of the announcement itself, Pickersgill issued a press statement calling it "an act of bad faith unequalled in the history of Canada." Smallwood was more moderate. He drove hurriedly from his farm to the CJON TV station, and there delivered an eight-minute address: "This is a sad day for Newfoundland, for our hospitals, for our schools, our rural electrification programs, our water and sewerage systems, and the other endless needs of our people. The last thing anyone on earth would guess would be that Mr. Diefenbaker or anyone else would put a time limit on Term 29."

The next day he stepped up the pace with a gesture in the grand style. To "mark the unspeakable betrayal of Newfoundland," he ordered three days of official mourning. All over the city, flags hung at half mast; the doors of government buildings were draped in black crêpe. On March 27, Memorial University students marched through the streets of St. John's bearing placards: "A Modern Judas Has Betrayed Us," "Secede," and "Diefenbaker, Thief and Faker." In the vanguard was the college band, playing "The Dead March from Saul." Dressed in a black coat and Homburg as "suitable for the occasion," Smallwood met them on the steps of the legislature. "The rest of Canada is ready to rise up in rebellion against Mr. Diefenbaker's betrayal of Newfoundland," he bellowed. "The entire responsibility rests with Mr. Diefenbaker." That night the students burned the Prime Minister in effigy.

At the Confederation anniversary dinner three days later, Smallwood was confident enough to mock his distant opponent: "I now make this offer," he told the guests, "if Mr. Diefenbaker will treat Newfoundland fairly and give us a fair deal, I'll resign Tuesday when the House opens." The magnanimity of the offer, and the likelihood of its being accepted, were reduced by his next sally: "I suppose Mr. Diefenbaker is nursing a grudge against me because I kept him out of five seats."

Ottawa, in fact, was already eager for a truce. Smallwood's imaginative histrionics, coupled with sympathetic articles about conditions in Newfoundland after ten years of union, had inspired genuine sympathy for the province. Almost no one understood Term 29; almost everyone believed that little Newfoundland was being hard done by. Letters of protest, particularly from fellow have-nots in the Maritimes and on the prairies, poured into M.P.'s offices. On a CBC "Nation's Business" telecast, Diefenbaker soothingly regretted "any misunderstandings that may have arisen," and promised "consideration" of a compromise settlement. Asked if he would meet with Smallwood, the Prime Minister replied: "I am ready at all times to meet with anyone who has a case to present."

Smallwood had no intention of letting his arch-foe off so easily. He intended to repay injury with insult. And the more he talked about Term 29, the less he needed to say about the loggers' strike, an issue which had already aroused bitter feelings between himself and Ottawa.

Confident that the Canadian public was behind him, Smallwood unleashed his full fury against the federal Conservatives. He launched a suit against Ottawa in the Exchequer Court for "breach of contract" on the issue of RCMP reinforcements, and a week later followed it with another suit to protest Ottawa's "unwarranted, impertinent interference" in attempting to place federal nominees on the St. John's Housing Authority, a body seventy-five per cent financed by Ottawa. When Public Works Minister Howard Green ventured to explain that this contretemps had come about because of Smallwood's failure to answer his mail, the Premier snapped back: "I didn't answer because I didn't want to offend the old fellow." Told of this, Green replied, "The man's impossible." In the meantime, work was halted on a five-hundred-acre, federal-provincial housing project in St. John's.

When Ottawa tried to reply in kind, Smallwood rolled effortlessly with the punches. After he was ordered to vacate Canada House (formerly the residence of Canadian High Commissioners and therefore federal property), Smallwood deliberately procrastinated in the hope, as he later explained, "they would kick me out. Then I would have had to put my luggage and furniture on the sidewalk, got my wife, children, and grandchildren to sit on it and arranged, shall we say, for some photographers to drop by." The Diefenbaker Government managed to avoid the trap, but in retaliation it stopped all repairs and repainting, so that the Premier for a time lived in the shabbiest mansion in St. John's.

So far, Smallwood had fired all his ammunition from long range. In a stroke of inspiration and daring, he now announced he would march on Ottawa. The whole country waited in fascination. For Smallwood, it meant a sortie into the heart of enemy territory, and his first star part on the national stage. Outwardly cocky, Smallwood was conscious of the risk he was taking. On the flight up from St. John's he rushed off the plane at each stop to snatch up the latest newspapers and to pace nervously around the terminal.

The rustic demagogue from the outports arrived at Ottawa's Union Station on April 8. A dense crowd of reporters, many of them primed with hostile questions, surrounded him as soon as he reached the platform. Soon the questions died and pencils raced across notebooks: "Even the Prime Minister can't bully me. He can kill me, but he can't bully me. We are just a poor little province trying to be modest, well-behaved little Canadians – but when you tread on a worm – it will turn." He lashed out at Browne as "the biggest slum landlord in St. John's." (The next day he retreated from the threat of a libel suit and described Browne instead as "a lawyer and for many years he collected rents, and maybe for himself, for some of the worst slums in the city.") Reporters bobbing in his wake, he then set off with Pickersgill to the Chateau Laurier.

That evening he took on four veteran Press Gallery reporters on the half-hour national television program "Press Conference." Between them, the journalists spoke perhaps three minutes. As one later explained to his caustic colleagues, "We were hypnotized." Smallwood was unstoppable. When one reporter was brash enough to correct his pronunciation of heinous as "haynous" to "heenous," Smallwood rapped back smartly by working "haynous" into his next three sentences. Making Diefenbaker's action on Term 29 sound like the worst insult to Newfoundland since Cabot sailed past without stopping, Smallwood stormed on: "Newfoundland's life is at stake. Term 29 must remain in force as long as water runs wet and grass grows green. . . . We put our faith in the people of Canada to see to it that justice is done to Newfoundland." The program pre-empted the first half-hour of the Stanley Cup finals; the CBC received fewer than a dozen complaints.

Not since the Confederation battles had Smallwood had such a good time. To Canadians, he had become a latter-day Pied Piper. As guest speaker at a meeting of the Ottawa Canadian Club the next day, he attracted the largest audience in the chapter's history. He needed barely five minutes to win the businessmen, civil servants, and diplomats over to his side. Confederation, he said, was "God's greatest gift to Newfoundland." But, "I am trying, under some difficulty these days to be a Canadian." Once the Term 29 issue was settled, he went on, flashing a broad grin, "Canada will be able to resume its glorious role of ten years of completely ignoring Newfoundland." When he had finished, bow tie askew and sweat pouring down his face, the audience gave him a standing ovation.

He ended his march of triumph with a full-scale press conference. He had nothing new to say, other than that: "If Mr. Diefenbaker maintains his present stand, then I'm going to fight him till the end – his end, not mine." The conference began at 3:00 P.M., and ended at five-fifteen. It had been the longest and best attended in the history of the Ottawa Press Gallery.

"He could sell Santa Claus a razor," wrote Clark Davey of the *Globe and Mail*, once Smallwood had departed. Charles Lynch of Southam News Services called it: "A display of virtuosity seldom matched in Ottawa." For two days Smallwood had held the nation spellbound, revelling in the publicity and in his role as underdog. As the Minister of Agriculture, Alvin Hamilton, commented astutely: "Joey's out to destroy Diefenbaker's image as the protector of the little guy, and he's damn smart." Insofar as he could, Smallwood had accomplished this.

In his own way and in his own style, Smallwood had done much at Ottawa. He had sold Newfoundland's case to the Canadian public. He had also sold his own. He left Ottawa as an accredited national character, a kind of Harry Truman with style. From then onwards, the nickname "Joey" appeared in headlines without any other identification, a status Smallwood, ironically, shares only with "Dief" among contemporary Canadian politicians.

Smallwood's conspicuous failure at Ottawa was that he brought Newfoundland not one inch nearer a better deal on Term 29. He could do this only by meeting Diefenbaker. This step he was far too adept a politician to take. It might settle the issue and rob him of his platform. On his trip to the capital Smallwood encountered Diefenbaker only by chance, when they passed one another in a corridor of the House of Commons. Each man stared straight ahead and neither broke his stride. "I would be nervous to meet Prime Minister Diefenbaker," Smallwood explained to reporters. "It might be disastrous for Newfoundland."*

Three months later, Finance Minister Fleming brought down in the Commons the necessary enabling legislation on Term 29. Other than a promise of "consideration [for] any special circumstances relating to the financial position of Newfoundland," there were no differences from Diefenbaker's original announcement. The payments would still end in 1962.

Between his own sortie and Fleming's announcement, Smallwood had called an uneasy truce. He had spoken only once, when he told the Rotary Club of Halifax, "We are not asking for the standards of Upper Canada. With luck and generous assistance from Ottawa, we could dare hope that twenty-five years from now Newfoundland would have almost as good services as Nova Scotia today." He had also met Diefenbaker.

The occasion was made for drama. On June 18, Diefenbaker flew down to St. John's to greet Queen Elizabeth at the start of her national tour. Smallwood was also waiting at the airport. Neither glanced in the other's direction, until at last Smallwood could no longer resist the temptation. With an air of supreme unconcern, and amid a barrage of flashbulbs, Smallwood marched up to the Prime Minister, stretched out his hand, and said, with a broad smile, "Hello there, Mr. Diefenbaker. We attribute the fine weather to you." Diefenbaker looked down. "Yes,

---

* Nor was Smallwood, while in Ottawa, able to persuade McGrath to quit the Conservatives, though he promised him a hero's welcome in St. John's and a provincial cabinet post.

it is fine." The two moved apart. It was the anniversary of the Battle of Waterloo.

Once the Term 29 bill passed the Commons, the battle royal resumed. Smallwood called the legislature back into session to tell them: "Mr. Diefenbaker, Mr. Browne, Mr. McGrath, all the members of the Tory Party in the House of Commons, all have punished Newfoundland, have cut Newfoundland's throat, stabbed her in the back."

It was not difficult to guess what Smallwood would do next. In anticipation, two of the four Conservative members in the legislature broke from their colleagues, moved their desks four feet away from them, and formed a new party, the United Newfoundland Party. Smallwood praised them as "patriotic men who put Newfoundland first." He followed this with an eight-clause resolution that condemned Diefenbaker's "violation of the sacred rights protected by Term 29." Unless everyone voted for it, said Smallwood, he had no alternative but to call an election and added, "Anyone with the smell of Diefenbaker on him is good and finished."

Finished or not, the two remaining Conservatives chose to go down fighting. In the debate on Smallwood's resolution, one of them, Rex Renouf, made a brave attempt to raise a flag of pan-Canadianism amid a sea of chauvinism. "A psychological wall, a psychological fence, is being erected around this province. We cannot be anti-Confederate, we cannot, we should not, hate Canadians. We should not hate mainlanders, we should not isolate ourselves from the mainstream that is running through the nation of Canada."

His plea fell on deaf ears. On Monday, July 29, 1959, the Newfoundland legislature met for the last time in the historic Colonial Building. (Next session it would reassemble in the newly built Confederation Building.) Smallwood had arranged for radio and television coverage of the debates, and loudspeakers carried the oratory to a crowd on the lawn outside, where a gaggle of small boys irreverently hurled pebbles against the legislature windows.

"This is a crusade to tell Canada how Newfoundland feels," Smallwood shouted into the bank of microphones on his desk. "It may take a while but we will never cease raising our voices against the injustice." He called for unanimous approval of the resolution. When the two Conservatives remained seated, Smallwood called an election "to ask the people to speak for themselves."

On August 20, election night, thirty-one of the thirty-two Liberal candidates were elected. Two United Newfoundland candidates unopposed by Liberals won, as did three Conservatives. As an issue, Term 29 swamped both the loggers' strike and the economic recession. Certain of victory, Smallwood used the campaign mostly as an exercise in politics. For the first time he experimented with television on a large scale, delivering five-minute speeches each night. In St. John's, where he ran with the successful intent of defeating Malcolm Hollett, the Conservative Leader, he canvassed by car and gave as many as six street-corner speeches a day. To reach those who remained indoors, a squad of Liberal workers telephoned householders and told them: "This is a message from the Premier," and then switched on a five-minute tape recording. Some listeners, who assumed the caller was Smallwood in person, tried to interrupt him with questions, and inspired Hollett to the best crack of the campaign: "That's typical of Smallwood, he never listens."

Even during the campaign the anti-mainland sentiment in Newfoundland had slackened noticeably, and once the election was over it quickly disappeared. In the rest of the country, more important issues arose to push Term 29 into the background.

Smallwood accommodated himself to the changed mood. He had promised, after the election, to make a cross-country tour "to tell the people of Canada our case on Term 29." As preparation for it he published, at a cost to the government of $100,000, a sixty-four-page, full-colour booklet, *Our Case*. The author was J. Wentworth Day, chronicler of royalty in such books as *The Bowes-Lyon Story* and *Lady Houston: The Richest Woman of England*. He described Smallwood as "a man of

immense energy, dynamic personality, and clean-cut ideas. Quick, decisive, with shrewd humorous eyes and the tongue of a statesman. He ranks
high in the Councils of the Commonwealth and wears the laurels of the
wise." Other pages described Newfoundland.

Aware that the affair had now run its course, Smallwood made only
three speeches, in Hamilton, Edmonton, and Toronto where in an address
to the Empire Club he brought an audience of businessmen to its feet
with his description of the International Wood Workers of America as
"the barracuda of the trade union movement . . . a savage shark, extremely
clever and experienced. They did a better job of brainwashing than anything this side of Moscow." On Term 29, he appealed to Canadians: "Here
is a small province, ancient and proud; let us end this bitterness." He kept
up his fire at Diefenbaker, and in the September 1960 issue of *Maclean's*,
scored him as "wrapped up in the seamless garments of a God. What he
needs is a big dose of humility."

Sheer persistence finally won Smallwood his point. Several premiers,
notably Duff Roblin of Manitoba, rallied to his side, and at the October
1961 federal-provincial conference Diefenbaker agreed to extend the $8
million payments beyond 1962 for another five years. "We'll take the
cash," said Smallwood. "We don't think it is being offered to us for the
right reasons, but we'll take the cash." The issue was settled once and for
all in May 1965 when, with the Liberals back in power, a new bill was
passed which committed the federal government to pay the sum in perpetuity. By this time, the $8 million accounted for barely five per cent of
the provincial government's annual revenues.

In one way or another, the vendetta lasted as long as Diefenbaker was
Prime Minister. For two years he and Smallwood squabbled over how
much each government should take on the abandoned U.S. base at Fort
Pepperell, an $85 million prize of real estate and buildings including a
four-hundred-bed hospital. They finally reached agreement when
Diefenbaker in October 1961 flew down to attend the ceremonial
opening of Memorial University's new campus. At the state dinner

Smallwood introduced Diefenbaker as "The Prime Minister of all Canada." Diefenbaker responded in kind by saying, "There shall be no fogbank in the Canadian family." During a reception at Government House, the two withdrew into an anteroom. Fifteen minutes later, they emerged smiling. Newfoundland would get four-fifths of the base and in return drop its two lawsuits before the Exchequer Court. (The suit over the St. John's Housing Authority had only nuisance value, but the breach of contract suit over the RCMP reinforcements might very well have been decided in Newfoundland's favour.)

A year later, there was another unedifying spat. It began when Diefenbaker gave Newfoundland's Lieutenant Governor, Campbell MacPherson, only a month's notice of the expiry of his term. Smallwood promptly took to the airwaves to protest "this callous treatment of Her Majesty's Representative." Ottawa hastily backed down, and allowed MacPherson the standard three months' notice.

In the federal elections of 1962, when he won six of the seven seats, and of 1963, when he won all seven, Smallwood dragged out the tired Term 29 issue yet again. In between elections he phoned Pickersgill almost every day to give advice on how to bring down the minority Diefenbaker government. On May 27, 1963, Smallwood stood in the Public Galleries of the Commons to watch the new Pearson Government begin its first session of Parliament, and inaugurate the Sixty Days of Decision. "This is a great day for Newfoundland," he said, "and for Canada."

The Diefenbaker Years were the unhappiest Newfoundland had known since Confederation. At a time when the prairies, and less dramatically so the Maritimes, re-entered the Canadian mainstream, offshore island and mainland drifted further apart. Though the feeling against outsiders subsided quickly, the loss of contact between St. John's and Ottawa was damaging psychologically as well as physically. The economic recession persisted as late as 1963, when unemployment remained as high as fourteen per cent.

Nevertheless, it is apparent that Newfoundland turned the corner during those years. In a cruel comment on how little difference unemployment made to the annual earnings of thousands of Newfoundlanders, the province in 1960, 1961, and 1962 recorded its greatest growth since Confederation: an exceptional ten per cent a year exclusive of inflation. With a start made on rural electrification, new dirt roads, vocational schools, the move of Memorial University to a capacious new campus, and the redevelopment of St. John's harbour to make it as modern as any on the East Coast, Newfoundland acquired at least the basis for a modern industrial state. As a harbinger of the future, Smallwood built a new, eight-million-dollar Confederation Building to house the legislature and civil service. A squat, buff-brick inverted ziggurat, the building's only claim to fame was its height: twelve stories, at the time the highest east of Quebec City.

Smallwood also turned a corner. He grew from a backwoods phenomenon to a national figure. After his triumphal procession at Ottawa in 1959, which coincided with Pearson's worst moments as Opposition Leader, federal Liberals seriously considered drafting Smallwood to head the party. His answer was as revealing as it was frank: "I am king of my own little island, and that's all I've ever wanted to be." Once called a Judas and accused of selling his country to Canada, Joey Smallwood, in the eyes of mainlanders as well as of his own people, was Newfoundland. Man and land could no longer be distinguished.

18

"We Are Only Loggers"

Once in power, every one-time revolutionary is bound, sooner or later, to be challenged by an individual or a movement as radical as he once was and is no more. For Joey Smallwood this moment of personal truth came early in 1959, when a strike by some twelve thousand loggers against the province's pulp-and-paper mills degenerated into the most bitter labour dispute in Newfoundland's history. Because of the particular way in which the strike developed, and because of the importance of the logging industry to Newfoundland, Smallwood was confronted with black-and-white alternatives: He could stand aside and let the loggers win, which they would have done if left alone, or he could intervene on the side of the management. He intervened and smashed the strike.

No decision Smallwood has made during his term as Premier has affected him more deeply; nor is there any decision he lives with less easily. Whenever the subject is raised, in public or private, Smallwood defends his action adamantly and vehemently; he never broaches the topic himself. Only once has he allowed his doubts to show. Shortly after he had intervened in the strike, he received a letter from one of his old socialist comrades on the *Call*, Richard Rohman, in which Rohman called him a "turncoat" and a "fascist." When he was next in New York, Smallwood called another colleague of those long-ago days, Philip Hochstein, and spent the evening in Hochstein's apartment on Central Park West, telling and retelling the story of the strike. "He seemed," Hochstein recalls, "to want my reassurance that he had done the right thing."

At no time was the loggers' strike just another labour dispute. In terms of social impact, its closest comparison in recent Canadian history is the strike at Asbestos, Quebec, in 1949. The fundamental issues were the same: autocracy versus democracy; social justice versus civil order. There were other similarities: Smallwood was as much a one-man ruler as Duplessis, and ruled a society as conservative as Quebec's had been a decade before.

The loggers formed the bottom layer of Newfoundland's social pyramid. Unlike the fishermen, whose lives were as hard, but whose exploits and tragedies were celebrated in scores of folksongs and "Come all ye's," they owned only a single ballad. Its opening lines were:

There is one class of men in this country
That never is mentioned in song.

The logging towns, inland from the harsh majesty of the coast, were sad and featureless – clearings in the forest astride a railway siding, or straggling along the bank of a river. The loggers were also the island's most docile and biddable workers. Unskilled, unorganized, and far more numerous than the supply of jobs, they constituted a classic source of sweated labour. Summer and winter they worked ten hours a day, in subzero cold, or amid swarms of blackflies, and for this they were paid $1.05 an hour. In the woods they huddled together in tarpaper shacks, furnished only with tiers of wooden bunks and rough blankets. At night they hung their clothes to dry round a single oildrum that served as heater, and in the morning they washed in water from an open barrel, kept outside, and often covered with icy sludge.

When the International Wood Workers of America came to rouse them, the loggers responded with all the power of a genuine protest movement. Though their strike was fought on the specific issues of rates of pay and hours of work, its real issue was human dignity. Their slogan, which echoed along picket lines strung across the lonely roads of central Newfoundland, was moving in its simplicity: "We are only loggers." It was coined by H. Landon Ladd, President of District Two of the IWA, after a retired logger heard him speak, and then told him: "What you say is right, and what you are trying to do is right. But you'll never get it. We are only loggers."

The IWA first entered Newfoundland in 1956, leaping across the country from its bastion in British Columbia, at the request of the president of one of the four quasi-company unions which then represented the loggers. Six months later, the IWA applied to the Provincial Labour Relations Board for certification as bargaining agent in Newfoundland; they supported their claim with the paid-up dues records of eighty-seven per cent of the loggers. Even this early the speed and efficiency with which the IWA had worked made it clear that a new force was being born in the province. Smallwood recognized its nature. "The midnight meetings in the camps with young men," he said later. "The young men came out with their eyes shining. They had a new religion. IWAism." In Smallwood's Newfoundland, there was no room for two secular religions.

Fittingly, in this struggle for the loyalties of rank-and-file Newfoundlanders, Smallwood was challenged by a man whose political skills in some measure equalled his own. Although Ladd, the IWA leader, lacked Smallwood's fluency, the sheer power of his personality dominated audiences. "You don't have to bow no more," he told cheering loggers, and he was astute enough to learn to say "bye" with the best of Newfoundlanders as soon as he crossed the Cabot strait.

Then in his mid-forties, Ladd was built like a truck driver, stocky and bull-necked, with piercing blue eyes, a cleft chin, and a shock of black hair swept up in a rough crewcut. He was tough, brash, and above all he was ambitious. Born in Vancouver, he had risen swiftly through the ranks of organized labour, and if he won in Newfoundland, the glittering prize of the international presidency of the IWA might be his for the taking. "He went to Newfoundland, and realized perhaps only subconsciously," a close labour colleague of Ladd's has said, "that he wanted to be another Joey Smallwood – a man of the people, but in power."

Ladd brought to his task exceptional talents as an organizer. When the companies closed their woods roads to union organizers, he ordered the IWA to hire planes and shower the camps with leaflets, or to crash twenty miles through the bush on snowshoes or skidoos. Sometimes he used a technique learned in British Columbia, and sent union men into the camps without food or bedding to dare the foremen to turn them away while the loggers watched. And in a stroke of genius, Ladd devised a strategy of his own. In each logging town he formed Committees of Six, and to give these continuity, since the loggers were constantly on the move, he decreed that at least half the committee members should be women. This was the first time in Newfoundland's rigidly patriarchal society that women had been given responsibility in public affairs. When their moment came, they responded with a discipline and fervour without which the strike could never have lasted so long.

As crucial to the outcome of the strike, and as particular to Newfoundland as the downtrodden status of the loggers, was the privileged position of the two pulp-and-paper companies: the Anglo-Newfoundland Development Company mill at Grand Falls, and the Bowater's mill at Corner Brook. These were the pillars of the provincial economy, and by far its largest employers. At no time could Newfoundland do without them, least of all during the depression year of 1959.

The mills were also the only industrial achievements of which Newfoundland could boast; to win them the province had already mortgaged its present and future. The AND mill, which began operating in 1906, owned the best timber stands in the island; the Bowater's mill, established in 1925, had had to be bailed out of bankruptcy by a government loan in the thirties. The concessions granted the two companies were unparalleled in North America. They paid no stumpage fees on company-owned land, undertook no conservation or reforestation, and paid virtually no taxes to the provincial government. Even so, neither operation was notably profitable, for although Newfoundland's trees were of high quality they were stunted, sparsely scattered, and expensive to exploit for lack of rivers or public roads.

For all that the pulp-and-paper companies took so much from the province, Newfoundlanders defended them with a passion which astonished mainlanders, particularly the journalists who, aptly, described the companies as "feudal empires." As unsettling to outsiders was that the paper mill workers in Grand Falls sided with management against their fellow workers in the woods. In fact, the mill workers in that company town boasted the best industrial jobs in Newfoundland; and were provided with trim houses and mainland-standard public services. In attitude and in affluence, they were middle class; they had little in common with the roistering loggers.

Within their fiefdoms, the pulp-and-paper companies were answerable neither to government nor to public. (The AND company, for example, owned outright half a dozen towns, a railway, a network of roads, a power station and a power grid, docks, and a fleet of ships.) Warned by their counterparts in British Columbia of just how tough a union the IWA was, both companies were determined to break it in Newfoundland. As one official said later: "It embarrassed us that the IWA was so moderate in its first demands. We knew damn well, and they knew we knew, that they would accept anything just to get established, and that the real crunch would come the second time round."

For a year, AND and Bowater's managed to fight off the IWA's attempts to win recognition as certified bargaining agent for the loggers. Finally, the Labour Relations Board ordered a supervised vote; the IWA won eighty-five per cent of the votes cast. In June 1958, bargaining began. The IWA demanded a twenty-five cent an hour increase, a work week of fifty-four hours, and improved working conditions, principally in the form of hot and cold water in the camps, and staple food other than beans. The AND Company turned down each request.*

To break the deadlock, the IWA applied to the government for a conciliation board. Its report was published in the first week of December and recommended, unanimously, a pay increase to $1.22 an hour. Both sides were also asked to seek out ways jointly to improve working conditions. Three days later, the IWA accepted the report. Although its own nominee on the conciliation board had signed the report, the AND Company rejected it. General Manager T. Ross Moore explained that the settlement would "cripple the entire AND operation."

Both sides now prepared for the trenches. The company piled reserves of sawn lumber in towering stacks outside the mill, and with equal foresight gave its mill workers a seven-cent-an-hour increase. The union chartered schooners to despatch food and supplies to the families of the men who would man the picket lines. The strike vote itself was a formality: 98.8% of the loggers in the camps voted in favour of the first walkout in the history of Newfoundland's forest industry.

The last union-company meetings took place in the AND staff house in Grand Falls. At one session Ladd asked if there were any terms that the company would accept. "Yes," came the reply across the table, "if you'll take a pay cut." Ladd walked out and the strike was on. It began officially a moment after midnight, January 1, 1959.

---

* Although two separate locals, 544 at Grand Falls and 545 at Corner Brook, were formed, because of the timing of the Labour Relations Board hearings, Local 544 was certified first. Negotiations began with AND, and it was against that company that the strike was staged. Ironically, AND was the better employer of the two. Had the IWA been able to strike first against Bowater's, the mill workers at Corner Brook, a union stronghold, would have backed the strike. Yet these differences were tactical; essentially the strike pitted loggers against both pulp-and-paper companies and the conditions which each of them allowed to exist.

So far Joey Smallwood had taken no action at all. For forty years hardly a leaf had quivered or fish leaped in the island without his commenting on it at length and fiercely taking sides. For a decade as Premier he had been the arbiter of all that happened and the instigator of most of it. Now, faced with the most dramatic single event since Confederation, Smallwood lapsed into silence. For the first time in his life he seemed paralyzed by indecision. He made no pretence of his dislike of the IWA, and never attempted to use his office to bring union and management together on neutral ground. Yet he had no love either for the pulp-and-paper companies whose extensive timber holdings and wanton cutting practices made his long-cherished third mill an impossibility.

Later, and understandably, organized labour accused Smallwood of having opposed the loggers from the start. With his weakness for refurbishing history, Smallwood lent credence to the accusation by telling a reporter: "I always intended to intervene. I just waited forty-five days for the right moment." The truth was that during the early days of the strike, Smallwood time and again rejected company demands that extra policemen be sent to the strike area on the grounds this would only incite the loggers to violence.

But if Smallwood hoped that the strike would resolve itself, as had so often happened in Newfoundland, by a quick collapse of organized labour, he was soon disappointed. The IWA had brought modern unionism to the island. The loggers were tough and hard, more than able to stand the strain of mounting picket lines on lonely, snowbound woods roads, and they were also disciplined and well-led. For the first time since Coaker, a force had arisen in Newfoundland that was completely uncowed by the established order. Moreover, the loggers were contemptuous even of the law itself, which they saw as simply another arm of management.

Technically, the woods roads which the loggers picketed were private property; day after day pickets were forced to stand aside to let through convoys of strike-breakers (mostly fishermen recruited by the company) under police escort. The loggers fought back with muscle-power, the only weapon they had. Day after day the newspapers reported these encounters: "Theft Damages: Three Loggers Charged"; "Assault Investigation Started: 15 Loggers Charged."

In the magistrate's court at Grand Falls, the mills of justice ground exceedingly fine: Lewis Rideout: $200 or two months for "obstructing a highway"; Archibald Snow, $250 or three months for "stealing a key valued at fifty cents from the pants pocket of James Farrell." The key belonged to an AND snowmobile. As the company hired more strike-breakers, the loggers retaliated: ignition keys were hurled deep into snow-banks; food and blankets disappeared from company bunkhouses. Blindly impartial, the law sided with management. Unlike strikers, company executives are rarely called on to jostle on the picket lines.

Slowly, and against every expectation, the loggers began to gain the upper hand. Outside the Grand Falls mill, the timber stacks dwindled steadily. Once the last log was gone the mill would close. On their lonely watches the loggers sang and stamped away the cold. Their wives, traditionally the weakest link in any strike, were as unyielding as their husbands. They walked miles carrying hot meals to their men on the picket lines, and on February 9 a crowd of them, "cursing something terrible," as a policeman reported, turned back a convoy load of strike-breakers as they tried to drive across the frozen Gander River. By February 12, those strike-breakers who had made it across the river and into the trees beyond began to stream out again. "You spend all your time on watch. You are always waiting for the strikers to attack, so you can't sleep," one of them explained.* On that same day, Smallwood at last broke his silence.

The pressures to act had built steadily upon Smallwood from the moment the strike began. Closure of the mills would mean economic disaster for

---

* Even more baffling to outsiders than the millworkers' backing of management was that, almost to a man, the strike-breakers in fact supported the strike. However, they were fishermen who had always gone into the woods in winter when there was work available, and they saw no reason to change the habits of centuries simply because the loggers had gone on strike. Newfoundland was too poor to afford labour solidarity.

the province, and both companies had made it abundantly clear that their threat to shut down was no bluff. Smallwood feared also that an IWA victory would transform Newfoundland's woods industry as it had British Columbia's, creating an élite corps of some three to four thousand full-time professional loggers. While such men would be well paid, they would put thousands of part-time loggers out of work, and close off the woods as a safety-valve for unemployed fishermen.

He also saw the union as a political threat, and Ladd himself as a potential Coaker. Scores of IWA members came from Coaker country on the Northeast Coast. For a decade now this had been Smallwood country, where his picture hung on kitchen walls; the union was trespassing on holy ground. Ladd had also been unwise enough to boast publicly that IWA's cell-like organization would spearhead a CCF drive in the province.[*]

Most of all, Smallwood was influenced by public opinion. If he led his province, he was also moulded by it. Overwhelmingly, Newfoundland opinion was marshalled against the loggers. It was they who had called the strike that threatened the economy; they who had attracted scores of mainland reporters who sent back stories which painted Newfoundland as poor and backward.

More potent a motive for public opinion than pride was the Newfoundlanders' deep-rooted horror for lawbreaking and violence. A. P. Herbert once called them "the most law-abiding people on earth." The society was too small and close-knit for crime to exist, other than in St. John's, and even there the court rolls recorded only the mundane peccadilloes of any seaport, drunkenness and prostitution. Unlike more advanced societies, Newfoundlanders looked on the police not as enemies but as friends and protectors, who dug trucks out of snowdrifts, rushed pregnant mothers to hospital, and passed news and gossip from one community to another. Ladd's accusation that the RCMP had acted as

---

[*] That this would have been successful is doubtful. Because all of its organizers were mainlanders, the IWA was already suspect to Newfoundlanders. Ever since, the same lack of local colour has prevented the NDP from gaining a foothold in the province.

strike-breakers aroused little sympathy, and each joust on the picket lines, each hijacking of company property turned public sentiment more firmly against the loggers.

From their pulpits, the clergy denounced the strike and called for an end to the civil disorder. All of Newfoundland watched horrified as what appeared to be a reign of lawlessness seized control of the central part of the island.

By early February, Smallwood had made up his mind to intervene. His opportunity to do so came on February 7. On that day, a band of 120 loggers set off from the inland town of Badger to raid a nearby woods camp packed with strike-breakers. They arrived just before midnight, smashed open the door, and herded the sleeping men outdoors. Some of these men, clad only in their underclothes, walked ten miles to the nearest shelter, in subzero cold. The next day, the RCMP rounded up seventy-seven loggers and marched them to Grand Falls, twenty miles away. This time some of the prisoners and policemen were frostbitten. "The whole thing is disgusting," declared the *Evening Telegram*. "Neighbour has been set against neighbour, and Newfoundlander against Newfoundlander."

Once he had made his decision, Smallwood acted as if he had never harboured any doubts at all. His goal was victory. He pursued it with the same single-minded commitment which had won him Confederation.

His first move was to make himself, for the duration, *de facto* Minister of Labour. As Premier and Minister of Labour, he then told Newfoundland what he intended to do.

On the evening of February 12, almost every man and woman in the province crowded in front of their television and radio sets to hear the familiar harsh voice at last speak out on the greatest issue of the day. Loggers listened in their outports and towns; Landon Ladd sat impassive in the IWA office in Grand Falls:

The IWA strike is a failure. The IWA is a failure. The IWA has failed the loggers of Newfoundland. In my opinion, the IWA never will and never can win.

We think and the government and people of Newfoundland think that the IWA are the greatest danger that ever struck Newfoundland. It is not a strike they have started, but a civil war. The IWA, since they came to Newfoundland, have brought nothing but trouble, torment, bad feeling such as we have never known. Entire neighbourhoods have been torn asunder; father torn from son; fishermen from loggers; settlements from settlements; union from union. There is hatred in Newfoundland tonight, bitter and ugly. There is more lawlessness, more violence, more lies, more falsehoods, more cheating in the past four weeks than we have seen in Newfoundland before. We see hate and suspicion and fear and force. This is what the IWA has set loose in Newfoundland.

How dare these outsiders come into this decent Christian province and by such terrible methods try to seize control of our province's main industry . . . spreading their black poison of class hatred and bitter, bigoted prejudice. How dare they come into this province, amongst decent God-fearing people and let loose their dirt and filth and poison. . . . Every decent Newfoundlander should feel that he has been made dirty by the presence of this wicked and mischievous body of reckless and irresponsible wreckers.

For inspired demagoguery, this was probably Smallwood's best speech. He struck every emotional key: "Christians"; "God-fearing"; "civil war"; "fishermen from loggers"; "class hatred"; and, above all, "outsiders." His opponents paid him their sincerest compliment. During the provincial election the following summer, an official from the Canadian Labour Congress, sent down to help out the fledgling labour party, took a tape-recording of Smallwood's speeches back to Ottawa and replayed them to union officials as models of the art of spoken propaganda.

In his speech, Smallwood had called upon the loggers to abandon the IWA and to join a new government-sponsored union, "independent of the pulp-and-paper companies, and strictly non-partisan," to be called the Newfoundland Brotherhood of Wood Workers. The legislature quickly passed an all-party resolution to approve the new union, and on

February 25, Smallwood flew out to Grand Falls to inaugurate it. He took with him his choice for the Brotherhood's first president, Max Lane, a Liberal member. "I have come," he said, "to free the loggers of Newfoundland from the tyranny of this foreign union."

The loggers turned their backs. On February 26, fewer than eight hundred, only a handful among them loggers, turned up for the Brotherhood's founding meeting, held behind closed doors at the Grand Falls Town Hall. That same afternoon, twenty miles away in Bishop's Falls, Ladd spoke to an audience of twelve hundred in the Star of the Sea Hall. Part of the crowd overflowed into a snow-covered field outside. "Here are the real loggers," bellowed Ladd, "and that's what counts."

Over on the mainland, powerful support mustered for the embattled union. The Canadian Labour Congress and the CCF Party denounced Smallwood's intervention; the IWA International office in New York wired a promise of "unlimited funds." Almost without exception mainland newspapers condemned Smallwood's stand.

If Smallwood was worried, he showed no sign of it. He stayed at the AND Staff House in Grand Falls for four days, a shirt-sleeved blur of energy as he snapped out orders and discussed strategy with political allies and company officials, all the while issuing optimistic bulletins to the press. Smallwood, however, was too astute to fool himself. When he left Grand Falls, he did so determined that, if he could not persuade the loggers to abandon the IWA, then he would use force to make the IWA abandon the loggers.

Back in St. John's, Smallwood told his anxious cabinet his plan. To stiffen the resolve of any who doubted it, he declared publicly: "There is not enough room in Newfoundland for the IWA and this Government. One or other must go."*

The last whispers of caution stilled, Smallwood plunged ahead. He

---

* He has often used this all-or-nothing technique in crises. As he has observed, privately: "When a cabinet knows its jobs are at stake, it unites them marvellously."

summoned the legislature back into session and handed it two hastily drafted bills. The first bore the prosaic title, "To Make Provision for Safeguarding the Public Interest in View of the Present Unsettled Conditions in the Woods Labour Industry." The sting was in the last clause: Certification granted the IWA by the Labour Relations Board was "void as of this date." In one stroke, Smallwood had wiped out the IWA as a legal entity. The Opposition applauded the bill. In Grand Falls, Ladd took to the radio: "Today will go down in the story of this island as a day on which freedom was stabbed in the back."

The second bill stuck the knife in deeper. It had been born two days before in Grand Falls. Working in his suite, the radio going full blast as always, Smallwood had suddenly shouted for quiet and leaned forward to listen as a young American lawyer-politician, Robert Kennedy, outlined for the CBC's "Project 59" his investigation into the hoodlum-ridden empire of James Hoffa.

"This gangster, this American criminal, tells the Canadian people in this special broadcast that his plans are to build an empire in Canada." Smallwood told the legislature. "I am ashamed to confess that I didn't know . . . Hoffa has already entered Newfoundland . . . the criminal has already established two branches in Newfoundland." His province would, he said, "hold up a torch to Canada" by smashing the Hoffa menace.

As a first step in the crusade, the province's labour laws would be amended so that "where any union exists in Newfoundland, a substantial number of whose superior officers have been convicted of such heinous crimes as white slavery, dope-peddling, manslaughter, embezzlement, such notorious crimes as these . . . it will be abolished by law. We will wipe it out . . . we will blot it off the face of this good Newfoundland earth." Such unions would be decertified by the government, without a public hearing, and any that attempted to continue to operate would be fined $5,000 and $500 for each member. The bill also banned sympathy strikes and fixed upon unions the "onus to prove" damages caused by a strike.

By the time Smallwood sat down, he had effectively made the Teamsters and the IWA seem as one. He had also enacted the most punitive anti-labour legislation of any post-war Canadian government other than that of Duplessis. The Canadian Labour Congress declared that the legislation "strikes at that rule of law which is supposed to be basic to western civilization," and appealed to Diefenbaker to disallow it.

Smallwood took the criticism in his stride. The Teamsters, he told the legislature, were "rats, crooks, criminals, scoundrels, the greatest collection ever made in the world since Hitler . . . a plague creeping into our decent island home." Hoffa could survive such rhetoric; nor did it affect the two Newfoundland locals of the Teamsters, neither of which Smallwood touched, then or later. Instead Smallwood aimed at an easier target. "He is in the Chamber here today, a full-time paid agent of the criminal Hoffa, representing the pimps, the panderers, the white slavers. He is their representative here in Newfoundland. Can we, in conscience, regard this man as an independent subject of the Queen?"

In the hushed chamber, spectators craned their necks. Smallwood identified the enemy: "I am referring to Daley, the President of the Newfoundland Federation of Labour. Larry Daley. Hoffa's man."

In the gallery Daley sat stunned and shaking. When his wife heard the news, she suffered a nervous breakdown. Later Daley challenged the Premier to repeat his words outside the privilege of the Chamber; Smallwood ignored him.

By now few Newfoundlanders stopped to count the human casualties. With his rhetoric Smallwood had swept the entire province into a frenzy against the outsider. "They Do Not Understand," ran the headline above an *Evening Telegram* leader; "They do not understand," said Education Minister Fred Rowe in the legislature of Canadian newspaper editorials; "They just don't understand us," said Don Jamieson in an interview with the *Toronto Star.* "After ten years, Canadians haven't a clue about us . . . there never has been any real attempt to embrace us or take us into the Canadian family."

The professional patriotism was backed by deep conviction. At heart, Newfoundlanders were still anti-Confederates, half-glad to be a race apart, embattled against all comers. As Smallwood, brilliantly for his purposes, put it: "Newfoundland's good name is at stake. The wolves are howling from one end of Canada to the other."

Forgotten, amid the emotion, was the nationality of the loggers.

It was into this maelstrom that Diefenbaker stumbled with his announcement on Term 29, on March 25. The two issues fed on each other. The full depth of Newfoundland feeling was soon made clear to the Prime Minister. Hoping to find some means of disallowing the anti-union legislation, Diefenbaker sent a "confidential" message to Lieutenant Governor MacPherson asking him to delay Royal Assent until the bills could be studied at Ottawa. Instead, MacPherson asked for advice from a friend in the provincial government and then gave Royal Assent immediately, before copies of the bills had reached the capital.

Once the IWA was decertified and stripped of its legal rights, the loggers could no longer hope for victory. Yet they refused to yield. More than three hundred jammed the town hall at Badger to cheer Ladd as he told them: "We're outlaws to everyone, but we'll bring Joe Smallwood to his knees." A week later, with calculated insult, Ladd staged a rally in Gambo, the Premier's birthplace. Six hundred loggers turned up to shake the rafters with their shouts: "When do we hang Joey?" "When do we burn the forests?"

For organized labour across Canada, the Newfoundland struggle had turned into a test in the epic tradition of the Winnipeg General Strike and the Regina Riots. The CLC launched a fund-raising drive from Halifax to Victoria, and for store clerks, stevedores, steelworkers, trainmen, and electricians giving became a matter of pride. More than $860,000 was collected, the largest strike fund in the history of Canadian labour.

By now, the strike had been on for nearly ten weeks. Not only had Smallwood failed to end it, but by his methods he had ranged an awesome ring of enemies against him: organized labour, mainland newspapers, the CCF, the Diefenbaker government, and even many federal Liberals.

Most politicians would have wavered. Smallwood simply bided his time and waited for his opportunity. It came on March 10. A violent clash between policemen and loggers at Badger ended with a man dead. He chanced to be a policeman. Smallwood made him into a martyr.

19

The Martyr

The tragedy at Badger was witnessed by only one man who was neither lawbreaker nor lawkeeper. In his account of the clash between loggers and policemen for the *Toronto Star* (which ended the friendship between Smallwood and Beland Honderich), the reporter Ray Timson wrote:

> A column of sixty-six policemen waded into a throng of striking loggers, clubbed two of them unconscious, flattened dozens more while wives and children screamed for them to stop. Nine of the loggers were arrested. Most of them had been beaten to the ground, hand-cuffed, and dragged to their feet.
>
> Towards the end of the riot one man taunted the Mounties: "You sure have guts, don't you?" The officer pointed and said, "Get that man now." One bounded into Mrs. Frances Piercey and knocked her down. "And he never looked back to see if I was all right."

Timson's story was flatly denied by the RCMP and denounced by Smallwood. No inquiry into the incident was made at the time, or later, but on the basis of all the available evidence, Timson's description was accurate.[*]

The tragedy was in fact a double one: An innocent man was killed, and he died in a fight that need never have happened at all. Although the elements of violence had been building for weeks, as the policemen grew more exhausted and exasperated, and the loggers became increasingly bitter and defiant, the catalyst which set them off on March 10 was a miscalculation by the police. As a direct result of that blunder, a policeman was killed; indirectly, the career of one of Canada's most distinguished public servants was ended abruptly, and a politician of great promise lost his chance to become Prime Minister. Out of this carnage, Smallwood wrested a personal victory.

Badger was the IWA fortress. It was a typical inland logging town of about a thousand. None of its buildings was more than two stories high, and its houses straggled in uneven rows along gravel streets. Badger existed because of a railway siding, and because of two woods roads which wound off from the centre of town into prime timber stands. All the men of Badger were full-time loggers.

Here, during the first week of March, the IWA chose to mass reinforcements recruited from among Bowater's loggers on the province's West Coast. The town overflowed with them, and on March 9 they showed their strength by stringing a two-hundred-man picket line across one of the woods roads. On the same day, in Badger itself, a car filled with non-union loggers was shoved off the road and its windshield smashed.

To control this ominous situation, the RCMP next day despatched a contingent to back up the ten-man detachment already on the spot. Smallwood sent out a squad of Newfoundland Constabulary, members of

---

[*] The most complete and impartial accounts of the incident were provided by police witnesses at the murder trial which followed it. The account given on the following pages is based on their testimony.

the St. John's city police. By late afternoon, a total of seventy policemen, commanded by RCMP Inspector Arthur Argent, had been concentrated in the community.

It was nightfall before the police were ready to move. Their first task was routine, and one which they had carried out dozens of times before. They were to clear a crowd of about 250 loggers who, together, with their wives and children, were blocking the main street of Badger. Argent formed his men into columns of threes and sent them swinging down the street. As the police approached, each one carrying a regulation night stick, lead-filled and bound with leather, the loggers fell back. Some of them scrambled away onto the snow-covered grounds of the Full Pentecostal Church; the majority drew back into a side road that led off towards the woods. In their military formation, the police marched past unhindered; their passage was marked only by a few nervous shouts and curses.

This simple objective achieved, Argent halted his men further down the main street, beyond the place where the crowd had stood. In another standard manoeuvre, he turned the column about and sent them swinging down the road once more. This time, however, a new order rang out from the head of the column. "Right Wheel" was the command, and in response the column turned off the main street and down into the side road where most of the loggers were packed between high snowbanks. Police and loggers were no longer face to face, but body to body.

Provided the police remained in formation, they could still jostle their way through the ragged crowd, accompanied by nothing worse than a second volley of insults. Instead, from the front file came the shout: "Get that man with a stick!" In an instant, the entire formation dissolved. Uncertain to which man among them the order was directed, or at which man among the scores of loggers standing knee-deep in snow it was aimed, policemen broke ranks to run into the crowd. Crowd control turned into riot.

In the pitch dark, policemen in dark blue uniforms and loggers in rough tartan lumberjackets grappled with each other. Five minutes later, one man lay on the ground, his skull cracked open by a three-foot birch billet. He was Constable Wilfrid Moss, a twenty-four-year-old member of the Newfoundland Constabulary.

Moss was rushed to the Lady Northcliffe Hospital in Grand Falls. He died next day without regaining consciousness. His assailant was never found. Although a murder charge was laid against Ronald Laing, one of the nine loggers arrested during the *mêlée*, it took a jury only fifty-two minutes to acquit him after a four-day trial in St. John's the following June.

In the Commons, Justice Minister Davie Fulton rejected Opposition demands for an inquiry and said that the RCMP had "conducted themselves with restraint under very difficult circumstances."

Smallwood had no doubts who was guilty. "The most cruel and brutal violence of the IWA. In four and a half centuries Newfoundland never saw anything like it," he told the legislature. "We greatly regret the real criminals were not arrested last night. All Newfoundlanders know who they are: Ladd, McCool, and Hall [IWA organizers]. They are the criminals. Up to now they have succeeded in evading arrest."

To emphasize the nature of the crime, Smallwood turned Moss's funeral into a state occasion. The dead policeman's flag-draped coffin was carried through the streets of Grand Falls, and then put aboard a train which stopped at each station on its way to the capital. In St. John's, the coffin was placed on an open hearse and borne through the streets in solemn ceremony, as crowds of silent, angry onlookers watched. Smallwood instituted a $600 "William Moss Memorial Scholarship" to be awarded each year to the son or daughter of a Newfoundland policeman.

Violence was answered by violence. In Grand Falls, frightened citizens, who expected the town to be invaded by marauding loggers, formed armed vigilante groups; a band of strike-breakers smashed into the IWA office at nearby Bishops Falls and reduced it to a shambles. In the woods the loggers talked of guerrilla war.

No matter the cause nor who was to blame for it, the labour dispute had degenerated into civil disorder. "The first duty of government is to maintain law and order," Smallwood told the legislature. "Without that there is nothing."

The RCMP was extended to its limit. Every available man in the province had been sent to the strike area, and many one-man posts had been closed. The last available reinforcements that could be spared from St. John's had been despatched, and the city was left with only eighteen policemen on each shift. If bloodshed broke out again, the police would be almost powerless to control it.

As early as March 8, Smallwood had made a start at restoring order. On his authority, the Attorney General, Leslie Curtis, telephoned Justice Minister Fulton at Ottawa to ask for RCMP reinforcements to be sent from the mainland. On the same day, Superintendent Arthur Parsons, commanding officer of the RCMP's "B" division in St. John's, put the same request to his superior, RCMP Commissioner Leonard Nicholson.

The decision that faced these two men, Fulton and Nicholson, was nerve-wracking. Too many policemen sent too soon might provoke the loggers to further violence; and brand the RCMP as siding with management. Too few men sent too late risked a reign of terror in Newfoundland.

As a team, and as individuals, few men were better equipped to make such a decision. Then forty-three, and the cabinet's youngest member, Fulton brought to the scruffy world of politics an aura of cold, intellectual brilliance and of unflinching personal integrity. Behind him lay a Rhodes Scholarship, an exceptional military career, and a string of political victories; within his grasp lay the Prime Ministership. In the public's eye, he stood on a pedestal almost unique in Canadian politics. But on top of that pedestal, there was little room for Fulton to manoeuvre.

With Nicholson, sixteen years older, the Justice Minister had developed an almost father-son relationship. If the popular image of an RCMP Commissioner is something of a cross between a drill-sergeant and a colonel of cavalry, Nicholson looked these parts: He was lean, ramrod stiff, silver-haired, with level blue eyes. Yet his personality belied his appearance: Nicholson moved easily in the company of journalists, civil servants, and diplomats, and possessed a dry, self-deprecating wit. From an ordinary policeman he had risen to command the 5,300-man force. He was within a year of retirement.

Two days after the requests came from St. John's, a reply went out from Ottawa. Oddly, it was made by Nicholson rather than by Fulton: "I am advised that changing situation . . . indicates reinforcements from outside province may not be needed."

Smallwood's reply was brusque: "Rather than desert the entire Grand Falls area to the tender mercies of irresponsible elements," he wired Fulton, "fifty additional men go to Grand Falls by train leaving here at noon. Under no circumstances will the Newfoundland Government yield to violence." That evening Wilfrid Moss was killed.

A few minutes after midnight, on March 11, Superintendent Parsons phoned his chief to report the riot at Badger. At the end of their conversation, Nicholson noted on his memo pad, "There seemed some hope that the clash might have the effect of showing the strikers that violence would not be tolerated."

At 6:00 A.M., Parsons called again. During the night, he reported, another hundred loggers had moved into Badger. "I must have more men, sir," he told Nicholson, "I can't hold off any longer." Nicholson immediately passed the grim news on to Fulton and was told to send reinforcements within the hour unless he heard otherwise. At 10:30 A.M., Nicholson set in motion the long-planned operation. A chartered TCA North Star trundled down the runway at Dorval and headed for the Maritimes to pick up fifty RCMP constables at Moncton, Halifax, and Sydney. The plane would arrive in Gander that evening.

In St. John's, Smallwood heard the news with relief. It was his only moment of comfort that day, for, unknown to him, a fresh chain of events had been set in motion. Half an hour after Nicholson had given the order to despatch the reinforcements, Fulton had summoned him over to his Parliament Hill office. There, to Nicholson's disbelief, Fulton ordered him to halt the North Star at Moncton. As justification, Fulton, for the first time, questioned whether the request for reinforcements met the terms of the RCMP's contract with the province. The key clause of that contract (standard to the eight provinces – all but Ontario and Quebec – where the RCMP acted as a local as well as national force) was No. 13:

> Where in the opinion of the Attorney General of the province an emergency exists within the province requiring additional members of the force to assist in dealing with such emergency, Canada shall, at the request of the Attorney-General of the province, increase the strength of the division as requested if, in the opinion of the Attorney General of Canada, having regard to other duties and responsibilities of the force, such increase is possible.

Clause 13 was ambiguous, Fulton argued. More important, a decision of such consequence could be made only by the full cabinet. The cabinet meeting, he added, would begin immediately. As soon as a decision was reached, he would telephone Nicholson.

By turns puzzled and angry, Nicholson returned to the RCMP Headquarters. As the hours slipped by without word from Fulton, Nicholson became more and more certain what the Government's decision would be. Alone in his office he made his own decision. However the letter of Clause 13 might be interpreted, there was no question in his mind as to its spirit. If politics were placed above the spirit of the law, he would resign to protect the honour of his force.

Fulton made his call at 5:20 P.M. The conversation was as bitter as it was short. Rather than risk the good name of the force by casting it in a role that could be misinterpreted as strike-breaking, said Fulton, the cabinet had decided to suspend the dispatch of RCMP reinforcements to Newfoundland. "Very well, sir," replied Nicholson, "you will have my resignation in the morning."

One of the finest public servants to serve Canada had voluntarily ended his own career. No one who knew Nicholson would have been surprised at his decision. The question now was whether Fulton would follow Nicholson, for he too had been overruled. At the day-long cabinet meeting, Fulton had argued strongly that RCMP reinforcements must be sent, for the sake of law and order and to fulfil the intent of the contract with Newfoundland. He had been backed by the Maritime ministers and by George Pearkes and Douglas Harkness, both former army officers. Ranked against them had been the prairie ministers and Labour Minister Michael Starr. The deciding voice had been Diefenbaker's. Persuasively and forcefully, the Prime Minister argued that sending the men would slander the RCMP as strike-breakers. The Prime Minister's argument prevailed. In making it, he had been motivated by his disgust at Smallwood's intervention in a labour dispute, and he had also been influenced by his own political memories. As a prairie Conservative, Diefenbaker had lost five elections because of R. B. Bennett's use of the RCMP in the Regina Riots, and Meighen's use of the Northwest Mounted Police during the Winnipeg General Strike. Newfoundland was a long way from Prince Albert, but in any clash between strikers and police there was no doubt where prairie sympathies would lie, nor, therefore, any doubt about the sympathies of a prairie Prime Minister.

Early next morning, Nicholson handed his letter of resignation to Fulton: "For God's sake, Nick, take it back," answered the anguished Justice Minister. When he asked why Nicholson had not told him before cabinet met that he would resign if the decision went against him, Nicholson answered, "I thought that would be improper."

The two close friends had a last painful duty to perform. That evening Fulton was to be Nicholson's guest at the monthly meeting of a private discussion club made up of civil servants, diplomats, and journalists. For his turn as host, Nicholson had arranged the meeting in the RCMP's officers mess. "Do you think we can go through with it?" asked Fulton. "If you can, I think I can," answered Nicholson. Both men played their parts well; none of the club members guessed what had happened.

In the afternoon, Fulton had finally accepted Nicholson's letter. For the Commissioner, it was a sad but noble end to his career. For Fulton it was an ashen moment. Unwittingly, he had driven his friend from public office, and he had damaged the reputation of a force to which he was devoted.

The following Monday, just before the Commons met, Veterans Affairs Minister Alfred Brooks and Pearkes begged Nicholson to change his mind. He shook his head. When the division bells rang to summon members of the Chamber, he walked alone down the marble corridor to take his place in the Officials' Gallery.

In the Commons, Diefenbaker spoke first, his voice tight with anger: "I feel impelled to say that the Premier of Newfoundland has greatly aggravated the present situation in that province by intervening in a labour dispute in a way which apparently goes beyond the usual role of government. The result, as might have been anticipated, has been a violent reaction on the part of the workers." This was tantamount to accusing Smallwood of causing the bloodshed, an open declaration of political war to which Smallwood responded on Term 29.

The first casualty of their political war was now announced. "With deep personal regret . . . particularly in the light of the close personal relationship which has existed," said Fulton, he had no course but to accept Nicholson's resignation. This he tabled in the Commons. Outside Parliament, the two men parted without rancour; a few weeks later they danced with each other's wives at the Governor General's Ball.

The second casualty was Fulton himself. At the time he saw no cause to resign, nor did he consider it. Later, when he realized that his admirers had unanimously expected him to do so, he came to question his own standards and conduct. Though the fine edge of his intellect remained, his zest and spirit were gone. A bright political career went into eclipse. At the 1956 Conservative Leadership Convention, Fulton had run third behind Diefenbaker; at the 1967 Convention he ran third once more. Few observers of that convention doubted that his resignation in March 1959 would have won Fulton the crown.

In St. John's, Smallwood made no comment on Fulton's statement. Up until this incident he had, ironically, been a great admirer of the Justice Minister. Nicholson he called "a true Canadian gentleman," and a year later repaid him the debt of honour. As the principal ornament of his mammoth Confederation building, a huge mural glares down on the main lobby, a panorama of Newfoundland history with real-life personalities, among them Smallwood and St. Laurent, cast as Elizabethan courtiers, Beothuk Indians, and Canadian servicemen. In the centre stands an RCMP officer: his face is Nicholson's.

Nicholson's resignation also handed Smallwood a political reprieve. He used it to counterattack Diefenbaker and, more important, to repair his relations with the federal Liberals, his only remaining political allies, which up to this point had been stretched near the breaking point by his open war against organized labour.

For a fortnight, behind the scenes, the Progressives in Pearson's office, Maurice Lamontagne and Allan MacEachen, supported by Paul Martin, had urged the Opposition leader to condemn publicly Smallwood's conduct. Against them in this battle between political need and principle stood Pickersgill who commanded a decisive advantage. He knew his leader's mind better than his opponents did. While they urged Pearson to act, Pickersgill, instead of demanding that he act in the opposite direction – by supporting Smallwood – argued instead that there was no need for him to do anything at all, since the legislation was a provincial matter and hence no concern of the federal Liberals. For a few days, as Pearson agonized over his decision, the outcome was sufficiently in doubt that Pickersgill spent one afternoon studying the Commons Chamber to pick out the best spot for himself and the four other Newfoundland Liberal M.P.'s to sit once they had bolted the party.

On March 13, Pearson at last broke his silence. "The policy in labour matters of the Liberal Party is firmly based," he said, "on the right of free collective bargaining through unions chosen by the workers themselves." This stand was based, he explained, on a 1937 statement by a Liberal Minister of Labour.

Pickersgill now turned to Smallwood for a reciprocal concession, and wrung from him a reluctant agreement to remove the most objectionable clause in the labour legislation, that which gave the government the right, without appeal, to decertify unions guilty of so-called "heinous crimes."

A week later, Pearson told the press: "I am very glad to learn that the Newfoundland Government is going to change part of the Act." His pleasure was short-lived. Before Smallwood's amendment (which would have transferred power of decertification from Government to provincial Supreme Court) reached the legislature, the CLC rushed out a statement expressing satisfaction that "Premier Smallwood is finally retreating in the face of pressure from outside." And Diefenbaker heaped coals of fire. "Action taken in haste gives rise to secondary thoughts," he declared in the Commons.

Readiness to admit error is among the least exercised of Smallwood's virtues, and the amendment died. Liberal anger and Pickersgill's dismay did, however, prompt him to wire Pearson: "REGRET FOR ANY EMBARRASSMENT I MAY HAVE CAUSED YOU."

By now closer to farce than tragedy, the ultimate irony of the crisis was that had the RCMP reinforcements been sent, they would have been superfluous. Demoralized by hostile public opinion, and grief-stricken by the killing at Badger, the loggers had abandoned their hopeless struggle. "Swallow your pride and take the jobs," an IWA organizer told a loggers' meeting at Deer Lake on March 20.

To get the jobs, the loggers joined Smallwood's Brotherhood; its membership climbed quickly to eight thousand. The Brotherhood needed only a week to win a contract from the pulp-and-paper companies; it gave the loggers a pay increase of five cents an hour. To hasten the return to normalcy, the AND Company announced a $150,000 road-paving program for Grand Falls, a $100,000 scholarship program for loggers' children, and, on May 18, a $500,000 students' residence for Memorial University.

Despised by the loggers and ostracized by organized labour, which refused to recognize it as a legitimate union, the Brotherhood survived for two years. It was an unfailing embarrassment to Smallwood, and it was finally laid to rest by a Royal Commission he himself had set up to investigate loggers' complaints about substandard working conditions. In its report, published on February 11, 1961, the Commission described the worst of the woods camps:

Dark and squalid hovels which would not be used for hen-houses except by the most primitive farmer. Dirt is everywhere. Rats are common. Dilapidation is the rule. There is nothing to do in the evenings but sit around on the bunks talking. The light is from a limited number of common, flat-wick kerosene lamps. Men have been pressed down to a dead level of a flat rate and have grown resigned. If a man kicks there are just now only too many to take his job.

No local paper bothered to comment on the indictment. From Toronto, Ladd said: "This vindicates everything we stood for." This time, Smallwood agreed with him: "Thousands of men in the woods are sweating with hate and frustration," he said. "It's enough to make a man commit murder." The murder had been committed two years earlier, in Badger.

Besides acting on the Royal Commission's recommendations, Smallwood used its report as an opportunity to dissolve the hapless IBWW and replace it with a real union, though one of his own choosing. As always, he wasted no time on recriminations or regrets. He did what had to be done. Through 1961, Smallwood negotiated behind the scenes with the International Brotherhood of Carpenters, Woodworkers and Joiners, an old IWA rival which had been knocking on his door since 1959. Then, in March 1962, the Carpenters suddenly announced that they had signed up a majority of Newfoundland loggers as members. The ballot was unsupervised, and its results were never published. Smallwood proclaimed it a victory for the loggers.

This coup brought the Canadian Labour Congress back briefly onto the stage. The Newfoundland loggers' strike, to this point, had been a decisive setback for organized labour in Canada. The CLC's attempt to persuade the federal government to disallow Smallwood's labour legislation failed. When it referred the issue to the International Labour Organization in Geneva, which quickly found the laws "not compatible with the generally accepted principles governing freedom of association," Smallwood coolly retorted: "What are they going to do, send in UN troops?" The ILO report was quietly pigeonholed. The CLC had been equally unsuccessful on the political front. In the 1959 provincial

election, it had backed the left-wing Newfoundland Democratic Party;*
all the NDP candidates lost their deposits, and between them amassed only
9,352 votes. (Nor has the NDP threatened Smallwood in any election
since, though in 1962 one candidate came within 254 votes of defeating
Smallwood's Labour Minister.)

In 1962, in the eyes of the Labour Congress, the IWA was still the official
bargaining agent for the loggers in Newfoundland. The Carpenters, therefore, were guilty of union raiding, and a protest to this effect was brought
before the CLC's annual convention in Vancouver in April. Before the
motion could be discussed, the Carpenters stalked out of the meeting and
out of the Labour Congress. "This is regrettable," said CLC President
Claude Jodoin. "There is no cause for them to walk out that way." Nor was
there: A year later the Carpenters paid their back dues, rejoined the fold,
and the Newfoundland affair was shelved. "With the exception of a few,
the trade-union movement is no longer a movement of idealism,"
Smallwood commented in the legislature. "The trade unions must not be
considered as a sacred vessel, as sacrosanct. They are all too human."

The end of the affair was more cheerful. Under the Carpenters, the
loggers eventually won most of the gains the IWA had fought for. By the
late sixties, the base woods labour rate had almost doubled, to $1.95 an
hour; the work week had been cut to fifty hours, and woods camps,
licensed by the government following the Royal Commission report, all
had hot and cold running water, oil ranges or hot air furnaces, and menus
which met a prescribed dietary standard. Because of mechanization, and
in particular the power saw, the Newfoundland logging force has dwindled to some five thousand. It constitutes today the élite corps the IWA
had planned, and which Smallwood had so violently opposed.

For ten years afterwards, organized labour remained powerless within
Newfoundland. Another strike, this one of hospital workers, was broken
by legislative action in 1967. But, by the end of the decade, trade unions
had regained their voice and strength, and launched a wave of almost

---

* This predated, by one year, the formation of the New Democratic Party.

continuous strikes in every area from fishing to teaching, from mining to the civil service. At its annual convention in Grand Falls in July 1971, the Newfoundland Federation of Labour listened to a specially-invited speaker: He was Earl Patterson, the Canadian president of the IWA, and the first Woodworker to make a public speech in Newfoundland in twelve years.

The common sense of ordinary Newfoundlanders soon reasserted itself, and even before 1959 was out the tide of emotion had ebbed. During the months of the strike Smallwood had exploited and sustained that emotion; the difference between those Newfoundlanders who had been swept up by it and the Premier was that he, ex-union organizer, ex-labour agitator, and ex-socialist stump orator, had known better.

In the loggers' strike, the revolutionary grown accustomed to power had faced his moment of truth. And he had ducked. When Smallwood stood up again it was as a conservative.

20

Power Without Purpose

By the time he turned sixty, Smallwood had built for himself a personal hegemony unmatched in modern Canadian politics. His defeat of Diefenbaker and destruction of the IWA ended all effective opposition to him within Newfoundland itself. At the federal level, where his closest contemporary comparison, Maurice Duplessis, had been weak, Smallwood was supreme. He won all seven federal seats in 1963, and again in 1965. In Ottawa, where Pickersgill was one of the most powerful members of the Liberal cabinet, he and Smallwood made a team whose path no federal minister or civil servant knowingly crossed.

Smallwood had also created for himself a double image. Through the mainland looking-glass, he was a folk hero, the "Kwame Nkrumah of Newfoundland," as Kildare Dobbs once put it, or "The Only Living Father of Confederation," who bewitched television viewers and charmed visiting reporters. "I'm a sort of tourist attraction," he explained. "Everyone who comes here wants to meet me. So I try to say something a little provocative, a little daring. They expect it, and they go away happy." To Newfoundland eyes, he was at one and the same time a populist autocrat, with enough of the common touch left to push a grocery cart unaffectedly round St. John's supermarkets and take his place in line at the checkout counter, and a despot who struck fear in the citizenry, and threatened the livelihood of any Newfoundlander who dared oppose him publicly.

The outside view was not so much inaccurate – Smallwood was the best entertainer on the Canadian political scene and its most passionate patriot – as out of date. Through the half decade after 1960, Smallwood rested on his laurels. The apostle of ceaseless change became the defender of the *status quo*. His love for country hardened into self-love. Although he held absolute power, he had never in his life been less certain what to do with it.

Smallwood was tired. Outwardly he did not appear to be so. Though "skin and grief" had mellowed to comfortable portliness and his hair had turned to silver, his abnormal energy and stamina were undiminished and his physical health was as radiant as ever. (His constitution is a minor medical phenomenon. He has been bedridden only four times in his life, and is almost immune to colds, viruses, and headaches.*) He could respond as quickly to a political challenge, and was as deadly as ever in debate. Once, when he drowsed off in the legislature, he crushed the Opposition's excited attempt to picture him as senile with the retort: "I don't know if it was because of advancing age or because of the dullness of the honourable member's speech. All I know was that I dreamed Mr. Greene was speaking, and when I woke up, he was."

Smallwood's lassitude instead was psychological. For more than a decade he had worked virtually alone, at a pace which would have

---

* As a boy he was twice hospitalized, with scarlet fever and pleurisy; in 1952, a severe bout of flu sent him to bed for three days, during which he held a full-scale cabinet meeting at his bedside to decide a new fisheries policy; in 1967, he had to leave the Confederation for Tomorrow Conference for an operation on a detached eye retina, and emerged ten days later to attend a federal-provincial conference on housing. Ironically, he is a mild hypochondriac, who lectures friends constantly on the dangers of smoking, and avoids eating sweets for fear of diabetes.

crippled most men, to build a new Newfoundland. By his standards, he had failed.

It was true that, by the mid-sixties, Smallwood could at last see around him tangible signs of progress. Provincial incomes had increased each year – to an average of $1,173 per capita by 1965. Unemployment had dropped to less than ten per cent. The Confederation Building had been completed; in 1961, Memorial University moved to a new campus, and in 1963 he proudly opened a Fisheries College, the first of its kind in Canada. There were two large new iron mines in Labrador, and a $30 million asbestos mine at Baie Verte on the Northeast Coast.

Yet the economic breakthrough remained out of reach. Newfoundland still lacked a paved trans-island highway, and the few cars bumped along narrow, nineteenth-century roads. Apart from a small scrap steel mill and an oil refinery, Smallwood had created no new industries. He still chased fruitlessly after a third pulp-and-paper mill. Through the mid-sixties his new industrial dream, the development of the Churchill Falls power project, remained on the drawing boards. In almost every phase of life, the island continued to drift far behind the mainland.

Nor had Newfoundlanders made the psychological breakthrough into the Canadian mainstream. Eroded by the impact of radio and television, the Newfoundland mystique was fast slipping away, and nothing of value had emerged to take its place. A unique and precious society was halfway to extinction. As the embodiment of that society, Smallwood mourned its passing and agonized over his own part in destroying it. This inner conflict, between aging radical and conservative by circumstance, he expressed most poignantly in a radio interview with John David Hamilton and broadcast as part of the CBC's "Canadian Mood" series in April 1965:

> The thing I fear most of all is a coarsening of our people through the impact of this so-called civilization. You have to make your choice; you have to make your decision. Are you justified in leaving people as they've been for centuries, almost in a mediaeval condition, living rather primitively – comfortably mind you, but primitively – without roads, without connections, without industries. It's all very idyllic you

know; it's attractive; it's nice to go and visit, but isn't it perhaps a little more than we have the right to do, just to say, "No, we will not open up these places, we will leave them as they are in their quaint isolation because it will be lovely for us to go and visit." How about the people in them? Is their becoming coarsened too high a price to pay for a higher standard of living, and is it really a higher standard of living after all? I don't know. I wonder. I'm not going to express too positive an opinion, but I do express some fears, some apprehensions, that our people will pick up most readily and most quickly, not the best features of visitors and tourists, but the smart-aleck, the wisecrack, the gag, you know, all the superficial things, rather than the quiet dignity, the quiet dignity of quiet people living in quiet places. This gives place to a certain veneer, a certain slickness, you know – the youngsters are the first to imitate, the first to see it, and all of us in Newfoundland that think about these things are getting to be a bit worried lest some of the sweetness, the sweetness of our outport life, the wholesomeness, the quiet dignity of it, will go – and it will be one of the great losses if it does go – it will be a terrible loss.

Besides his emotional involvement in the old Newfoundland, Smallwood became a conservative after 1960 for the uncomplicated reason that he was no longer a raw idealist of twenty, but a practised politician in his sixties. He moved increasingly with men of conservative bent: Pickersgill, Winters, John Doyle, and the businessmen who flocked to his banner after the defeat of the IWA. The average age of his own cabinet was now more than sixty. As if it were an intimation of his own mortality, he hated to let anyone retire, so that tired warhorses lingered on, to relive with him the epic battles of Confederation over long lunches in the Premier's private dining room.

Above all, Smallwood became a conservative because he could no longer summon up the imagination or intellectual daring to offer his people an alternative. After fifteen years of visions and experiment, he had run out of ideas. Baffled by problems he had expected to solve long ago, he fell back on the tried and tested. In politics he became a reactionary; in education, where he staunchly defended the archaic denominational system, he allied himself on the side of those who opposed reform. Between 1959 and 1965, except in Labrador, where his purpose was plain and daring, Smallwood attempted only two important policy initiatives. Each was an attempt to turn back the clock.

In October 1962, Smallwood called a provincial election, and launched his campaign with "the greatest fishery program the province has even seen." Before polling day, he staged a mammoth fisheries convention in St. John's; its twenty-two hours of proceedings were covered live by the province's network of private television stations.

Fifteen months later, in January 1964, a federal-provincial conference on the fisheries, the first of its kind in Canadian history, was held in Ottawa at Smallwood's insistence. He accomplished this coup by cajoling Pearson, just before the 1963 federal election, into signing a letter which Pickersgill had drafted and which promised "a federal-provincial program for fishery development to be founded on the principle that national action for the fishery should parallel the action already being taken, and action to be taken, for agriculture." To forestall any sober second thoughts at Ottawa, Smallwood farsightedly published Pearson's letter in the local newspapers.

"The Newfoundland fishery is moving deeper and deeper in the direction of an insuperable welfare problem," Smallwood's brief to the Ottawa conference began. "Low incomes, lack of alternative opportunities, lack of capital, lack of equipment and supplies – all lead inevitably to lower production and a gradual deterioration of the human resources. Year by year, the industry and the families engaged in it are further demoralized and depressed."

His diagnosis was as honest as it was perceptive. Some fifteen thousand Newfoundland inshore fishermen scraped out a living by working barely three months of the year; their methods, except for a few innovations such as nylon gill nets, had been unchanged for centuries. They earned an average of $850 annually, two-fifths of it provided by government payments of one kind or another.

But his cure was as unsound as it was outdated. The inshore fishery could be revived only by a ruthless rationalization that would cut the number employed in it by as much as three-quarters. Instead, Smallwood proposed to keep the fishery alive and intact by wholesale federal subsidies. To do this, he asked Ottawa to institute a guaranteed price for salt cod, as well as a fish marketing agency patterned on the wheat board. Both proposals were rejected by the Ottawa conference. Although, beginning in 1965, other sections of Smallwood's program, such as a subsidy for small boat building, a credit and insurance scheme, and a twelve-mile limit were implemented, the central concept – that Newfoundland's ancient inshore fishery could be perpetuated into the late 1960s – was quietly abandoned.

Instead of their coastline, Newfoundlanders turned towards the open sea. On February 1, 1965, only a fortnight after the Ottawa conference ended, the giant British company, Bird's Eye, a subsidiary of Lever Brothers, announced it would develop a major new plant to be supplied by twenty deep-sea trawlers. Although this venture ultimately failed, as did that of another British firm, the Ross Group in St. John's, major international companies such as B.C. Packers, Atlantic Sugar and Booth Fisheries all built plants and with them trawlers and draggers to take Newfoundlanders back, after a century's absence, to the Grand Banks.

A more flamboyant instance of Smallwood's conservatism – and more dramatically, of the power he wielded at Ottawa – came with the great flag debate of 1964. To satisfy his own nostalgia and that of most Newfoundlanders, Smallwood single-handedly secured a major change in what was perhaps the most important single piece of legislation of the Pearson years.

In this encounter, Smallwood drew much of his strength from straight political leverage. Within the minority Liberal government, the seven Newfoundland M.P.s formed the third largest provincial caucus. Had they bolted the party, Pearson's Maple Leaf flag would almost certainly have been defeated. As important, however, was Smallwood's own personality, and the nature of his personal relationship with Lester Pearson.

Few men were more dissimilar than Smallwood and Pearson; each man, though, admired and respected the other. Pearson warmed to Smallwood as a genuine patriot and as the champion of his province, and he marvelled at the Premier's political prowess. Smallwood for his part, while he despaired of Pearson's inability to strike at an opponent's jugular, was awed by his talents as a statesman and diplomat. Even during Pearson's worst moments as Prime Minister, Smallwood permitted no disloyalty towards him among his own subordinates.

Thanks to Smallwood, Pearson hugely enjoyed his campaign visits to Newfoundland. On his return he would relate with amused detachment his multiple adventures in Smallwood's kingdom. One such began with Smallwood's fierce enjoinder to him as they rode together through the streets. "You're not waving enough, Mr. Pearson. Wave." Then, as the motor cavalcade rolled on, after Smallwood had cheerfully explained that they were passing through solid Liberal territory, Pearson found himself waving at an onlooker who in return shook his fist and spat on the sidewalk. "We'd better," hissed Smallwood, "put him down as undecided."

Because of his affection for the Prime Minister, and because he relied so heavily on federal largesse, Smallwood, in contrast to his battle over Term 29, contained his argument over the flag within well-defined limits. He fought with all his might for what he wanted; once he had won it, he held faithfully to the bargain he had struck with Pearson.

At issue was the future of the Union Jack, Smallwood's beloved ensign and Newfoundland's unofficial flag. "I will continue to advocate," he had said as far back as February 13, 1962, long before the flag issue arose, "until I die, at least while I have life left in me, I will advocate the Union Jack." His advocacy of the Union Jack was as trenchant when, two years later, Pearson announced to a hostile Royal Canadian Legion audience in Winnipeg that he intended to create a new and distinctive Canadian flag.

By May of 1964, parliamentary observers took it for granted that Pearson intended to seek parliamentary approval for his Maple Leaf flag alone. There was no mention of the Union Jack. Typically, a Canadian Press story, carried by the St. John's *Evening Telegram* of May 21, declared: "Pearson is ready to stand or fall on the Maple Leaf flag."

Smallwood's first reaction was of alarm. "Reports pouring in to me from all over the province convince me that the Newfoundland people demand that the Union Jack, or Red Ensign, or both, be kept as the flag of Canada," he told reporters.

Soon he was angry. "Newfoundland," he said, "will continue to fly the Union Jack if we are the last place on earth to do so." On the evening of Saturday, May 22, he phoned Ottawa, and since Pickersgill was out of town, his wrath was expended upon the Newfoundland M.P., Charles Granger. Unless Pearson declared publicly he would retain the Union Jack as co-equal to the new flag, Smallwood told Granger, he would refuse to fly the Maple Leaf flag above any government building in the province and, to show his feelings, would the following Monday ask the legislature to condemn officially the new flag. He took it for granted, with ample reason, that the Newfoundland M.P.s at Ottawa would cross the floor on the issue.

A few hours later, Pickersgill returned to the capital and mounted a hasty rescue operation. He recalls it as "a quite exceptionally hectic week-end," during which he alternated between long-distance calls to Smallwood and personal visits to Pearson at 24 Sussex Drive. By late Sunday evening, Pickersgill had forged a compromise, aided by his unspoken but understood threat to resign if Smallwood pushed his point too far. The compromise was confirmed in a telegram Pearson sent to Smallwood and preferring action to discretion, Smallwood read it out to the legislature: "WE HAVE NOT DECIDED WHETHER THERE SHOULD BE A ROYAL PROCLAMATION TO ESTABLISH THE NATIONAL FLAG AND A SEPARATE PROCLAMATION TO RECOGNIZE THE UNION JACK AS THE SYMBOL OF CANADA'S MEMBERSHIP IN THE COMMONWEALTH OF NATIONS AND OUR ALLEGIANCE TO THE CROWN BUT THERE IS NO QUESTION OF OUR INTENTION TO RECOMMEND THAT BOTH BE RECOMMENDED BY THE QUEEN."

At Ottawa, Diefenbaker taunted the Prime Minister: "One flag for show and one for Joe." And the resulting two-flag resolution set the stage for the long flag filibuster which brought the Pearson government to the brink of defeat.

Smallwood kept his side of the bargain. He lavishly praised the Maple Leaf in public. It and the Union Jack, the official provincial flag and sentimental favourite of Newfoundlanders, fly together above Smallwood's ranch, and above all provincial government buildings.

Smallwood himself has mellowed. On an afternoon in September 1967, he walked down the steps of the Confederation Building with a visiting federal minister. As the two paused to look up at the Union Jack and the Maple Leaf flags flying outside, Smallwood turned to his companion: "It is sad, but it is true," he said, "the Union Jack doesn't mean much to young Newfoundlanders today."

Even so, like most Newfoundlanders of his generation, he remains a devout Monarchist, determined to die as he was born, a British subject. At the federal-provincial Constitutional Conference in February 1968, he made an emotional plea for Canada's last royal links with Britain: "If we had to choose between the Crown and this great Canadian family," he said, "it would be a sore choice to make."

A foot-high Union Jack stood at one corner of his desk*: aside from an oil painting of Churchill Falls the only permanent fixture on Smallwood's office walls was a glossy reproduction of Annigoni's portrait of the Queen.

---

* Smallwood's desk was a marvel of inspired disorder. A sluggish letter-writer, his standard reply when questioned about a letter he had failed to answer was, "It's right in front of me." This was almost invariably true; the letter was lost amid the pile of state papers and personal memorabilia that cluttered his six-foot, glass-topped desk. Among the mementoes were: a silver-topped inkwell used by Sir Robert Bond; a porcelain bust of Wesley; a model of the silver shovel used to open the Churchill Falls project; a medallion from the Girl Guides of Canada; a colour photograph of himself in doctoral robes; samples of rock from asbestos, copper, lead and zinc mines; statues of Laurier and Macdonald; a bust of General Booth; a golden key to celebrate the opening of the College of Trades and Technology. To one side of the desk was Smallwood's prized electronic gadgetry: black, green, pink and grey telephones by which he could, among other things, instantly call any member of his staff, cabinet ministers and deputy ministers. Behind all this sat Smallwood, stockinged feet on his desk.

For Smallwood, the spat over the Union Jack and the fight for the fisheries development program were welcome respites from the dullness of life without political or intellectual challenge. "I'm bored with this job," he told an incredulous visiting reporter. "It hasn't seized me, it really hasn't, these last two or three years."

He was also lonely, to a degree almost no one guessed. A mild misogynist, he was ill-at-ease and uncomfortable in the presence of women. Years of absolute power had brought him scores of hangers-on but few friends, and fewer still whose affection he could be certain of once he departed from power. Frustrated by the lack of any outlet for his energy and enthusiasm, Smallwood from 1959 onward began more and more to devote himself to himself. The long-time Puritan became a late-blooming hedonist.

In character, he embraced hedonism as if it were a long-running political campaign. Picasso-like, he flung himself into a series of periods during which he acted as if the subject that had caught his fancy was the only one in the world. He pursued art and archaeology through scores of glossy, coffee-table books; amassed a vast collection of classical records, and shot hundreds of reels of home-movie footage. He installed an indoor swimming pool at his ranch, and for a time no member of the cabinet could be certain of catching the Premier's ear unless he turned up complete with swimming trunks. He even took up riding. In 1963, clad in ten-gallon hat and spurs, he helped drive a herd of cattle flown in from Saskatchewan to their new pastureland on the Burin peninsula.

Smallwood's most durable, and most costly, pastime was farming. His first glimpse of the green and gentle farmlands of Britain back in 1927 had left him convinced, as he once informed his startled cabinet, "Nobody was anybody who did not come from the land." He romanticized the landed gentry, and added to his library such works as *English Life and Character* and *Memories of Old Gloucestershire*.

His own career as a country gentleman began in 1951 as a joint venture with his son-in-law Ed Russell. Together they cleared land on the desolate Brigus Barrens, forty miles from St. John's. Until he built his own house there, Smallwood spent his weekends in a winterized packing case outfitted with a cot, and a space heater. For all that he spent on it – "I can't afford to retire," he once said, "I owe too much money" – the farm was a financial disaster. Hens failed to lay, pigs sickened with monotonous regularity, and mink, because of inadequacies in their diet, failed to breed.

Nevertheless, Smallwood went down in style. He installed a six-foot-high plaster of Paris horse, which he had rescued from a defunct harness shop in St. John's, on a bluff above the farm, from which the animal surveyed his domain. For a time, until the venture failed, he raised and sold pheasants. Struck with the idea of raising sheep, he collected a flock from around eastern Newfoundland and imported a shepherd from Scotland who in his spare time read Homer, in Greek. Smallwood was in his element as he strode around, crook in hand, a sheepdog behind him – until the first heavy fog when the animals, who had never before been herded, set off in all directions for their original homes. The next week, Smallwood rounded them up once more, and set them firmly back on the barrens where they remained – until the next fog. At this point, he bowed to the inevitable.

As much effort went into Smallwood's "Newfoundland House," an arrowhead-shaped, twelve-room bungalow which he built upon the side of a hill overlooking his farm. Together the two properties are worth not less than $500,000, of which at least two-thirds is still owed to the banks. In 1960, Smallwood set out to build his house with a $13,700 federal government mortgage; since this was plainly insufficient, he hit upon the idea of accepting all the gifts that contractors and suppliers offered and in return he donated the property to the province to be used, after his death, as a residence of future premiers.

The plain, brown, shingle-roofed house, built around a vast triangular living room, is furnished with an eye for comfort rather than style. It is cluttered with the memorabilia of a lifetime: a rare, seal-oil lamp that once belonged to Clara's ancestors; a silver napkin ring of Coaker's which Smallwood uses at every meal; two fine Krieghoffs presented by the mining magnate M. J. Boylen; a huge portrait of Smallwood as patriarch with his grandchildren. Smallwood's self-esteem is unconcealed: a bronze bust of the Premier stares down the steps to the library; the walls of the corridor leading to his bedroom are lined with photographs of himself in the company of such notables as Richard Nixon and Francisco Franco.

Smallwood's own nook is in one corner of the huge living room, beside a picture window where, barricaded behind stacks of books and papers, he has installed his favourite, dark-brown, reclining armchair, a draftsman's table and light, and a battery of telephones. He spends most of his time at home there, reading, scribbling notes, barking orders into the telephone, and spinning tales to his grandchildren, who all live nearby and have unimpeded run of the house. Downstairs in his private library, a mahogany-panelled room half as large as the living room, Smallwood has stacked his books two deep. His prizes are the best collection of Newfoundland books, prints, and drawings in the world, including an original copy of the *Golden Fleece*, Sir William Vaughan's seventeenth-century account of life in the colony's first settlement, and a prime assortment of books and papers on his hero, John Wesley. Both collections will be the property of Memorial University.

As his own contribution to Newfoundlandiana, Smallwood, in the early sixties, began to collate a biographical dictionary of seven hundred outstanding Newfoundlanders. The work is not yet completed. Instead, late in 1966, he conceived the idea of bringing out Volume Three and Volume Four of *The Book of Newfoundland*, to span the thirty years since Volume One and Volume Two. He took five weeks off to work on the project, and personally edited each of the more than one thousand pages. The books appeared in November 1967, and the set sold for fifteen dollars. Their content was less remarkable than the speed with which they were produced.*

Already more Monarchist than the Queen, Smallwood in his sixties became more attached to ceremony than a regimental sergeant-major. He

---

* One striking difference between old and new was that this time Newfoundland businessmen cheerfully contributed $137,000 worth of advertising.

resurrected the tradition of formally presenting the Address in Reply to the Speech from the Throne to the Lieutenant Governor in a ceremony at Government House, and made Newfoundland the only parliament of the Commonwealth where all members wear morning coats to the opening day of each legislative session. He created a new tradition of state banquets for such notables as John Kenneth Galbraith, Farley Mowat, and Donald Gordon, and once spent $13,500 to celebrate Portugal Day by flying a troupe of entertainers over from Lisbon.

With the self-conscious compulsion of one who still thought of himself as a social outsider, Smallwood delighted in the baubles of status. He collected a dozen university degrees – two of them, from Dalhousie and the University of New Brunswick, garnered in a single day. He joined innumerable fraternal societies, among them the Orange Lodge and the Shriners, and studied avidly their arcane rules of procedure. He insisted upon being listed on the programs of all government functions with his full title: "The Hon. Joseph R. Smallwood, P.C., D.C.L., LL.D., D.LITT, M.H.A.," and a period misplaced provoked his wrath. Other honours flocked in unsought. When a whale was trapped inshore at Burgeo, it was nicknamed Moby Joe – until Moby Josephine was found to be more appropriate. Mr. and Mrs. Leonard Hynes of Twillingate, the parents of Newfoundland's 500,000th citizen, named their son Bernard Joseph and accepted a thousand dollar government cheque. The numerals for the general government telephone exchange, 5639, spelled out JOEY.

Smallwood's vanity made him an easy target for ridicule. Yet he honoured Newfoundland as much as himself. He talked Eleanor Roosevelt into opening the new Memorial University in 1961, and lured John Kenneth Galbraith (with a promise of a day's tuna fishing) into presiding over a Thinkers' Conference in 1965. His most spectacular attempt to put Newfoundland on the map came in 1967, when he proposed that Charles de Gaulle turn the sod at a proposed pulp-and-paper mill, partly financed by French capital. In Ottawa, the proposal was eagerly considered, since it meant de Gaulle would step on "Canadian" soil before landing at Quebec. The idea was quietly pigeonholed when an External Affairs official recollected that the owner of the mill was John Doyle.

Alone at the pinnacle of power, Smallwood began to draw apart from his own people. His trips abroad, to every country of Western Europe, to North Africa, the Middle East, India, Japan, and twice right round the world, became longer and more frequent. For his personal transportation, he acquired a twin-engine Otter, officially designated as a "water bomber" for forest fire control, and which at $450,000 cost more than the personal plane of the Premier of Ontario. He toured the province infrequently and attended only functions where he would be star and principal speaker. He relied more and more on second-hand information and on stored memories.

Yet, in characteristic paradox, Smallwood remained the most approachable politician in the country. Journalists, local or mainland, could reach him at any hour. At his office, or in his home, federal ministers or corporate vice-presidents still found themselves upstaged in mid-interview by a fisherman determinedly demanding instant action on a job, a misplaced pension, or an unemployment insurance claim. On behalf of any Newfoundlander, whatever his rank, Smallwood acted as a one-man ombudsman in tireless and explosive battle against a bureaucracy he himself had created. His own, private nickname for rank-and-file Newfoundlanders was "The Ragged Arsed Artillery." As a former gunner, he never felt superior to others still in the ranks.

Nor had advancing years added pomp to his passage. To inspect construction projects he splashed happily through mud up to his ankles, or clambered up scaffolding like an elderly but eager monkey. He abhorred stylish dress as if good tailoring were sinful, or worse, undemocratic, and once, for no apparent reason, he lashed out at textbook salesmen for dressing up like "archbishops in mufti." His own rare attempts at sartorial dignity were unsuccessful. Resplendent in a new suit, he turned up to greet the Queen at Gander Airport but marred the overall effect by a two-inch gash in his trousers through which glared a bright white pair of boxer shorts.

Smallwood's contempt for hypocrisy was as strong as ever, and his candour undimmed. In one memorable aside, which earned him a frosty stare the next time he and Premier John Robarts met, he told Tom

Alderman of *The Canadian*: "I'll be gone and some stuffed shirt like John Robarts who reads his speeches from a prepared text will be in. God – let's hope Newfoundland doesn't progress so much it gets a *Tory* like Robarts for Premier."* When one prominent St. John's citizen inquired about the likelihood of a certain cabinet minister being appointed to the bench, Smallwood replied with a grin: "Oh, you know X, even I couldn't appoint *him* a judge." At a Government House reception, Smallwood inquired of a prominent local Conservative, "Do you think I could get away with making Pickersgill President of Memorial?" The reply was noncommittal.

Perhaps the quintessential Smallwood of the sixties – part public entertainer, part folk hero – was best captured in the saga of his march on Moscow.

On April 18, 1965, together with former Vice-President Richard Nixon, Smallwood flew to Helsinki to inspect the plant of United Paper Mills of Finland, a company that was a proposed partner in the latest paper mill venture and for which Nixon was acting as legal counsel. Once their business was done, Nixon suggested they drive across the border to Leningrad and go on to Moscow by train. They toured the Kremlin, Lenin's tomb, paused to gaze at the plaque which marked the grave of the IWW Leader Bill Haywood, whom Smallwood had interviewed forty years before, and then pushed on to Moscow University. There the vice-rector, as Smallwood later related to the legislature, "engaged in a very insulting and provocative speech of welcome to both of us, but aimed essentially at Nixon." In his own reply to the rector, Smallwood proposed that Nixon and Khruschev run for the presidency of each other's country, "which joke didn't go over very well, or very enthusiastically." Late that evening, on impulse, Smallwood and Nixon set off to call on the deposed Premier. They got as far as his apartment building, where female commissionaires halted their progress; as a calling card, Nixon, who was the principal mover of the sortie, left a scribbled message of greeting. After a stopover at Gallipoli, to take in the ceremonies which marked the fiftieth

---

* Amity was quickly restored: Robarts put it down to Joey being Joey.

anniversary of the allied landing, Smallwood came home to St. John's, to a hero's welcome.

By now, whatever he did was news. Except for Diefenbaker, he was the most quotable public figure in the country, and an inexhaustible source of good copy. Television might have been created for him. He accepted every invitation to be interviewed and entranced viewers with his provocative quips and tall tales of the old Newfoundland. On one memorable occasion, he accomplished the near-impossible feat of reducing W. A. C. Bennett, the Premier of British Columbia, to bewildered silence during a half-hour TV debate between the two of them. A Canadian public, starved for heroes, took him to its heart. In *Saturday Night*, Kildare Dobbs described Smallwood and René Lévesque as the country's only genuine heroes, "passionate, brave, magnetic, witty, intelligent, and full of guile."

His own public more often saw, and experienced, the other side of Smallwood's character. He was far too powerful a personality to be contained within the tight little world of Newfoundland, or to be constrained by her gentle uncompetitive people. The single-minded dynamism and willpower that Smallwood applied to industrial projects or to politics he applied, with equal lack of restraint, to human beings. In public, he was openly contemptuous of his subordinates; in private, he tolerated no personal relationship except sycophancy. Once, in the legislature, he shouted to a minister, who had risen to reply to a question, "Sit down, don't answer that." He made public policy on personal impulse. After the President of the Newfoundland Federation of Labour called him a "dictator" for his 1959 labour legislation, Smallwood refused for four years to accept the Federation's annual brief to the Government. Quick to score off others, Smallwood tolerated little humour at his own expense and his colleagues, when they ribbed him, did so with painful circumspection.

The effect of such bullying was destructive even to those not directly involved. "I have detected for some little time now," commented the

Opposition Leader James Greene in a speech to the legislature on February 13, 1962, "and seen instances in many places of a fear coming over our people, a fear of many people in many walks of life that they cannot stand up publicly and take their place in the public life of this country, cannot make their voices known for fear of repercussion." Another Conservative Member, Rex Renouf, said in March 1964, "There is, I cannot say how, this fear, this nervousness. I don't know how it commenced, but somehow or other the people of this province feel it, whenever anybody remotely connected with themselves is in government employment."

Fear in itself was nothing new in the island. For centuries, Newfoundlanders had suffered the untrammelled power of "fishing admirals," of merchants, of colonial governments, and of clerics. But systematic intimidation by a political machine which responded to the will of a single man was new and terrifying. Political debate, once a bawdy Newfoundland art form, was driven underground, to be voiced only in taverns and private homes. The Official Opposition, resigned to perpetual defeat, lapsed into silence. The miasma of fear pervaded everywhere: in anti-government letters to the editor that were signed only by "interested citizen," "Terra Nova," and "Housewife"; in pallid newspaper editorials and, even more tellingly, in the timidity of the local outlets of the CBC which, unlike the commercial media, were beyond the reach of direct political pressure. Businessmen, once the community's natural leaders, withdrew themselves from involvement in political affairs. Unlike Laval under Duplessis, Memorial University remained as inarticulate as it was politically impotent.

To oppose Smallwood in public was to risk financial retribution. The entire economy rested upon government spending, and this, whether federal or provincial, Smallwood controlled. He used the power of the purse with little restraint. Friends were rewarded and enemies persecuted. If Newfoundlanders feared Smallwood, they did so with good reason.

As much as fear, corruption had been a constant in Newfoundland politics. Under the Liberal Government of the late fifties and early sixties, it became an institution. The Liberal Party's demand for election funds was insatiable, and the penalties for niggardliness were severe. A mainland construction company, which forwarded a contribution of $15,000 instead of the requested $30,000, was refused contracts for three years. A tavern owner, who refused to pay his annual assessment after it had been doubled to $3,000, was stripped of his licence within a week; he held out for six months before capitulating. Most people paid without quibbling. In the 1966 provincial election, Liberal spending exceeded $300,000, a staggering amount for so poor a province.

Except where federal funds made public tenders mandatory, the government's purchasing and construction policies were tailor-made for favouritism. A clutch of companies of inscrutable heritage, among them Bonavista Catering, and the oddly titled but flourishing Sanitary Products Limited, secured an astonishing volume of government business. Between 1958 and 1965, when, to the relief of his Departments of Finance and Public Works, Smallwood halted the practice, some $100 million worth of construction contracts was awarded without open tenders, and on a cost-plus basis to two firms, both barely distinguishable from the Liberal Party. The system used was leaseback, a tax-saving device common in private industry but which cost government ten to twenty per cent above normal tenders.*

The real cost of corruption was moral. Cynicism by government invited public cynicism. The sale of liquor licences, as Greene once commented in a debate, "is a matter so unconcealed, done with such candour, that it really surprises." One Liberal candidate went to court to claim a $32,000 payment promised him in return for a cocktail bar licence. The case was dismissed.

Not least because he knew it would increase his hold on those around him, Smallwood threw open the doors to conflict of interest. As one colleague was moved to comment, in private, "Every king needs to have some courtiers whom he can afford to despise." Ministers held partnerships in law firms which depended upon government business; they were

---

* Even so, the practice could in part be justified. Only by granting contracts to Newfoundland-owned firms could Smallwood hope to build within the province industries capable of competing on an even basis with mainland competition.

owners or shareholders in firms which sold products and supplies to the government, and which competed for government contracts. The Liberal Party operated almost as a state within a state. Its brotherhood took privilege for granted, and enjoyed the best the province had to offer, from luxurious weekends at government-owned hunting and fishing lodges, to free airplane trips and tuna-fishing expeditions.

As king, Smallwood stamped out the slightest sign of opposition. Journalists who dared to write critical articles or who failed to give a speech by the Premier its due were denounced in the legislature as "scallawags," "drunken fools," "scoundrels," and "mischievous-minded persons with poverty-stricken minds." The *Evening Telegram* was offered, but refused, $60,000 of government job printing if it would drop Horwood as political columnist. The *Sunday Herald* dismissed a journalist hostile to the government after a cabinet minister protested to the management.

Acquiescence was justified. Smallwood in full fury was a terrifying figure. Convinced that two hapless Company of Young Canadians volunteers had entered the tiny outport of Brig Bay to spread NDP propaganda, he despatched to Pearson a blistering letter demanding their removal. The two soon departed. In 1965, in the midst of a headlong rush to complete the trans-island highway and so fulfil an election promise, Smallwood exploded in outrage after the town council of Deer Lake protested that an asphalt boiler was being set up in the town's main street. If the boiler were removed, the entire paving schedule would be ruined, he said, and he would "throw in the sponge, resign, get out." The boiler remained where it was, spewing out noxious fumes. "What else can we do?" the mayor of Deer Lake asked reporters.

Only rarely did outsiders see their folk hero cast as a domestic tyrant. The most notable such occasion was Smallwood's encounter with Donald Fleming during the 1962 federal election, an incident that aroused sufficient outrage among the Canadian public to affect materially the outcome of the election. At the time Smallwood thought it no more than conventional small-arms fire.

On June 6, Fleming flew to St. John's to speak to the local Rotary Club. The company had already assembled at the Newfoundland Hotel when Smallwood, elsewhere in the building, learned that Fleming would be speaking about devaluation of the dollar, the principal issue of the election campaign. In a towering rage, he scribbled out a note to the luncheon chairman, threatening that if Fleming spoke, "or even gets to his feet," the Government would cancel its invitation to host the Rotary Convention the following week. At the chairman's embarrassed but urgent behest, Fleming remained seated. Once back on the mainland, the Finance Minister let fly. At a press conference in Halifax he called Smallwood "dictatorial," and added, "I feel sorry for the officers of Rotary." They had told him, he said, "We have to live here, and we're all in business."

Through the balance of the campaign, Diefenbaker, happy to score off his old opponent, made the St. John's incident an integral part of every speech, and taunted Pearson for his failure to repudiate Smallwood. Aware of the damage done the Liberal image, Pearson had in fact done what he could to make amends. After Smallwood's outburst, Pearson got his aide, Tom Kent, to telephone Pickersgill to ask him to try to wring an apology from Smallwood. Well aware of the limits of his influence on the Premier, Pickersgill declined to make the attempt.

Fleming, however, could take care of himself, and he lived elsewhere. The most vivid example of the changed nature of Smallwood's hold upon his electorate was the letter he sent during the September 1966 provincial campaign to the voters of Stephenville, a town threatened by economic collapse after the closing of the U.S. Air Force base there.

The minute [they] left it became my job to save that part of Newfoundland from unemployment, destitution, dole, despair, and finally the disappearance of much of its population. . . . Will you help me to do it? Or do you want to send me a message saying, "Stop. We don't need your help." . . . That will be the answer you will give me if you elect the Tory candidate, or the Independent Liberal candidate. If you want to send me a message saying: "Yes, Joe, we want you to keep on working hard for this District and the people in it," the only way you can send me that message is to elect the Liberal Party's candidate.

The heavy-handed blackmail of that letter paralleled Smallwood's "not one red cent" speech to the voters of Ferryland seventeen years earlier. The difference between the two incidents was not so much the Liberal victory in Stephenville in 1966, compared with Greg Power's defeat in 1949, as that the Conservatives this time could find not a single voter prepared to sign an affidavit of protest.

In the 1966 election, Smallwood reached the apex of his political power. He reduced the hapless Conservatives to three members out of forty-two; he already held all seven federal Liberal seats. Behind him lay seventeen years of unchallenged authority: ahead of him lay the plaudits of the Centennial Year.

Yet the basis of his power was beginning to crumble. A generation was coming of age to whom Confederation was simply a chapter in the history books, and the Valdmanis saga was something their parents occasionally laughed about. Confronted by the students of Memorial University, Smallwood for the first time in his life faced an audience that was beyond his power of communication and persuasion. These young Newfoundlanders saw their Premier not as a revolutionary, but as a reactionary.

In only one area of policy during the first half decade of the sixties did the old "crazy radical" show his true colours. In far-off Labrador, Smallwood pursued his own vision of the north.

21

The Land Joe Gave to John

If God, as the saying goes, gave Labrador to Cain, then He must have had Joey Smallwood in mind when He made it.[*] The land fulfils the man. Its size, the vastness of its resources, and the mammoth problems of developing them match the scope of Smallwood's imagination, and his gifts as visionary, builder, and promoter. Labrador's other advantage was to be untouched. Whatever Smallwood has built there will stand as a permanent monument to him.

"Our northwest territory," as he likes to call it, captured Smallwood on his first visit there, in the summer of 1949, when he toured the Iron Ore of Canada project at Knob Lake, and flew over the Churchill Falls. Ever since then, he has been obsessed by it, at times to the disadvantage of insular Newfoundland, for even Smallwood has only so much energy to spare. As Smallwood sees it, Labrador is the one lucky break that nature gave to Newfoundlanders, a compensation for their climate, isolation, and sparse natural resources. "It is our chance, perhaps our one chance," he has said, "to give something back to Canada for all she has given us. It

---

[*] Another version of the familiar aphorism is: "God made the world in six days, and on the seventh, sailed inshore and hurled rocks at Labrador."

is our chance to stand on our own feet, to do something ourselves. You don't think we like accepting welfare cheques, do you?"

In recognizing so early the psychological as well as economic importance of Labrador, Smallwood was once again too far ahead of his people. To most Newfoundlanders, his northern vision was too nebulous, and his chances of realizing it too doubtful to take seriously. The bleak, cliff-bound shoreline was all they knew of Labrador, and even there the once-flourishing Labrador fishery had died away. When Smallwood came to power, the land beyond the coast had scarcely been explored, an endless, unpromising expanse of stagnant marshes and barrens, splashed with pink-grey rocks, and interspersed with stands of stunted spruce. In winter the temperature fell to sixty below zero; during the short summer, a man could scarcely breathe for dense clouds of mosquitoes and blackflies. Only Smallwood believed that anything could be done with such a country, and only he would have dared try. In Labrador, down to the mid-sixties, Smallwood was as much a solitary visionary as he had been at the start of the Confederation campaign.

No aspect of Smallwood's development of Labrador has been more controversial than his choice of the mining promoter John Christopher Doyle as his principal partner. He has defended Doyle frequently and hotly, and perhaps never so expressively as in an exchange with the Conservative Leader Malcolm Hollett in the legislature in May 1959:

> SMALLWOOD: He is the greatest promoter in this century in North America. What Newfoundland needs is exactly this kind of promoter.
>
> HOLLETT: He made a fortune.
>
> SMALLWOOD: Let us hope he makes ten, provided also he gives us fast development . . . that is the system, that is the incentive, to get industry rolling, to get production started, to get men employed. Lord Rothermere, Sir Eric Bowater, name them, all of them the same, Beaverbrook. If John Doyle makes a fortune out of

> promoting and getting development in Labrador he
> will only be doing what Jules Timmins has done.
>
> HOLLETT: Surely the Premier is not putting Doyle on the same
> level with Timmins and Rothermere?
>
> SMALLWOOD: They are all promoters . . . the promoter becomes
> respectable after he has made his fortune. Whoever
> became a millionaire in this world today by teaching
> Sunday School?

Neither John Doyle nor Joey Smallwood resembled a Sunday School teacher.

A large measure of Doyle's undoubted charm, and a major reason for his appeal to one so impatient with hypocrisy as Smallwood, was that he never pretended to be more than he was – a hustler who hit several jackpots. His other outstanding characteristic was an enormous zest for living. Rotund and manicured, he was a connoisseur of wines and foods, who flew prize Newfoundland salmon to London to be smoked properly, and then had it flown back again. In his expensively rather than impeccably tailored suits, he looked like the cartoon image of the mining promoter and lived up to it by puffing on as many as twelve *La Primadora* cigars a day. His tastes ran to the raffish baroque, and were displayed to greatest effect in his personal four-engined DC-6, its interior fitted with mahogany panels, purple and grey plush seats, and a crystal chandelier which eventually had to be removed for fear it would be shattered by turbulence. In addition, the plane boasted a bar, a kitchen, and a bathroom complete with shower. In his Ottawa penthouse, he installed and exuberantly played a vast Three Manual Allen Organ, while at the El Panama Hilton, of which he was part owner, he set up what was reputedly the largest organ in the world, a composite of instruments from the Warner Brothers' Theatre in Atlantic City, and Loew's Theatre in New Rochelle. As hostelries, he fancied Le Crillon in Paris, the Savoy in London, the Drake in New York, and the Queen Elizabeth in Montreal.

Until his path crossed Smallwood's, Doyle's career was much like that of scores of other moderately successful, immoderately lucky promoters. Born of Canadian parents in Chicago, in 1911, he worked his way

through the University of Chicago and served overseas in North Africa
and Italy, where he acquired the rank of Captain and a fluent command
of French and Italian. After the war, he plunged into mining promotion,
and in 1949 bought up a small, 108-year-old company in Joliette,
Quebec, which he renamed, "because it sounds the same in French and
English," Canadian Javelin Foundry and Machine Works. As such, the
company became a legend to penny-mining investors. Doyle also
acquired the Boon-Strachan Coal Company of Montreal, and it was in
search of business for that firm that he flew to Newfoundland in 1952.

His timing could not have been better. Valdmanis's star was on
the wane, and the Premier needed a new partner. Smallwood was also
new enough in office and uncertain enough of his own talents to be
awed by a captain of industry.* Best of all, Doyle arrived at a moment
when Smallwood had something more substantial to offer than rhetoric –
a genuine, and large, iron ore deposit in Labrador.

Although it is not an honour enshrined on its boardroom wall, the credit
for Doyle's ascendancy in Labrador belongs to the Iron Ore Company of
Canada. The presence of specular hematite ore in Labrador had first been
noted in the 1860s by an Oblate missionary, and later confirmed in 1896,
through a survey undertaken by Dr. A. P. Low of the Geological Survey
of Canada. Although Low found millions of tons of ore, he wrote sadly:
"This area may long remain one of the undeveloped resources of the
country." Quite aside from the lack of markets, the reason was the prohibitive cost of extracting the mineral from that bleak wilderness. After
World War II, the situation changed radically. Economic expansion and
defence spending created an almost unlimited market for steel. At the
same time, the Paley Report, though in fact wrongly, predicted a worldwide shortage of iron ore, as well as of other minerals. This fortuitous

---

* He has never entirely lost this trait. A conspicuously unsuccessful businessman himself, Smallwood has always been impressed by anyone who has
succeeded in the one field where he failed.

combination of demand and supply inspired the Canadian mining magnate Jules Timmins to join forces with a consortium of U.S. steel producers to form the Iron Ore Company of Canada, and launch the first Labrador iron ore project at Knob Lake, astride the northern Quebec-Labrador boundary. It took five years and $250 million to develop the mine. When completed, it was a milestone in Canada's postwar resources boom comparable to the oil discoveries in Alberta, the uranium rush to Northern Ontario, and the aluminum smelter at Kitimat, B.C.

Under the terms of its lease, Iron Ore of Canada was required to return to the Newfoundland Government ten per cent of its 24,000 square mile Labrador holding every five years. In 1952, the company picked the wrong strip to relinquish. In one of the classic blunders of Canadian mining history, the company handed back a 2,400 square mile strip to the south of Wabush Lake, chosen because it was supposedly barren of mineral deposits. In fact, as the Newfoundland Deputy Minister of Mines, Claude Howse, noticed when the company officials pointed the territory out to him on an unedited company map, the land around Wabush showed magnetic anomalies similar to those in known ore deposits in land nearby retained by the company. Howse reported this to Smallwood. As soon as the deal was concluded, Smallwood transferred the Wabush territory to the government-owned corporation, NALCO. What he needed now was someone to develop it. Within a month Doyle was knocking at his door. On his trip to Newfoundland, Doyle had chanced to sit next to Howse. By the time the plane landed in St. John's, he had lost all interest in coal.

Doyle exerted all his salesman's charm and skill upon Smallwood. Even more persuasive, he offered an advance payment of $250,000 in cash. As one minister remembers: "It was the first time anyone had actually given us money instead of taking it." In exchange for Canadian Javelin shares, Smallwood agreed to sell NALCO to Doyle, and with it the Wabush ore.

Although this particular scheme foundered when, in what was to become a familiar pattern, the Montreal and Toronto stock exchanges

delisted Canadian Javelin for "failure to comply with a request for information deemed to be in the public interest," Doyle evolved a new plan.
Instead of NALCO, he was given rights to the key Wabush Lake section.
In the summer of 1954, his geologists confirmed the existence of up to
two billion tons of ore. As Doyle exuberantly put it, it was as if "Iron
Ore of Canada had invested $150 million in Canadian Javelin" – the $150
million being the cost of the company's railway from its Knob Lake mine
to the tidewater port of Sept-Îles, which passed less than fifty miles from
Doyle's property.

That same summer, the Knob Lake mine reached completion. On
August 1, Smallwood and Maurice Duplessis met at Sept-Îles. As 275
American and Canadian bank and corporation presidents, vice-presidents,
and board chairmen watched, the two Premiers pressed buttons which
sent carloads of ore mined on either side of the border swinging sideways
to dump into a waiting ore-carrier bound for Philadelphia. The next such
ceremony, Smallwood resolved, would be all his own.

To bring off a second mine, and one which unlike Knob Lake and its
satellite town of Schefferville would be entirely within Newfoundland-
Labrador, Smallwood needed Doyle. No other promoter of substance was
interested. While the deposit at Wabush was huge, it was low grade, its ore
thirty-five per cent compared to Knob Lake's fifty-five per cent. In addition to the heavy costs of ordinary mining development, to market such
ore would require an expensive process of beneficiation (to upgrade the
iron content) and pelletization (to reduce the raw lumps to concentrated
pellets that could be readily refined in the blast furnaces). Such extra costs
made exploitation uneconomic, even for Iron Ore of Canada, which had
its own thirty-five per cent ore deposits and which, because owned by
steel companies, had an assured market for its product.

To Smallwood it was unthinkable that the first major mineral discovery in the province, since the base metals find at Buchans a half-century
earlier, should remain undeveloped. That the experts all forecast failure
only, predictably, strengthened his resolve. Together with Doyle, he set
out to develop Wabush.

Almost the least of their problems were the traditional ones of finance and economics. Much worse, they were outsiders trying to break into the traditional horizontal monopoly by which the North American steel producers controlled their own sources of iron ore. To raise the money he needed to develop the mine, Doyle would have to first secure, as collateral, long-term sales contracts from the U.S. steel producers, the only customers able to absorb his vast output; they in turn had no intention of helping an outsider to break their own cartel.

It took Smallwood and Doyle six steel-nerved years to break the ring during which they engaged in a massive and perilous game of bluff. With one hand Doyle negotiated with German and British steel producers and thereby sent shivers of alarm through boardrooms in Pittsburgh, Cleveland, and Hamilton at the prospect of trans-Atlantic competition; with the other, he tried to bring Wabush as close to production as he could on his own, and so compel the steel companies to deal with him. Although he pared costs as much as he could, Doyle's outlay mounted to some $5 million, a sum which he, or Canadian Javelin investors at least, stood to lose unless the steel producers could be bluffed into a deal.

Smallwood's initial contribution was his rhetoric. He described Wabush Ore as "so rich a man could scoop it up in his bare hands," and called it, in more familiar style, "the world's greatest iron ore discovery." More decisively, in 1955, he unlocked the doors to Newfoundland's treasury.

The crucial decision demanded of him in 1955, and which began his real partnership with Doyle, was the promoter's request for a government guarantee of a $16.5 million bond issue, a sum that equalled half the total provincial debt. It was also the amount Doyle reckoned he needed to build a spur railway to the mine. The magnitude of the risk, since if Doyle failed, Newfoundland would be for practical purposes bankrupt, staggered even Smallwood. For months Doyle argued and pleaded with him. He won in the end by a bluff of his own. Without the bond guarantee, said Doyle, he would have to abandon the project. As Smallwood remembers the choice, circumstances forced him into "Beggars can't be choosers."

Once his mind was made up, Smallwood cast away all doubts. In the debate on the bond guarantee, he lauded Doyle as "brilliant, industrious, able," and balanced this with his blueprint for survival if Doyle defaulted: "We won't have any hesitation or remorse. We shall just sell it, just sell it at once, to the highest bidder." The debate was highlighted also by Smallwood's claim that the *Société de Banque Suisse* had invested $4.8 million in the venture, an outburst that forced the wardens of Zurich to explain that the sum involved nothing more than the purchase of Canadian Javelin stock by an unnamed investor. The bank did not disclose that the investor was Doyle.

By April 1956, Doyle had twice announced "firm agreements" to sell ore to a syndicate of German steel companies, as well as a new set of negotiations with British steel producers. Of the bond issue itself, only $2 million was sold. Doyle explained that he halted sales after he had discovered that the bonds were being snapped up by steel companies trying to win control of Canadian Javelin; a subsidiary reason was that the New York Stock Exchange disbarred Stahl, Miles, and Company, the investment house handling Doyle's issue.

Nevertheless, the project rolled forward. In 1956, serious negotiations opened between Doyle and the North American steel producers; in 1957, a new company, Wabush Iron, was formed to buy out Doyle and itself develop the ore. Though the final agreement was still two years away, the extent of Doyle's victory was staggering. In return for the Wabush ore property, the steel producers (a consortium which included American, German, and Italian companies, as well as Canadian-owned Stelco and Dosco) agreed to give Doyle a $2.5 million down payment, and annual royalties beginning at $1.8 million and rising to a maximum of $3.2 million after five years. On a shoestring, he had pulled off one of the great coups of postwar Canadian mining.

For Newfoundland and Smallwood, Doyle's coup in fact meant two new mines. On May 3, 1959, Smallwood delightedly told the legislature that now that pelletization had been proved feasible, Iron Ore Company of Canada had decided to develop its own low-grade deposit at Carol Lake, four miles from Wabush. "I've always wanted to move a mountain," said Smallwood on July 12, 1962, as he pressed a plunger to set off seventy-five tons of dynamite embedded in a hill above Carol Lake. Soon afterwards, Iron Ore of Canada began shipping ten million tons of ore south each year.

Two years later, on July 20, 1964, Smallwood presided at the formal opening of Wabush Iron's $235 million project. "Never in the history of Newfoundland's industry," he told the assembled dignitaries, "was so much owed to the effort of one man." Unhappily, Doyle heard the praise second-hand. He was that day detained in Hartford, Connecticut, awaiting sentence after pleading guilty to a violation of the U.S. Security Regulations. A week later, Doyle jumped bail rather than serve a three months' jail sentence.

Perhaps the best, and certainly the most eloquent, description of Doyle's style as promoter was written by the referee appointed by the New York County Supreme Court in 1961 to settle Javelin stockholders' claims against their president. "Doyle's development of Labrador," he wrote, "affords an epic tableau of economic pioneering in the Canadian wilderness, accompanied by all the usual features of pioneering; swashbuckling, lawlessness, disdain for convention, crude improvisation, even commercial piracy . . . and by the applications of normal United States standards of corporate morality, appears at best devious and doubtful, and at worst, corrupt and venal." Doyle himself, the referee continued, "emerges from the tableau less like Cecil Rhodes and more like Erroll Flynn portraying that role."

Under Doyle's tutelage, several members of the Newfoundland Government were introduced to the intricacies of penny-mining speculation and, aided by advance notice of the erratic gyrations of Canadian Javelin stock, the wiser ones netted small fortunes. (Insider trading in shares of the eminently respectable British Newfoundland Development Company Brinco was equally heavy. At the 1966 federal-provincial conference, when Ottawa announced the abolition of taxes on private power utilities, a move which materially benefited Brinco, one Newfoundland minister stunned a federal cabinet member by telling him: "I guessed this was coming a week ago and bought up ten thousand shares. How much do you think they'll go up?" The federal minister managed not to hear the question.)

Smallwood was no more disapproving of this than he was of patronage*. As for Doyle's difficulties with the law, he viewed these as minor skirmishes in an epic battle for development. "I hope some day," he told the legislature, "to tell the full story of the fantastic war of opposition to John Doyle on both sides of the border." Smallwood had the steel companies in mind.

In fact, a large part of the opposition came from within Doyle's own camp. He collected about him a picaresque collection of characters whose motives – a share of the lush Wabush royalties – were as uncomplicated as their activities were unscrupulous. One last-minute flight check of Doyle's DC-6 showed that the hydraulic system had been slashed; during one flight, an engine burst mysteriously into flames. Some of the lawsuits his associates launched against Doyle seemed less those of injured claimants than of disappointed suitors.

More credible opponents were investors in Canadian Javelin and the stock exchanges. Canadian Javelin was delisted by the Canadian exchanges in 1953 and by the U.S. Securities Commission in 1956, which estimated that boiler-shop operation that dumped quantities of Canadian-Javelin stock on the U.S. market, had cost American investors $30 million. The Commission lodged a suit against Doyle for violation of security regulations, and then dropped the suit, and removed Canadian Javelin from its restricted list after Doyle agreed to a ban on boiler shops and to open his books for inspection. Smallwood became party to this agreement after a Commission official, Edward Jaegerman, flew to St. John's in June 1959 for a day of talks with Smallwood and his cabinet.

Early the next year, Doyle was once again entangled in the law. He was arrested in his suite at the Queen Elizabeth Hotel and spent the night in jail. The next day bail was set at $100,000. Doyle wrote out a cheque, and, while he waited in the courtroom, two policemen drove to the nearest

---

* Smallwood, it came to light, after he left office, had himself heavily invested in Brinco, aided by an interest-free loan from the Bank of Montreal.

branch of the Royal Bank of Canada and cashed it in dollar bills. The suit was as flamboyant as the gesture. James Benning, convicted in 1951 as a Russian spy and later acquitted, charged that Doyle had defrauded Canadian Javelin of $4.8 million worth of stocks which he had transferred through the *Société de Banque Suisse* to the European Fiduciary Corporation of Liechtenstein. In St. John's, Smallwood said, "I find it hard to believe, and I am shocked." The case was thrown out of court.

Other legal troubles remained. In 1960, Doyle settled out of court a suit against him by Canadian Javelin's Vice-President, Victor Geffine, for alleged non-payment of $6.8 million worth of commissions. Geffine subsequently was made President of Javelin's subsidiary, Canadian Jubilee. In July 1961, Doyle ended a three-year-old suit before the New York Stock Exchange by agreeing to pay shareholders' claims of $3.8 million worth of company funds. In May 1963 the Department of National Revenue filed a claim against him for non-payment of $3.6 million worth of back taxes. Then, on August 7, 1963, a judge at Hartford, Connecticut, opened a sealed grand jury indictment against Doyle and three associates on eleven counts of violation of security regulations. Doyle had known of this indictment four months earlier, and forewarned Smallwood of it. Even for him, Smallwood's reaction was impetuous. As he recorded in his diary:*

April 24, 1963: Tonight JCD phoned from Toronto. He's in trouble again. Court in New England. I phoned Lanford, U.S. Consul General. Am to phone Robert Kennedy tomorrow.

April 25: Tried to get Kennedy on phone. Wired him.

April 26: Wire from Robert Kennedy. Went to New York and left for Washington.

April 27: Saw Robert Kennedy in his office. About three-quarters of an hour. Very pleasant. Very keen and I would say, a very bright fellow.

The Attorney General was also unyielding. He flatly rejected Smallwood's appeal that he halt the court proceedings, and rejected as

---

* Smallwood has kept a diary, or more accurately an *aide-mémoire*, for every year since 1962, and sporadically for a few years before then.

well his claim that the U.S. Securities Commission had given Doyle a guarantee against further proceedings. Kennedy made no comment on Smallwood's conduct in attempting to interfere, on behalf of a friend, in the legal processes of another country.

The origins of the Hartford suit were obscure. The alleged offences took place between 1955 and 1959, long enough ago for the cases against the other three defendants to be dropped. The eleven counts against Doyle remained, and on February 3, 1964, he pleaded guilty to a single offence, that of "causing" fifty unregistered shares to be mailed to an investor. In delivering sentence Judge Emmett Clair noted that Smallwood and six of his ministers had taken out affidavits claiming that Jaegerman had promised Doyle legal immunity against old offences during his 1959 visit to St. John's, a claim that Jaegerman flatly denied. The judge also observed that testimonials to Doyle's character had been composed by Associate Defence Minister Pierre Sévigny, Chancellor of Memorial University Lord Thomson of Fleet, members of the Newfoundland Supreme Court, as well as "editors of newspapers and religious personages." He went on to comment, "If the law means anything at all it means that all persons must comply with it." He then sentenced Doyle to three months and a $5,000 fine. On July 20 Doyle jumped bail and forfeited his $100,000 bond.* Publicly he explained, "If you don't feel you have done wrong, would you accept it?" Privately he made it plain that once in jail he feared that disaffected shareholders would lay fresh charges.

On the day of the judgment Smallwood expressed full confidence in his partner: "Mr. Doyle will be back and forth to St. John's in the normal way. His decisions will be carried out to the letter." A week later, in a show of confidence, he flew off from the federal-provincial conference at Ottawa aboard Doyle's DC-6. In his stand he was motivated as much by gratitude as by loyalty and friendship.

---

* The Canadian-U.S. extradition agreement excludes security violations.

Until Doyle brought off Wabush, and indirectly Carol Lake, development of Labrador's iron ore had benefited Quebec to the virtual exclusion of Newfoundland. That province secured most of the employment at Knob Lake as well as two new towns, Schefferville and Gagnonville. Thanks principally to Doyle, by the mid-sixties Newfoundland had two mines of its own, a 240,000 horsepower power station at Twin Falls built to serve them, and two townsites. Even these advances had been painfully won. The two ore companies, Wabush Iron and Iron Ore of Canada, had each at first wanted to build their own wholly owned railway spur lines which would have run about a mile apart, over some forty miles. Common sense and what Smallwood described as "the greatest castigating you ever heard" finally prevailed over private enterprise and a single, jointly owned line was built. Smallwood failed, however, to get the rival companies to agree on a sharing of municipal costs, so that instead of a single townsite each company built its own two tiny clearings, four miles apart in the midst of a total wilderness. These towns were Labrador City, with a population of six thousand, and Wabush, with about four thousand. That Wabush should be the smaller of the two precipitated Smallwood's most violent clash with the steel companies and his first battle with Quebec. His only allies in that fight were Pickersgill and Doyle.

Wabush was the smaller town because it lacked a pelletizing plant similar to the one built by Iron Ore Company at Labrador City. Instead, the Wabush Company announced that its plant, designed to employ some two hundred, would be situated at tidewater, at Pointe-Noire, Quebec, on the Gulf of St. Lawrence.

Incensed at the prospective loss of a desperately needed industry, Smallwood launched into a bitter battle to keep the plant in Newfoundland. It began, as he recorded in his diary, on February 19, 1963. "Keith Benson and two of Pickands-Mather [the company building the Wabush mine] lawyers over tonight. Benson 'broke' that Wabush Iron intend to build their pelletizing plant at Pointe Noire. I told him this means war."

Though Smallwood did not know it then, he had almost no room to manoeuvre. Wabush Iron had already promised to put the plant at

Pointe-Noire. Straight economics dictated the decision. It was strengthened by the Quebec Government's leverage as a major steel purchaser,
and by the opportunity given Wabush Iron to curry favour at a time when
Quebec planned to build its own steel mill to compete with private steel
companies.

Three weeks later the crisis boiled over:

March 7: Letter from Keith Benson. A crude attempt by him to bluff,
bully, and blackmail me into accepting Pointe Noire for their pelletizing plant. Tonight had Miss Duff come to the flat and I dictated a
scathing letter to Benson. Phoned JCD at Montreal and read both
letters. He phoned Benson and told him he'd have to give in.

March 8: Jean Lesage from Quebec this afternoon on pelletizing
plant and for three quarters of an hour we had it hot and heavy. He was
beside himself. Threatened and wild talk. I told him he was wasting his
breath. The plant was going to Wabush. Wants to see me and I agreed
to meet him in Montreal Saturday next week. He told me that the
power deal was off. He'd tax our ore as it entered Quebec. In fact –
war. I have never been more determined to win.

March 16 [Montreal]: 9:30 A.M. met Jean Lesage at his suite, Queen
Elizabeth. We talked alone till 12:30. One hour on pelletizing plant.
One hour on Hamilton power. One hour on politics and bicultural-
ism, etc. He surrendered absolutely on pelletizing plant when I stood
resolutely for Wabush Lake. He is now all for the power scheme. He
will make a joint statement at Ottawa later at a federal-provincial conference. He is going to burn his bridges in this election.

Smallwood was sadly mistaken. For Lesage had, in fact, retreated not
one inch on the pellet plant. Nevertheless, Smallwood proudly told the
legislature, on April 26, 1963: "The pellet plant will go to Wabush . . . I
am prepared to stand or fall on this." He stood, as he soon discovered,
alone.

May 6: Bob Winters phoned. [V. W.] Scully [President] of Stelco had
seen him on pellet plant. I gave him no encouragement. Pickersgill

phoned. Walter Gordon had phoned him to say [Frank] Sherman [President] of Dofasco had made a friendly approach on pellet plant.

May 8: Winters phoned again today on behalf of Scully of Stelco. Also wired me. John Sherwin of PM [Pickands Mather] in Cleveland phoned. JWP [Pickersgill] phoned from Ottawa.

May 16 [Ottawa]: John Sherwin at 9:00 A.M. All he had was the same old stuff on pellet plant. I said No. At Doyle's new flat.

June 18 [Ottawa]: House of Commons. Lunch with Pickersgill in his office. Dinner at Rideau Club. Pickersgill, Mitchell Sharp, and [Bud] Drury. We talked over pellet plant and Doyle's project and the hydro project, all with a view to a satisfactory compromise. Phoned Doyle who arrived from Montreal.

June 19 [Ottawa]: Pickersgill came at 9:00 A.M. for one hour on pellet plant. Emotional. In the House of Commons Walter Gordon getting a hard time and I half think he deserves it.

At that meeting in Smallwood's Chateau Laurier suite, Pickersgill, with tears in his eyes, told him that his battle for the pellet plant was hopeless. Wabush Iron had told the cabinet that if Smallwood continued to insist that they locate the pellet plant in Newfoundland rather than in Quebec, they would instead move the industry out of the country entirely, to Erie, Pennsylvania. Faced with a possible loss of a major industry for Canada, the federal cabinet was now overwhelmingly against him, Pickersgill sadly told Smallwood. Pickersgill also added a sage word of advice. By surrendering on the pellet plant Smallwood would store up credit which he could draw on to extract federal aid on other projects. Smallwood was enough of a realist to see the sense in making the best of a bad defeat. Because of his public outburst, however, a face-saving compromise was needed. Doyle provided it:

June 20: Over to Doyle's. Then lunch with Pickersgill in his office. JCD's tonight, and we worked out a good compromise for Wabush. I told it afterwards to Pickersgill, who likes it. [Smallwood misread Pickersgill as much as he had Lesage. Pickersgill was noncommittal about Doyle's proposal.]

June 21: Lunch with Pickersgill. At 12 noon I met John Sherwin of Pickands Mather and Scully of Stelco in my room at my hotel, and we came to a final agreement on the pellet plant and NALCO.

The agreement gave Wabush Iron the right to locate the pellet plant at Pointe-Noire; in return, the company handed back, free of charge, NALCO, a much-travelled corporation that Smallwood had sold to Doyle back in 1957, and which he in turn had sold to Wabush Iron. "We wanted it back, we got it back," Smallwood told the legislature in July 1963. NALCO had yet one more journey to make. In November 1964, it was sold once more to Doyle, in return for Canadian Javelin stock.

For several years after the Hartford affair, nothing changed in the Smallwood-Doyle partnership, except that Doyle sold his DC-6, acquired an unlisted phone number, and never again crossed the border. Smallwood was too certain of his power to care about public reaction to his being linked to a bail jumper and a fugitive from justice.

Through 1965 and 1966, Smallwood stuck by Doyle in two grubby political scandals that rocked the Liberal Government at Ottawa. The first of these, which became known as *L'Affaire des Six*, was touched off in October 1965 after a Quebec Social Crediter, Dr. Guy Marcoux, charged that six *Créditiste* members had been offered by the Liberals a bribe of $25,000 to support the Pearson Government after the indecisive election result of 1963. The plot to do this, Marcoux charged, had been hatched at a party held in Doyle's Windsor Hotel suite on election night; following the party two Liberal organizers, both close friends of Doyle, had contacted the *Créditistes* and offered them the bribe. Marcoux described how one Liberal organizer, after meeting the *Créditistes*, "ran to the airport to rejoin Joey Smallwood, Pickersgill, John Doyle, and others who were waiting for him in Doyle's private plane." Marcoux provided no concrete evidence to support his accusations. The circumstantial evidence was powerful. The six *Créditistes* had in fact in 1963 signed a statement, given to the Governor General, that they would support Pearson.

The party leader, Robert Thompson, had charged at that time that "rather handsome" Liberal money had been offered to them. The scandal died a natural death. Canadian Javelin produced flight records to show that neither Smallwood nor Pickersgill was aboard the plane on any of the days mentioned by Marcoux. Smallwood's only later comment was: "Mr. Pickersgill had absolutely nothing to do with it. Absolutely nothing. I had nothing to do with it, absolutely nothing."

As the odd man out, Doyle's name cropped up in another grubby, federal scandal. Four months before the Gerda Munsinger affair broke in the Commons, a newspaper, *Le Journal de Montréal*, ran an article which recounted how at a suburban Montreal party given by Doyle a journalist had been handed a confidential file marked "MUNSINGER." During the inquiry itself, Gerda's girlfriend, Jackie Delorme, stated she knew Doyle, an association Doyle promptly denied.

The net effect of these scandals was to show that Doyle moved with familiarity in the murky world of Quebec politics that flourished before the Quiet Revolution. The gross effect was to damage still further his credibility as an industrial ambassador for Newfoundland, and therefore his usefulness to Smallwood.

After the Hartford incident, Doyle resigned as President of Canadian Javelin. He lingered on as a "consultant," at an annual fee of $50,000. A year later he was elected Chairman of the Executive Committee. His troubles with the law continued. The National Revenue Department pressed a claim for $2.6 million in alleged back taxes; the Montreal Stock Exchange, in August 1966, delisted a Doyle subsidiary for failure to file an annual report. That same year a Canadian Javelin Shareholders Protective Association attempted to wrest control of the company from Doyle. Their bid to do this, at the September 1966 annual meeting in St. John's, was forestalled when dissident stockholders discovered that every available seat on incoming flights had been booked.

Doyle bounced back into the news in 1967. In April of that year, in order to block any further takeover attempts and as collateral for a government-backed bond issue for Doyle's proposed linerboard mill at Stephenville, Smallwood arranged for the Newfoundland government to acquire temporary controlling interest in Canadian Javelin. The U.S. Securities Commissioner, Ed Jaegerman, repeated his denial of any commitment not to prosecute Doyle, and Smallwood exploded: "He is an unmitigated liar, an unadulterated scoundrel and a liar." To this Jaegerman replied, "I just sort of pity him. I assume he took parliamentary immunity when he made the statement."

Through the balance of the decade, as Doyle's mill project edged painfully forward, public attention shifted toward another U.S. promoter Smallwood had acquired, John Shaheen. His relations with Smallwood remained close. Just how close, Newfoundlanders discovered once the Conservatives took office. Lest there was any doubt, Smallwood in one of his first post-retirement columns for the *Daily News*, quoted the epigraph, "Let Us Now Praise Famous Men," and went on praise Doyle: "He has one of the stoutest hearts, one of the most courageous temperaments I have ever seen . . . his name will go down in history as one of the great industrial promoters in North America."

22

"A Grand Imperial Concept"

As a builder and a dreamer, Joey Smallwood's only rival among con-temporary Canadian politicians is the Mayor of Montreal, Jean Drapeau. The Churchill Falls power project is Smallwood's Expo 67, the most grandiose and daring of his ideas in the wilderness.

Although only Smallwood has made them his passion, the falls have cap-tured the imagination of every man who has seen them, from John MacLean, the Hudson's Bay Company factor who discovered them in 1839,* to René Lévesque, who, in 1961, wrote lyrically of "the small field where the perpetual spray of the cataract made strange beds of southern flowers and shrubs grow out of place on the barren sub-polar steppe."**

---

* MacLean stuffed a piece of paper with his name on it into a glass bottle which he left at the site. Every white man who visited the Falls followed his example until, in 1961, the bottle was removed for safekeeping. It is now one of Smallwood's most prized possessions.

** The falls were originally called the Grand Falls and then the Hamilton Falls

As Lévesque suggested, a large part of the waterfall's fascination is that it looms almost out of nowhere. At its source high on the central Labrador plateau, a vast saucer of rock remarkable only for its enormous annual rainfall and snowfall, the Churchill River is no more than one among countless streams inching their way towards the sea. But when it reaches the deep gorge of the Beaudoin Canyon, the riverbed drops sharply away; in the space of sixteen miles, the water tumbles a thousand feet. At the waterfall itself, the drop is 246 feet, half again as high as Niagara. The prospect there has been best described by Henry G. Bryant who, in 1891, was the second white man to reach the site.

> A single glance showed us that we were before one of the greatest water-falls in the world. Standing on the rocky brink of the chasm, a wild tumultuous scene lay before us, a scene possessing elements of sublimity and with details not to be comprehended in the first moments of won-dering contemplation. Far upstream, one beheld the surging, fleecy waters and tempestuous billows dashing high their crests of foam, all forced onwards with irresistible power towards the steep rock, whence they took their wild leap into the deep pool below.
>
> Turning to the very brink, and looking over, we gazed into a world of mists and mighty reverberations. Here the exquisite colours of the rainbow fascinated the eye, and beyond the seething cauldron the river reappeared, pursuing its turbulent career past growing cliffs and over miles of rapids.

As much as beauty, the falls epitomize naked untamed power. Their hydro potential is seven million horsepower. Despite their size, development is a relatively simple engineering feat. Low dykes can dam a catchment area of 27,101 square miles – three and a half times the size of Lake Ontario – and channel the overflow into tunnels bored in rock near the falls to send them smashing down on underground turbines. At site, the power is as

---

until 1965, when Smallwood changed their name to honour Sir Winston Churchill. To avoid confusion, the current name – Churchill Falls – is used throughout.

cheap as any in the world. The nearest market, however, is seven hundred miles away, far enough to deter all but the most stubborn dreamer.

As with iron ore, the apparent impossibilities of exploiting the Churchill Falls potential only whetted Smallwood's appetite. He first conceived the idea of developing them in 1952, as part of his drive for new industry. By this time he had pounded on corporate doors across Canada and the United States and had uncovered only a single prospect – John Doyle. Out of instinct, by tradition, and by necessity, he looked instead to London.

"I'm just a little man from a remote corner of the Empire," said Smallwood as he checked in at the Savoy Hotel in August 1952. The next day he unleashed a tide of oratory at a meeting of the British Federation of Industries. "I am here to offer you the biggest real estate deal of the present century," he said. "Labrador, the last remaining storehouse of natural wealth and natural resources on the North American continent." He called for a consortium, "in the tradition of the East India Company, the Hudson's Bay Company, the great land companies of merchant adventurers," to develop Labrador.

He used the right words at the right time. Britain's experiment with austerity was over, and so also were the years of Empire. Now on the brink of what Britons hoped would be a "New Elizabethan Age," the *Western Mail* proclaimed, "LABRADOR CAN BE NEW ELDORADO," the *Daily Mail* headlined, "LABRADOR CALLING BRITAIN," and even the pulse of *The Times* quickened as it wondered, "Whether from the strictly economic point of view or from that of the wider question of commonwealth relations, Britain can afford to be left so completely out of the race." Smallwood was deluged with private letters, from retired Army officers proffering their services, to a nurse who volunteered to set up a nursery in the new colony. Scores of letters contained money orders. These Smallwood returned and waited instead for the investors to call.

Entry to Britain's financial establishment, however, could be achieved only at the top. Two people opened the doors for Smallwood: Sir Eric Bowater, Chairman of the Corner Brook pulp-and-paper mill, who had

long been interested in Labrador's extensive stands of spruce, introduced
him to the merchant banking house of N. M. Rothschild's. Independently, Lord Beaverbrook, who had been Smallwood's host for a two-week
holiday in Montego Bay the year before, sent him to the grandest door of
all, Number 10 Downing Street. That meeting – the little man from the
remote corner of Empire confronting the greatest personality of the age
– is among the most treasured of Smallwood's memories. Years later,
when negotiations on the falls were at the point of collapse, his opponent,
René Lévesque, in a moment of astonishing perception, realized how
much it had meant. "Joey's crazy but he means it," he remarked to a colleague. "He's totally genuine. He won't nationalize Churchill Falls as long
as Churchill is a shareholder."

The Prime Minister waved Smallwood into an armchair, offered him
a whisky and a cigar, both of which he declined, and asked him to tell his
story. "I like it," said Churchill. "It's a grand Imperial concept." With a
nod to the sensibilities of the age, he added: "And I don't mean
Imperialist." When Smallwood left he carried with him a copy of *Closing
the Ring*, the fifth volume of Churchill's chronicles of World War II.
Inscribed in the flyleaf was: "To J. R. Smallwood, from Winston S.
Churchill." Apart from his seal of approval, Churchill's practical contribution to the project was to put Smallwood in touch with his financial
adviser, Lord Leathers. Later he stretched the Exchequer regulations to
allow the export of sterling to start exploration work at Churchill Falls.

The main activity took place at the House of Rothschild's. On
August 19, 1952, Smallwood was invited for lunch at its offices in New
Court. He received a salute from a derby-hatted doorman, and was
ushered into the mahogany-panelled "Partners Room," where, among
the memorabilia of two hundred years of banking, hung a framed receipt
for two million pounds loaned to Wellington's army. Smallwood sat in the
guest's chair at the head of the table, "not in the least awed," recalls one
director, and while he lacked the finesse of most Rothschild guests, "he
was no more of a rough diamond than Rhodes." Smallwood had also
done his homework, and, the director remembers, "it was his reference to
Rhodes that caught Anthony's [de Rothschild] attention." In between the
grouse and the strawberries and cream, he outlined his proposal. By long

custom, Rothschild's lunches ended at 2:00 P.M. Smallwood kept the company until 3:00 P.M.

As always for Smallwood, selling his idea was the easiest part. During the actual negotiations, he twice despaired of securing terms acceptable even by his own generous standards, and had to call on the good offices of Lord Leathers and St. Laurent to keep the project alive. After the last meeting at Rothschild's, Edmund de Rothschild, then heir to the firm, and today its senior partner, went with Smallwood to the library in New Court and pulled out the *Times* map of Labrador. Across it was printed "UNEXPLORED." It was, recalls Rothschild, "rather exciting." It was also faintly absurd. Rothschild later wrote that to celebrate the signing of the contract, "I decided the funniest show in London would be the one to go to, Bud Flanagan's *Crazy Gang*, because the whole project as envisaged seemed so remote."

On March 31, 1953, the Newfoundland legislature passed a bill to incorporate British Newfoundland Development Corporation, a tight consortium of family and financial connections, including Rothschild's Rio Tinto Company Limited, Anglo-American Corporation of South Africa, and English Electric. (This last company was the only one then interested in the Churchill Falls; the others were concerned only with mineral and pulpwood rights.) Later the consortium was expanded to include another twenty-three firms, among them *Compagnie Financier de Suez*. For assets, Brinco had fifty thousand square miles of Labrador, and another ten thousand square miles of Newfoundland, an area larger than England. Apart from potential mineral deposits, the territory included two major power sites and an estimated fifty million cords of prime black spruce. In return, the consortium was committed to spend a spare $250,000 a year, and to pay the Newfoundland Government annual royalties of eight per cent. As the Opposition pointed out, Smallwood had indeed given Brinco the biggest real estate deal of the century.

Twelve years later, Brinco's accomplishments amounted to a small two thousand ton a day copper mine at Whalesback on the Northeast Coast of Newfoundland. The Churchill remained a lonely northern river. "It is high time," Churchill wrote to the Rothschilds in 1956, "the Churchill Falls had a bridle." The following year, Smallwood told a New York audience, "Power from Churchill Falls will one day light the lights of Broadway." No paper bothered to report his prophecy.

"He never for one instant, and he alone, never gave up hope." So Edmund de Rothschild, the only member of the original consortium who has maintained a personal interest in the project, remembers Smallwood's defiant optimism during those years when there was precious little to be optimistic about. Endlessly he rhapsodized the splendour of the project, harassed Brinco for action, pounded on doors in New York, in London, and across Canada. When none of the doors opened, Smallwood simply packed his bags once more and, like a wandering minstrel, set off in search of new customers, in the New England States, Ontario, the Maritimes, and Quebec.

The breakthrough came in 1962, when three events brought Smallwood's dream suddenly close to reality. In Ottawa, the Diefenbaker Government, for the sake of British Columbia's Columbia River project, suddenly reversed the long-standing national ban on long-term exports of power. In Sweden, technology had conquered the problems of long-distance energy transmission. Most important of all, a customer large enough to absorb Churchill Falls power had at last appeared: Consolidated Edison, the giant New York State utility announced that it was prepared to take up to two million kilowatts of power a day, or half the full Churchill Falls output. By itself, a sale of such a size made the project feasible.

All these strands were pulled together into a credible whole when Robert Winters was appointed Chairman of Brinco in June 1963. Until Winters arrived, Brinco amounted to little more than a letterhead. Within a few months, he had assembled an outstanding managerial team and persuaded top-flight Canadian and American engineering firms to form a new company, Canadian Acres-Bechtel, to carry out the actual construction. He had also launched the first full-scale engineering survey of the site, and opened intense negotiations between Newfoundland, Quebec, and Consolidated Edison.

At stake was the largest industrial project in Canada since the construction of the Canadian Pacific Railway and the largest single hydro project in the Western World. It would employ up to seven thousand men, export $60 million worth of power annually, and involve the construction of thirteen hundred miles of high-voltage lines, the longest in the world, from Labrador to New York. To do all this would cost $1.5 billion, more than the St. Lawrence Seaway.

Winters's own career and reputation matched the size of the project. Tall, impeccably groomed, and perennially tanned, with the even good looks of a movie star portraying an industrial executive, he had been described at different times as an "Eisenhower with brains" and "a George Hees with brains." Twice, in the mid-fifties and again in the late sixties, his charm made him a prospect, at least to some sections of the party and business community, for the Prime Minister's Office. Winters's brains had taken him, the son of a Lunenburg, Nova Scotia, dragger captain, to MIT, a rising business career, and finally into politics as a protégé of C. D. Howe. After the Liberal debacle of 1957, he chose, from a score of offers, the Chairmanship of Rio Tinto Mining Company, a major shareholder in Brinco. This connection brought him into the Churchill Falls project.

In sum, Winters was a first-class engineer. He made decisions easily: like C. D. Howe, he got things done. He also exhibited the limitations of his type. Essentially, he was an uncomplicated businessman without subtlety or imagination. In the peaceful political dovecotes of the 1950s, these defects mattered little; in the 1960s, when Winters had to deal with the leaders of a new Quebec which responded to imperatives other than those of economics and finance, they became crucial.

For Smallwood, accustomed to one-man rule, the subtle arts of diplomacy and empathy came even less easily. The hardest part was to get on with Jean Lesage, a politician as proud and as unyielding as he.

Although Smallwood and Lesage were to part as bitter, abusive enemies, they met, if not as close friends, at least as close allies. As a fellow-Liberal, Smallwood applauded Lesage's surprise election victory. Of Lesage's performance at the July 1960 federal-provincial conference, he said: "He towered head and shoulders above everyone else, and I mean everyone."

The next year they agreed to start talks on the touchy question of delin-
eating the Labrador boundary, since as Lesage commented, "Where we
touch we don't exactly know." (This was literally true, since the boundary
line, which followed the Labrador watershed, shifted with the seasonal
rise and fall of the water in lakes and marshes.) When Consolidated
Edison emerged as customer for the Churchill Falls power, Smallwood
quickly passed the news on to Lesage: As he recorded in his diary after a
meeting in Quebec City on December 19, 1962:

> Jean Lesage called for me at 6:15, Chateau Frontenac. We went to
> Garrison Club for dinner. I outlined Con Ed-Brinco deal. He is
> tremendously interested. We had a v. pleasant chat on politics, etc., and
> then he walked me back to the hotel.

The first break in good relations came ten days later. On December 29,
Quebec nationalized private power companies in the province: Among
them was Shawinigan Engineering which in turn was a twenty per cent
shareholder of Brinco's operating subsidiary, Churchill Falls (Labrador)
Corporation. Quebec had, overnight, become one-fifth owner of
Newfoundland's most valuable asset.

"Talked on phone to Jean Lesage, JWP, Curtis *re* Lesage's announcement of Shawinigan shares," Smallwood wrote in his diary. The entry was
too brief. In fact, for the best part of an hour Smallwood castigated
Lesage, accusing him of bad faith and of nationalizing Shawinigan for the
sole purpose of acquiring its Churchill Falls holdings.*

All through the following spring, Smallwood's hostility towards
Quebec deepened as he battled with Lesage over the pellet plant at
Wabush. In one retaliatory blow, he shelved the plan for a joint border
survey. But by late 1963, as the power project seemed about to become a
reality, he submerged his differences.

---

* In June 1964, in order to strike a more equitable balance between the two
provinces, Brinco floated a special issue of a million shares, a device which
reduced Quebec's holdings to sixteen per cent and allowed Newfoundland to
pick up a five per cent ownership.

During the early negotiations with Quebec and Consolidated Edison, which Winters initiated in the fall of 1963, Smallwood was only an enthusiastic and impatient onlooker. He assumed that an agreement was imminent, and that he would be asked to do no more than approve those policies which would affect Newfoundland directly. Events conspired to rob him of the triumph which seemed so near.

In theory, the plan to develop Churchill Falls was simple enough. Brinco would develop the power, drop off a small amount to serve local Newfoundland needs, and sell the remainder to Hydro-Quebec. In turn, Hydro-Quebec would sell half to Consolidated Edison via lines to Rouse's Point at the New York-Quebec border, and use the remainder itself.

In practice, the negotiations turned into what René Lévesque once memorably described as "three statistic-ridden years only a Benedictine economist could unravel."

The trouble was that the four parties concerned – Quebec, Consolidated Edison, Brinco, Newfoundland – each spoke a different language. Only Consolidated Edison's was uncomplicated. As one vice-president said, "There's a lot of politicking going on up there. We're waiting for everyone to return to their senses so we can get back to business." Winters, for all his ability, antagonized the Quebec team by his manner and appearance, which symbolized the old English-speaking dominion over Quebec's business affairs. He often ducked hard-knuckled bargaining to rely on an old-boy network rarely equalled in Canadian commerce. Lesage was a former fellow federal minister; Harlan Forbes, the Chairman of Consolidated Edison, was a fellow MIT alumnus and close friend; the Hydro-Quebec Chairman, Jean Claude Lessard, was a former federal deputy minister and another close friend; and as for Smallwood, the two had been confidants since 1946. But the quiet revolutionaries across the bargaining table were unimpressed by Winters's ability to pick up the phone to call Ottawa or New York and address a minister or corporation president by his first name. They were impressed by the exorbitant price Brinco demanded for Churchill Falls power.

At the head of the Quebec team was Lesage, a figure of formidable presence, and one of the most powerful Canadian politicians of the day. Behind him were ranked Lévesque, intense, dynamic, and driven by a fierce national pride that was to reach its logical and defiant conclusion in separatism; Michel Bélanger, a brilliant technocrat in his mid-thirties; Lessard, an accomplished but impressionable civil servant; and Douglas Fullerton, an Ottawa financial counsellor and one of the ablest personages behind the scenes of government. Ironically, in view of the role he was to play, Fullerton had been born in Newfoundland, though he left there as an infant.

Self-confident, and swept up in the excitement of the new order they were creating, the Quebec negotiators were both more and less than the team of hard-headed technocrats they thought themselves to be. They failed, conspicuously, to recognize the difference between the corporate shell of Brinco (which Lévesque called "a sort of medieval Hudson's Bay kind of set up"), and the totally new team Winters had assembled. The name Rothschild, evocative of colonial past, was so unsettling to them that Edmund de Rothschild, a gentle and unmercenary banker whose real passion was botany, diplomatically excluded himself from all meetings with the Quebec group.

Smallwood himself was another sticking-point. Because of his associations with Doyle, and his one-man style of rule, he uncomfortably reminded the quiet revolutionaries of Maurice Duplessis. "Joey's just a concessionaire of a property Brinco's trying to develop," Lévesque told a journalist in an undiplomatic aside. For his part, Smallwood had for so long absorbed himself in Newfoundland's problems that he had little time left over to care about or understand those of others. "The French Canadian is one of the most lovable human beings in Canada," he told the Quebec journalist, Solange Chaput-Rolland, "but collectively he deserves a swift kick."

The key stumbling block, however, was price. Winters's opening offer to Quebec was three mills per kilowatt for power delivered at the border, a figure so high the Quebec team wondered if he could be serious. Their counter-offer was 2.1 mills. After painful recalculation, Brinco dropped its price down to 2.65 mills. Quebec, in turn, refused to go higher than

2.3 mills. On January 7, 1964, after a trip to New York for talks with Consolidated Edison and Hydro-Quebec, Winters in his diary reflected the miasma of depression which hung over the negotiations: "Waldorf. We spent two hours of exhaustive but not too productive discussion. It's a frustrating situation." The two sides were deadlocked and the negotiations so promisingly begun were already on the point of collapse.

Fullerton on February 3, 1964, suggested a daring and imaginative solution. "In studying the figures," he wrote in a private memorandum to the Quebec cabinet, "we cannot but become aware of the very heavy additional costs of building, financing, and operating the Churchill Falls as a private company." These costs, including taxes and higher debt charges, Fullerton estimated to account for forty per cent of the Brinco's selling price to Quebec. On that basis, he continued, Brinco was "an expensive anachronism." Since all major power projects were now publicly owned, Fullerton proposed that Brinco should be nationalized and the Churchill Falls developed jointly by a Quebec-Newfoundland crown corporation. The cost of the takeover he reckoned at some $30 million. The Quebec cabinet quickly endorsed Fullerton's suggestion, and made it the basis for a new bargaining position. The risks of nationalization were awesome. Winters was certain to resign, and no replacement close to his stature was in sight; investors, already unsettled by Quebec's takeover of private power companies, were bound to react adversely. Yet only with Brinco, the middleman, out of the way could Quebec buy the power at a price it could afford, and only then could the Churchill Falls project proceed.

The proposal was first broached by Lévesque at a meeting with Winters on February 17. Later Winters wrote in his diary: "René's office, 9:30 A.M. to 10:45 A.M. He now seems bent on public ownership, which cannot succeed. He has quite an irresponsible attitude to public policy." Winters's reaction was predictable. The crucial question now was how would Smallwood react?

On the day Lévesque spoke to Winters, Smallwood was three thousand miles away to the east. A fortnight earlier he and John Doyle had taken off on a trip to Rabat, Fez, Vienna, and finally to Stockholm to inspect a laboratory there that was processing samples of wood from Doyle's holdings in Labrador. In Stockholm, just before noon on

February 18, Smallwood was called to the telephone. Rothschild was on the line; he reported the nationalization offer and told Smallwood that Winters was flying out immediately to London with a full report.

Already the idea of nationalization was virtually dead; had Quebec deliberately wanted to kill it, the province's approach could scarcely have been more effective. Smallwood, the creator of Brinco and the man who would have to nationalize it and bear the prime political and financial consequences, was to be told the idea, second-hand, by Winters, head of the company he was expected to nationalize. Such tactlessness under-scored the essential flaw of the proposal. It amounted to extra-territorial nationalization by Quebec of Newfoundland property in a partnership that would comprise, as Smallwood put it, "One elephant, one mouse." Instead, late at night in Smallwood's suite at the Savoy Hotel, he and Winters jettisoned the scheme. After their conference, each man opened his diary. Smallwood wrote: "Two hours talk to 1:00 A.M., with Winters on Churchill Falls deal: Quebec's attitude and the need for me to save the project." Winters noted happily: "He will resist any attempt by Jean Lesage to operate Churchill Falls as a crown company."

The last chance for the nationalization scheme rested with Lesage's ability to sell it to Smallwood. On March 1, the two met for a long after-noon conference at the Queen Elizabeth Hotel in Montreal. By the time Lesage left the room, the concept of nationalization was dead and buried. Confident that he held all the high cards, Lesage had thrown them in Smallwood's face. As he should have anticipated, Smallwood threw them back. In his diary Smallwood wrote angrily: "He wants Brinco out, Newfoundland and Quebec jointly to develop Hamilton; the border changed; Newfoundland to absorb 4,000 men from Quebec; Quebec materials to be used. I said NO." On such terms, Newfoundland would indeed be a mouse beneath an elephant. Not even for Churchill Falls would Smallwood accept them.

Talks on the Falls sputtered on for another three months. In an attempt to stave off collapse, Winters persuaded Smallwood to negotiate once more with Lesage. The two Premiers quartered in different Montreal hotels: Lesage at the Windsor, and Smallwood at the Ritz-Carlton. Since a face-to-face encounter between the two would have resulted in disaster, Winters spent the afternoon doubling back and forth between them. By the end of the day he had wrested a compromise agreement. Lesage agreed to drop his demand for the use of Quebec materials and Quebec manpower. (In fact, these were redundant. Economics alone dictated that Quebec would dominate both fields.) He had also secured what was called a "concomitant" agreement – "we got tangled in the semantics of that," he recalls – on the boundary issue. Newfoundland would receive ten thousand square miles of barren Quebec territory in the north and, in exchange, grant Quebec ten thousand square miles in the south of Labrador, which encompassed the headwaters of five rivers that flowed into the Gulf of St. Lawrence. At the end of the day, Winters wrote in his diary: "He [Lesage] said boundary would have to be arranged concomitantly; project must be nationalized. Other points as well as much criticism of Joey. Added that Churchill Falls must proceed and that I was the only one to do it."

This settlement got the negotiations back – but on a track that led nowhere. At the federal-provincial conference at Quebec City in the first week of April, Lesage and Lévesque made a last bid to convince Smallwood of the virtues of nationalization. During a recess, the three withdrew into a small room in the Quebec Parliament Buildings, where Lévesque once more explained the cost benefits of the takeover to Smallwood, and added, "You're crazy not to nationalize." "And I'm crazy if I do," Smallwood replied. The two then turned to the window and stared silently as a group of Laval students paraded in front of them, bearing *Québec Libre* signs.

Without nationalization, Brinco could reduce its price offer no further than 2.55 mills. Quebec refused to go higher than 2.3 mills. On June 23, Winters made his last offer to Lesage. A fortnight later, Lesage telephoned Winters and Smallwood who was then in Athens. "I have bad news for you," he told each of them, and that evening, he informed the Quebec Legislature that talks with Brinco had been broken off. Winters told a hastily called board meeting in Toronto: "We are ready to continue negotiations. The difference in price is so narrow, a small fraction of a mill, there must be ways and means of bridging the gap." He calculated the annual value of the gap at $20 million. At Quebec City, word was leaked to the press that the government estimated the money saved by nationalizing Brinco would be $20 million a year.

Winters has called the failure to reach an agreement to develop the Churchill Falls in 1964 "one of the worst blunders of Canadian economic history." Every circumstance then was ripe: the power would have gone on stream in 1968, half of it for export to the United States; interest rates at that time were low, reducing the project's cost, the economy was slack, and construction would have absorbed unemployment. In each year that has passed since, the cost of the project has risen, and its net benefit to the nation has dwindled.

Smallwood reacted to this blunder, not to say tragedy, as he has to every other setback. If one road led nowhere, he would try another. And if necessary, he would go down it alone. He would develop the Churchill Falls if it broke him, Quebec, and Brinco.

23

"This Is Our Waterfall"

The collapse of the Churchill Falls negotiations left Smallwood in a state of unsuppressed fury. Quebec's intransigence, as he saw it, had deprived Newfoundland of the industry and employment it so desperately needed, and had robbed him of his monument. As powerful a motive for his anger was that Quebec claimed sovereignty over his beloved Labrador. For the next two years he treated Quebec as if it were an enemy country.

The quarrel over the boundary reopened an old wound, and one which has never fully healed. From earliest times, the Labrador coast had belonged by custom to Newfoundland, and formal jurisdiction over the littoral was vested in the colony by Britain in 1809. Through the nineteenth century, as many as six hundred vessels a year sailed from the island to prosecute the Labrador fishery. But there were few "liveyers" or permanent settlers and no local government. Such schools as existed were those of the Moravian Brethren, a small German missionary sect; the only medical services were those provided by the Grenfell mission. Not until the early twentieth century did either Quebec or Newfoundland evince the slightest interest in the empty interior of Labrador. Quebec fired the first shot.

On December 5, 1902, Alfred Dickie, a Nova Scotia mill owner who was cutting wood around Lake Melville in central Labrador, received a letter from the Quebec Minister of Lands, Mines, and Forests which protested that he was operating a business without a Quebec licence. Dickie wrote back that he had assumed that he was operating in Newfoundland. Quebec lodged a formal complaint at Ottawa that Newfoundland had expanded its jurisdiction into the interior. In turn, Ottawa sent a note to London to protest at the colony's "encroachment upon the territory of Quebec." Newfoundland denied the charge. By now accustomed to the island's fractiousness, Colonial Secretary Joseph Chamberlain suggested that Canada "take steps to obtain a legal decision in the matter." In 1904, the Canadian Governor General, Lord Minto, replied: "It was the request of the Province of Quebec that the question of the boundary . . . be submitted for decision to the Judicial Committee of the Privy Council." The mills of the Privy Council ground with glacial speed. Not until 1926 was Quebec's case finally heard.

Few cases in international law have been examined and argued more exhaustively. The documentary evidence filled five thousand pages and eight volumes; oral presentations accounted for another sixteen hundred pages. Determined to hold on to its mainland territory, Newfoundland fought harder, and with greater skill. The colony was represented by Sir John Simon, who buttressed his case with maps dug from libraries all over Europe and with sprightly quotations from the Bible, among them: "Every place whereon the soles of your feet shall tread shall be yours: from the Wilderness and Lebanon, from the river, the River Euphrates, even unto the uttermost sea shall your coast be."

Quebec was represented by Antoine-Aimé Geoffrion, who introduced himself as "retained by Quebec specially." In that cause, he delivered a thirty-thousand-word speech. On the central issue of ownership, however, he only said, "The reasons why it [Labrador] should fall to Canada may and should all be given by Canada."

Quebec was ill-served by the Canadian argument. Canada readily granted Newfoundland's jurisdiction over the coast but claimed everything inland. In reply, Simon pointed out that since Canada had made no greater attempt than Newfoundland to administer the interior, there was no reason to draw the boundary at the shoreline. In the absence of other guidelines, he argued that the shoreline constituted "a territory with defined sea frontage which stretched to the height of land," that is, from the coast to the central Labrador plateau.

On March 1, 1927, the Privy Council delivered its verdict: "Having considered the facts put before us with the care necessary in a matter of such grave importance [we] have come to the conclusion that the claim of the Colony of Newfoundland is in substance made out." Their decision expanded Newfoundland's territory by 112,826 square miles – more than twice the size of the island itself. Quebec reckoned the loss slight: In 1924, the Newfoundland Prime Minister, during a daylong meeting at the Windsor Hotel in Montreal, had offered Labrador to Premier Louis Taschereau for $15 million. The offer was declined.

After that the boundary issue went underground. It bubbled up briefly during the negotiations that led up to Newfoundland's entry into union. Five years later, however, Premier Duplessis tacitly recognized the demarcation when he and Smallwood instructed the Iron Ore Company of Canada to calculate royalty payments from its Knob Lake mine according to the amount of ore mined on each side of the existing border. A decade afterwards, the issue was revived as a back-eddy of the Quiet Revolution.

The most extreme and forceful Quebec argument was put forward by the Laval University geographer, Henri Dorion, in his book *La Frontière Québec-Terreneuve*, published in 1963. Dorion proposed a joint Quebec-Newfoundland condominium over Labrador on the grounds that the Privy Council decision was unfair and injudicial. In a speech to the Quebec City Fleur de Lys Club on December 18, 1964, Dorion proposed that Quebec compel Newfoundland to redress the boundary by taxing Newfoundland ore coming south to Sept-Îles. "I admit it's not a very nice thing to do," he said, "but it's the only way Quebec can force Newfoundland to accommodate its needs."

Resources Minister Lévesque was more realistic: "They won and we lost on the damn thing," was his comment. Yet the boundary issue bedevilled the Churchill Falls negotiations. The difficulty was that Quebec could buy Churchill Falls power only at the price of recognizing the existing boundary since whatever the point at which Brinco turned over the power to Quebec would, patently, be the boundary line. In the legislature, Opposition Leader Daniel Johnson made certain that Lesage knew what was at stake. "The people of Quebec," he said, "will never accept this loss of their territory." Sensitive to the political overtones of the issue, Lesage made an agreement to develop the Churchill Falls contingent upon a redress of the boundary. Since without Quebec's participation the power could not be developed, Lesage was justifiably confident he held the high cards.

Though Lesage was then at the height of his power and prestige, for Smallwood, he was no more intimidating an opponent than Diefenbaker had been. And there was nothing Smallwood enjoyed more than a fight against odds. He first attempted to resolve the crisis precipitated by the collapse of negotiations by seeking a way to market the power without selling it to Quebec. He persuaded Winters to ask the Quebec Government to allow the transmission lines to go through the province directly to the Consolidated Edison system. Lesage refused. Smallwood even considered demanding that Prime Minister Pearson designate the transmission route through Quebec as federal territory but was talked out of it by Pickersgill.

Smallwood smothered his disappointment and set off on a new tack. On the map at least, Churchill Falls power could be brought to market by two routes: west through Quebec; or east and south, across the Strait of Belle Isle to Newfoundland, across the Cabot Strait, through the Maritimes and on to the New England states. The eastern route was far longer, more expensive, and fraught with technical difficulties. Yet if Quebec was no longer willing to be either partner or participant, it was the only route left. Smallwood spent the next nine months trying to defy economics and geography.

As early as February 18, 1964, the day he was told of Quebec's demand to nationalize Brinco, Smallwood conceived the idea for what became known as "the Anglo-Saxon route." While in London, he called on the firm of Preece, Cardew, and Ryder, the world's experts on underwater power transmission, and collected from them a list of major underwater links, the longest a fifty-five-mile cable between the north and south islands of New Zealand. By contrast, the Anglo-Saxon route involved a nine-mile hop across the Strait of Belle Isle, and another sixty-two miles across the Cabot Strait.

On May 13, Smallwood gave the first public inkling of what he had in mind. Hoping to pressure Lesage, he told the legislature that Churchill Falls power could be brought to market by routes other than through Quebec, and that "the project does not have to be controlled by a single authority outside Newfoundland." Two days later, to emphasize his stand on the boundary, Smallwood changed the official name of the province to Newfoundland and Labrador. "We want the world to know," he said, "that Labrador belongs to us."[*]

Once the Churchill Falls talks had been broken off, Smallwood was confronted with a more immediate problem. Winters wanted to resign as chairman of Brinco. Frantic at the prospect of the complete collapse of a project once so close to fruition, Smallwood used all his powers of persuasion to convince Winters to stay. As bait, he held out the prospect of the eastern route. (In fact, Winters at no time considered it worth serious consideration.)

From this point on, and encouraged by some surprisingly optimistic technical studies on the economic prospects for the eastern route, Smallwood operated on sheer bluff. He hired Preece, Cardew, and Ryder to carry out a $100,000 engineering survey of the project and flew to Boston for talks with potential customers at New England power companies. Certain that what he wanted to happen would happen, if necessary

---

[*] Smallwood's territorial sensitivities also extended downwards. On June 25, 1964, he sent two divers to place a brass plaque of the Newfoundland coat-of-arms in sixty-three feet of water on the floor of the Grand Bank. Back on land, one diver reported: "We saw thousands of codfish."

by sheer willpower alone, Smallwood threw caution to the winds. "I have no interest in reopening negotiations with Quebec," he said in London on October 26, 1964. "This is one of the great days in Newfoundland," he declared a month later. "We are freed of the clutches of Quebec." In Quebec, where the idea of underwater transmission was dismissed out of hand, Lesage was unperturbed: "Mr. Smallwood can entertain all the lovely plans he likes," he said.

Smallwood, by this time, had become disenchanted with Brinco's and Winters's lack of interest in his project. He even went so far as to open talks with a New York financial house, Dillon, Read and Co., on ways in which Newfoundland might nationalize Brinco, a stunning reversal of his previous stand. Winters icily told him, "I don't regard it as one of my roles in life to be manager of a nationalized project." As a further complication, Smallwood also named Doyle as his selling agent for the power. "I don't know which side has been worse and which better," Winters confided to a reporter, "but it has been awfully difficult."

Early in December, Smallwood received the final Preece, Cardew, and Ryder report. On December 14, he presented it formally to the Brinco board of directors. The subsequent press conference was strained. Smallwood said almost nothing, and Winters limited himself to the enigmatic comment, "Mr. Lesage has said the door to negotiations is still open, but I have told Mr. Lesage I am not now in a position to negotiate."

Willpower and bluff had taken Smallwood as far as they could. The final report showed that the eastern route would cost a prohibitive $350 million more than the direct route through Quebec. Even the technical problems were almost insurmountable. To bridge the Cabot Strait would require eight insulated cables, each a ponderous 5.5 inches in diameter and strung eight thousand feet apart. Because of the Strait's 290-fathom depth, and the hazards of ice and of ocean currents, the cables could not even be designed without two years of trials.

Smallwood fought back in the only way he could. On February 1, 1965, he flew with Winters to Boston to address a meeting of the New England power companies. For an hour, he held the executives spellbound and then sat back to hear their reply. It was no. "They're just bluffing, Bob," Smallwood told Winters as they left the room together. Winters broke the news again to him, gently but firmly.

For six weeks, Smallwood mulled over his defeat, and then on March 10, he asked Winters to come down to St. John's. At a full cabinet meeting Winters set out in detail the case against the eastern route. Over lunch in his private dining room, Smallwood accepted the inevitable. "I'm going to have to swallow very hard," he told Winters. "I want you in the House to help me." In the legislature that afternoon Smallwood explained, "Brinco shares the Newfoundland Government's strong desire" to sell Churchill Falls power "to our sister province of Quebec." To which Winters tactfully added, "This is the cheapest way and the best way." Confident that an agreement was near, Smallwood launched a $250,000 advertising campaign in U.S., European, and Japanese newspapers offering industries "large blocs of power."

Agreement, however, was far from near. Smallwood had two more years to wait. By now, Consolidated Edison had lost interest and had dropped out of the project. This left only Quebec to absorb all the vast output of Churchill Falls, a circumstance that required a complete rejuggling of delivery schedules. Nevertheless, Quebec's own power needs had changed radically; Hydro-Quebec officials forecast these would double, to 14.2 million kilowatts a day by 1975, and warned publicly that without Churchill Falls power the province would be "on power rationing by the early seventies."

Yet Brinco and Quebec remained far apart on price. They were finally brought within reach of reconciliation on July 25, 1965, when after a year of lobbying by Smallwood, Winters, and Pickersgill, the federal government agreed to abolish taxes on privately owned utilities. "I expect the deal to be signed within a few days," said a delighted Smallwood. Lesage was more cautious. "There are still difficulties to be overcome," he said.

Prime among these was the boundary. In May 1965, determined to repay Smallwood for the verbal excesses of his Anglo-Saxon route period, Lesage announced that there would be no agreement on

Churchill Falls, "without a rectification of the Quebec-Labrador bound-ary." This drew from Smallwood a withering return blast: "There will be no change, and I repeat, there will be no changes, no modifications, no amendment, no change whatsoever in the boundary between Labrador and Quebec – not now or at any time."

Once more the matter was deadlocked; the two Premiers glared at each other across their defended border like a pair of bulls, as shortsighted as they were strong. Feelings ran so high that a Newfoundland Senator, Alexander Baird, told a surprised Upper Chamber: "We Newfoundland-Canadians don't want to fight, but by jingo if we have to, then I say we have the ships, the money, and the men." To this Senator Maurice Bourget retorted: "And the fish."

Common sense, and an uncharacteristic show of diplomacy by Quebec's Revenue Minister Eric Kierans, prevailed. In June, Kierans got agreement on a face-saving compromise. The boundary itself would remain unchanged but Newfoundland would allow Quebec to tap the headwaters of the five rivers flowing into the Gulf of St. Lawrence. In return, Newfoundland would be allowed toll-free use of the shortest route through Quebec territory to bring the power from Labrador to the island of Newfoundland.

In May 1966, Brinco's final offer was approved by Hydro-Quebec and passed on to the provincial cabinet. Since an election was in progress, the decision was postponed. On June 6, an astonished Daniel Johnson found himself Premier of Quebec. Smallwood heard the news with shock. At best, it meant another delay; at worst, since the Union Nationale was more nationalist than the out-going Liberals, the change of government could spell the end for Churchill Falls.

Yet the economics of the project remained constant: Quebec had to have the power. There was no other source in sight. Smallwood recovered his confidence, and in the midst of his own election campaign announced he would fly to Churchill Falls on September 6 to inaugurate the start of construction. Faced by a forbidding silence from Quebec City, he can-celled the flight. Instead, once his election was won, Smallwood took off on a round-the-world trip, paid for by the hundred-dollar deposits of the grateful Liberal candidates.

On October 7, when Smallwood was two-thirds of the way around the globe, and had just checked into the Erawan Hotel in Bangkok, a messenger ran up with a telegram. It was from Brinco's chief executive officer, and read: "QUEBEC HAS AUTHORIZED HYDRO-QUEBEC TO SIGN LETTER OF INTENT TO PURCHASE CHURCHILL FALLS POWER STOP DO NOT BURN BANGKOK." "Glory Hallelujah," shouted Smallwood to the first reporter to reach him. "Praise God, from whom all blessings flow." After fourteen years he had won. For Newfoundland, Churchill Falls meant some $20 million a year in royalties (one-tenth of the then provincial revenues); a chance to compete for seven thousand jobs a year, and the prospect of developing, exclusively for the province, the more than three million horsepower potential of the downstream Churchill River. And Smallwood had his monument. A fortnight later he came home to a hero's welcome.

Surprisingly, the Quebec decision included no mention of the boundary. Instead, to protect his political rear, Johnson established a Royal Commission, chaired by Professor Dorion, to study the territorial integrity of Quebec – principally the Labrador boundary. "They can appoint twenty-eight Commissions or 128 Commissions, for all I care," was Smallwood's unruffled comment. He could afford to be phlegmatic. He found dealing with the cool pragmatist Johnson a welcome change after Lesage.

Smallwood had still to settle old scores with the former Premier, and in September Lesage handed him the chance. In the legislature he announced that while in office he had conducted secret negotiations with Smallwood on "boundary concessions." Smallwood came roaring back: "If Mr. Lesage is quoted correctly, then he is an unmitigated liar. A shameless and scandalous liar from head to toe. In private, in public, I rejected, repeatedly, categorically, in Jack-blunt fashion any demand to change the Labrador boundary by a single inch." The following day, a shaken Lesage admitted the talks had involved not boundary changes, but only "permanent leases" to the headwaters of the five rivers. Smallwood did not bother to reply.

On July 17, 1967, as the cataract thundered behind him, and 450 guests airlifted in from Montreal and St. John's looked on, Smallwood stood in the midst of the work camp Brinco had hacked out of the Labrador forest, and plunged a silver shovel into a square of moss held in place by spruce logs to begin officially construction of the Churchill Falls power project. Among the audience were Edmund de Rothschild, Winters, Donald Gordon, former president of the CNR and the new president of Brinco (whose appointment six months earlier Smallwood had cheered with the shortest telegram of his career: "HURRAY STOP JOEY"), and Winston Churchill, grandson of the author of *The Closing of the Ring*.

It was his moment of glory, a time for platitudes and plaudits. Instead, Smallwood launched into a tirade. His message was the same one he had preached for fifteen years. Labrador belonged to Newfoundland. "We are completely selfish, let there be no mistake about that," he bellowed into a bank of microphones. "This is *our* river, this is *our* waterfall, this is *our* land. . . . We are developing it mainly, chiefly, principally for the benefit of Newfoundland. Newfoundland first, Quebec second, the rest of the world last."

Smallwood had good reason to be tactless. No sooner had the Churchill Falls deal been signed than Hydro-Quebec had claimed the agreement gave Quebec priority in the provision of men and materials. Smallwood issued an adamant denial, and Hydro-Quebec beat a hasty retreat. Nevertheless, sheer economics made it clear that Quebec would dominate the project. Few companies in Newfoundland were large enough to win construction contracts at the Falls; despite a crash training program Smallwood had inaugurated, the Newfoundland labour force was woefully unskilled. Only two-thirds of the men at the site were Newfoundlanders and almost all of these were raw labourers. Almost to a man, Quebeckers held the supervisory and managerial posts. As for materials, the buses which drove guests round the site for the opening ceremony had been brought up by rail from Sept-Îles; the safety helmets handed out to visitors bore the label: *Approuvé par le Ministre du Travail du Québec.*

Yet Smallwood's wrath was aimed not so much at Quebec as at Brinco, the company he had once saved from nationalization. A week earlier Brinco had outraged him by preventing a member of the Newfoundland legislature, Tom Burgess, from visiting the campsite to talk with his own constituents. (Burgess, a former Steelworkers organizer, intended to campaign for his old union.) He was incensed equally by Brinco's proposal to charge Newfoundland as much for power bought at the site as it charged Quebec for power delivered at the border, a hundred miles away. Even as he spoke, Smallwood had in his pocket affidavits from eighteen Newfoundland workmen protesting that they had lost jobs or had been denied promotions by French-Canadian foremen.

For all his threats, Smallwood knew full well that he could not afford a public fight with Brinco. Delivery schedules were so tight and profit margins so slight that any further delay could wreck the project. The most he could do was make the gesture of appointing Burgess to the Newfoundland Power Commission, and open a government office at the company workcamp to hear workers' complaints. Smallwood also made his personal feelings clear enough. One day in September 1967 he refused five successive long-distance calls from Donald Gordon. The two were usually the closest of friends.

Smallwood had won his fight for Churchill Falls. Negotiations between Brinco and Hydro-Quebec dragged on for two more years until, on May 12, 1969, Premier Jean-Jacques Bertrand tabled in the legislature the completed agreement, signed the day before by Lessard and Donald J. McParland, who on Gordon's death had succeeded him as president, and who was himself killed in a plane crash six months later. Under the agreement Hydro-Quebec, beginning in May 1972, would take delivery of 29.1 billion kilowatt hours of power a year for forty years, with an option to renew for a further twenty-five years. The balance of the output, 2.7 billion kilowatt hours a year, was reserved for local use.

On December 12, 1971, six weeks after Smallwood had fought his last election, the first power from Churchill Falls was delivered, well ahead of schedule, to Hydro-Quebec. That same month, another chapter in the story ended. The Dorion Commission, in an eighteen-volume report, handed in its study of the boundary controversy. The issue, as the

Commissioners saw it, was dead. "Quebec's cause is compromised," the report concluded, by the province's failure to protest the boundary in 1949, when Newfoundland's entry into Confederation had "sealed" the Privy Council decision of 1927.

For all Smallwood's achievements there, Labrador remains apart from Newfoundland, in spirit as much as in geography. In the 1971 election, Labradorians' conviction of neglect brought the splinter New Labrador Party within an ace of capturing all three of the mainland territory's seats.

Labrador's potential remains vast, particularly the 1.7 million horsepower sites on the Lower Churchill River and a massive uranium deposit discovered by Brinco which could become the basis for a one billion dollar uranium enrichment complex.

"If we are not big enough, if we are not daring enough, if we are not imaginative enough, to colonize Labrador, someone else will do it," Smallwood had warned during a legislature debate in March 1966. By the time the Churchill Falls project was completed, that challenge was no longer his. It belonged to the new Newfoundland he had created.

24

"They Know Not Joseph"

The hardest decision any successful politician ever faces is how and when to quit. The more successful he is, the harder it becomes. Few go with aplomb; few have gone as awkwardly as Smallwood. Confronted by the dilemma he sketched so accurately himself, neither "to hang on like Diefenbaker, an old man past his prime" nor yet "to step down at a time when people would say I did it just to avoid being humiliated," he let his options slip away until humiliation became inevitable. Yet at the end, if there was little grace in his departure, there was grace in his consistency. Smallwood went down the way he had come up – fighting.

There were, by the late nineteen-sixties, plenty of conventional reasons for Smallwood to retire. He was nearly seventy; except for Bennett in British Columbia, "the other bookend of Confederation" in Smallwood's phrase, every other premier was in his thirties or forties. One by one his own contemporaries slipped into retirement, or died. Newcomers who might have been his sons or grandsons took their places around the cabinet table. With the birth of Natasha Rachel Harvey in August 1970, Smallwood himself became a great-grandfather.

His health remained as phenomenal as ever. Even so he tired noticeably at the end of a long day and his office hours dwindled to a leisurely
ten to four. Lunch, once a sandwich and a cup of tea on the run, turned
into an elaborate three-course ritual, starting with sherry and ending
with kirsch or kummel, shared with close colleagues in his ornate private
dining room in the Confederation Building.

He was still, when need be, the consummate politician. When a rebel
ex-minister, John Crosbie, suggested that the $2.6 million budget for
mothers' allowances might be better spent on other priorities, Smallwood
lunged effortlessly for the jugular: "I would rather resign, quit, fold the
government right now than be party to stabbing 50,000 Newfoundland
mothers in the back." On a platform, despite a marked tendency to
ramble, he could still upstage anyone around: his performance in the
National Film Board's film *Little Fellow from Gambo* won him the Best
Actor award at the 1970 Canadian Film Awards.

These skills, though, were the accumulated store of a lifetime's experience, no longer an art constantly renewed. He listened less and less
often. His monologues and speeches were more and more often sorties
into the past to conjure up the great names from Newfoundland history
– Bond, Morine, Coaker, Morris, Squires – to whom he expected to be
compared. He looked the part of a living historical personage, and even
his fabled memory had lost its edge. He would sometimes tell the same
story to the same person three times in a single day. His audiences listened
politely, but they were no longer in awe. "A new crowd's growing up," he
said early in 1969, "and they know not Joseph."

This new crowd, much more than the ebb and flow of popularity, or
the shifting fads of political style, was the real reason Smallwood should
have retired. By the late sixties, he had accomplished his life's work.
Newfoundland's revolution had happened, a static society had become a
dynamic one. For this triumph, which has no parallel in Canada outside
Quebec, Smallwood paid the ultimate price. He had created a society that
no longer needed him and knew it.

Shortly before noon on November 27, 1965, a road crew rolled the last square foot of blacktop into position on the Trans-Canada Highway. After generations of isolation, Newfoundlanders had a paved road that stretched the 565 miles from coast to coast. The most glaring material disparity between island and mainland had disappeared. That event, more clearly than any other, marks the transition from the old Newfoundland to the new. "The Trans-Canada Highway, more than the outports," the British novelist John Masters wrote in the *Daily Telegraph*, after a visit in 1970, "is today Newfoundland. It carries the busloads of young people emigrating to Toronto. American tourists flash by, going fast, and uprooted villagers, like children of Israel, crawl along it to their new homes, going slowly."

The revolution, for which the completion of the highway serves as a convenient starting-point, had evolved through two distinct phases. The first wave, beginning in the mid-sixties, was a classic uprising of expectations, catalyzed by continuous and visible improvements in transportation, communications, housing, health, public services and education. In 1967, the average per capita income of $1,287 was still the lowest in the country. Yet it was sixty per cent of the national average compared to fifty-one per cent at Confederation.

A society conditioned to accept survival as its highest possible achievement began to recognize, and to learn to cope with, the inevitability of progress. In the process, Newfoundlanders shook off the psychological *malaise* left by centuries of privation and intensified by the depression that began in the 1920s and by the humiliations of surrendering self-rule in the 1930s, and of abandoning nationhood in 1949. Before long, they came not just to expect more, but to demand it as a right, not as a privilege extended by Smallwood, or by anybody else.

If the foundation of the revolution's first phase was economic, the core and substance of its second stage, which as yet is incomplete, was social and cultural. At stake was the survival of a people, a province, and a particular way of life. Progress meant homogenization, the disintegration of the Newfoundland mystique, the dismemberment of her culture, humanist and Celtic, passionate and parochial and above all, fragile.

Once painfully defensive about their particularities, Newfoundlanders by the 1970s had developed an almost extroverted pride in them. They expressed it in a rash of books and plays and historical and anthropological studies and articles; in a flurry of Newfoundland specialty stores opening in mainland cities; in the permanent Newfoundland collection established at Toronto's Picture Loan Gallery; in artist Christopher Pratt's meticulous reconstructions, as silk-screen prints, of nineteenth-century Newfoundland stamps; in the songs of Harry Hibbs, whose records, *Maclean's* estimated, sold as many copies as those of Anne Murray and Gordon Lightfoot put together.

Pride, as Newfoundland broke out of the prison that history, economics and geography had locked it in, led to aspiration. "This jazz about fear pervading the province," said student leader Rex Murphy in 1969, "is a hangover from the past." For the first time since Coaker stormed out of the northern outports at the turn of the century, fishermen formed a union and stood on picket lines at Burgeo under signs that read "Never Again Will We Beg." Memorial University's Extension Service nurtured into life co-operatives, district councils, community associations, the first instruments of rural democracy Newfoundland has ever known.

"We have lived so long under a superman," the Deputy Mayor of St. John's said in a public speech in mid-1970, "that we have lost all capacity for initiative." Initiative, in fact, had died in Newfoundland long before Smallwood ever reached power. It had not so much been taken from the people, by fish merchants, clerics, politicians, as eagerly surrendered to them. It had been stifled, even more, by "the poor bald rock" itself, by an environment that could offer its population no more than a limited and unchanging and unchangeable good; an ethic that held that if no one could succeed except at the expense of others, then it was better that no one should succeed.

Smallwood's achievement, his unlikely revolution, was to create the conditions in which initiative could be reborn. By bluff, bullying and iron will, he kept the society going until the moment when, as he had written in the *New Leader* forty years earlier, it was no longer true that "most of the time and energy and ability of most of the people are caught up in the mere attempt to get enough food, clothing and shelter to enable them to continue existing."

Yet, ironically, in the last years of his rule Smallwood became for a majority of Newfoundlanders an obstacle, at once symbolic and substantive, in the way of their pursuit of excellence and the exercise of initiative. From the late sixties onwards his struggle was no longer sanctioned by an other-directed cause such as Confederation or projects such as the Churchill Falls. Instead he fought increasingly for himself and his place in history. The voters let him know how they felt in the 1968 federal election when six of his seven Liberal M.P.'s were defeated. They removed the last obstacle in the 1971 provincial election. For Smallwood, the first defeat, because it was wholly unexpected, hurt the deeper. For months afterwards he blocked out the reality, inventing explanations or magnifying minor causes. He never let his guard down in public and perhaps only once in private, when he told a friend: "They finally had the guts to vote against me." At the last, Smallwood may have been out of step with his people; to the last no one understood them better.

Smallwood's career reached its peak in 1966 and 1967. In the former, he won the greatest electoral triumph of his life, in the latter he was applauded from coast to coast as "the only Living Father of Confederation."

Because he expected the 1966 campaign to be his last, Smallwood prepared for it with a thoroughness equalled only by his 1958 contest against Diefenbaker. He used heavy-handed blackmail to woo the voters of Stephenville, who were hard hit by the closing of the giant USAF base in return for votes. When the occasion demanded, he thundered out in his best bravura style: "They do this every time," he said, when the hapless Conservatives claimed he planned to wipe them out, "They whine, they cry, they snivel, they beg for mercy on bended knee."

To achieve precisely that objective, Smallwood himself ran against an incumbent Conservative and shifted one of his most popular ministers, Fred Rowe, from a safe Liberal seat to a Tory riding. He hired George Elliott of MacLaren Advertising to help organize the campaign and, on

Elliott's advice, muted his oratory and appeared in only three of fourteen TV commercials. More significantly, he executed his first major cabinet shuffle since 1949. In place of exhausted veterans, he brought in attractive newcomers: Ed Roberts, then twenty-five and Smallwood's former executive assistant; John Crosbie, thirty-five, a member of one of the island's best-known families; Aidan Maloney, forty-seven, former fish-plant manager and Deputy-Minister of Fisheries; and Alex Hickman, forty-two, a prominent lawyer. In addition, more than half the Liberal candidates were newcomers to politics, and so many were in their twenties and thirties that the party was nicknamed "Kiddies Corner."

On September 8, 1966, Smallwood's political tide reached its high water mark. Newfoundlanders, the new young middle class in the growing towns as much as the baymen in the outports, gave him 65% of their votes and all but three of the forty-two seats. At the same time, all seven federal seats were held by Liberals, two of them confirmed at by-elections in that year. No other Canadian politician had ever held such total electoral power.

From there, Smallwood strode on to the glory of Centennial Year. In a country hungry for heroes Smallwood was given national acclaim as an historical figure, a passionate patriot and a politician without equal. Within Newfoundland itself, he moved from triumph to triumph. In July, he presided over the realization of one of his dreams, the official start of construction at Churchill Falls. On the outskirts of St. John's another dream, Memorial University, had become a physical reality. Two years before he had made it an institution unique in North America by providing free tuition and paying students up to $100 a month to attend.* In August, he opened the first north-south road through the centre of the province, to the new $200 million power development at Baie d'Espoir.

---

* Smallwood liked to boast that Memorial, with its students' salaries, was unique in the Western Hemisphere. He contracted this claim of uniqueness after meeting Soviet Premier Aleksei Kosygin at Gander, on his way back from a trip to the United States. Kosygin heard Smallwood's claim and then corrected him: "There is one other in the Western Hemisphere, the University of Havana."

A month later, he opened a $14 million shipyard at Marystown. At the close of 1967, Smallwood, along with other incumbent Premiers, was made a Privy Councillor for life, and proudly hung the inscription on the wall leading to his bedroom. He was offered a Senate seat and gleefully refused, saying "I'm too young to die."

Nation and province had no more laurels left to give, and there were no more electoral prizes to be won. Occasionally, to tease his opponents, Smallwood would drop hints about retirement, and then spoil the effect by noting that all his ancestors had lived hale and hearty into their eighties. Others, however, had decided that the moment to depart was at hand.

On August 6, 1967, Smallwood and Pickersgill drove together down the long dusty road to the Baie d'Espoir power site, to preside at its official opening. Alone in the car, they talked easily of politics, provincial and federal. Abruptly, Pickersgill changed the subject. "Joe. I'm thinking of leaving politics. There's a post coming up that interests me." A month later he left the federal cabinet to become President of the Canadian Transport Commission. Smallwood, in the interim, had telephoned Pearson, who said tactfully that the decision was Pickersgill's; Smallwood then offered Pickersgill a higher salary to become special adviser to the Newfoundland Government, a job that Pickersgill, as tactfully, declined. A personal alliance of fourteen years, without equal in Canadian politics for intimacy and effectiveness, was over.

Some of the loss could be measured in specifics. Since the Liberals' return to office in 1963, Pickersgill had stretched the letter of every act and statute to make Newfoundland Ottawa's favourite province. He dotted the island with rural post offices. As Transport Minister, he commissioned three new ferries and authorized $14 million worth of improvements to the ferry terminals on either side of the Cabot Strait. He provided subsidies to bail out struggling Eastern Provincial Airways, which eventually developed into a thriving regional carrier, and directed the National Harbours Board to take over responsibility for St. John's harbour and thus for its annual deficit.

The larger part of the loss was private and immeasurable. Smallwood's closest and ablest personal adviser was gone, one whose counsel was all the more important because it was given by an equal and accepted as such. The two continued friends, and met and dined regularly whenever one or the other was in Ottawa or St. John's. But there were no more lengthy, thrice-weekly telephone calls. Smallwood rang Pickersgill only twice to ask for political advice: once on a minor matter, once to establish the constitutional niceties of whether or not a minister running for party leadership against the premier had to resign. (Pickersgill said no.) The reason was pride. Any call from Smallwood would sound too much like a call for help, for he no longer had anything to offer Pickersgill in return.

Almost from the moment of Pickersgill's departure, Smallwood could have benefited from his advice. In fact, even before going, Pickersgill had cautioned him against his first political move, a decision to call a provincial by-election in Gander for October 1967. Smallwood lost the district, for the first time since Confederation. A month later, in a federal by-election held to fill Pickersgill's old seat of Bonavista-Twillingate, the Liberal majority was slashed from 6,400 to 1,700.

One reason for the abrupt change was the remarkable resurgence of the Conservatives. The new leader, Gerald Ottenheimer, brought to island politics the style and skill of one educated at London University and the Sorbonne. Instead of wasting his energies, as his predecessors had, in headlong personal assaults on Smallwood, Ottenheimer set out to outflank him with a series of progressive policy proposals. By touring the outports, and publicizing their grievances, he began to drag the party out of its St. John's fastness. The ablest Opposition Leader Smallwood encountered in his career, Ottenheimer was forced to step down for personal reasons in 1970. He returned, however, to run and win a district in the 1971 election.

The basic reason for the change, though, was that the expectations of Newfoundlanders had run ahead of the capacity of economic progress to fulfil them. As a Conservative campaigner in those by-elections, later an M.P., recalls: "For the first time, we could sense that people actually wanted to listen to what we had to say. We didn't really have all that much to say, but we knew they were at least beginning to think about possible alternatives."

Expo year, and its preamble, had given Newfoundland's economy a major stimulus. Community halls, recreation centres, libraries, and hockey rinks went up all over the island. An Arts and Culture Centre, one of the handsomest in Canada, was built in St. John's. Unemployment in 1967 averaged 8.4%, half the figure it had been five years previously.*

Late in that year, all this progress came abruptly to a halt. A slowdown in the mainland economy became a full-blown recession once it reached Newfoundland. By March 1968, one-sixth the entire population, or 87,059 persons, were receiving assistance from the provincial Department of Welfare. That same month, unemployment jumped to twelve per cent. In his budget of April 1968, Smallwood was forced to raise taxes on everything from gasoline to chocolate bars.

The worst blows fell on the fishery. From an average of 35¢ a pound for cod blocks, prices collapsed to a low of 21¢. The production costs of the average Newfoundland plant were 26¢ a pound. The entire industry staggered and two major plants, the four-month-old Ross-Steers operation in St. John's and Northeast Fisheries in Harbour Grace, owned by Bird's Eye of Britain, closed. The cause of the collapse was cyclical: high prices in the prime U.S. market attracted competitors from Poland, East Germany, South Africa and South America who dumped their products, forcing prices down to the point where the small, undercapitalized Newfoundland plants could no longer compete. To make matters worse, the U.S. market itself declined when the Pope proclaimed the end of meatless Fridays. To save the island's fish plants from total collapse, Ottawa moved in with a deficiency payments scheme. After U.S. fishermen protested to Washington against foreign dumping this was altered to an inventory support program.

Federal assistance mitigated the worst, but it could not touch the core of the problem. In past times of economic troubles, Newfoundlanders

---

* Newfoundland's *lowest* unemployment rate in any post–Confederation year was 7.9%, in 1966.

had retreated to the outports, where an inshore fishermen could always survive. After the economic recession of the late fifties, the total number of fishermen in Newfoundland had jumped, by almost half, to a postwar high of 22,615 in 1964. The collapse of fish prices meant that this escape-valve no longer existed; even if it had, Newfoundland's expectations had been raised beyond the subsistence income and unemployment insurance style of life of the outports.

Smallwood's own escape-valve from the burdens of governing had always been the game of politics. The federal Liberal leadership race presented him with the opportunity to do so.

Late in January, the federal Minister of Justice, "wearing this small hat and leather coat. I thought he looked odd but I didn't like to say so," reached St. John's on a cross-country tour to brief the provinces for the forthcoming federal-provincial conference. Smallwood's conversion to Pierre Elliott Trudeau was instant, and total. "Beside him I feel like a clumsy elephant with arthritis," he said. He saw also in the urbane, self-assured French-Canadian intellectual, the man he would have liked to be himself.

At the Constitutional Conference in February, Smallwood announced he would officially declare Newfoundland a bilingual province. This gesture ended his rift with French Canada, initiated by his battle with Lesage and Lévesque over Churchill Falls. As Smallwood at least recalled, his and Trudeau's views on the constitution were a perfect match. His own view was, "For Quebec as a province, not one jot or tittle more than any other province, but for French Canadians, everything."

The other consequence of their meeting was more to the political point. At the April leadership convention Smallwood delivered to Trudeau three-quarters of the eighty-four Newfoundland votes. A delighted observer of the scene, Smallwood sat in Trudeau's box at the convention. A week later, at the 135th annual dinner of the St. George's Society in St. John's, he signed autographs, "Joseph R. Trudeau Smallwood."

Outwardly, he had caught successfully the next wave of power at Ottawa. In fact, and Smallwood was slow to recognize this, the intimacy of the Pearson-Pickersgill years, of chummy personal calls and private meetings, was gone forever. The new regime at Ottawa was technocratic and rational, two virtues towards which Smallwood had never aspired. Instead of grandiose schemes and salesmanship, the new government demanded plans, flow charts, cost-benefit studies. These neither Smallwood nor his civil service could provide. Under pressure from Ottawa, he hired his own squads of experts.

More significant than skirmishes over blueprints, Smallwood had lost political influence at Ottawa. Though he remembered his debt to Smallwood, Trudeau, unlike Pearson, had no need of Liberal reinforcements from Newfoundland. And for many of the new men around Trudeau, Smallwood's style was an uncomfortable reminder of a political dictator they had once fought on their own territory, Maurice Duplessis.

If Smallwood's role at the Liberal convention earned him few credits, it resulted in unmistakable debits. The month before Trudeau arrived in St. John's, Smallwood and his chief lieutenants had agreed to back Trade and Commerce Minister Robert Winters. Smallwood, in fact, had called Winters just before Christmas, urged him to enter, and promised support. Winters told friends a few days later that this was the call which decided him to enter the campaign. The kinship with Winters, which went back as far as Smallwood's first pre-Confederation visit to Ottawa and which had become closer through the fight for Churchill Falls, was obvious, and he was the personal choice of most of the Newfoundland delegates.*

But Smallwood, once converted to Trudeau, brooked no arguments. On the plane up to Ottawa, he harangued delegates on Trudeau's virtues: "He alone can win an election." At the convention itself he sent aides to order Newfoundland delegates wearing "Winters" buttons to replace them with "Trudeau" buttons. The Newfoundland delegation

---

* Though by no means of all: one of Smallwood's members, just before leaving to support Pierre Elliott Trudeau at Ottawa, christened one of his newborn twins, "Pierre."

returned to St. John's with many of its members furious with their leader's bullying, and humiliated by their own mute acquiescence. Of those who resented being treated as voting fodder, none was angrier than John Crosbie.

Crosbie had arrived full-blown on Newfoundland's political scene in 1966. Independently wealthy, an outstanding lawyer who had graduated top of his class at Dalhousie University, he had pursued a conventional career until he ran for Deputy Mayor of St. John's, and won in a landslide. Smallwood recognized a comer, and invited him into the cabinet. Apart from the evident political benefits, Smallwood had reasons deep in his own history. For John Crosbie was just that, a Crosbie, scion of one of Newfoundland's historic families. His grandfather, Sir John Crosbie, a cabinet minister, was remembered, aside from scandals, for the memorable utterance: "The people want branch lines and they shall have them. The voice of the people is the voice of God." His father was Chesley Crosbie, Smallwood's friend in hard times, who had financed the *Book of Newfoundland*, backed the piggery at Gander, and who had rebuilt the family fortunes in large measure from contracts provided by Smallwood. Of Crosbie's two years in the cabinet, a former colleague recalls: "It gave Joe a sweet, special pleasure that he, one of the ragged-arsed artillery should have serving under him a natural-born general."

Generals do not readily take orders from ex-privates. For a full year before he quit, Crosbie left little doubt of his dissatisfaction as he mocked Smallwood, with astonishing indiscretion, round the St. John's East cocktail circuit. The stories all found their way back to Smallwood, but he took no action. He could not afford to. As Minister of Municipal Affairs, and later of Health, Crosbie came to dominate the cabinet. A glutton for work, he won arguments by force and sheer dogged persistence. At the same time, outside the cabinet, investors and businessmen looked to him for leadership and sanity. As the government's financial troubles deepened, Crosbie became that rarity in any Smallwood cabinet, the almost indispensable man.

To leave, Crosbie needed a reason. Smallwood provided it by proposing to advance a bridging loan of $5 million to the New York promoter

John Shaheen to help advance the search for capital for the oil refinery Shaheen planned to build at Come-by-Chance. Inside the cabinet, Crosbie locked into battle with Smallwood over the unsecured loan. When Smallwood forced through the measure, he quit. With him went a colleague, Minister Without Portfolio Clyde Wells. "I have found that in your administration," wrote Crosbie in his letter of resignation, "there is but one master. Anyone who does not accept the opinions and decision of that master is suspect."

Smallwood's response was savage. He called Crosbie "a rat" and then accused one of the most highly regarded members of the Crosbie family of having importuned Shaheen for construction contracts. Under the threat of a libel suit, Smallwood withdrew the charge the following day.

The reason for this intemperance was Smallwood's anguished recognition of the impact the dual resignation would have on Liberal fortunes in the federal election then underway. Already, there were ominous signs of trouble. Trudeau had made his decision to go to the polls on the basis of a Liberal party survey taken two days after the Leadership Convention. It showed the party winning handily across the country, but being crushed in the Atlantic Provinces. Smallwood himself told a friend during his visit to Ottawa, "I've got to get out. I've become a liability to the Liberal Party."

The liability was far heavier than even he had guessed. On June 25, 1968, in the greatest political upset since Confederation itself, the Conservatives won six of the seven federal ridings, and fifty-three per cent of the vote. Only Jamieson, in Burin-Burgeo, the most isolated riding of all, survived, as he put it, "a hell of a beating." Transferred to provincial districts, the results would have given the Conservatives 31 of the 42 seats. The *Daily News* headlined its morning-after editorial, "The Smallwood Era is over in Newfoundland."

Smallwood's first response was cocky. "The tide has gone out," he told reporters the next day, "but it will come back again." Then he retreated into himself, taking his humiliation with him. To block out the reality of rejection by his own people, he invented reasons. Some were valid: an underground anti-Catholic campaign had swung the Pentecostal vote to the Conservatives.* Newfoundlanders liked Robert Stanfield and many mistrusted Trudeau as too urbane, too flashy and a French Canadian to boot; times were hard and unemployment was high; Smallwood himself had alienated many voters by the unrestrained personal assault he had launched in mid-campaign against Frank Moores, the Conservative candidate in Bonavista-Trinity-Conception, as "the latest of a family that has robbed Newfoundlanders blind for centuries."

Within a few weeks Smallwood was haranguing his cabinet colleagues with a list of eighteen reasons for the debacle. Omitted from it was the one that equalled all the others put together – himself. One individual had the courage to put it to him straight. A week after the election, Smallwood visited the outport home of a close friend. "Joe," said his host, as soon as the first pleasantries were over, "I've got something unpleasant to say, and I want to get it over right away. I've been around the bay; the people are saying you're another John Diefenbaker." Smallwood turned his back, stared out the window for a full minute and then swung back. "Do you think I would be such a fool?"

A week later he announced that a convention would be held the following year to pick a new leader for the Liberal Party.

---

* Always hypersensitive about the political influence of the churches (he never forgot that Catholic opposition had almost defeated Confederation), Smallwood meticulously wooed the Pentecostal vote in succeeding years. In 1971, before his last election, an amendment to the BNA Act was moved in the House of Commons by Jamieson: it proposed to add the Pentecostal Assembly to the official list of denominations named in Newfoundland's Terms of Union.

25

"The Wrong Hands"

Smallwood's decision to hold a leadership convention had been impulsive and personal. The election results had disorientated him. The aura of invincibility was gone. For the first time since taking power he no longer automatically commanded events or created them. Instead, like all mortal politicians, he had to ride them out as best he could.

In making his decision, Smallwood had not consulted his cabinet, nor gone through the formality of asking the advice of the party executive. The result was confusion, among the faithful as much as among his enemies. Within a fortnight a "Draft Joey" movement sprang up and issued a manifesto imploring him not to resign. Then Fred Rowe, the senior minister and Smallwood's standby successor for a decade, made up his own mind to run and announced his candidacy formally in January 1969. Crosbie followed soon after. Smallwood, meanwhile, held his options open with a series of uncharacteristically delphic statements: "Nothing and nobody" could persuade him to run except "a strong indication the party will fall into the wrong hands." At the annual Liberal Ball early in 1969, he said he would not "be dictated to by any man who could actually taste ambition . . . no man is going to boot me out." If the public was confused, so was Smallwood. Crosbie could almost certainly beat

Rowe. The question was, if the party were not to fall into "the wrong hands," into whose could it be pressed?

As an opening response to the election setback, Smallwood shuffled his cabinet. Three veterans were pensioned off on the grounds of ill health.* Besides Roberts, the most prominent of the newcomers was Bill Rowe, then twenty-six, son of the senior minister, married into one of the island's most prominent families, a lawyer and a former Rhodes Scholar.

Offsetting the reinforcements, Smallwood lost another member before the year was out. Tom Burgess, an Irish immigrant and former Steelworkers organizer, decided that "Smallwood doesn't give a damn about Labrador" and left to become an independent. The previous May, Smallwood had half-expected Burgess to sweep out in the wake of Crosbie and Wells. He kept him out of harm's way by sending him on a mission to Ottawa to discuss broadcasting coverage in Labrador with the CBC.

In rhetoric that was both emotional and effective, Burgess articulated the grievances of Labrador: a conviction of isolation, political as much as geographic, and, more concretely, the twenty-five cents a gallon tax on gasoline in a territory where there were only twenty-five miles of road; the eighteen cents a pound flight surcharge on all food transported in; the forty per cent of jobs at the Churchill Falls site (nearly all of the skilled ones) held by non-Newfoundlanders. To quell the rebellion, which had been swelled by cancellation of a chipboard mill John Doyle had intended to build there, Smallwood, on January 13, 1969, flew to Happy Valley. He was greeted at the airport by a sign stuck in a snowbank – "No More Promises. The Tide is Still Out." In a raucous two-hour meeting at the high school, he faced a hostile crowd and catcalls – "We don't love you anymore." He ended, coat off and sleeves rolled up, with

---

* When two of these protested publicly that they were in fact in fine fettle, the third, Dr. James McGrath, gravely explained to the press, "I'm sick enough for all three of us."

a standing ovation. The performance was a triumph. Labrador's grievances remained.

By now, Smallwood thought he had found his solution to the succession:
he would remake the Liberal Party, or more accurately, he would make it.
Long romanticized in the press as "a machine" the Liberal Party in fact
added up to an ill-disciplined, inefficient agglomeration of personal
alliances. Grace and favour rather than organization and policy was its
glue. It was innocent of such formalities as constituency associations,
nominating conventions* or even a constitution. In each community,
local notables acted as link between Smallwood and the people; they
passed up information and passed back petty patronage. In fact, these local
chieftains, who won status by their presumed ability to dispense patronage, had little say in who got what. Decisions, down to road repair jobs
and school bus contracts, were made almost entirely by Smallwood
himself and an inner coterie.

"My last great task, the task to which I will devote every ounce of
energy, every waking moment," said Smallwood, "will be to make the
Liberal Party into a great mass movement, down deep in the hearts of
Newfoundlanders." In an historical mood, he observed that "the first
Newfoundland Liberal, the first pioneering Liberal" was Lief Erickson.
Thus assured of their antecedents, 1,250 delegates assembled at the
Beaumont-Hamel Armoury in Grand Falls on September 28, 1968, for
the party's first convention in nineteen years. They drafted a constitution,
elected ex-M.P. Richard Cashin instead of Smallwood's nominee, as pres-
ident, and heard Smallwood say, "For the past twenty years I have

---

* Nominating conventions were first introduced in 1966 to pick candidates
for two federal by-elections. To Smallwood's chagrin, his nominee for the
seat in Grand Falls-White Bay-Labrador was defeated. He never had much
luck with the system: at the first nominating convention held for the 1971
election, his son Bill failed in his attempt to become party candidate in
Labrador South.

selected, I must admit it, ninety-nine percent of the candidates." From now on, he assured them, democracy would decide. The goal of party membership, he went on, should be 100,000.

Nine months later the Liberal Party counted 8,000 members. It had lost its first president. "The party is on a self-destructive course," said Cashin, and resigned. It was uncertain whether the leadership convention would be held at all, still less who would contend it. The explanation was simple: Crosbie's strength was growing and Smallwood had yet to find a successor other than himself.

In part, he had created the problem himself. His two-decade tenure of absolute power had created a vacuum of talent. Smallwood, if immodest, was not far off the mark when he said, "It so happens I'm the only one who has the experience to be Premier." Except for Don Jamieson, whose sights were fixed firmly on Ottawa, there was not a politician of stature in his forties or fifties to be found in the island.

Among the politicians who came to the fore in the late sixties, under Smallwood's tutelage or in opposition to it, and who will dominate Newfoundland politics now that he is gone, there were common denominators so strong as to make them almost a separate class. All were very young, in their twenties or thirties. All were rich, and an astonishing number were millionaires. Several, Crosbie, Cashin, Moores, were the sons of famous families. All had been educated at mainland or international universities.* Almost all were lawyers. Most significantly, except for the stocky and mercurial Cashin, whose rollicking rhetoric echoed that of his uncle, Smallwood's old anti-Confederate opponent Peter Cashin, and perhaps also Clyde Wells, none were recognizably Newfoundlanders. All the others could have fitted comfortably anywhere inside the rising class of North American managerial politicians.

The ablest of the group was Ed Roberts. At the University of Toronto he had demonstrated budding political talent by becoming Editor of *The*

---

* Not entirely by coincidence, three, Crosbie, Moores and Roberts, attended the same private school, St. Andrews in Aurora, Ontario.

Varsity. After an apprenticeship in Pickersgill's office he became, at twenty-four, Smallwood's personal assistant. A ruthless backroom operator, he turned this post into perhaps the second most powerful in the province. Cool and shrewd, his formidable intellect backed by an exceptional memory, Roberts had two qualities rare in the unprofessional hurly-burly of island politics, the self-discipline to work regular twelve-hour days and a detached sense of timing. In the early years, he and Smallwood developed a father-son relationship. Their friendship frayed as Roberts matured into a political personality in his own right. It broke when he tried to leave and Smallwood prevented it. Many of Smallwood's last acts in office amounted to a frantic search to find a candidate who could deny Roberts the succession.

In 1969, however, Roberts was not a potential candidate. He was only twenty-eight and a loner, moreover, who had not learned how to suffer fools patiently. Instead, he advanced the claims of Aidan Maloney, a gentle, perceptive man who had made his mark in the portfolios of Fisheries and of Community and Social Development. Smallwood himself thought highly of Maloney. His political flaw, though, was lack of ambition. A year later he left the cabinet to become first president of the Canadian Saltfish Corporation.

One who had no doubts at all about his readiness to succeed was John Crosbie. His formal attack began March 10, when a "Crowds for Crosbie" movement was launched in Grand Falls. Its style, as much crusade as campaign, was immediately apparent. Crosbie himself, by his tenacious courage, inspired fierce loyalty among his supporters. His spear carriers were students and the businessmen, lawyers and housewives of Newfoundland's rising middle class. The crusade was also well managed and well heeled. Crosbie brought in mainland organizers whose experience had been gained at the federal Liberal convention the year before. For funds, he turned to his brother Andrew, manager of the family's far-flung business empire (and a man whose own political ambitions would before long divide the house of Crosbie).

The audited expenses of Crosbie's six month campaign amounted to an incredible $529,624. Indirect expenses amounted at least to another $100,000. Smallwood, when his turn came, would spend somewhere between $600,000 and $700,000. His funds were calculated with less precision, and regular party finances were used at will.*

That Crosbie, unlike previous opponents, could match Smallwood dollar for dollar mattered, but it was not critical. Vast sums were squandered, by both sides, to pay individuals for the routine chores of driving cars, acting as scrutineers, and cheering in "spontaneous" demonstrations, which elsewhere in the country were performed freely as a matter of course. Crosbie's campaign, for all its effectiveness, had a serious weakness: it posed a direct challenge, not just to Smallwood's political position, but also to his place in history. Crosbie, whose bulldog tenacity was matched by an equal measure of unsubtlety, never realized this. As he toured the province, he attacked Smallwood's industrial policies, on which the government had been founded for two decades, and Smallwood's style of leadership. He thereby invited the Liberal Party to reject the man who had created it. The irony of Crosbie's tactics was to make it almost certain that Smallwood would run, and thus to keep him in power for another two and a half years.

"I'm an unusual person, no doubt," said Smallwood with heavy-handed sarcasm. "I don't like being booted out, cast aside. When someone tries to kick me, I kick back." Crosbie, his former cabinet colleague, had kicked him now for a full year. The only two in the party who could reply in kind were himself and Don Jamieson.

The former broadcaster, Smallwood's old adversary in the Confederation wars, had been appointed Minister of Supply and Services after the 1968 federal election, and had quickly made his mark in Ottawa. The first native-born Newfoundlander to have done so, Jamieson, in the process, had made himself into a power independent of Smallwood. A

---

* These sums can be compared to the $440,000 which represented the largest budget of any of the 1968 claimants for the federal Liberal leadership. On a per capita basis, the expenditures of Crosbie and Smallwood amounted each to a national equivalent of $20 to $25 million. In all, during the three years 1969-71, the Liberal Party of Newfoundland expended close to $3 million.

deft politician, a fluent and indeed an inexhaustible speaker on every conceivable topic, as passionate a Newfoundlander as the Premier, Jamieson could clearly win the convention in a walk against Crosbie, and perhaps even against Smallwood.

In the autumn of 1968, Smallwood had sought out Jamieson in Ottawa, pleaded with him to run, and promised his support. Jamieson kept his counsel. By the spring of 1969, the climate had changed. Jamieson had been promoted to the major portfolio of Transport; any move to Newfoundland now would be at best sideways. At the same time Crosbie was on the rampage and if Smallwood quit he would indeed open himself to the charge he was doing it to avoid being humiliated, for Newfoundland's ship of state was visibly sinking.

"I have always known that Joe had guts," a former colleague remembers of those desperate months in early 1969. "I never realized until then that they were made of pure steel."

The recession of the year before had continued and worsened. By April, fifteen per cent of the work force was unemployed. In his spring budget, Smallwood was forced once again to raise taxes, and to slash $27 million from government spending. Memorial University's budget was cut from $13 million to $9.7 million. The principal victim was Smallwood's beloved free tuition program, cut back to those who could pass a means test. Students marched through the streets led by a jeep towing a trailer that bore a black coffin and the banner FUNERAL FOR EDUCATION.

As serious as the recession itself was the shortage of money to pump-prime recovery. Smallwood's industrial speculations had escalated the per capita provincial debt to $1,400. The capital markets were shut tight. Nor could he wheedle funds from Ottawa. The capital was deep into its anti-inflation freeze. Smallwood's pleas for assistance for his Come-by-Chance oil refinery were vetoed. The new Department of Regional Economic Expansion (DREE) was enmeshed in developing its new theology of "growth centres." In the meantime, the $200 million bootstrap development of the west coast which Smallwood had hoped to negotiate under the previous development doctrine (Fund for Rural Economic Development) was scrapped. One year after its birth, DREE had still to spend a dollar in Newfoundland.

Newfoundland's self-confidence, born of the Centennial year boom and excitement, was collapsing. In its place there was uncertainty, and bitterness. In past times of trouble, when the price of fish was low and of flour high, Newfoundlanders had fallen back to that hard core of the Newfoundland mystique, endurance. As columnist Ray Guy wrote in the *Evening Telegram*, "We should follow the example of the baymen who have learned at least one thing in four centuries. And that is endure, endure, endure. Sometimes the mute endurance of rocks, sometimes the roaring endurance of a stout bull . . . sometimes the fluid endurance of the waters around us that only look soft."

Under the impact of modernization this mystique was losing its vitality, and its symbols. After a year-long battle, the *Newfie Bullet* was pensioned off, its place taken by shiny, anonymous CNR buses which made the cross-island run in fourteen hours, instead of the train's twenty-four, wind and weather permitting. On July 2, 1969, the seventeen-car Caribou No. 102 left Port-aux-Basques to make the last run to St. John's. It was, wrote Guy, "a Presbyterian wake, not an Irish wake."

Once credited for every gift to Newfoundland, including those from God and Ottawa, Smallwood was blamed now for every failure and setback no matter what its origin. He was criticized as much for the industries he failed to create, like the Come-by-Chance refinery, as for those which he did create and which polluted the countryside, like the ERCO plant on Placentia Bay. To a degree which has few parallels in Canadian politics, he became the target for personal abuse.

As if to make up for its long quiescence, the press turned on him savagely. The columns of the *Evening Telegram* in particular, the largest and most influential paper in the province, became a daily diatribe. In response to a press he considered hostile, Smallwood produced the *Newfoundland Bulletin*, a monthly governmental hagiography distributed free to 50,000 homes. Later, he initiated a daily fifteen-minute "Conversation with the

Premier" on Radio Station VOCM, stopping in to record his message on his way to work from Roache's Line.

The endless battering had its effect. In private, Smallwood spoke lovingly of retirement and of the "great history of Newfoundland" he planned to write. Pride stopped him. So also did a visceral dislike, closer to hatred, of Crosbie, whom he saw both as a traitor to the party and as a representative of the merchant class he had once crushed, now reaching back for power. So also did simple joy at the prospect of a rousing political battle. And so finally did the fact that there was no one else who could beat Crosbie.

There were moments of respite from the pressure. In January, Smallwood flew to Washington to attend the inaugural ball of his former travelling companion, Richard Milhous Nixon. On March 31, ceremonies marking the twentieth anniversary of Confederation rolled round. The Prime Minister in his speech (read for him by Jamieson, since Trudeau was forced to cancel out for Eisenhower's funeral) called Smallwood "the b'y who built the boat of Confederation, and who for twenty years has sailed her." Smallwood said in reply that Newfoundland had at last lost "her infamous curse, her inferiority complex," and added "Newfoundlanders are impatient to say to Canada, 'Here is more than you are giving us.' When that day arrives, Newfoundlanders will be so proud and vain they will be impossible to live with."

But the critical decision could not be avoided. Early in May, Smallwood called on Jamieson in Ottawa. He and the Transport Minister circled one another warily. Once more, Smallwood asked him to run and pledged his support. But in contrast to the year before, there was no urgency in his plea. Jamieson promised an answer in three weeks. Jamieson was well aware that by agreeing to run he would pre-empt Smallwood. He was equally aware that Smallwood's support might be so extravagant that he might never be able to re-emerge as a leader in his own right.

Smallwood now set out, with two travelling companions, on a round-the-world tour, through Europe, India, Thailand, to Hong Kong (where he tried to cross into Red China and spent an hour arguing with a stone-faced Chinese consul). It was in Hong Kong, at the Peninsular Hotel, that he made up his mind. Well after midnight he woke up his two companions, announced he would run and, pacing back and forth, shooting out phrases, set out his strategy. A mammoth petition would be organized, to be signed by 100,000 Newfoundlanders, and brought to his office in a wheelbarrow. Bowing to the will of the people, he would agree to run. This scheme was never implemented: advisers pointed out that it was Liberal delegates rather than citizens who mattered.

From Hong Kong, while his travel-mates continued on to Taiwan, Smallwood flew non-stop to Montreal. In the Queen Elizabeth Hotel he met Jamieson. Once more the offer was made. This time, as soon as Jamieson refused, Smallwood wasted no time on further entreaties, but immediately launched into an elaborate description of his own campaign.

On July 3, on a province-wide television hookup, Smallwood announced the leadership convention would be held October 30–November 1. He said nothing of his own plans. A fortnight later he ended the suspense. He would be a candidate, he said, and wage "the greatest political campaign Newfoundland has ever known." (Fred Rowe dropped out of the race a week later.)

From the start, Smallwood made plain the nature of that campaign. "What will be on trial," he said at his opening meeting on August 14, "is not only Joey as leader, but Joey as Premier of Newfoundland. And when Joey is on trial, the party he leads is on trial." When a member of the audience shouted, "This sounds like the fight for Confederation all over again," he nodded agreement from the platform. In one day, he barnstormed through nineteen Conception Bay communities, heralded by a truck with a public address system blaring out Newfoundland ditties.

Like Confederation, this was civil war. The cities, the young, the educated, the wealthy were with Crosbie. Smallwood had the outports and the party machinery. "I'm still a bayman" he said at one meeting, and, reaching back to the simpler certitudes of twenty years earlier, damned the "Water Street merchants." At the hamlet of Gilliams in the Bay of Islands he was almost booed off the stage, but came roaring back – "Newfoundlanders may get mad at Joey, but deep down in their hearts they love Joey" – and had the audience cheering on its feet.

Crosbie's campaign, by contrast, was smooth and conventional. He flooded the airwaves with sixty-second radio commercials. A "Youth for Crosbie" movement was created, his headquarters distributed slick pamphlets and buttons and ordered red and white mini-skirted uniforms for a corps of Crosbie hostesses.

Still maturing as a politician, Crosbie spoke in generalities of "planning" and "priorities." He was feeling his way towards the concept of rational, comprehensive, economic development, that would be enunciated a year later by the federal Department of Regional Economic Expansion and by the Conservative Opposition.

Smallwood's approach was easily caricatured, and endlessly so, by the local press, as one of helter-skelter, industrial promotion. ("He's looking for a gypsy-caravan factory," wrote Guy when Smallwood visited Roumania.) Yet it encompassed both a philosophy and a dream. "Newfoundland cannot afford to be strictly logical if she is to catch up," he said in one legislature debate with Crosbie. He admired Doyle and Shaheen for their daring and imagination, but he had few illusions about businessmen. "This free enterprise system is only a big laugh. A joke. It's not free and it's not enterprising. It's pap-fed, it's nursed, it's coddled by governments who lash out with the thousands of millions of dollars." Nor had he any illusions about the magnitude of the problems facing Newfoundland, whatever style of development was attempted. During the Throne Speech Debate, on March 3, 1970, he expressed, with tears in his eyes, the essence of his philosophy.

> If the young people leave, we're dead. How do you make New-
> foundland an exciting province? With caution? With prudence? With
> conservatism? That's death, that washes us down the drain . . .
>
> There isn't a tougher job anywhere than governing Newfoundland.
> I couldn't stand the thought of five centuries going down the drain. It
> can happen, and we could cease to be even a memory.

If simple vanity often prompted Smallwood's violent reactions to criticism of his industrial policies, so also did a conviction that the caution his
critics urged could lead to the destruction of his beloved Newfoundland.

With the press overwhelmingly on his side, Crosbie easily won the
battle of words. But he lost where it mattered, among the delegates who
would decide the convention. The mechanics required that each of 41
districts hold a meeting to elect 36 delegates. Smallwood's strategy was to
pack these meetings with his own supporters, who would elect a slate
committed to his cause. Crosbie, once he realized what was happening,
responded in kind. The district meetings turned into continuous trench
warfare (the vote counting at one lasted for six hours), each side rounded
up supporters by pressure and with money. One especially costly tactic
was to rent every available bus and taxi for miles around a meeting place,
so that none was left for the other side.

Smallwood swept three of the first five association meetings. A week
later, Crosbie triumphed in St. John's Centre. By October 3, the count
was Smallwood 189, Crosbie 89; a week later it closed to 439 to 215; by
October 13, it stood at 565 for Smallwood and 233 for Crosbie. The outharbour districts were reporting now and by the time the last meeting was
over, Smallwood had close to 1,000 delegates and Crosbie a bare 350.
Provided the delegates stood by their pledges, the issue was settled.

The three weeks of district elections had split the Liberal Party almost
beyond healing. Families were divided: the sons and daughters of cabinet
ministers campaigning for Crosbie, their parents standing staunchly by
Smallwood. At this juncture, a third man thought he saw the chance to
become a candidate of reconciliation. On October 13, Alex Hickman,
the Minister of Justice, a competent unaggressive lawyer who had
attempted to play the role of mediator between the old guard and the
rebels, announced he would run. Without money, organization, and
entering too late to contest the association meetings, Hickman was
scarcely a serious contender. Yet his defection publicized still further the
divisions within the party. In another intemperate outburst, Smallwood
announced that Hickman, because he had demonstrated lack of faith
in the leader, must resign the cabinet. On the anguished advice of his
colleagues, the Premier backed down and said only that "It would be

dishonourable for anyone to try to persuade committed delegates to change their minds." Since these delegates were Hickman's only potential source of support he judged that the statement "impugns my integrity" and quit anyway. With his cue lines better prepared, Smallwood kept his head when another colleague, Finance Minister Val Earle, announced his support for Hickman. "He's as welcome back as the flowers in May," he said of Earle.

The convention was the largest political assembly in Newfoundland's history. One thousand five hundred and seventy-five delegates, alternates and ex-officio party members streamed into St. John's. For some, it was their first visit to the capital. They arrived in Sunday suits for the occasion, some accompanied by wives to guard them from the fleshpots of the city. At the airport and the bus terminals, squads of Smallwood, Crosbie and Hickman supporters pressed campaign kits into the delegates' hands, and tugged them off to hospitality suites where beer cases staggered toward the ceiling and bottles of rum were massed like armies behind the bar. Hickman, dubbed "Mr. Clean" by the press, offered only coffee and sandwiches; even his own supporters preferred the hospitality suites of others.

For Smallwood, the press of people and the challenge of the contest were, as always, like a shot of adrenalin. He moved among the delegates like a populist monarch, remembering names by the hundreds, swapping stories of battles and chicaneries long ago, waving his repartee like a sceptre. Since the hotels were filled to overflowing, his managers had hired seventeen sleeping cars from the old *Bullet*, drawn up on a siding at the station. He announced he would sleep there himself, president of "The Loyal Order of Sleepers" and issue certificates, "I Slept with Joey."

At noon on Friday, October 31, Smallwood handed in his resignation as party leader. That afternoon, he went down to the St. John's Memorial Arena, on the shore of Quidi Vidi Lake, to deliver his speech. The steamy arena was packed, the floor a forest of black and red (Smallwood), red and white (Crosbie) and yellow (Hickman) banners, posters and streamers. When Smallwood's name was called, the doors at either end burst open and in marched three bands, led by squads of cheerleaders and majorettes. For eight minutes they rocked the hall, while Smallwood's army cheered and whistled, waving their long spearlike "JOEY" banners, sending plastic boaters with his name soaring into the air.

"This is the great gathering I always dreamed of," he said as the hall stilled. He likened the power of the Liberal Party to "the surge of the mighty Churchill River." He pledged himself "to devote my energy, my skill, my experience to reunite and to reconcile," and paraphrased Lincoln, "with malice towards none, with charity for all, let us proceed to bind up the Party's wounds."

He was lucky in his opponents. Hickman, flat and uninspired, begged the audience to "give a little fellow from Grand Bank a chance to serve you." Crosbie, as his supporters screamed their lungs out, was nervous. He sweated heavily under the klieg lights and muffed many of his best lines. Yet he caught the core of the issue: "It is always painful when a great political figure has accomplished the purposes needed to be accomplished at a certain time, and then fails to relinquish his power." He spoke of the need for "priorities," for order in governmental affairs, for an end to patronage, and brought his supporters to their feet with his peroration, "I am a Liberal by conviction, a reformer by preference, and an opponent of abuse of power and bullying."

On Saturday, the voting took more than three hours. The mood of the crowd, incited by the speeches and by rumours of bombs and stolen ballots, was edgy. At last, at 5:45 P.M., on a platform backed by a huge banner bearing the provincial flower, a red and black pitcher-plant, the Chairman of the Convention, Herman Batten, tapped the microphones, called for order and in a monotone read out the results. "John Crosbie, 440 . . . T. Alex Hickman, 187 . . . Randolph Joyce (a student candidate) 13 . . . Joseph R. Smallwood, 1,070 . . ."

In a great bullroar of triumph, joy, and relief, Smallwood's army surged up from the floor of the auditorium and massed against the wooden boards to the right of the platform where the Premier sat in his candidate's box. Exultant, he moved slowly through the crowd, two burly constables pushing ahead, his wife clinging to his arm, four of his grandchildren riding in the rear on the shoulders of other constables. Hand after hand thrust out to be shaken, a woman, sobbing, put her arms around him, "We did it for you, Joe."

On the podium, his head almost hidden behind the bank of microphones, Smallwood began to speak. "A great victory for Liberalism . . . the majority has decided . . . let us go forward together." The words in between, and all those afterwards, were lost. From the far end of the arena a chant, angry and menacing, had begun. "We want John. We want John. We want John."

As Smallwood's phalanx, its mission accomplished, swept out of the hall, the Crosbie supporters, students and middle-class businessmen, took their place on the floor. Girls wept openly, young men cursed and shouted into reporters' microphones, "This means two more years of tyranny."

In ragged ranks, they marched back and forth before the television cameras, chanting "Ho Ho Ho Chi Minh," arms raised in the Hitler salute. They burned party membership cards. Above the podium, a bearded student spat. His spittle hit a cabinet minister.

Quick to passionate anger, Newfoundlanders make poor haters. The spectacle on the convention floor had brought the open hatred of Chicago's Democratic Convention to the provincial backwater of St. John's. His moment of triumph robbed from him (television gave as much coverage to the demonstration as to his victory), Smallwood left the auditorium deeply shaken. He drove straight home, attending none of the victory parties planned for him. The next day he said on CBC's *Weekend*, "They're the same as young people everywhere. They know what they are against. They don't know what they are for."

Whatever the numbers of the final vote, or the way it had been achieved (Smallwood had hoped for 1,300, instead forty per cent of the party rank and file had voted against him), Smallwood had won convincingly. Once more, he was the unquestioned leader, able to be magnanimous even if magnanimity risked being interpreted as weakness. Instead he ripped open the Party's wounds.

Vengeful in the wake of the student demonstrations, the cabinet met four days after the convention and at Smallwood's urging, voted overwhelmingly to refuse a post to Val Earle, the minister who had backed Hickman. Nor was Hickman, though open to offers, invited to return. A year later Smallwood boasted, "not even the vestigial remains of Crosbieism are left in the party." He had achieved this at the cost of seven ministers or members. Crosbie, Hickman and Earle all eventually joined the Conservatives. Clyde Wells left politics to tend his law practice. Tom Burgess went on to found and lead the New Labrador Party.

Even those closest to him were growing restive. By early 1970, Maloney and Roberts, friends and allies, had become exhausted and disgusted by the endless quarrels within the declining empire. Maloney was offered, by Fisheries Minister Jack Davis, the post of president of the new crown corporation established to market fish, The Canadian Saltfish Corporation. At the same time Roberts was approached by his friend Tom Kent, Pearson's former policy secretary and at that time Deputy Minister of Regional Economic Expansion, with the proposal that he become Newfoundland Regional Director for DREE. When Smallwood learned of the news he telephoned Trudeau and protested angrily against federal raiding of his cabinet. After weeks of negotiations, he agreed to Maloney's departure, but not to Roberts's.

Had Roberts gone, even on outwardly amicable terms, the government would have been reduced to a shadow. Only a single minister of recognized stature, the likeable but youthful Bill Rowe, would have been left. Smallwood never forgave what he considered to be Roberts's disloyalty; he forgave his own dependency on him even less.

Yet this dependency could not be avoided. As the process of government became increasingly complex and specialized, expertise became essential. Smallwood, more by default than by design, was forced to delegate authority. He could no longer run the government, as one journalist put it, "like a bicycle repair shop." Decision-making came to rest increasingly on three young ministers: Roberts, Bill Rowe and John Nolan, the last a former broadcaster who rose to the occasion in the heavy portfolio of Economic Development.

Even so, by the power of his personality, Smallwood could still, whenever he chose to, settle an argument on his own terms. And those terms were still industrial development, "Develop or Perish." As soon as the convention was over, Smallwood turned his attention to the most grandiose of his current schemes, an oil refinery to be created by John Shaheen at Come-by-Chance. Against the opposition of Ottawa, the oil industry and the Opposition and press in Newfoundland, he fought for two years, and in October 1970, the deal was signed.

Whatever the cost-benefit defects, the refinery was on, and Smallwood had his vindication. That same season two other successes came his way: The Iron Ore Company of Canada announced a $150 million expansion of its Labrador properties and on November 2 after two years of wrangling, mostly over oil and silica leases (the former held by John Doyle), Ottawa and Newfoundland signed an agreement to create a second national park in the province, at Bonne Bay on the west coast.

The Conservatives, meanwhile, were encountering the same personality divisions which, a year earlier, had come close to sundering the Liberals. Early in 1970, the party leader, Ottenheimer, stepped down. For replacement, the party turned to Ottawa, and to Frank Moores.

Of the half-dozen Conservative M.P.'s elected in 1968, three – Jim McGrath, Jack Marshall and John Lundrigan (the man Pierre Trudeau told to "fuddle-duddle") – had gone on to make a considerable mark in the House of Commons. Moores, by contrast, had been close to invisible. Then thirty-seven, the son of a wealthy fish merchant family from Harbour Grace, he was cool, affable and, most important, blessed by good fortune. He had won the 1968 election at least partly out of public disgust at Smallwood's personal attack on him. In Ottawa, he set a record for non-attendance in the Commons, turning up at eight per cent of its daily sittings. Even so, he was elected President of the National Progressive Conservative Association in 1969, as successor to Dalton Camp; he was supported both by the Camp faction and by Diefenbaker loyalists, each of whom were anxious to avoid another confrontation. In St. John's in May 1970, he effortlessly won the provincial leadership, over four other candidates. Once more Moores disappeared from public view. Still an M.P. at

Ottawa,* he made few public pronouncements and instead set about reorganizing the party from the ground up.

The trouble, though, was mostly at the top. One of the losing candidates at the convention had been Hubert Kitchen, a former school principal turned professor of education at Memorial. A passionate and emotional outharbourman, Kitchen was out of place in the St. John's-centred party, all the more since, as he saw it, power was passing back to new representatives of the old mercantile class. He quarrelled openly with Moores, then took his troubles to Smallwood at a meeting at his Roache's Line home. Moores expelled him from the party. In the summer of 1971, Kitchen joined the Liberals and was named to the cabinet. On the way over he passed Crosbie heading in the other direction. Newfoundland's political gavotte, which would bemuse outsiders after the election, had begun.

The Kitchen affair left the Conservatives in disarray. Coupled with Smallwood's industrial successes, it presented him with his most promising opportunity in four years, either to call an election or to leave with his head high.

Smallwood in fact had begun thinking about retirement again almost the moment the Come-By-Chance deal had been settled. That fall, by wheedling $25,000 out of local businessmen, he had engineered the purchase in London of the papers of Sir John Duckworth, a nineteenth century Newfoundland Governor, which he presented to the provincial archives. In this literary mood, he revived the notion of writing a history of the island. He promptly called an old literary friend, announced he planned to resign immediately and suggested that the two of them set up in partnership. Until his enthusiasm waned, Smallwood had got as far as

---

* Camp, with Moores's support, planned to run in the by-election in Bonavista-Trinity-Conception that Moores's retirement would open up. He changed plans, however, after careful soundings made it plain he could not win against the "carpet-bagger" issue. Moores then stayed on as M.P. – he did not officially retire until September 1971 – performing for a year a unique dual role as a member at Ottawa and as leader of the provincial party.

planning the apartments the pair should rent in London and Lisbon while they dug through old records.

But politics soon supplanted history. Late in October Smallwood called a day-long meeting of his ministers and close advisers. He told them the results of a survey carried out by Contemporary Research Ltd., of Toronto. It showed the Liberals well in the lead in the popular vote. Translated into seats, it would give the party twenty-eight to thirty of the forty-two, a clear win though modest compared to the triumphs of the past. Of the men around the table all but one, a junior minister, voted to postpone an election. Their consensus was that economic conditions would improve enough to make a major victory certain.

Hindsight is a tool of the trade for historians but for a practising politician it is the most futile of exercises. Just over a year later, Smallwood was asked if he regretted not calling the election at a time when he would almost certainly have won it. He answered: "Yes. And if my mother had married the King I would be . . ., and so on. I only regret losing it when I did call it."

Apart from an abortive attempt to conjure up a platform for the eventual campaign by a so-called Master Plan Conference held in St. John's the following February, Smallwood gave no further thought to election plans until the summer of 1971. By then, the second stage of Newfoundland's revolution was in full ferment.

26

"It Started in Burgeo"

WE BELIEVE ABSOLUTELY AND UNCHANGEABLY IN THE RIGHT OF ALL WORKERS OF HAND AND BRAIN TO ORGANIZE THEMSELVES AND TO BARGAIN COLLECTIVELY. THIS RIGHT IS ALMOST AS BASIC AND PRECIOUS AS LIFE ITSELF. So ran the telegram Smallwood sent to the president of the newly formed Newfoundland Fishermen's Union (on November 5, 1970) after a fish plant owner in Burgeo had refused to recognize the union's existence.

The rhetoric rolled out as munificently as it had a half century earlier when he stumped New York for Norman Thomas. It echoed the words he had used in 1951 when he had formed the Newfoundland Federation of Fishermen in a hopeful but unsuccessful attempt to recreate Coaker's movement. As an exhortation it was almost as powerful, though coming this time from the side of the angels, as those he had delivered in 1959 against the Woodworkers. The difference was that there was no longer purpose behind the rhetoric. The members of the fishermen's union knew it, their votes cost Smallwood three seats in the election the following year. Smallwood knew it too. Through the six-month battle of Burgeo which nearly destroyed the union he spoke scarcely a word. Instead, as a gesture, he donated $125 to the union strike fund.

That gesture, awkward and not much appreciated, described accurately the role that circumstances compelled him to play. Even if Smallwood had wanted to intervene, there was little he could have done. Burgeo itself was no more than the noisiest evocation of what was going on all over the island. The green-and-black "It Started in Burgeo" bumper stickers on the cars of union sympathizers were no more than a handy symbol for a social transformation underway long before as dissent, open and unafraid, took the place of Newfoundland's long tradition of mute apathy.

This was the second phase of the province's revolution. It diminished Smallwood's power in two ways. In straightforward political terms, a passive, hierarchical society that could be dominated by a single, charismatic figure had matured toward a conventional, pluralist society. The second consequence was more personal. On the foundation of the modest prosperity he had won for them, Newfoundlanders were "seeking human excellence" in the phrase he had used in the *New Leader* in 1924.

From Cape Race to Cape Ray this new-found confidence found new voices. Sometimes it spoke through individuals, like Vic Hollett of Arnold's Cove who travelled to St. John's carrying in protest a bottle filled with the polluted water of Placentia Bay. Or Olga Spence who organized a human blockade at Hawke's Bay to protest a dusty, pitted road and who said of Smallwood, "If he were here, I'd take him by the collar and shake him." (Mrs. Spence was a woman of Herculean proportions and Smallwood declined the invitation.) More often the confidence was expressed collectively, through the thirty-three regional development associations and improvement committees, the first rural democracies in Newfoundland's history who took on planners and politicians alike and through the uninhibited protests of Memorial University students and the equally uninhibited satire of the daily press, as biting as any in the country.

The loudest voice was that of organized labour which, beginning with three simultaneous strikes late in 1969, emerged from its long, post-IWA silence. In 1970, members of the St. John's Constabulary shattered tradition by marching off their beats to protest the disciplinary suspension of thirty-two officers and won their case. Long-quiescent unions such as those of civil servants, prison wardens and hospital laboratory technicians all threatened strike action to back up wage demands. In 1971 the dam broke, there were fourteen separate strikes and a million man-hours lost. Among them were walkouts by school teachers (the first in their history), by fluorspar miners in St. Lawrence who manned picket lines from April to September, by Buchans steelworkers who stayed out from June to November, and by electricians who held out for twelve weeks even though five thousand construction workers were idled. "Public protest," agonized the Anglican Lord Bishop, "is coming close to being used to replace the proper executive authority of elected representatives and government departments."

Smallwood understood his people far too well not to recognize what was happening. "For fleeting moments," as Professor Peter Neary has written (*Journal of Canadian Studies*) of his last year in office, "the old radical gleam could be seen." He brought down legislation to grant the right of collective bargaining to the Fishermen's Union, and legislation to take over management of forest lands. That same year, his Minister of Health, Ed Roberts, setting a precedent one province after another picked up, revised the Medicare Act to introduce penalties against doctors who submitted false claims.* Nor did Smallwood, despite heavy criticism, waver in support for his Minister of Welfare, Steve Neary, former labour leader and a maverick populist possessed, as Smallwood put it, "of a brilliant heart." Even so, after twenty-three years in office, of which more than a decade had been spent hobnobbing almost exclusively with the rich and the ruthless, he could change only so much. The Liberals, as Professor Neary put it in the same article, "were laden with decades of privilege and encrusted with barnacles of compromise."

---

* Roberts, in his campaign to halt Medicare's exploitation, disclosed that one physician had managed to claim for 88 consultations in a single four-hour period. Some of the reported incomes scandalized the public: $142,688 for one general practitioner; $131,541 for one surgeon. The equivalent, in each case, of the total annual income of one hundred inshore fishermen.

In the 1940s, Smallwood himself had overturned Newfoundland's power structure. Now he had to stand back and watch it happening all over again. The painful irony was that the two most powerful agents of social change in Newfoundland, the Fishermen's Union and, more profoundly, the Extension Service of Memorial University, were each hostages from his own past, born out of the ashes of initiatives he had attempted, too early and too hopefully, during his first heady years of power.

By the late sixties, Smallwood's Federation of Fishermen had dwindled almost to a letterhead. Dependency upon government had robbed it of credibility, its membership had dropped to bare 2,500. The movement which took its place stood on its own feet, and made its own mistakes.

The Northern Fishermen's Union, as it was first known, was formed in the northern peninsula outport of Port au Choix, on May 2, 1970. In this raw little town looking out on the Gulf of St. Lawrence, as in scores of other settlements, fishermen grumbled about their lot and about the price that merchants paid for their fish. The difference was that in Port au Choix there was a parish priest who listened.

At thirty-four, Desmond McGrath was an activist Catholic with the looks, and much of the style, of Philip Berrigan. He was burly, uncomplicated, at ease amid the rough language of his parishioners. "You're chicken," he said, when fishermen complained about merchants' prices. "What you need is a good union so you don't have to put up with this kind of crap." When the fishermen asked him to lead the union, he replied, "You haven't the guts to follow through. You'll leave me high and dry." Until at last they committed themselves.

Within two months, membership swelled from an initial 200 to 700, each bearing a blue and white tin badge. On November 7, the union signed its first agreement, with the Fisheries Products plant in Port au Choix. For the first time in Newfoundland history, fishermen and plant workers had been welded into a single bargaining unit.

The sophistication and drive the union demonstrated were the product of McGrath's most important convert; his classmate at St. Francis Xavier University, the former M.P. Richard Cashin. Ginger-haired, once described as the "Scarlet Pimpernel" of the movement, Cashin was one of the ablest orators in the province. After his defeat in 1968, his career had gone into decline. Then, breaking ranks with his own class (independently wealthy, he belonged to one of the island's oldest clans), he had found himself and a new career. He acted as lawyer for Placentia Bay fishermen in their pollution damage suit against ERCO, and wrung a $300,000 settlement. After that, he joined forces with McGrath. From the platforms of Star-of-the-Sea and Loyal Orange halls, the two spread the word. McGrath offering the vision of dignity and strength through unionism, Cashin the fire and brimstone.

From the start, Cashin realized that any union confined to Newfoundland alone would be too small to survive the inevitable clashes with fish companies. In the fall of 1970, he and McGrath travelled to Ottawa and there discovered the god-parent they were looking for in the 40,000-member Canadian Food and Allied Workers, an industrial union which had branched out to organize a number of Maritime fish plants.

Renamed the Newfoundland Fishermen, Food and Allied Workers, the new union held its founding convention at the Hotel Newfoundland in St. John's in April 1971. Delegates elected Cashin as President, and listened as Smallwood, the principal guest speaker, reminisced of his own days as a union man. By then, union membership, testament of one of the most remarkable organizing drives in Canadian labour history, stood at close to 7,000. The union came formally into existence that June, when a bill granting fishermen the right to collective bargaining was passed by the legislature. "After Confederation and Churchill Falls," said Smallwood, "this is the third-proudest moment of my life."

But the fledgling union had to struggle to survive. It was already locked into battle with the most powerful fish merchant in the province, and the most stubborn. Their confrontation became, as Cashin put it, "a fight, not for wages or working conditions, but for human dignity."

"I'm not anti-union. I just think that in certain circumstances unions are not practical, and rural Newfoundland is one of them. You haven't the local leadership to run them intelligently, with all due respect to the people – I'm very fond of them."

That statement, which resounded across province and nation in the summer of 1971, could have been uttered only by Spencer Lake, fish merchant and squire of Burgeo. His power was less the product of size (he operated three medium-sized plants) than of location, Burgeo was wholly isolated, without roads and reachable only by sea. Within the community, Lake was not only the fish plant owner, he was also mayor and most of the stores belonged to him.

Lake's obduracy was his own, but at the same time he was something of an apotheosis of his class. Still handsome in his fifties, urbane and bluff, he was the son and grandson of fish merchants, and had married into another powerful mercantile family. He was also one of the most efficient managers in the province, having developed a line of proven products marketed under the brandname "Caribou" in Gloucester, Massachusetts. Since coming to Burgeo in 1953, Lake had transformed the community. He himself lived in luxury, surrounded by a menagerie that included a stable of riding horses, and a trio of South American llamas.

Only too well aware of Lake's strength and personality, Cashin and McGrath had hoped to avoid a conflict. Instead, their hand was forced by local militants, mostly young men who had served on inland lakers, and become members of the hard-nosed Seafarers' International Union. The battle of Burgeo split families, pitted brother against brother and neighbour against neighbour in a small closeknit community where feuds, once begun, lingered on for decades. Most of all, though, the strike was a war of generations – the old preferring the certitudes of paternalism, the young the potential of democracy.

The certification vote itself was won by the narrowest of margins, 105 to 65, with 35 abstentions. Lake went on radio to appeal to his workers not to join. As more substantive assurance he hiked plant wages from $1.36 to $1.50 an hour. Six months of negotiating produced a single advance, agreement to add one statutory holiday. A conciliation board recommended a seven cents an hour increase, which Lake flatly rejected.

On June 4, 1971, after the mid-day dinner break, the men of Burgeo Fish Industries failed to return to the plant. Instead, they set up a ragged picket line on the gravel road outside, carrying signs, "Local 1243, NFFAWU on Strike" and "Never Again Will We Beg." The struggle had begun. "This is not just a fight in Burgeo," Cashin shouted at a raucous meeting in the Anglican Parish Hall. "This is a fight to change a system that has kept Newfoundland down for centuries."

"They should mind their own business," said Lake, "rather than going round stirring up trouble in communities where there is full employment."

The events that followed had a quality of Grecian inevitability. Neither side, once the confrontation had begun, could yield. Nor could either side win. Lake could never again recreate the cap-in-hand acqui-escence of the past. As for the Union, it could defeat Lake only at the cost of his leaving Burgeo and of closing down the plant that kept the town alive.

The Union won the opening skirmishes. It blocked Lake's first attempts to break the picket line, and even extended the strike to his Gloucester subsidiary. He then secured a court injunction restricting pickets at Burgeo to a token four, and, by hiring schoolchildren on holiday and older workers, managed to reopen the plant.

Goaded to desperation, men marched to the centre of town and in a two-hour orgy did $25,000 worth of damage to Lake's stores. In the wake of this violence, Smallwood broke his silence. Lake, he said, was "making a very serious mistake" in trying to buck public opinion. He appealed to him to reopen negotiations with the union, and to agree to a joint meet-ing between himself, the union leaders and members of cabinet. Lake refused. On September 3, Smallwood tried again. He flew to Burgeo and tried to talk Lake into walking with him to the union headquarters. Once again the rejection was absolute.

On November 1, the strike reached its foreordained, futile conclusion. "There is nothing for me to do here," said Lake. With that, he closed the plant, stepped aboard his 65-foot yacht, *Limanda*, and moved to the island of Ramea, site of the largest of his fish plants.

On December 17, in the wake of the provincial election, Smallwood moved at last. He announced that the government would expropriate the Burgeo plant. It would be operated for an interim period by the Research Productivity Council of New Brunswick, which would lay the groundwork for an eventual co-operative.* Smallwood's belated intervention had been prompted less by concern for union rights than by political benefits. The union vote would be crucial in a by-election.

Except that they were fishermen instead of loggers, the substance of the Burgeo strike was identical to that of the IWA strike in 1959, a struggle by those at the bottom of the pyramid against a social and economic system that held them in serfdom. The outcome though was different – the fishermen had won. In some ways, their victory was hardly more than Pyrrhic. The struggle had exhausted the union's energy and much of its credit. Unorganized fishermen in other parts of the province, fearing a similar battle that would leave their communities divided and torn, began to see the union as a threat as much as a protector. These problems can be surmounted. For the union had expressed the power of Newfoundlanders to change their own lives by direct action.

The other instrument that taught Newfoundlanders how to change their own lives had also originated in Smallwood's imagination. Back in 1949, as one of his first legislative acts, he had transformed Memorial University College, and its modest two-year liberal arts program, into a degree-granting university. Memorial must become, he had said, "a true people's university." In 1959, dissatisfied with progress, he returned to the attack. He took issue with the president who wanted the university to remain small and élite, and said: "Every Newfoundlander who wants to

---

* Because of the change of government, this agreement was never consummated. Instead, on March 4, 1972, the new Conservative administration bought up the plant and at the same time signed a contract with the Fishermen's Union on virtually the same terms offered to Lake one year earlier.

go has a right to go." Memorial, he added, should become "an Extension Department with a university tacked on to it, not the other way round." He was thinking of the co-operative and community work of St. Francis Xavier University in Antigonish.

It was not until 1965 that Smallwood backed his words with action. Up to then, though he wheedled Eleanor Roosevelt into opening the new campus in 1961, his attention to education had been sporadic. To him as to most Newfoundlanders, who lacked the Scottish scholastic traditions of neighbouring Nova Scotia, book-learning had never seemed all that important. The reason for the change was that renegade Scot, John Kenneth Galbraith, whom Smallwood had badgered into attending a Thinkers Conference. "It is often said that under-developed countries require massive infusions of capital," Galbraith told his audience. "They do not. They require massive infusions of education." As Smallwood recalls, "I knew Galbraith was right the moment he said it." A month later, without informing let alone consulting any of the faculty, he ordered afternoon classes cancelled and students and faculty assembled in the auditorium. There he announced that all tuition fees would be abolished and student salaries introduced, $50 a month to those from St. John's and $100 a month for those from out of town.*

Smallwood's next move was to find a new president. His methods this time were even less conventional. He first offered the post to Galbraith and to Lady Barbara Ward Jackson (who for a time considered it seriously). Then, mortal offence to the faculty, he advertised in Canadian, U.S. and British newspapers. Among those who replied were an Anglican bishop and several graduates of correspondence colleges. At last, on June 8, 1966, he announced he had found his man. The new president would be Lord Stephen Taylor of Harlow, a tall, shaggy-browed peer who had been successively surgeon, author, Parliamentary Secretary to Herbert Morrison, developer of Harlow New Town and arbitrator in the

---

* Budget exigencies forced steady retrenchment in these schemes: eventually a means test tied to the federal Canada Student Loan Plan was used as the basis for choice. Even so, Memorial's student aid programs remain among the most generous in the country.

1963 Saskatchewan doctors' strike. In Newfoundland's case, the terms finally agreed on, Taylor had never heard of Memorial until Smallwood called him out of a House of Lords debate, included a $30,000 salary, a new house, a pledge of freedom from political interference and the promise of support to develop a major university.

A shrewd political realist, Taylor acted mainly as public personality and speechmaker. The intellectual driving force, as Memorial aspired upwards, has been M. O. Morgan, the Academic Vice-President, a tall, reflective native Newfoundlander. Under his creative tenure, several departments, notably education, engineering and marine biology, moved towards first rank. The University's Educational Television Centre developed what is probably the most extensive off-campus program in the country. By 1971, by means of videotapes recorded at the centre and circulated throughout the province, seven university-level credit courses were provided to adults in twenty-six remote communities.

By then, Memorial's 141-acre campus had come to resemble a separate city, impressive if architecturally undistinguished, on the outskirts of St. John's. Enrolment was more than 7,000; a separate college was being planned for the west coast city of Corner Brook; an expansion program announced that year included the building of a $40 million dollar general and teaching hospital.

Smallwood's general performance in the field of education, though he earned comparatively little credit for it, was one of the most substantial in his record. In 1968 he accepted the controversial recommendations of a provincial Royal Commission and persuaded the churches to abandon many of the privileges granted them by the constitution (the Terms of Union) in favour of state-run education. In the process, a tangle of 270 school boards was reduced to 40. He created institutions such as the Fisheries College and the College of Trades and Technology and dotted the island with vocational schools. From $4 million in 1949, the province's annual budget for education increased to $140 million at the end of Smallwood's term.

Smallwood's own relations with Memorial, however, became increasingly ambivalent. He held to his pledge not to interfere. He boasted to visitors about its growth, and showered it with funds. But he visited the campus only on ceremonial occasions. Student audiences, articulate and irreverent, were the only ones he ever feared and never learned to master.

That same ambivalence, the pride and distrust of a patron towards a protégé grown up, marked his attitude towards Memorial's single most creative department, the Extension Service, the very reason he had wanted to build a university in the first place. This Extension Service has been the catalyst of change in the communities that were once Smallwood's private domain, the distant and half-forgotten outports.

If the outports were the quintessence of Newfoundland, they also described its limits. From the beginning, these isolated hamlets had lived by an ethic of egalitarian individualism. Few sought to improve their lot, fewer still to improve the lot of the whole. For generations, every attempt at community development and co-operation, like Smallwood's own efforts at Bonavista in the thirties, had foundered on the bleak facts of economic deprivation and social apathy.

Nowhere in Newfoundland in the mid-sixties were these facts more distressingly apparent than on Fogo Island. Five thousand people lived on this gaunt, tree-less lump, nine miles wide and a dozen miles long, which lay ten miles off the northeast coast. But they lived sealed off from one another, by religion and race, in ten tiny settlements. No one on Fogo ever spoke of the island as their home; instead they would name their own outport, Joe Batt's Arm, Seldom Come By, Stag Harbour or Tilting. Each had its own one- or two-room denominational school. A child could grow up without visiting a community five miles away. Since the closing of the last commercial fish plant, sixty per cent of the fishermen had been on welfare. A single future remained for them, resettlement at the government's discretion.

Such was the unpromising territory that Memorial's Extension Service, in 1967, chose for its experiment – the introduction of a new concept of community development. The ingredients, instead of money and blueprints, would be self-realization and citizen participation. The first step towards this was self-awareness. To promote it the Memorial team used film and videotape as tools to create channels of communication within and between the communities.

The approach was the product of two remarkable individuals. Colin Low, a senior producer with the Challenge for Change unit of the National Film Board, co-director of *Labyrinth* at Expo 67, conceived the imaginative use of the new communications technology. The development philosophy was that of Donald Snowden, Director of Extension, who had emigrated from his native Manitoba to the Arctic, where he established the first co-operatives among the Eskimos, and then in 1964, to Newfoundland. A bulky, restless Renaissance figure, at once a romantic and a pragmatist, Snowden transformed the extension service into the most dynamic in the country.

The six hours of film that the Film Board and Memorial produced on Fogo in 1967 constitute a landmark in social documentary. Invited for the first time to express themselves openly, the islanders poured out their hopes and frustrations to the cameras and microphones. "We let the co-operatives we had here before perish in our midst," said fisherman Andrew Brett. "We know we are not educated and we kept our tongues still. We should never do that." Of the prospect of resettlement, another fisherman said, "I've lived in towns and cities and I don't want to move. I'd miss the sea." The Fogo Process, as it came to be known (the technique has since been used all over North America), amounted in essence to the slow, painstaking, assembly of social consensus. Each individual interviewed could edit any part of the interview he wished. Each strip of film was shown first in the community where it had been shot; only with that community's approval was it shown in neighbouring hamlets. Eventually, the lengthening films were screened for the decision makers – politicians and civil servants. Their comments were recorded, and played back on Fogo.

Slowly the island came to life. An Island Improvement Committee was formed, with representatives from every community. A fishing co-operative was established, in its first year it attracted twenty-eight members. Four year later, membership had grown to 829. A co-operative shipyard, set up in 1968, launched its first longliners the following year; by 1971 it had produced twenty-one. From there the co-operative branched out to take over management of a small, abandoned fish plant, then talked the government into laying plans for a new multi-purpose plant. The single most dramatic development came about on August 12, 1971, when the CN coastal boat *Glencoe* steamed into Fogo Harbour, carrying in her hold the pre-fabricated parts for a new Central Junior Senior High school. In a clean break with the past, the school would go up in the exact centre of the island.

For all its progress, Fogo may not survive. Its economic base remains precarious. The advances in education and public services may in the end hasten the drift of young people to the mainland. The difference is that this would happen now by the free and expressed choice of Fogo Islanders. For that, in five years, is how they have come to think of themselves.

By 1972, the Extension Service had become a major force in the province. Apart from its achievements on Fogo, it had nurtured into life thirty-three local development associations and community improvement committees, the first fledgling democracies in outport Newfoundland. Its fieldworkers, a team of hard-driving idealists, operated on every coast and in Labrador. The Service organized courses on everything from art appreciation and tourist development to public speaking and business administration, for a public that ranged from police constables and bank clerks to union organizers and co-op administrators. It fulfilled in every act Smallwood's old dream of a "people's university."

Fogo and Burgeo are microcosms of the post-Smallwood Newfoundland. The brave beginnings they represent have yet to be fulfilled. Standing in the way are the same economic problems Smallwood agonized over for a quarter-century as Premier; the same threat to Newfoundland's existence as a unique society that he has fought his entire life.

27

"Jobs, Four Letters, J-O-B-S"

M any times I have returned from the mainland, with its cities, its highways, its great industries and rich agricultural land" said Smallwood on his last day in office. "And I've wondered how to keep this island going."

In Newfoundland, more than anywhere else in the country, the social change Smallwood struggled to come to terms with was produced by, and in turn reacted upon, economic change. Despite all the economic gains since Confederation the society remained, in George Perlin's phrase, "a broadly-based pyramid with a very narrow apex." At the top were the parvenu millionaires and the old families, these still astonishingly wealthy and even more astonishingly influential; just below was the new middle-class of professionals, enjoying, in Canada's poorest province, the highest salaries in the country;* at the base of the pyramid almost one-half of the population lived below the poverty line of $3,000 a year compared to one-third in the nation as a whole. These interest groups competed: the

---

* In 1968, Newfoundland doctors earned annual salaries of $31,000 compared to a Canadian average of $29,181; lawyers, $28,500 (compared to $23,597) and engineers and architects, $24,400 (compared to $22,707).

old families closed ranks against the new middle-class; the professionals saw in the wage increases won by organized labour a threat to their standard of living. Their class rivalries were made more acute by the shortage of resources.

With the fastest growing population in the country (roughly doubled since Confederation to some 530,000) and the least resources, the province was caught in an economic vise.* An average annual unemployment rate of less than ten per cent was a major success, and even this figure masked the massive under employment in the outports. "When I die," Smallwood once said, "If they find anything inscribed on my heart it will be jobs, four letters, J-O-B-S." To create them he sought industries, the larger and more grandiose the better, and at virtually any price.

Smallwood liked to describe himself as a self-taught economist. A colleague described his comprehension of finance as "alternating between the non-existent and the erroneous." What Smallwood really was and had always been, was a salesman, pushing ideas at investors, at promoters, at Ottawa, at his own people. As a salesman, though, Smallwood was almost unique: he thought up his own products.

No aspect of his record created more controversy than his industrial policies, for his wheeling and dealing brought promoters and construction millionaires so close to the centre of government that at times they were almost indistinguishable from it. Still, he did create jobs, by means of nearly $2 billion worth of industries, few of which – Churchill Falls,

---

* In stark statistical terms Newfoundland's struggle seemed hopeless. The 1970 per capita incomes of $1,784 amounted to 54% of the Canadian average ($3,092) compared to 60% four years earlier – despite all the federal funds poured in during this period. These statistics are, as always, distorted. There was far less real poverty in rural Newfoundland than in mainland cities. Non-cash income (including self-built houses on self-owned land) closed the gap. So also did the style of life that included free hunting and fishing, freedom from pollution, a relaxed work style that included leisured lunches at home and random holidays on most fine summer days, and finally, maids for the middle class.

the Labrador iron ore mines, the Marystown shipyard – would otherwise have existed. Indeed, many of his faults had more to do with style than substance, which is why his failures attracted more attention than Nova Scotia's disastrous heavy water plant, or Manitoba's Churchill Forest Industries. (A comparative study of regional development in Newfoundland, P.E.I., Nova Scotia and Manitoba by Philip Mathias of the *Financial Post* gave the highest marks, in fact the only marks, to Newfoundland.)

Smallwood's style of development for which, in spite of all the criticism, he never apologized, and which he never changed, reached a kind of climax in his last years with the Come-by-Chance oil refinery. Creative, controversial, financially wayward and flamboyant, the project epitomized Smallwood's solution to Newfoundland's never-ending problem of jobs, jobs, jobs.

In 1965, Smallwood had used the occasion of a two-week holiday in Puerto Rico to study that island's "Operation Bootstrap" development program. He was particularly taken by the giant 100,000 barrel-a-day oil refinery, and an associated petrochemical complex that the program had created. As far back as 1957, he had tried to establish a small 14,000 barrel-a-day refinery to serve the island's own needs. He approached Imperial Oil, who answered that the market was too small to justify a plant. Instead, following what was by now a well-worn path, he turned to promoters. A New York entrepreneur, John Shaheen, responded, and built the plant at Holyrood, on Conception Bay. In 1966, searching this time for a multi-million dollar complex that could supply international markets, he turned to Shaheen once more.

The concept the two evolved was breath-taking. At the bleak Placentia Bay outport of Come-by-Chance there was an ice-free harbour that, uniquely along the Eastern seaboard, was deep enough to handle the vast tankers of 200,000 tons or more that were becoming a feature of the international oil trade. Why not, Smallwood and Shaheen reasoned, ship cheap crude oil from the Middle East to Come-by-Chance, process it there, and then ship it out again in smaller tankers headed for U.S. ports? Few but Smallwood could have conceived such a plan, and few but Shaheen could have pulled it off.

"He's the world's greatest salesman," Shaheen's personal friend, Richard Nixon, once told Pierre Trudeau. Then in his early fifties, the son of an Illinois farmer, Shaheen's cool, urbane manner matched his skills as a gambler. He made the first of his several fortunes, some of them lost again, by selling airport insurance machines. Swiftly he moved up the promoters' ladder, through chemicals, pulp and paper, petroleum, and broadcasting. Along the way, he picked up an invaluable ally in Nixon who when out of office acted as his lawyer and who, on reaching the White House, named Shaheen to the Presidential Committee on Information.

As it turned out, the principal opponent of the Shaheen-Smallwood scheme was not so much John Crosbie, who left the cabinet because of it, as the government in Ottawa. Ottawa, urged on by a plaintive oil lobby, was appalled by the proposed financial underpinnings for the project. The refinery, in effect, was intended to become a tax-free haven. A provincial crown corporation was to be created, to be free of all federal and provincial taxes. This corporation would actually own the plant. Shaheen would operate it, and collect his profits in the form of a management fee. Newfoundland, meanwhile, would loan Shaheen the first $30 million of the $125 million development capital required.

Finance Minister Edgar Benson blocked the tax loophole by a budget amendment. Ottawa's concern was that the highly publicized venture would set a precedent one province after another would copy. After several months of negotiations, Smallwood wrung a concession that allowed quick depreciation for the provincial crown corporation that would build the plant for Shaheen.

Shaheen, for his part, had come up with both a source of supply and a market. The supplier was British Petroleum. As for marketing, Shaheen concocted the idea of shipping refined high-octane jet fuel in bond direct to U.S. airports for sale only to international airlines. In this way, he would avoid both customs duties and the U.S. quota on oil imports. The balance of the refinery's output, principally heating oil, would be sold in Eastern Canada and Europe.

The search for the $100 million worth of outside capital took two years. By early 1970, after scouring the United States, Europe and mainland Canada, two promising sources, one in London, the other in Paris, had been identified. Smallwood and Shaheen set out to play one against the other. Early in March, along with a contingent of ministers and civil servants, Smallwood flew to Paris for talks with a syndicate of investors while Shaheen went to London. Halfway through his Paris meetings, Smallwood was called to the phone. Shaheen was on the line to report that the British group were ready to sign. That afternoon Smallwood, without telling his hosts, slipped out of the Crillon, passing up a dinner at Maxim's arranged for the evening. After two days of talks in London, the deal was set. A group of British banks would raise the money, backed by the British Government's Export Credits Guarantee Department. In return, the Corporation demanded that all equipment used in the refinery be British-made.

With word of his success going ahead of him, Smallwood flew back to St. John's to be greeted at the airport by student demonstrators carrying signs: "Don't sell our birthright," "Judas." One student spat straight into his face. To assuage public opinion, Smallwood brought Shaheen to Newfoundland in April for a two-day, televised session of the legislature. Under hostile questioning, the promoter conceded little that was new. Asked why he had decided to invest in Newfoundland, Shaheen looked straight into the camera and replied: "I was attracted by the honest, stable, political climate."

The last strands, including a delayed commitment by Ottawa to build a $20 million deep-water wharf, were tidied up, and on August 10, 1970, four years of talks and deals were consummated. In the cabinet room of the Confederation Building, Smallwood and Shaheen signed a construction agreement with the British company, Procon Ltd. For the occasion, he used the pen with which Prime Minister St. Laurent and the Newfoundland delegation had signed the Terms of Union on December 11, 1948. Six weeks later, Smallwood staged another ceremony.

This one consummated the financial arrangements with the British bankers. The highlight of the occasion was the return to the Newfoundland Government of a cheque for $5 million, repayment of the bridging loan which had triggered Crosbie's resignation two years earlier.

When construction began at Come-by-Chance the following spring, a two-mile long line of cars filled with job applicants formed outside the site gate. Once opened, the refinery itself would employ only about 450 workers. The promise of the spin-off petro-chemical industries, intended as the principal source of employment, remained as remote as when Smallwood first conceived the scheme. For this Smallwood had given Shaheen, among other sweeteners, an option to buy the plant for $10 million, and freedom from all provincial taxes. But industries, however many Smallwood won, were never going to be enough. At the opening of the Marystown shipyard, on August 27, 1967, he had sketched out the problem with his typical candour.

> One-third of Newfoundlanders cannot make a decent living. They have nothing to do except for a few weeks each year when they catch fish or lobster, or pick berries or work on the roads. What are we going to do with them?
>
> There will be no more shipyards. There will be only three or four new mines. There will be only one or two more pulp mills. What are we going to do with one-third of our people?

More than two years passed before anyone, at least publicly, grasped the significance of his analysis. Then, on February 6, 1970, Jay Parker, President of the Newfoundland Board of Trade, delivered a speech which became a landmark in public discussion. He had thought the unthinkable, and said it. The province's inescapable problem, Parker said, was "economic overcrowding . . . We have a fairly healthy economy for perhaps 380,000 people, but little possibility of expansion." The other 120,000, he suggested, should be assisted to move to the mainland. "We have got to persuade these people to move for their own sakes . . . for how can anyone live decently by working 95 to 100 days a year?"

This speech, its thesis as taboo as Confederation had once been, raised a storm of protest. The Board of Trade disassociated itself from its President's remarks, as did Memorial's Department of Commerce when one of its professors voiced the same view. Smallwood's own response was mild. "We've got to achieve a breakthrough," he said. "Otherwise there will be no growth, only decline, ending perhaps twenty years from now with a population half as great."

A year later Don Jamieson, in an act of remarkable political courage, told the Learned Societies' annual meeting in St. John's that Newfoundland faced the prospect of becoming "a glorified geriatric ward" and "a tourist mecca." Its population, he said, was likely to "siphon off" to perhaps 300,000. The most gloomy forecast was that of British novelist John Masters. "Some 520,000 people survive here by determination, hardihood and moral stamina on an island that is by 20th century standards, unlivable," he reported to the *Daily Telegraph*. He suggested that natural resources might support 50,000, with as many again employed as curators and guides "for a world wilderness park . . . a place of refuge, solace and challenge for industrial man."

Depopulation, and with it the breaking of the island's spirit, was the nightmare Smallwood had fought unceasingly. He no longer had any answers. They would have to come from others.

"A progressive development plan for Newfoundland must do three things. It must make more jobs available. It must help people to increase the efficiency of their operations. It must help people to take advantage of improved opportunities." Thus the Canada-Newfoundland Special Areas Agreement of August 9, 1971, laid down a five-year blueprint for development, and sought to usher a new economic order into the province.

The DREE agreement, negotiated between Smallwood's Department of Community and Social Development and the federal Department of Regional Economic Expansion, provided for an infusion of $110 million worth of federal funds, $76.6 million in direct contributions and $34.1 million in loans. (To those would be added assistance available under ARDA, and incentive grants for new and expanding industries.) The approach the agreement demanded was a one hundred and eighty degree departure from Smallwood's style, it was rational, systematic, planned. In painstaking detail, funds were divided among eight selected "growth areas," encompassing about half the island's population. The idea was to equip these areas with all the basic services – schools, water and sewer systems, roads, residential subdivisions, industrial parks – and so create a climate favourable to industrial development. "Industries," the agreement read sternly, "cannot be conjured out of air." As alternatives to magic, it suggested: "The fishery is still the key . . . The mining industry may far exceed its present level of development . . . commercial agriculture has only just begun to make an impact . . . Travel and recreation will become increasingly fast-growing sectors . . . The province's home market pro-vides demands for many products which at present are brought in from outside." Newfoundland, for example, imported 85 per cent of all its building materials, down to wooden ribs for longliners and wooden boxes for packing fish.

For some, DREE's plans for Newfoundland – a subsidiary agreement called for the establishment of a joint federal-provincial Newfoundland Development Corporation – were hardly an improvement over Smallwood's. The Opposition DREE critic at Ottawa, Newfoundland M.P. Jim McGrath, called the Special Areas agreement "a glorified public works scheme." Others complained about slowness, about excessive secrecy, about the sudden influx of planners "from away" (a number of whom turned up in high places in the province's own Department of Community and Social Development). In a paper presented to the Learned Societies in June 1971, Professors Peter Neary and Sidney Noel compared it to "the ghost of the Commission of Government," an alien bureaucracy come to make decisions for Newfoundlanders.

In fact, for all the outward rationality of its attack, DREE's blueprint, at its heart, was almost as much a gamble as Smallwood's. Nor was the concept novel; the British Commission of Government had tried much the same approach, though in a far less developed economy, and with far less money, in the 1930s. The gamble was that planned development, helped by lucky breaks like a possible oil strike on the Grand Banks, could turn "the end of the line" into a viable economy for half a million people.

If it were to have any hope of success, the fishery was indeed as DREE had diagnosed, "the key."

To the end of his career, few criticisms made Smallwood angrier than that he had neglected the fishery. In straightforward statistical terms the assistance he provided or, more commonly, secured from Ottawa, was considerable. Thirty-eight of thirty-nine operating fish plants were built during his term of office while total government assistance amounted to not less than 65 per cent of the total income generated by the industry. In some communities, Parzival Copes had estimated in the *Canadian Journal of Political Science*, "the total amount of government assistance has exceeded the local incomes."

Smallwood's object of concern, though, was the *fishermen*, not the fishing industry. Convinced that the fishery itself was gone beyond recall, nursing his own memories of the human misery it had caused, he sought to create industries that bore no relationship to the sea. (He had more personal reasons for his preference: the quest for giant industries represented an exciting challenge, and their achievement brought glory.) At the same time, well aware that it provided his own political base, Smallwood perpetuated the uneconomic inshore fishery, supplementing annual cash incomes of $500 to $1,500 with seasonal unemployment insurance and welfare, and with direct support through programs which included a 50 per cent rebate on salt purchases, and a subsidized bait service.

If Smallwood did little, others did less. Ottawa consistently focussed its attention on the prosperous B.C. fishery. Fishermen themselves encouraged their sons to leave and fish merchants used massive government assistance not to make improvements but to minimize their risks (all but two of the province's fish plants were mortgaged to the government).

The brutal truth was that although Newfoundland sat on top of the richest fishing grounds in the world, and sold its products to the richest market in the world (the U.S.), it remained inefficient, uneconomic and uncompetitive. The sea's harvest was still dumped onto the market in its rawest form for quick sales, while the shelves of Newfoundland supermarkets were crammed with canned and processed fish products from

Japan, Europe, and the United States. Marketing skills and distributing organizations were almost nonexistent. Attempts at diversification and quality control were sporadic. And despite all the advances in gear and equipment, the production costs of the oldest fishing method of all, from an inshore skiff or trapboat, remained by far the most efficient: 3 ¾ cents per pound of fish caught, compared to 6 or 7 cents for the largest trawler.

No single challenge to the post-Smallwood government and to the hopeful planners in DREE will be greater than reform of the fishery. As a legacy to his successors, Smallwood created the instrument by which a comprehensive reorganization might be achieved, the Canadian Saltfish Corporation. A federal crown company established early in 1970 to market the province's saltfish output, it has since branched out to species such as herring, salmon and arctic char. "I can foresee the day," said Smallwood, during the debate to establish the Saltfish Corporation, "when the entire industry: processing, packaging and marketing, may have to be nationalized."

By the 1970s, the fishing industry accounted for only about six per cent of the gross provincial product, but it provided some 16 per cent of the province's jobs. From a peak of over 22,000 in 1964, the number of fishermen had declined, by 1972, to perhaps 15,000. Rationalization could stabilize employment at about 10,000 earning year-round salaries, with perhaps half as many again employed in packing and processing plants. Yet just as far-reaching reforms were beginning to be considered, it became apparent that even these employment levels could not be maintained, unless the ocean's resource itself could be preserved.

Since the early sixties, the annual groundfish catch in the northwest Atlantic has averaged about two million metric tons. This constancy masked a disturbing trend: the annual harvest was being maintained only by a progressively heavier investment of boats and gear. From an average catch per vessel ton of 15,000 pounds a season in the mid-fifties, the catch had dropped to 10,000 pounds.

As always, the inshore fishery was the most seriously affected, all the more since Soviet and East European trawlers had moved in by the score to scoop up dwindling stocks. Over the five years from 1967, the inshore cod catch dropped from 270,000 quintals* to 108,000 quintals. The annual harvest on Labrador's Hamilton Banks dropped by more than half over four years to 440 million pounds. Even more dramatic was the decline of the salmon fishery. Decimated by Danish fishermen who had discovered salmon feeding grounds off southern Greenland, it dropped from 7 million pounds in 1963 to 2.5 million pounds in 1971.

"The Newfoundland fishery is going downhill on a toboggan," Gus Etchegary, President of the newly formed Save Our Fisheries Association (SOFA), told the Commons Committee on Fisheries in May 1971. He urged, among other measures, extension of the twelve-mile limit to all areas of Newfoundland and the banning of gill nets on offshore banks. Ottawa, in reply, undertook to lobby at the 1973 Law of the Sea Conference for the delegation to Canada of full responsibility for managing all sea resources of the Continental Shelf.

Much of the damage, though, remains irreparable as the struggle for economic survival becomes more difficult. The once plentiful haddock have vanished from the Grand Banks. The future of the Atlantic salmon will, almost certainly, be confined to sport fishing. The stocks of most major species, from cod to herring, are already at or beyond their maximum yields. Expansion will have to be achieved through diversification into new species such as the queen crab, shrimp, hake and pollock, and the misshapen grenadier.

Like Quebec, with which it has so much in common except political power, the Newfoundland that Smallwood leaves Canada as a legacy is fighting a battle for cultural survival. Much of the old Newfoundland is already gone, or like the 140-year old frame church at Quidi Vidi just outside St. John's, is preserved as a museum for tourists. The schooners have gone from the outports. The seal fishery is virtually over. The canned music of Nashville has replaced the "come-all-ye's" derived from English and Irish ballads and Christmas mumming is fading into memory.

---

* A quintal is 112 pounds.

In St. John's many of the old, squat, brightly painted wooden houses have disappeared, more will be obliterated by a planned arterial road linking the harbour with the Trans-Canada Highway.

Inside Newfoundland, the old conservatives fighting change have been joined by many of the young people, searching for a cause and for identity. Their principal target has been Smallwood's program of resettlement, which, in a paradox as striking as any in his character, struck at the foundation of his own political base, for it moved the baymen towards the towns. His program, involving a shift of population relatively as great as any that had taken place in North America, will eventually reduce pre-Confederation Newfoundland's 1,200 settlements to perhaps 350. This shift is turning Newfoundlanders away from the sea, the element which, J. D. Rogers wrote in his *Historical Geography of Newfoundland*, "clothes the island like a garment, and that garment contains the vital principal and soul of the national life."

"We are painted by our critics as murderers, destroying beautiful, unspoiled villages," said Smallwood in defence of the program. "On a summer day, there's no finer place in the world, but how many of those who criticize would want to live there year round?"

Perceptively, Smallwood had separated romantic rhetoric from year-round reality. A typical romantic critic was the author Farley Mowat, who at a state dinner Smallwood tendered him in 1966, said of resettlement, "It is altering our state of being. Newfoundlanders look increasingly in a direction that has no connection with the past ... in danger of being lost are personal pride, personal belief and dignity." A year later Mowat left the outport of Burgeo to return to Ontario.

A substantive criticism was that of the economist Parzival Copes, who calculated that only 14 per cent of those relocated had moved to designated growth centres, only another 10 per cent to potential growth centres. Most people, in truth, had shifted from one declining community to another.

In sad irony, the outports are being discovered just as they are dying. A trickle of refugees from the North American urbanscape have begun to migrate to coastal Newfoundland. Settlements like Fogo Island, supposedly doomed, have taken on new life, and in a curious yet profound way, these communities somehow seem more adapted to the much heralded "post industrial age" than the frenetic industrial centres of the mainland.

Despite all the erosions, the core of the Newfoundland character endures. The North American Calvinist ethic has never penetrated here. In its place a gentle, wry humanism prevails. If their culture is to survive, if they are not to be demoralized by too rapid change, nor homogenized by too much progress, Newfoundlanders will indeed have to choose in Jamieson's phrase between a "way of life" and "a standard of living." Like the people of Fogo, they will have to choose for themselves. On October 28, 1971, they took their first collective step into an uncertain new era – they defeated Smallwood.

28

The End of the Beginning

"Most politicians regard defeat as part of the game, but not Joe," a close associate of Smallwood's told the *Globe and Mail* early in 1971. "He lives in mortal terror of being rejected by his beloved Newfoundlanders."

The lion, that winter, was growing old. By now his age was part of his person, his thinning pure-white hair as much a symbol as his bow-tie had once been. The years were exacting a harsher toll – he had become prey to an old man's doubts.

One critical decision was demanded of him, the timing of the twentieth election* in his fifty years of politics. He could not bring himself to make it. As the year drew on and as the months beyond which the election could no longer be postponed grew fewer, surveys taken regularly by the Liberal party revealed a dramatic, and, for Smallwood, a disastrous, shift in public opinion. Still he evaded the moment of commitment.

---

* The U.S. presidential campaign of 1924; the 1932 campaign for the House of Assembly; the 1946 election to the National Convention; the two Confederation referendums; eight federal and seven provincial elections.

As late as the end of August, five weeks before the election date of October 28 was finally set, Smallwood had yet to order a single substantive preparation for the campaign. The principal television clips, put together by a Toronto company working round the clock, arrived ten days *after* the three-week campaign had begun. "It was like watching a disaster happen, that you knew was going to happen, that you knew could be avoided, and about which you could do nothing," one of his chief advisers recalls. "He seemed to be waiting, almost literally, for a miracle." That was the essential difference between the Smallwood of 1971 and the Smallwood of all the earlier campaigns. Then he had not waited for miracles, he had created them for himself.

He tried. But as if he were an aging actor attempting a comeback, the gestures were right but the timing missed. The first week in February, he staged a two-day "Master Plan Conference" at the Arts and Culture Centre in St. John's to build a platform for the campaign. Thrown together at the last minute, the meeting teetered on the edge of farce. Regional Economic Expansion Minister Jean Marchand, billed as the star guest, unguardedly told Ottawa reporters he had never heard of it, then hastily announced he was delighted to be coming. Smallwood's two-and-one-half-hour speech ended with the hall half empty. His ministers one by one came sheepishly to the podium to intone into the cameras (the entire affair was televised) a series of makeshift "major new programs" ranging from $52 million worth of roads to sixteen new airstrips.

His opening shot a failure, Smallwood instead found himself under fire. The week after the conference, teachers all over the province quit their classrooms to protest protracted wage negotiations. Their strike idled 13,500 students and left as many parents infuriated (as much with the government as with the teachers). From then on the labour unrest never ceased; it reached a bitter apogee at Burgeo, a stalemate for which Smallwood once again drew as much blame as the participants.

In tandem with these labour troubles, which blighted hopes of the recovery upon which Smallwood had based his strategy of a 1971 election rather than holding one late in 1970, the economy itself faltered. At the former U.S. Marine base at Argentia, 700 were idled. In July Canadian Vickers announced it was pulling out of the Marystown shipyard. By early August the province's two pulp and paper mills had each closed for some fifty days in order to reduce inventories. Late that month, Bowaters announced it would close Machine No. 7 in its Corner Brook plant, a move that would leave 1,200 unemployed. Even more serious in political terms, the fishery, despite record high prices, staggered into one of its worst seasons. The July cod harvest was 47 million pounds, down from 78 million the year before.

In May, the unemployment that Smallwood had assumed would dwindle away had reached 16 per cent. By July it had dropped only to nine per cent, as high as it had been for the same month in the year Newfoundland joined Confederation. Even Trudeau's visit in August, plagued by poor weather, won no converts for Smallwood.

"This poor old gent," wrote Ray Guy, normally Smallwood's severest critic, in his *Telegram* column. Well used to criticism and well able, ever since he learned the art standing on a soapbox at Manhattan street-corners, to give back more than he got, Smallwood had never before encountered pity. Once he let the iron mask of pride drop for an instant, and asked for compassion. "I've just been reading a book on Diefenbaker," he told a member he encountered by chance in the corridor leading to the legislature. "God how I hated that man. He was unfit to be Prime Minister. But they should have let him go decently."

That member, of all people, was John Crosbie, and it was the first time the pair had met in nearly two years. Crosbie promptly reported the conversation to the press. He quoted Smallwood as saying, "I'm only leaving when I'm cock of the walk again," which Smallwood denied. Smallwood for his part claimed that Crosbie had smiled in agreement with his estimate that the Conservative leader, Moores, could not win a seat – a gesture that Crosbie, by then a Conservative, also denied.

Their public performance in the Legislature was no better. The session opened March 22 and dragged through until June 3. In one of their endless head-to-head debates, Smallwood called Crosbie a "bully boy," and was told in return that his management of the House was "foul and despicable." But these exchanges were man-to-man, no longer man-to-boy. Conscious that his capacity to inspire fear had dwindled as much as his capacity to inspire awe, Smallwood, in one revealing gesture, threatened to clear the public galleries when spectators laughed at a sally by one of his opponents.

The session reached some kind of nadir late in May, with an exchange of blows between Smallwood's son Bill and an Opposition member. Bill Smallwood stalked across the floor to deliver a punch square in the face of the Conservative whom he judged had insulted his mother by citing an article in the *Alternate Press* that named Mrs. Smallwood as owner of a slum property in the city. The next day Smallwood defended his son's actions on his daily radio show. Three Conservatives sought to have him cited for contempt. When the Speaker rejected their motion, they accused him of bias and were evicted. In protest, the entire Opposition walked out of the House. In a flash of his old style, Smallwood used their absence to ram through forty-two pieces of legislation during the next two days.

The public was not amused. Its attention instead was caught by the continued economic disorders and by the squalid and equally continuous scandals the Opposition were bent on unearthing. The latest of these had to do with nine liquor stores rented by the government from anonymous owners at twice their commercial value. "Our information is that the owner is someone close to the Premier," said Crosbie. No one came forward to deny the allegation[*]. Titles to the properties were held beyond reach of prying eyes in the St. John's branch of the Royal Trust Company.

---

[*] On June 30, 1972, the report of a Royal Commission appointed by the new Conservative administration disclosed that the leases were held by Investment Developers Ltd. Smallwood, O. L. Vardy, and Arthur Lundrigan were named as equal shareholders. Subsequently, Smallwood stated that though a shareholder, he had neither known of this nor approved.

As a further precaution, the purchases had been made through a mainland bank, beyond Newfoundland jurisdiction.

With considerable skill, the Conservatives moved in to exploit the electorate's new mood. Moores, all but invisible since his election as leader the year before, re-emerged to issue a series of well thought out policy programs ranging from fisheries to tourism and economic development. In a brilliant stroke, the party threw its nominating conventions open to the general public. Some 20,000 people turned up (all but nine of the conventions were contested) and most stayed on to become party workers. Crosbie joined the party in June (Hickman and Earle had come aboard the previous year) and it gained further substance with the return of Gerald Ottenheimer. For the first time since Confederation, Smallwood faced an opposition that looked and acted like a credible alternative.

He meanwhile had taken stock of the inescapable fact that his own presence was making the Liberals look less and less credible. A survey taken in April, while it gave the party a comfortable 47-25 lead over the Conservatives, showed Smallwood himself trailing the party by eight points. Coupled with the massive 27.7 per cent of the electorate who declared themselves undecided, this was grounds for serious concern. Angrily, Smallwood dismissed the poll as "rubbish." This was for show; he remained enough of a realist to act on it.

His strategy was to make himself less conspicuous by filling the bill with star players. To do so, he played the single high card on which he had never slackened his grip, the Premiership itself. With the practised skill of one who had promised senatorships by the score on the road to Confederation, Smallwood set out to woo fresh recruits. In July and August, he executed a series of cabinet shuffles that swept out most of the last remaining warhorses. Into their places he brought eight newcomers, each clutching ambition like a sword. Among them were two former Conservative leading lights, Hubert Kitchen and Noel Murphy, the Mayor of St. John's, two of the province's best-known lawyers, and the site manager of Churchill Falls. If it still lacked depth, his cabinet had at least the semblance of a new look.*

Smallwood reserved his biggest ploy, though, for the backroom. On September 1, with unconcealed delight, he announced that the manager of the Liberal campaign would be Andrew Crosbie.

With that announcement, the public became aware of a rift in the house of Crosbie that in fact was already a year old, a passionate rivalry between two powerful and wealthy young men who chanced to be brothers. Each had been successful in his own sphere and for each only a single worthwhile prize remained.

Andrew, at thirty-eight the younger by two years, was handsome, gregarious and self-assured. He looked as much the Kiwanian as his brother, except that while John grew long sideburns ahead of the fashion and was occasionally known to appear at cocktail parties wearing hippie beads, Andrew exuded the bluff prince-Hal energies of a hunting-fishing businessman. He was perhaps the wealthiest man in the province.** Yet he had

---

* By midsummer 1971, Newfoundland's political tableau resembled the last stages of a long and savage game of chequers. Returning to attack the Liberals as crowned kings were Crosbie and Hickman. At the other end of the board, now Liberal cabinet ministers, were Hubert Kitchen, former President of the Progressive Conservative Association, and Noel Murphy, a former Conservative leader. At the same time, once nominations closed, few of the principal players were in their right places. Moores had jumped from his hometown of Harbour Grace to a riding in Corner Brook. Smallwood had left Corner Brook for the outport riding of Placentia East. Three other ministers had shifted ridings, while Smallwood's son Bill made an unsuccessful attempt (his nomination papers arrived twenty minutes late) to switch from his district to a more favourable one in Labrador.

** He contended for this title with Arthur Lundrigan, owner of a construction empire on the province's west coast. The local judgement was that the Crosbies and the Lundrigans divided the spoils of Newfoundland between them much as Spain and Portugal had once divided those of the New World.

spent nearly all his life in the shadow of his brother. John won academic laurels, Andrew dropped out of college. John won public acclaim as a lawyer, as a cabinet minister, as a gutsy opponent to Smallwood, Andrew quietly nursed the family business interests. As quietly, he nursed his own political ambitions. Less intellectual, but more subtle and possessed of far more *nous* than his brother, he made sure to place as many irons in the fire as possible.

He had put the first iron in, more accurately, it was put in for him, in 1968. In July of that year, six weeks or so after John had stormed out of cabinet, and a few days after the Liberals had been decimated in the federal election, Andrew had called on Smallwood to discuss his multifarious business enterprises. In what was even then a well-polished routine, Smallwood had switched the conversation to politics, talked of his own plans for retirement, made flattering references to Andrew's potential, and ended the meeting by offering him a cabinet post. The offer was declined.

To give himself a political base, Andrew Crosbie bought a newspaper, the *Daily News*, which in 1968-69 produced some of the best investigative reporting of any paper east of Toronto. To hone his political skills, he had discussions with Bill Lee, former executive assistant to Paul Hellyer, and one of the shrewdest political operators in Ottawa. After John had gone down to defeat, Andrew drew closer to Smallwood. He became a regular visitor at Roache's Line and an influential, if unofficial, adviser. Smallwood, in mid-1970, dangled the premiership before Andrew, who turned it down. In mid-1971, he yielded at last to Smallwood's urgings and came out into the open. As manager of a victorious campaign, he could look forward to being Smallwood's chosen candidate in the next leadership race.

Apart from money and the family name, Andrew Crosbie brought with him a managerial competence of a high order. The trouble was, there was at that point little to be competent about. No organization existed, no poll captains or riding managers had been picked, nor had any radio and television commercials or publicity brochures been ordered. With the election already past due, the Liberal strategy team had yet to receive the word to go into action. It was not until the last week in August that they discovered why Smallwood had kept silent so long.

Early that month, the Toronto pollster Martin Goldfarb had flown into St. John's carrying with him a copy of his latest survey. He took the document directly to Smallwood who read it and reminded Goldfarb tartly that the terms of his contract required him to report to the Premier alone; he was to disclose his findings to no one else. Goldfarb left town without discussing the survey with any member of Smallwood's inner team. After his departure, they asked Smallwood about the results. "Not much difference, a couple of points down, nothing interesting," he replied. Each time he was pressed for details, Smallwood gave the same evasive replies. Whenever asked for the document he had either "forgotten to bring it from home," or had "left it at the office."

"We knew damn well something was wrong," one member of the group recalls. "It wasn't just the obvious pretence of not having the report, or of not knowing the exact figures. It was rather that he suddenly ceased to talk election. Here we were, two months away at most, and it had become a non-subject."

Within this core group of half a dozen, which met almost daily for lunch in the Premier's private dining room, relations were becoming more and more strained. Through the year Smallwood had lost two more loyal veterans, Les Curtis, Justice Minister since 1949, by retirement, and Bill Keough, Labour Minister since 1949 and author of the Confederate battle-cry "the last forgotten fisherman on the Bill of Cape St. George," by death. Only two of those who remained (Al Vardy, Deputy Minister of Economic Development and Smallwood's closest friend, and Fred Rowe) were on their way to pasture. The three young ministers, Ed Roberts, Bill Rowe and John Nolan, and Andrew Crosbie were jockeying tenaciously for the succession.

About the group hung the atmosphere, at once stale and tense, of a court in exile. They had all seen far too much of one another. Each knew the others' ambitions and knew also of the tortuous plots and intrigues by which these were pursued. They were all the more suspicious because Smallwood used Vardy, a sour, enigmatic figure, as a stalking horse to play the rivals off against each other. Day after day, they listened to Smallwood's monologues with barely concealed impatience, yet no one dared risk an open break, for without his support no leadership convention could be won. And in the end, they came to realize that Smallwood trusted none of them, for he would not tell them what was in Goldfarb's poll. (Aware that some in the inner court would have accepted defeat with equanimity as the one certain way to ensure his retirement, Smallwood feared that unfavourable survey reports would be leaked to the press.*)

By the end of August, the group's exasperation with Smallwood's silence had changed to a growing nervousness that silence concealed not some convoluted plan, but a vacuum. "We really began to wonder," one of the group remembers of those unreal days of late summer, "whether in some incredible way he thought he could avoid having an election at all." Unable to bear the tension any longer, one minister arranged a business trip to Toronto. While there he called Goldfarb, pretended he had seen the survey (which Goldfarb took for granted) and carefully stage-managing the conversation, managed to extract the vital figures. The shift, as Smallwood had claimed, indeed was of only a few points. It was the nature of the shift that stunned: the undecideds were coming off the fence, and they were coming down, almost unanimously, into the Conservative column. The survey was already two months old. The trend it uncovered pointed straight to defeat.

Armed with this information, the group confronted Smallwood. The first week in September, at a strategy meeting held at Andrew Crosbie's inland hunting lodge, they wrung from him a commitment for an October election. He would not, however, be pinned down even then to

---

* Smallwood also became alarmed at the possibility of leaks caused by outsiders listening, inadvertently because of cross-talk, to his telephone conversations and ordered his senior ministers and advisers to install scramblers on their phones.

a specific date. At last campaign preparations were set in motion, though still at a measured place. Two major efforts, a twelve-page comic book and a half-hour television program, were thrown together after the campaign had begun.

By the end of September the thought that Smallwood, unbelievably, might try to avoid having an election at all had spread to the public at large. John Crosbie urged "civil disobedience" to force Smallwood to call an election. Senator Eugene Forsey, the constitutional expert, diagnosed the situation as unusual, but concluded that Smallwood was within his rights in postponing the voting as late as November 30 (the date the Legislature had been called into session following the election of 1966). As suspense began to dissolve into farce, Smallwood finally broke his silence. At a press conference held late in the afternoon of October 6, he announced that the election would be held October 28.

Just two days after he announced the election, Smallwood was called by Goldfarb. He reported his latest poll taken by telephone the week before. It showed, Goldfarb said, that Liberal strength had continued to dwindle. Translated into figures it gave the party 23 seats. This downward trend had continued since early summer. The message was clear, unless the trend could be halted and reversed, Smallwood faced not simply defeat but humiliation.

A leader cannot afford to show uncertainty lest the troops panic. Through the three-week campaign Smallwood told no one of the survey. One of his campaign advisers recalls that every few days or so, he and Smallwood would go over the list of the forty-two districts[*] and come up with an estimate of 28 or 29 Liberals elected. Then they would be "really tough," go over the districts once more, and reduce the Liberal count to

---

[*] There were actually 41 districts, one of which, Harbour Main, elected two members. For simplicity's sake, the figure of 42 is used throughout. The boundaries of these districts had remained unchanged since a gerrymandered redistribution in 1962. At the extremes of mal-distribution, there were close to 20,000 voters in the largest St. John's riding, compared to a scant 3,500 in the smallest outport districts.

27 or 28. Then, "just for the exercise" Smallwood would go back to the electoral map, "let's be ridiculously pessimistic" and himself reduce the number to 23. That done the pair would dismiss the last figure and get back to serious calculations.

If Smallwood alone knew how close defeat really was, almost all observers reckoned he would lose in the popular vote. Five years separated him from his last campaign. By delaying the election until the last possible moment he had given the impression of being afraid to face the public. Nor had he created any issues to distract attention from his own person or from the indifferent record of his administration. The electorate that would judge was sixty per cent urban, one-quarter under twenty-five. These Newfoundlanders were being asked to vote for a great-grandfather of seventy-odd, a figure from the history books who insisted upon intruding into the present, an improbable Ulysses seeking a newer world in a mauve shirt and a maroon silk jacket (bought in Thailand). Yet he would not yield. The fine edge was off his energy and his oratory but nothing had corroded the iron will.

For Smallwood, the one bright spot on the electoral map was that a majority of Newfoundland's 42 districts lay in outport country. These were his only hope of eking out a victory. The new Newfoundland of the cities and towns he had lovingly fashioned would have to be abandoned. Instead he must return to the old, to the coves and tickles and harbours that had won him Confederation, where yellowing photographs of a lean and hungry man with black hair and rimless glasses lingered on parlour mantelpieces, and where they remembered all that man had done. And so he went out to them, alone.

"A phantom moving among the fishing villages," a visiting mainland reporter wrote of Smallwood's campaign. Except that there were no schooners anymore, not so many settlements and that the men and women who rushed to shake his hand or hug him had grown old, twenty-five years might have melted away. Entirely by himself except for a driver-cook, in a white minibus with JOEY painted on either side in large capital letters, he crisscrossed the island bringing the word back to his people. For two weeks no reporters, not even Liberal workers, had the faintest idea where he was, or where he was heading. Instead, a truck, its p.a. system blaring "I'se the B'y" would pull up by a jetty, or in front of a general store, the signal that half an hour later Smallwood's bus would appear. In one day, bettering the pace of Confederation, he gave twenty-five speeches.

His rhetoric, as much as his style, conjured up memories of battles long ago. "God Almighty saw this little fellow Joey and raised him up so he could bring a bunch of stiff-necked Newfoundlanders into Confederation." So did his campaign mementos, among them $20,000 worth of buttons, on one side a garish three-dimensional portrait of himself and the legend, "Would the lady on the other side please vote Liberal." When the curious turned the button over, they found themselves looking in a mirror. Smallwood's mentor, Squires, had used this same device in 1928. The buttons prompted John Crosbie to make one of the campaign's better sallies. He held up a broken one and told his audience, "The glass is cracked, just like the government."

Smallwood's appeal, for thanks, for auld lang syne, could succeed only if those to whom it was directed knew for sure that it was being made for the last time. The Liberal strategy of emphasizing the imminence of Smallwood's post-election retirement (a difficult one since it invited the rebuttal, why vote for a man about to step down?) had been unhinged just before the campaign opened. John Crosbie had taunted Smallwood about being a liability to the Liberals, drawing the proud reply, "I am the Premier, and if elected I will remain Premier for the full five-year term." To counter this gaffe, Andrew Crosbie hastily put together a half-hour film, *The End of the Beginning*, its title a delicate nuance. Played twice in the campaign's last week over a province wide television network, it opened with Smallwood in the legislative chamber of the old Colonial Building where the National Convention had met, and closed with an evocative sequence showing him leaving his desk in the new Confederation Building and walking out of the chamber. The last frames showed the massive doors swinging shut behind him. The message that went to the bays was unmistakable – your champion is going, send him out with his head high.

In the last week of the campaign, Smallwood emerged from his seclusion as abruptly as he had entered it. He stormed into St. John's to canvass door to door. On radio open-lines he took on all comers. The old debating skills surfaced undimmed. When one radio caller shouted, "You've got to go. Your idiotic economic policies have put Newfoundland in the hole," Smallwood smoothly replied, "I think I'll put you down in my doubtful column." He drove to Arnold's Cove, close by the new oil refinery, to tell an enthusiastic audience of the achievements since Confederation, and to assure them, "This is the last election for me." In Corner Brook he beat down a knot of hecklers and told the crowd, "It's easy to see the tide has come back in."

Once confident of victory, the Conservatives, in these last days, could sense the returning current. Smallwood had promised a campaign "as clean as a hound's tooth" and they had not believed him. Instead, with their ammunition prepared for, as Moores put it "the dirtiest campaign in our history," they waited for Smallwood's classic frontal attack. Discomfited by his wraith-like strategy, it was ten days before they changed their own. Even so, they staged their best-financed and best-organized effort ever.* In rally after rally, they outdrew Smallwood – by as much as three to one in Corner Brook. Behind the slogans, "Join the Moores Team" and "The Time has Come," they flooded radio and television with sprightly commercials. Against charisma, they had mustered professionalism.

Election day, October 28, 1971, the feast-day of St. Jude, patron saint of lost causes, was clear and sunny, a flawless summer day that somehow had

---

* The Liberal campaign chest, at some $1 million, was about three times as large. One businessman contributed $200,000. In addition, the Liberals made unrestrained use of the machinery of government, communities were showered with fire trucks, overnight road paving, wharf repairs, street-lighting, anything and everything that was quick and visible.

stumbled into autumn. Conscious that the moment was historic, Newfoundlanders flocked to the polls. In some communities, 90 per cent of the voters had cast their ballots in the first two hours. Spokesmen from rival parties issued identical estimates, Liberals and Conservatives would each win thirty seats.

At 8 P.M. counting began. At the Liberal campaign headquarters on the Portugal Cove Road, bottles were stacked high for a victory party. The Premier, reporters were told, would arrive as soon as the results were known.

The first flash, at 8:20 P.M., came from White Bay South, deep in the heart of outport country. Incredibly, it gave the Conservative, running against Bill Rowe, the lead. A few minutes later the first returns came in from Corner Brook, as unbelievably, the Liberals were ahead. These counts quickly righted themselves, but a pattern had been set. At 8:37 the first member, a Conservative, claimed victory, and another three minutes later. At 8:45 P.M. the first Liberal (Roberts) was elected; one minute later a third Conservative, John Crosbie, won in St. John's West. Liberal hopes of holding anything in the capital were smashed. Fred Rowe, the first of seven cabinet ministers, went down in Grand Falls. The Conservatives swept nearly all the Catholic districts of the Avalon Peninsula. Tom Burgess triumphed for the New Labrador Party in Labrador West.

Yet the outports were holding. Their majorities were cut, among them Smallwood's own, but still they were in the Liberal column. When counting ended at 2 A.M. the Liberals and Conservatives had each elected 18 members, Burgess was in, and five seats were undecided.

Out on the Portugal Cove Road, the Liberal victory dissolved into tears and a drunken brawl. From Smallwood there was only silence. Through the long evening he circled the city in his chauffeur-driven limousine, the radio turned up high, jotting the results on a pad. In the small hours, he drove the forty-five miles back to Roache's Line. He said not a word to the press.

Next morning, the counting continued. When it ended, the Conservatives had won 21 seats, one by a margin of eight votes, the Liberals 20,
while Burgess, as he exultantly put it, had "got 'em where I want 'em."

The post-Smallwood Newfoundland had spoken. Fifty-six per cent of
the electorate had voted out its Premier of twenty-three years. It had
done so with a conscious deliberation that caused third-party candidates
to be wiped out everywhere, except in Labrador where the Conservatives
ran a distant third to the New Labrador Party.

Even in defeat Smallwood had broken records. Some 85 per cent of
those eligible to vote had done so, a turnout that was almost certainly a
record in Canadian politics.* Among those determined to defeat
Smallwood, the young, the educated, the middle class, the townies and,
the most important element in the final results, organized labour, this
high turnout had been expected. The surprise, and the reason the final
margin was so narrow, was that the Smallwood loyalists had also flocked
to the polls in unparalleled numbers.

In the fine weather of election day, the old, the poor, the outsiders, the
baymen had marched out for their man. His trumpet might be uncertain,
but he was still the only champion they had. They did it out of loyalty, out
of gratitude, out of memory for what he had once been, and, a deeper
emotion than any of these, out of a realization that after two decades
during which he had not needed their votes because victory was certain
anyway, they at last had a chance to repay him.

Their ranks were thinned by Smallwood's own program of resettlement, by modernization, and by death. Yet, just as he had said, from Cape
Chidley to Conception Bay, the old Coaker country of the northeast
coast, citadel of the old Newfoundland, every district but one had held
for Joe. These harsh and beautiful coasts had been his windy Troy. It was
here that he raised the banner of Confederation in 1946. And it was here,

---

* The turnout among registered voters was 88 per cent. However, since
Newfoundland electoral law does not restrict the ballot to those who have
registered, the actual turnout among those eligible was lower, but impossible
to calculate exactly.

more than a quarter of a century later, that Joe and the baymen made their last political stand. The last for Joe, because he had to quit now. The last for the baymen because redistribution will shrivel their political influence, and because resettlement, modernization and death will continue to thin their ranks. The old Newfoundland had failed to give Smallwood victory but it had saved him from humiliation.

29

The Last, Last Hurrah

Newfoundlanders awoke on Friday, October 29, expecting to hear at any moment that Smallwood had resigned. Only twenty Liberal members had been elected to the Opposition's twenty-two (including Burgess). He and the party had been overwhelmingly rejected in the popular vote.

Instead, there was silence. Stunned by the defeat, he stayed out of sight at Roache's Line. Inquiring reporters were told, "He's not available." He spoke only to close friends. In these conversations he would lapse into prolonged silences, then excitedly explain that three or four seats would be changed "for certain" by recounts, or rail against the university students who had voted against him by nearly three to one.*

On Friday afternoon he drove in secret to television station CJON in St. John's. There, having ordered the studio crew to tell no one

---

* Against the urging of his campaign advisers, Smallwood had arranged for the votes of Memorial students to be counted in their home districts rather than in St. John's, where they would have merely added to the huge Conservative majorities.

of his presence, he taped an hour-long interview with broadcaster Geoff Stirling.

That tape, played at nine o'clock that evening, gave Newfoundlanders their first sight of their Premier in more than twenty-four hours. His voice was subdued, his style almost introspective. The defeat had happened, he said, "because of everything we have done since Confederation, people no longer remember the past." His own campaign, he added with a flash of his old fire, had "saved the Liberals from clear defeat." About the future, he was studiedly enigmatic. Since supply had been voted for the year, there was no need to call the legislature into session, and the government, if it chose, could stay in office until March 31, 1972. "I'm not saying we will do it. I'm only saying that proper constitutional authority exists." In the meantime, no decisions would be made until recounts had been completed, as well as an examination of "alleged irregularities" in certain districts.

The effect of this was to reduce his opponents to blind fury. Conservative spokesmen demanded he step down in response to the evident will of the majority. They talked publicly of petitions, to the Lieutenant Governor and to Ottawa, to force him out. Students planned demonstrations and the press raged. Moores flew in from the west coast to a tumultuous welcome and a cavalcade through the city. "It is pathetic and shameful," he said, "to see this man going to any extreme to retain personal power."

By the weekend, St. John's was a hotbed of rumours – that Burgess had been offered cabinet posts by both sides; that potential defectors, again from both sides, were being enticed with sums running into tens of thousands of dollars; that several cabinet ministers were threatening to resign if Smallwood did not. The presence of John Doyle added fuel to the flame. He had flown in by private jet, accompanied by Burgess, who told reporters, "I have often knocked Mr. Doyle, I admit." During the flight, however, he had discovered him to be "a gentleman."

Many of the rumours were groundless, some were true, others were premature. The point was that the narrowness of the election outcome had created too many opportunities for intrigue for either side to resist.

Such intrigue, moreover, was second nature to even the most circumspect
of Newfoundland politicians. Since Confederation, the economics and
sociology of the island had changed almost beyond recognition. But the
style of its politics had changed scarcely at all. Bond, Coaker or Squires
would all have felt entirely at home in the autumn of 1971. It was mainland Canadians, accustomed to having the manoeuvrings of politics
carried out under a cloak of rectitude and platitude, who were confused.

"What you have to understand about Newfoundlanders," a visitor from
St. John's told a CBC radio audience in Ottawa in mid-January, "is that we
like to think of our politics as being quite separate from our government."
It was, her interviewer allowed, the best explanation so far of what was
going on in the tenth province.

By then, obscure Newfoundland backbenchers had become household words as far west as Victoria. From the election onwards, the mainland press gave Newfoundland almost as much space and attention as the
province had received up to then in the twenty years since Confederation. The *Globe and Mail*, in editorial after editorial, hectored, ful-
minated and despaired. The CBC repeatedly prefaced its television and
radio news with Newfoundland items. Some kind of climax was achieved
by the *Montreal Star*, which bannered the front page of its February 29,
1972, edition with the headline, "Moores Ready to Open House," in the
confident expectation that its readers knew who Moores was and that
they cared that the legislature was about to meet in Newfoundland.*

Smallwood, of course, was the star attraction, but even without him
the Newfoundland scene became compulsively fascinating. Jaded by the
characterless managerial style of their own politics, mainlanders waited
for daily instalments of a saga that read like a cross between *The Last*

* *Montreal Star* readers, however, were no doubt fascinated to learn that
Moores, earlier the same day, had said the Legislature would *not* open, and
that once assembled it dissolved immediately for a general election that
replaced a by-election Moores had already announced but which, on
reflection, he. . . .

Hurrah and *The Godfather*. For under the bravura theatricality and flamboyant rhetoric carried over from Ireland, or drifted north from the Boston States, there were less pleasant undertones of intrigue and betrayal, of clannish vendetta handed down from father to son that might have found their way from the Mediterranean.*

The personal feuds thrived because there were no discernible differences between the parties. The Conservatives, for example, were largely an urban party unlike their counterparts elsewhere simply because the cities were the centres of opposition to Smallwood. And while this absence of ideology was hardly unusual, there were in Newfoundland no formal party structures to compensate for it by providing discipline and continuity. Nor was there any tradition of politics as public service. As Moores commented, "There is a stigma attached to politics in Newfoundland which must be removed."

Smallwood had given island politics its only coherence. He had polarized the public into those who hated him and those who loved him. He had introduced the first semblance of ideology since Coaker, and had provoked in return the beginnings of an opposing ideology: reformist, technocratic, managerial.

The imminence of his departure dissolved this fragile structure. Right to the end, Smallwood remained the only major figure able to command unquestioning loyalty; a loyalty that he returned in equal measure, often to his own political cost. (John Crosbie, in recognition of his dogged courage, also commanded a core of supporters, though it was much less numerous.) Within Liberal ranks, there was no single unquestioned successor and a half-dozen claimants jostled for position. As for the Conservatives, Moores, though ostensibly the victor, had made little impact on the public at large. His position, moreover, was challenged by many in the party who believed that his leadership had robbed them of a clear-cut victory.

---

* Few recollections of the author, in earnest pursuit of comprehension, are more vivid than that of a small social gathering at which one of St. John's most highly regarded citizens said of a well-known politician, "I would never trust him because of what his grandfather did" – an analysis that everyone present accepted as reasonable.

This was the noisy, turbulent stage upon which Smallwood played his encore. For a quarter of a century, he had dominated it as star actor, scriptwriter, producer and director. He still understood politics far better than anyone else around. In the end, it was perhaps only the late entrance of one of his players, an Opposition defector who lingered too long in the Florida sun, that robbed him of his goal of retiring undefeated as Premier.

The astonishing thing about Smallwood's mastery was how quickly it re-emerged. His legendary recuperative powers were undiminished. Once the shock of defeat had dissipated, which took about a week, he was again seized by the excitement of a challenge against odds. The Conservatives he shrugged off as "a bunch of babies." His comments in private about many members of his own party were only slightly less scathing.

There were other reasons for his recovery. For one thing, his objective was, for once, limited. At no time did he seek to remain permanently in office. Instead he hoped to hang on long enough to hold a convention at which he could hand over the reigns of office to a successor satisfactory to him. To achieve this, he needed to hold the Conservatives at bay for about three months.

For another, Smallwood's mind was no longer distracted. The year-long wait for an election he might lose was over. He had lost, but he had not been humiliated. He had after all won, as Prime Minister Trudeau delicately expressed it, "six and a half elections." Whether for or against him, his magnetism had pulled people to the polls in record numbers. He had even managed to collect six thousand more Liberal votes than in the 1966 election.

For the first time in his life, Smallwood acquired, at least by his frenetic standards, qualities of disengagement and detachment. Nothing surprised observers more than the ease with which, when the moment could no longer be postponed, he finally put aside the cares of office. His delight on the day he stepped down was not the carefully rehearsed pose of an actor, but the honest relief of someone from whom an impossible burden had at last been lifted. Instead of going through the acute decompression symptoms everyone had expected, he bobbed happily back to the surface. Within ten days of leaving office, he had bought one hundred new and second-hand books and had plunged into the task of writing his "great history" of Newfoundland.

For the first few days after the election, Smallwood stayed mostly in seclusion. On Saturday, October 30, he helicoptered to Swift Current to spend the day with Don Jamieson at his summer home. On Sunday, he met briefly with Burgess at the Confederation Building. "It's our turn to howl now," said Burgess. Earlier in the day he had met also Moores and Crosbie. He received, from both sides, promises of a cabinet post and of immediate assistance to Labrador, including improved medical services and a better school bus system. On Monday, using a statement that friends had written for him, Burgess announced he would support neither side, but would vote "for legislation that benefits the people of Labrador, and all the working people of Newfoundland."

That same day, Smallwood flew to Ottawa for talks organized some weeks before, about the Marystown shipyard. In the evening, he and Jamieson dined privately with Trudeau at 24 Sussex Drive. The discussion discreetly steered clear of the election, instead it focussed on Smallwood's post-retirement literary plans.

The next day, November 2, Jamieson issued a statement. "The Premier has assured me he will leave office if no changes occur as a result of the recounts and I fully support his decision." Smallwood was far from pleased, since the declaration cramped his scope for manoeuvre, but he told reporters, "I fully concur," and added, "I have no desire to hang on if I don't have a majority."

The statement deflated a situation that was threatening to turn ugly. In St. John's that morning, Moores had said he was considering legal action to force Smallwood from office. He added darkly, "We want to keep physical action out of it." Press stories magnified the public unrest. These reported that Doyle had been in contact with several Conservative members. Doyle explained that he had done so "purely out of courtesy." He denied he had tried to "woo" them into Liberal ranks.

A second calming influence was that of Senator Forsey (a native Newfoundlander), who pointed out that Smallwood was entirely within his rights to remain in office until the recounts were completed. "It would be pretty foolish to have to change the government again if two or three seats changed."

Disquiet dissolved into normalcy. The weekend papers devoted most of their front pages to protests by Memorial students against the Amchitka blast. On Monday, November 8, the defeated ministers resigned their portfolios. Three days later, Smallwood set a limit to his own tenure by announcing that a Liberal leadership convention would be held February 4-5. On Friday, Burgess held a joint press conference with Moores to announce that, "in the best interests of Newfoundland," he would support the Conservatives. (The two had reached agreement at a meeting in the Chateau Champlain in Montreal the previous weekend.) With this commitment, the Conservatives had a clear majority of 22 members, a position strengthened by judicial recounts completed in five districts, all of which confirmed the election night results.

On November 23, the peaceful interregnum fell apart. Supreme Court Judge Harold Puddester cut short the recount in the district of St. Barbe South. This was the riding where the margin had been narrowest of all, a majority of eight votes for the Conservative. One hundred and six ballots were missing, Puddester disclosed. They belonged to Poll No. 13 in Sally Cove, and they had been burned accidentally on election night.

The bizarre accident at Sally Cove, which left even the indefatigable Senator Forsey at a loss for words beyond, "there is no precedent in history for this," brought the entire Newfoundland political process to a halt. Both sides lodged opposing court suits: the Liberals to have the election in Sally Cove declared void; the Conservatives to have their candidate declared elected. In the meantime, Conservative strength was cut to twenty, and Burgess, though officially committed to the Conservatives, was once again the kingmaker. Even in the unlikely event that Smallwood did nothing to exploit the situation, he could legitimately remain in office for another five or six weeks until the court cases were settled. This would leave him only a month to go before his self-imposed retirement deadline of February 4.

The political manoeuvres that now ensued became so intricate and convoluted that even the principal players were hard put to unravel them. Only the mystery of Sally Cove itself was easy to solve. The explanation, as established by a magisterial inquiry, was that Deputy Returning Officer Olive Payne had accidentally cast the ballots (55 for the Conservative, 50 for the Liberal and six spoiled) into her wood and oil stove while clearing out the rubbish of election night.

Ever since the weekend immediately following the election, Smallwood had known, via his well-tended grapevine, of the missing ballots at Sally Cove. Well aware of the possibilities their absence opened up, he had carefully maintained his lines of contact with Burgess. Dealing with Burgess, as all who attempted it discovered, demanded an endless supply of patience and good humour – though not necessarily of cunning. The real problem was, there were two Burgesses.

One of these was best described, by a cabinet minister, as "an Irish soldier of fortune," slim, good looking, with a gift for oratory and a refreshing lack of pretension about his motives who had bounced around the world from Australia to Africa, landed in Labrador as a carpenter's mate, married a trapper's daughter and then risen to become an international organizer for the Steelworkers. He had skipped from the expectant arms of the NDP to those of the Liberals, left them to become an independent, then formed and led his own New Labrador Party.

The other Burgess was a confused populist. He had been elected in the affluent but isolated mining towns of Labrador West, where talk of "special status" helped while away the long winter evenings. Elsewhere in the territory, the party had drawn its support (one candidate came within 83 votes of winning) from the poorest communities in the province, the tiny fishing hamlets strung along the length of the coast. Burgess was dazzled by the press attention, as much national as local, given him, and by the reporters' continued description of him as a "kingmaker."

In the wake of the election, heady talk bubbled of a new left-of-centre party that might sweep together the New Labrador Party, the Fishermen's Union, co-operatives, organized labour and the remnants of the NDP. What this hopeful movement lacked most obviously was a leader – a Smallwood, in fact. Instead, as spokesman, it had Burgess. He caught the idealistic mood in his first post-election statement. "The doctors, the lawyers, the big fish merchants, the owners of big construction companies are the people who have been getting the most out of Newfoundland. They have the biggest incomes in Canada. The rest of the people have the smallest."

The movement never got out of the living rooms and hotel rooms where it was endlessly discussed. Yet Burgess never forgot that the possibility had been there. His wanderings around the political map were to be erratic beyond belief. They were made more so by the constant tug of conscience.

Immediately after the election, Burgess had taken the advice of his idealistic friends and had refused to commit himself to either party. He quickly wobbled off that virtuous course.

After Sally Cove, the bidding between himself and Smallwood became intense, and so complicated that Smallwood at one point told reporters, "Newfoundlanders should get down on their knees and pray that Burgess does not hold their fate in his hands." That was precisely where Burgess held Smallwood's fate. One of Burgess's demands was that Smallwood promise not to run Liberals against NLP candidates. Smallwood could hardly accede, since this would have meant junking the two Liberals elected in the other Labrador seats. One of these, Joe Harvey, became so suspicious that Smallwood might do just that, that, "to make the old man sweat, he was making me sweat," he arranged a meeting with Moores which the press conveniently heard about. Smallwood hastily reassured Harvey of his fidelity. Those who needed assurances now were the NLP's own candidates. Burgess at one point proposed to Harvey that he join the NLP, which would have meant abandoning Burgess's own man in that seat.

By Christmas week, when these initial manoeuvrings ended, all the players were back in their original places – except that Burgess, without the public's knowing it, had moved considerably closer to Smallwood. He spent a weekend in Montreal with a prominent Liberal businessman. Late in December he flew to Florida for a holiday, his expenses paid by a Liberal supporter.

Smallwood, meanwhile, had made even quicker progress on another front. The district of St. Barbe South where, it seemed then virtually certain, a by-election would have to be called, was a stronghold of the Fishermen's Union. And the Union was in the market for favours. (The Burgeo plant had been closed for more than a month since Lake's departure, putting a heavy drain on the Union's resources.) On December 17, he announced that the government would nationalize the plant and reopen it; in return the Union's attitude towards the Liberals changed markedly.

The Conservatives, having knocked impatiently at the door for nearly two months, were becoming uncomfortably aware of a shift in the political climate. They knew also that as many as four of their own members had been in direct or indirect contact with Liberal emissaries and that one of these had even telephoned Smallwood himself twice to discuss, in blurred tones, the best party in which to seek his fortune. (The Conservatives knew this for the uncomplicated reason that the member told them.) Trouble in the ranks was compounded by disharmony at the top. John Crosbie upstaged Moores by an endless stream of public statements. Roberts took to calling the pair "co-leaders" and Burgess, after one meeting, told reporters, "I couldn't tell who was in charge."

By late December, Smallwood had a half-dozen irons sizzling merrily in the fire. On the 22nd, aboard a jet chartered by Doyle, he flew south to Florida where he owned a condominium apartment at Clearwater. Nearby, also enjoying the southern sun, was Burgess. There, a firm schema began to be developed. Burgess would join the Liberals and, after a few days, he would announce he planned to run for the leadership with Smallwood's support.

Before leaving, Smallwood had settled one other affair. Since the election, the common barroom gossip had been that Smallwood was delaying his departure because he needed time to clear out sensitive documents. What he really needed, was time to create some new ones.

Since late October, *habitués* of the Holiday Inn in St. John's had grown
used to watching the comings and goings of the portly resplendent figure
of John Christopher Doyle. Not for many years had the mining promoter
graced the city with his presence for so long a period – not, in fact, since
the last time Canadian Javelin had been under attack.

Since the mid-sixties Doyle had also stayed pretty much out of the
headlines. The heady days of developing iron ore mines and the harrow-
ing days of battling the U.S. Securities Exchange Commission were far
behind him. His style, though, was much as ever, his apartment on
Sherbrooke Street in Montreal encompassed three kitchens and eight
bathrooms. So also was his intimacy with Smallwood. Ray Guy, in one of
his deftest shafts for the *Evening Telegram*, wrote that the Premier, whenever he was in trouble, phoned "Doyle-a-Prayer." It was not far from the
truth. Late in 1969 Smallwood had said, in heated exchange with John
Crosbie, "I wish I had one hundred, one thousand John Doyles to help
develop Newfoundland."

For numbers of Newfoundlanders, one John Doyle was more than
enough. At times it became hard to tell where government began and
promoter left off. Of Canadian Javelin, *Barron's Weekly* commented in
April 1971, "In effect it has been the chosen instrument of provincial
economic policy, a role in which it has pledged its own resources, plus
whatever it can borrow, to grandiose and chancy development schemes."*

The latest such scheme, Doyle's giant linerboard mill at Stephenville,
was certainly chancy and grandiose. Even so, as critics of the Smallwood-
Doyle partnership tended to overlook, it would also develop the
province. The mill would be the third-largest in the world, it would
provide a use for Labrador's endless stands of spruce (on which Doyle
held concessions for some sixteen million acres) and, when completed in

---

* The problem of distinguishing between province and promoter was made
more difficult by such circumstances as that in the summer of 1971 when
Smallwood's long-time Justice Minister, Leslie Curtis, resigned from the
government. He joined a law firm whose principal partner, until then, had
been handling Doyle's accounts. The partner promptly joined the government as Justice Minister while Curtis took over on behalf of Doyle.

mid-1972, it would employ close to two thousand people. Originally, the project had been expected to cost $120 million. By the end of 1971 this figure had escalated to around $200 million, the precise figure depending upon a number of factors, notably the purposes for which estimates were made, and by whom.

Smallwood's original pledge had been $53 million of provincial funds. Later he raised this to $58 million. In June 1971 he pledged a loan of another $24 million. Three weeks after the election, giving scarcely a thought to the propriety of such an act by a government almost certain to leave office shortly, he advanced the last $9 million of the June commitment. (Smallwood gave as little thought to the post-election propriety of appointing Liberal faithful to the public service.)

Now Doyle needed another $30 million, of which all but $6 million would be used to enable him to pay back the $24 million loan of the previous summer. But this time the cabinet, more precisely its two youngest members, Roberts and Bill Rowe, balked. Both members of Smallwood's inner team, the pair had long been rivals for the leadership. Now, far from unaware how the record might look once the Conservatives arrived, they forged a close alliance. Enraged by their obduracy, Smallwood called them "The Bobbsey Twins." Day after day they argued that the loan should be given only if it were accompanied by a back-up agreement which would prohibit its being used without the province's approval. Unable to drive a cleft between the Roberts-Rowe twins, Smallwood took matters into his own hands. On December 10, Doyle's son came to the Premier's Office carrying in his briefcase the papers covering the provincial guarantee of the bond issue. Unbeknownst to any of his ministers or civil servants, Smallwood signed the documents – without any backup agreement. Shortly thereafter, Doyle left for Germany.

It was not until a fortnight later, on December 24, when Smallwood was in Florida, that Roberts and Rowe discovered what had happened. From financial sources, they learned that Doyle had raised $30 million in Germany on the strength of the province's guarantee, and that he had deposited the money at the Banque Nationale in Paris. Immediately, the two got in touch with Doyle by phone. Threatening to quit the cabinet and thus bring the government down, they demanded that the money be placed in trust, to be used only with the province's authority. Several hours later, Doyle phoned back and agreed to the terms. The bulk of the money was deposited in the security of a St. John's law firm, the balance in a Montreal bank.

Smallwood was furious about the erosion of his own authority, and embarrassed by what he considered a grievous insult to Doyle. From this point on he became an implacable opponent of Roberts as successor. It became almost as important to him to block the man who had once been his closest confidant as it was to extend his own term of office. (Oddly, though Rowe had fought the loan as vociferously as Roberts, scarcely any of Smallwood's wrath was directed towards him. Smallwood in fact at one point urged Rowe to run, promising him the same $100,000 campaign fund offered to Burgess.)

Many of the details of Smallwood's last favour to Doyle were uncovered after he had left office and the new government had taken over. John Crosbie, the new Finance Minister, secured a return of the $24 million guaranteed loan under threat of legal action. During the subsequent election campaign Crosbie announced that the government would buy up Doyle's holdings in the mill and operate it itself, and this step was taken shortly after the Conservatives were returned in March.

In the palmier reaches of Florida the progress was a good deal smoother. There Burgess, as a friend later put it, "was taken to the top of the mountain." If he jumped, the Liberals would have a majority, 21 to 20 pending a settlement in St. Bathe South, and could remain in office at least until the legislature assembled.

The plan the two agreed on was for Burgess to return to Newfoundland the first week of January, and to time his announcement before the Supreme Court ruled on St. Barbe. This timing was critical. The point was that if Burgess jumped *before* the Supreme Court decision, the Liberals would have enough members, 21, no matter how the court ruled. If in fact, as everyone expected, the Court ordered a by-election in the contested district, Smallwood counted on picking up the seat. But even if the by-election were lost, or the Court awarded the seat to the

Conservatives, the Liberals, with Burgess, would still have enough members to remain in office, call the Legislature into session, and put the onus on the Conservatives to defeat them and force a general election with the Liberals still holding the advantage of being in office.

For Burgess, the chief problem was how best to explain his switch. Smallwood coached him carefully and, aware that the best plans go awry, wrote out his explanatory statement. It said that Burgess, after a month's association with the Conservatives, had come to realize that the party was incompetent to govern. He therefore had decided to rejoin the Liberals, whom he had left three years before because of a disagreement with the Premier. Since the Premier was now stepping down, the way was clear for him to return home. As Smallwood said later, "I rather liked the last part. I thought it up myself."

Early in January, Smallwood flew back to St. John's. Burgess was due to return a few days later. In Smallwood's mind, the prodigal son was cast for two roles; he could certainly give the Liberals enough members to justify their remaining in office and he might possibly mount a strong enough challenge to halt Roberts's bid for the leadership. But during Smallwood's absence, that bid had gained momentum. Though he had still to announce his candidacy, Roberts had now the vocal support of Bill Rowe and the tacit support of Jamieson. Given his formidable drive and tactical skill (Roberts, who won over 80% of the vote in his district, was the only Liberal to increase his majority since the last election), this combination would almost certainly prove too much for Burgess, no matter how well coached. As reassurance, and in the event that Burgess, at the last moment, failed to deliver his side of the bargain, Smallwood set out in search of an alternative. By the second week in January, he had found him.

On Monday, January 10, Richard Cashin, President of the Fishermen's Union, telephoned Smallwood on routine union business. Smallwood asked Cashin to join him for lunch at the Confederation Building. On the other side of the table were Roberts and Rowe. A politician of proven skills, possessed of Celtic charm and oratorical powers few of his contemporaries could match, Cashin was a considerable power in the land. Why not, Smallwood proposed, as the "Bobbsey Twins" looked on impassively, run in St. Barbe South? With his union background, Cashin would be certain of victory there; after that he could storm into the convention as the man who could win the next election. Cashin promised to think it over, and began to map out his strategy.

That evening, January 10, Smallwood stood on the brink of one of the most remarkable political comebacks of his career. The Supreme Court was due to hand down its decision on St. Barbe South the following day. If the Court ordered a by-election to be held, as both Liberals and Conservatives took for granted, Smallwood had an unbeatable candidate in Cashin. He also had Burgess, although the maverick was taking an unconscionably long time wending his way back from Florida.

At the same time, his opponents, the Conservatives, were on the verge of collapse. Two days before they had staged a putsch against their leader. While he waited impatiently for Burgess and for the St. Barbe by-election, Smallwood knew that his opponent Moores was close to being finished.

Moores had been in trouble with his own party ever since the election. Twice he had flown out of the province on vacations. Whether he was absent or present it was John Crosbie who grabbed most of the headlines. Many in the ranks felt his leadership lacked decisiveness, not a few showed it by their readiness to parlay with the Liberals. Shortly after the election, Moores's position had been damaged further by a story in the *Daily News* of November 10, which linked him to an alleged scandal involving the bankruptcy of a Toronto brokerage firm, Malone Lynch Securities. The story claimed that Moores, the day before the company was delisted, had withdrawn from the firm $200,000 of his own funds. In reply, Moores explained that the money was a trust fund for his family, which, dissatisfied with the firm's performance, he had moved elsewhere.

A worse blow fell on Moores on January 7th, while he was on vacation in St. Lucia. The press reported that his wife Dorothy had filed a divorce petition before the Newfoundland Supreme Court claiming grounds of adultery and mental cruelty. In a province where religion and the family still anchored society, the political impact of a divorce would be devastating.

That weekend, with Moores still out of the province, a group of dissident Conservatives met to consider the party's and their leader's political future. Led by John Crosbie and John Carter, both later to become cabinet ministers, they concluded that with Moores in charge the Conservatives could not hope to win either the by-election in St. Barbe or a succeeding general election. The next day, Sunday, January 9, the rebels forced a meeting of the full caucus. A vote taken at the end of the long heated meeting showed ten of the twenty elected members demanding Moores's immediate resignation. Only four stood by him. (The others were neutral or absent.)

On the Monday, while Smallwood wooed Cashin, Moores flew back to St. John's to fight for his political life. That afternoon his wife withdrew her position. "I am not divorcing my husband," she said in a formal statement. "I believe as I always have that he is the best man to be Premier of Newfoundland." The rebels, though checked, were far from beaten. A second full caucus was scheduled for the following day.

A week behind schedule, having made a slow passage northwards via Montreal, Burgess now reappeared in the province. He telephoned Smallwood early Tuesday morning to report that he was ready to make his announcement. But to Smallwood's dismay, Burgess said that he first must go to Labrador, to convince his New Labrador Party executive to support him. To Smallwood's remonstrations, Burgess replied, "I must do it." He promised to call back late that same evening.

The two Burgesses, the soldier of fortune and the populist, were warring that day within a single man. On Tuesday evening, he spoke to his own executive and won their support. But he did not telephone Smallwood until well after midnight. All was going well he reported, but added, this time to Smallwood's barely concealed fury, that before he could make a public announcement he would have to secure the approval of the party executives in the two other Labrador ridings. He would, he promised, phone back in the evening (Wednesday).

That day, January 12th, spent waiting for Burgess's call was perhaps the most frustrating Smallwood had ever spent. Time and again he jumped up when the telephone rang to find it was only a journalist or a cabinet minister on the other end of the line. And they were all demanding to know when he planned to announce his resignation. The reason was that the Supreme Court had handed down its decision on St. Barbe South. In one stroke, the two judges had virtually settled Newfoundland's political future.

The decision came down at 5:30 P.M. on Tuesday, January 11 – just as Burgess was making his rounds of Labrador and as the Conservative rebels waited to challenge Moores in full caucus. The opinion was unanimous: "to declare an election void under these circumstances" as one of the judges put it in his written statement, "would leave the door open to the possibilities of practices which could invalidate any future election." The Conservative candidate in St. Barbe South, the winner by eight votes on election night, who was ahead by just two votes when the recount was halted, was formally declared elected.[*] The decision restored Conservative strength to twenty-one, and gave them a clear majority once Burgess's vote was added – an addition that no one, at that time, had any reason to doubt would be made.

For the Conservatives, the effect of the Supreme Court judgement was to puncture the putsch against Moores; its members recognized they were dealing now with a certain Premier. (John Crosbie paid for his part in the rebellion. When Moores announced his cabinet line-up he placed Crosbie third in line behind Alex Hickman in the post of unofficial deputy premier.)

---

[*] The Supreme Court based its decision on the interpretation that the election itself was valid, no matter what may have happened afterwards. Smallwood gave no thought to appealing the decision since, pending the inevitably lengthy outcome, the Conservative candidate would rightfully have taken his seat.

The impact upon the Liberals was as decisive. Ed Roberts had announced his candidacy for the leadership on Tuesday. To hasten things along, Jamieson issued a statement that since the Conservatives now had a majority, he expected Smallwood to resign, "if not on constitutional grounds, then certainly on traditional grounds."

Yet Smallwood would not give up. By Wednesday morning, he had received Burgess's first call reporting success with his own executive, and the promise of a second call that evening. Burgess was late, desperately late, but he was not yet too late. His belated defection would even the standings 21-21. Smallwood would have at least the constitutional right (which Senator Forsey, to the annoyance of the Conservatives, confirmed) to call the Legislature into immediate session and there seek a vote of confidence. While he could not win such a vote, or elect a speaker, he would be able to secure a dissolution and a general election with the Liberals still the government.

From the moment the Supreme Court decision was announced, Newfoundlanders hung by radios in cars, houses, offices, restaurants, waiting to hear Smallwood announce his resignation. Instead there was silence. On Wednesday evening, they found out why. Frank Moores told them. A New Labrador Party member had tipped off the Conservatives to Burgess's intentions, and Moores in turn attacked Burgess in a public statement.

The full equation was more complex in fact than Moores let on. The Conservatives had also discovered that one of their own members planned to make the jump in tandem with Burgess, a double jump that would give Smallwood not just parity but a majority. To ensure this member's loyalty until the tempting moment had passed, Conservative workers locked him in a hotel room and stationed one of their number as a chaperon during the critical twenty-four hours.

By midnight Wednesday, Smallwood had still to make any announcement. While he waited the pressures mounted. Among the public at large, disgust at Burgess had turned to blind fury at Smallwood. The next day, he was scheduled to speak to the St. John's Rotary Club. Memorial students planned to demonstrate at the hotel and the police feared an outbreak of violence.

Might-have-beens are for historians; politicians deal with facts, lucky or unlucky according to the breaks. Smallwood stayed up till one o'clock then turned in to sleep. He took for granted that the delay in the call from Labrador meant that Burgess had failed. He was right.

In his own riding, Burgess's charm had succeeded. In the coastal tidings of Labrador, seat of the populist wing of the party, his passionate pleas were met by equally passionate rebuttals. If he jumped, the party would not follow, but would oppose him on his own ground. A man almost broken, who in the space of forty-eight hours had managed to alienate every political party in the province, Burgess could not bring himself to report failure to Smallwood. Instead he called a journalist friend at Radio Station VOCM in St. John's, and through him spoke to Moores who in turn told the press, "Mr. Burgess has assured me he will stick by his commitments." At 3 A.M., the journalist phoned Smallwood at Roache's Line, woke him up, and told him that the last thread holding him to office was gone.

There was nothing more to be done and Smallwood wasted no time. "It was like a huge weight had been lifted from me. I had to get out right away." Early on the morning of Thursday, January 13, he cancelled his engagement with the Rotary and instead called a press conference for 4 P.M. In the morning he met with the party caucus, in the early afternoon with the cabinet.

Half an hour before the start of the press conference, television crews set up their equipment in his eighth-floor office. Smallwood greeted the reporters, most of them by name, then read a thousand-word prepared statement to the cameras and microphones. "It is our plain and simple duty to vacate office," he said. He had delayed doing this only because two Opposition members had approached him about joining the Liberal Party.

His voice was hoarse from the strain of the day before, and twice he came close to tears. He spoke of the "marvellous privilege" of having had an opportunity to build Newfoundland. He warned, "We remain in eternal danger of being washed down the drain. It is an unending battle to keep Newfoundland going." Asked to describe his own record, he said: "I leave it to the verdict of history to describe my work." At the meeting's end the reporters, many his bitter opponents, applauded him. His old enemy, John Diefenbaker, seemingly unconscious of the irony, commented: "He could have had a greater place in history if he had withdrawn gracefully once defeat became inevitable."

Smallwood's formal moment of departure came five days later on Tuesday, January 18. It was just two and a half weeks short of the date he had set for himself. The days in between he had spent clearing out his personal mementos and memorabilia as well as some 400,000 papers, documents and letters.

On the morning of his last day in office, Smallwood went on two radio open-line shows in St. John's, and unleashed a flood of nostalgia and affection. "There'll never be another Joey Smallwood," said one caller; a woman explained that her three-year old son said in his nightly prayers, "God bless Mummy, Daddy and Joey."

Shortly before noon he drove up, for the last time as Premier, to the Confederation Building. He took a last look at his bare office, handed the keys to his staff, then took the small private elevator to the ground floor. From there he went to Government House to hand in his resignation to Lieutenant Governor E. J. Harnum and to recommend that Moores be invited to form a government. But he did not wait to shake hands with his successor. Instead he lunched privately at the Holiday Inn with several cabinet ministers and his two private secretaries, one of whom, Muriel Templeman, had been with him since 1949. To kill time before his plane left, he drove out of the city, as far as Pouch Cove, where he had established a co-operative society in the thirties. At 6:25 P.M., since a strike by controllers had grounded commercial aircraft, he boarded a twin-engine

Aero Commander lent him by Roberts who had been using it for his leadership campaign. (In one final irony the government's twin-engine Otter, which otherwise would have been made available to him, was being used that day to fly John Crosbie back from Halifax to attend the swearing-in of the new cabinet.) The next day Smallwood flew on from New York, south again to Florida.

With Smallwood gone, Newfoundland political life rolled on its wayward way, the undertones of tragedy submerged by those of farce. Three days after his re-conversion to the Conservatives, Burgess announced they had "broken faith" with him (the offer of a cabinet post had been cancelled). This loss to the new government was balanced when a Liberal member, faced with the dreary prospect of opposition instead of the cabinet position he had expected, announced he would resign his seat. Lest he change his mind, the new government promptly re-appointed him to the magistracy.

The count in the Legislature was unbalanced once again when a Conservative backbencher, Hugh Shea, apparently convinced that ownership of a grocery store automatically qualified him to be a cabinet minister, bolted the party to become an independent. At the end of January, Shea and Burgess made the only perambulation across the political map left to them, and joined the Liberals. This reinforcement, which many in the party saw more as hindrance than help, created yet another parliamentary precedent – in a two-party House the Opposition now had more members than the government. No one was particularly surprised by Burgess's move, nor by his subsequent announcement, since it came from one who had already demonstrated the worst sense of timing in Canadian politics, that he would contest the party leadership. Shea's defection though brought political passions back to the boiling point. With more foolhardiness than sense he tried to explain his position to an audience of Memorial students, who pelted him with rotten eggs and tomatoes. He had to be escorted from the stage under guard.

On Friday, February 4, 1972, a bitterly cold night with flurries of snow on the wind, Smallwood put a formal end to fifty years of active politics. More than a thousand Liberals crammed into the former USAF drillhall at Pleasantville on the outskirts of St. John's. They stood and cheered as Smallwood, dabbing a handkerchief to his eyes, came up the centre aisle while the band of the Church Lads Brigade played his 1969 convention theme song, *Hello Joey (Dolly)*.

His daughter Clara sat beside him on the platform, his grandchildren clustered in the front rows. The daughter of a Liberal senator presented a bouquet of twenty-three red roses, one for each year in office. Then Smallwood settled back to listen to Jamieson's hail and farewell. "People have said he is illogical; he is the most logical man I know. He recognized that for Newfoundland, the only logic was to fly in the face of logic, to make the illogical, logical." Smallwood wept again when the sheaf of telegrams were read out, from Pickersgill, Pearson, Trudeau and, for him the most touching of all, from Louis St. Laurent who had signed the Terms of Confederation with him, and who had turned ninety just three days before.

The surroundings, bleak and cavernous, blunted the sharp edge of emotion. Smallwood himself was nervous, shifting from hand to hand the cards on which he had that morning written his notes. He spoke for too long, nearly an hour, and dwelled too long on the familiar litany of his post-Confederation achievements. Still, the message came through. "Unless you keep your party to the left of centre, the party will die. Keep it always a people's party, a party of the toiling masses . . . make sure it stays where it belongs – in the hands of the people."

When he had finished the crowd rose as one, many clambering onto chairs for a last look. A veteran backroom worker, Joe Ashley, rushed to the platform, put his arms around Smallwood and sobbed openly. Women pushed through the mob to hug him and shake his hand. Two burly party members hoisted him to their shoulders and carried him to the new car, a Rambler, the party had given as its farewell gift. Smallwood's grandchildren scrambled inside, and slowly it pushed towards the exit, and out into the cold stormy night.

Next day, the Liberal Party of Newfoundland chose its second leader since Confederation. Ed Roberts won on the first ballot, with 564 of the 663 votes cast. Burgess collected a token 82. Smallwood cast his own ballot early in the afternoon and left before the winner was announced. "I was tired," he told reporters who questioned his absence during Roberts's victory speech. "I was bored" was his private explanation.

No longer leader, Smallwood set about learning the arts of statesmanship befitting a retired politician. (To prepare for this role he had several years earlier listed his profession in *Who's Who* as 'Statesman.') At the first post-convention caucus he monopolized discussion as if nothing had changed, but gradually he checked his ready flow of advice. When Roberts offered him his pick of Opposition seats in the legislature, he chose one in the back row, closest to the door. He made no public statements, though he poured out thousands of words for his new column in the *Daily News*, dictated in batches of as many as ten a day. He planned to say nothing in the legislature, "unless they attack me," and to resign his Placentia East seat as soon as the political climate shifted and the Liberals could hope to win the by-election.

None of this restraint proved necessary. On March 2, Premier Moores called an election for March 24. His way had been paved by the resignation of a Liberal member which permitted the Lieutenant Governor to grant a dissolution since the Opposition could no longer claim to be able to form a government. The Conservatives easily won the election by a clear majority of 33 seats to nine. Among the losers were Burgess, "a washed-out politician" in his own words, and Shea.

Smallwood resigned his seat at the start of the campaign and planned to take no part in it. Liberal candidates entreated him to speak on their behalf, and so halfway through the campaign he reappeared to make his final entry onto the political stage he had dominated for so long. He ranged up and down among the outports of the northeast coast and on March 23, on the eve of election day, gave his last political speech. The magic of his name pulled five hundred to the schoolhouse of Western Bay to hear him, in a two-and-one-half hour oration, praise his own record and damn the Conservatives as "men of high intelligence and cold-blood, . . . puppies and cold-blooded merchants." When he was finished the crowd mobbed him, burly fishermen fighting back tears, one of them telling a reporter, "I loved that man like a brother. What a man he is. God what a man."

To ease his retirement (Smallwood's pension as Premier plus interest on investments including a string of service stations in Quebec left him comfortable but not affluent), Smallwood had been offered a Senate seat and an Ambassadorial post. He refused both offers out of hand. Instead, he planned to write two books, his own autobiography, which he announced at a press conference in Toronto late in March, and a two-volume history of Newfoundland that would focus on the economic and social life of the colony, the dominion, and the province. To work on the history he planned to spend six months each year outside the province, burrowing through archives in England, Spain, Portugal and France. He told friends he had gone back to writing, his "first love." "I would like to think," he said, "that one day someone will read my book on Newfoundland and say, 'this historian, wasn't he also for a time a politician?'" (The tug of politics lingered: on the advice of his publisher Smallwood set aside the history he had planned to write first, and instead plunged into writing his autobiography.)

In this book I have tried to describe and analyze Joseph Roberts Smallwood, and to catalogue and assess his record. To be truly understood, though, the man had to be experienced, and felt. More than a personality or public figure, he was a phenomenon. His character slips through the net of easy descriptive nouns like "demagogue," "populist," "orator," "visionary," or of adjectives like "iron-willed," "demonic," "humorous," "passionate," "courageous."

The force which shapes and determines the careers of most politicians is, in Harold Macmillan's phrase, "events"; politicians react to events, uncertain, once these events are history, whether their performance made any difference to what would have happened anyway. Smallwood created events. Newfoundland is different because he was there, a statement that can be made about only a handful of other politicians, and about no other Newfoundlander.

His character was shaped by his family and his childhood; it was developed by a lifetime's experience of direct action, and tempered by the circumstances of the particular society in which he lived. In that complex of influences there were two forces which pushed him forward and over every obstacle: an ego and a dream.

The ego made him impervious to criticism; it gave him the strength to go on when no one believed in him or his ideas. It produced in him also a quality of unrestrained hardness, one that compelled him not just to defeat his opponents but to crush them, not just to control those around him but to dominate them.

The dream sprang from his love, absolute and unqualified, for Newfoundland. "The blind patriot" was the term he liked best to describe himself. More than upon the people, he focussed his love upon the place, upon "this poor bald rock," upon the *idea* of a society that refused to give up in the face of all economic and geographic reality, "Like the mother of a crippled child, proud of hardship, finding a substitute in pride for all we had not otherwise." To the end, his values were those of an engineer rather than a humanist. He spoke often of roads, and bridges, and industries, much less often of "quiet people living lives of quiet dignity."

There was also, beneath the self-confident exterior, the rich humour and the zest for life, a quality of tragedy. He was the object of more public love than any contemporary Canadian politician, yet his private life was lonely and he could count, or keep, few genuine friends among the thousands who sought his favours. Hubris, the overweening pride of ancient kings, made him cling to power so long that a society that owed almost all it had to him was left with no choice but to reject him, for he had become an obstacle to the progress of his own people.

To Smallwood the politician, and to Smallwood the man, there was a quality also of unmistakable greatness unique in his society, and very possibly of genius. He was not so much a propagandist as a communicator with a matchless command of the spoken word (he called one errant colleague "a man of cupidity, stupidity and malignant self-esteem"). By his insights, he taught others to think about themselves and about their society.

He inherited, or more precisely he seized for himself the inheritance of, a society that was broken, demoralized and apathetic. He leaves to his successors a society that is vibrant and dynamic, full of problems still but full also of possibilities. His imperishable achievement was to give his people the self-confidence to "seek human excellence." The generation of Newfoundlanders that defeated him are the beneficiaries of his life's work. Their achievements will be his memorial.

Afterword

Nearly a decade after his death and almost a quarter-century after he left politics, Joseph Roberts Smallwood remains the great white whale of the Newfoundland imagination. Like Pierre Trudeau, like Margaret Thatcher, like John F. Kennedy he has continued to be a presence long after his last, last, last hurrah.

That Smallwood remains a force in Newfoundland's political imagination, as a hero and, roughly equally, as an object of derision, is scarcely surprising. He built most of what is there now, but he built it *his* way, imposing his vision, his prejudices, his biases upon his people. More unexpectedly, his presence can also be detected in Newfoundland's artistic imagination. Many artists would recoil from any such suggestion. Many explicitly reject him. For most of today's artists, painters, sculptors, novelists, playwrights, filmmakers, singers, actors, comics, and entertainers, Smallwood represents variously the past, the exaggerated, the hyperbolic, not to mention the buffoonish and the dictatorial. There is a parallel between the dismissive attitude of Quebec's cultural elite towards Jean Chrétien and that of Newfoundland's towards Smallwood.

One interconnection is obvious enough. Without Smallwood there would be no artists in Newfoundland, or very few, perhaps just the occasional, economically self-sufficient genius like Christopher Pratt, or a pioneering scholar like the late George Story, whose seminal studies of Newfoundland speech were sustained by, and shielded by, tenure. Perhaps the best recognition of this debt has come from the painter Gerald Squires. In the mid-1960s, he came back to Newfoundland from Toronto – an unusual occurrence for that time. Once returned, Squires realized that Smallwood's program of resettling the outports into "growth centres" was destroying the tender, close-knit way of life of which he himself was a product. Squires's outrage inspired a series of savage, surrealist outport scenes, *The Boatman*, which is perhaps his finest work. In a 1998 interview with a *Globe and Mail* reporter, Squires recalled, "Here was me trying to rediscover this wonderful culture, and here it was falling apart." Then he added, each word dragged out reluctantly, "But if Newfoundland hadn't changed, I couldn't be here. In my father's time there was no room for a painter."

These artists matter. There are proportionately far more of them in Newfoundland than anywhere else in Canada: visual artists like Squires, David Blackwood, Christopher and Mary Pratt; novelists like Kevin Major, Wayne Johnston, Patrick Kavanagh, Edward Riche, Bernice Morgan, Joan Clark, and Paul Bowdring; poets like Mary Dalton and Michael Crummey; singer/songwriters like Ron Hynes, Anita Best, and Pam Morgan; actor/playwrights like Andy Jones and the *This Hour Has 22 Minutes* crowd of Mary Walsh, Rick Mercer, Greg Thomey, and Cathy Jones; comics and talkers like the CBC's Rex Murphy; and all the musical groups from Great Big Sea to Buddy Wasisname and the Other Fellers to the Irish Descendants to the Ennis Sisters. The "Newfoundland" section in St. John's bookshops is almost as large as the "Canada" section in Toronto stores. The LSPU Hall, "Newfoundland's national theatre" in the description of Andy Jones, is the liveliest and edgiest community theatre centre in the country. Mary Dalton, also a professor of literature at Memorial University, has compared, with only slight exaggeration, the contemporary cultural ambience of Newfoundland to that of Renaissance Venice. Outsiders, like the painter John Hartman and the novelist E. Annie Proulx, have been drawn to Newfoundland irresistibly.

Placing Smallwood among these creative, anarchic individuals seems ridiculous. But it's not that far a reach. Smallwood's aptitude for story-telling, above all the telling of tall tales, and his sheer joy in the English language – he described an opponent as guilty of "cupidity, stupidity and malignant self-esteem" – are the primary sources of Newfoundland's cultural expression.

Much more to the point, it is the artists who have reached out to him. Time and again Smallwood has been the subject of their works. This has happened to him more often than to any other modern Canadian public figure. Thus, Pierre Trudeau has – so far – inspired just one play, Linda Griffiths's entrancing *Maggie and Pierre*, and Mackenzie King has inspired one novel, Heather Robertson's *Willie*, while both (and many others) have been the subjects of Michael Hollingsworth's extended series of plays about Canadian history. The one Canadian political personality who outranks Smallwood as a catalyst for artistic creation is Louis Riel, who offers artists the unmatchable raw materials of martyrdom and madness. By contrast, Smallwood's creative count is two novels, two plays, and one film. Quite soon after leaving office, Smallwood became the central character in *Joey*, a play by the Rising Tide collective that toured the country; later, author/actor Kevin Noble, who had played the principal part, rewrote the work as a one-act play that also toured widely and that was restructured as a CBC television drama. In 1992, playwright Tom Cahill's *The Only Living Father* premiered in St. John's and then toured the province. Smallwood also appeared in a 1992 feature film, *The Secret Nation*, written by Ed Riche and starring Cathy Jones.

The most perceptive portrayals of him are contained in two novels. The first to appear was *Clapp's Rock* by William Rowe, a former cabinet minister who used his inside knowledge to paint a vivid portrait of a monomaniacal and machiavellian premier named Percy Clapp who in all his characteristics was pure, late-vintage Smallwood. In 1998 came Wayne Johnston's superb *The Colony of Unrequited Dreams* in which Smallwood appears as himself, from childhood to early middle age, part factual, part fictional. Johnston captures marvellously the young Smallwood's energy, drive, ambition, wit and crazed love for Newfoundland. But his

Smallwood is far too reflective and introspective to have ever done what Smallwood actually did – drag his people into the twentieth century and then rule over them like a medieval monarch.

Near the end of Johnston's novel, his fictional Smallwood reflects on his life's achievements. It is here that the interconnection between Smallwood and the imagination of Newfoundland artists becomes not just close but intimate. Smallwood's interior monologue begins: "I did not solve the paradox of Newfoundland or fathom the effect upon me of its peculiar beauty. It stirred in me, as all great things do, a longing to accomplish or create something commensurate with it. I thought Confederation might be it, but I was wrong." And it continues: "Perhaps only an artist can measure up to such a place or come to terms with the impossibility of doing so. Absence, deprivation, even despair, are more likely than their opposite to be the subject of great art, but they otherwise work against greatness."

There's a certain professional conceit in this presumption of the superiority of that which is created out of the imagination over that which is created tangibly in the marketplace, whether economic or political. Individual Newfoundlanders searching for jobs, decent incomes, and education for their children might have a different measure of value. The quality that comes through most strongly in those ruminations of Johnston's is that of *rivalry*. Newfoundland's artists and Smallwood are rivals for the role of storyteller about their own society. The purpose of these stories is not just to entertain or to educate but to create the conditions for Newfoundland's survival by describing and defining it. For three decades, Smallwood *was* Newfoundland, so far as the rest of the world was concerned. Today, for most outsiders, it is the society's artists who *are* Newfoundland.

The original text of this edition – it is the second edition, published in 1972 shortly after Smallwood had stood down as premier, in order to extend the chronicle beyond the original, 1968 edition – ends with Smallwood attending the February 1972 leadership convention that elected his former aide and cabinet minister, Ed Roberts, his successor as party leader. The text notes that soon afterwards Smallwood resigned his seat. He took no part in the election that followed in March 1972 and that was won handily by Conservative Frank Moores. Thereafter, concludes this part of the text, he "set about learning the arts of statesmanship."

Not quite. Thanks to Moores's natural indolence, his government began to unravel. Victory for Roberts in the next election became a distinct possibility. In one of the most destructive acts of his political career, Smallwood set out to ensure that this would not happen – to make certain, in other words, that no Liberal could succeed him as premier. In his 1989 biography *Joey*, Harold Horwood, a novelist and naturalist, and one of the "Bolsheviks" around Smallwood during the Confederation campaigns and then his fierce critic as columnist for the *Evening Telegram*, offered an explanation as good as any for Smallwood's descent into King Lear-style ranting at someone he'd once treated like a son: "There can be no doubt he resented Roberts's superior intellect and education, at least unconsciously." Smallwood demanded a second leadership convention. It was held in 1974. He ran against Roberts, and lost badly. A year later, he gathered two hundred of his old-guard party members and at a convention in Gander proclaimed the creation of a new Liberal Reform Party. In the 1975 election, Smallwood's rump managed to muster up seventeen candidates, and, with the financial backing of mine promoter John C. Doyle and eccentric media magnate Geoff Stirling, ran a reasonably substantial campaign. This effort was enough to elect four Liberal Reformers, Smallwood among them. It was more than enough, as was the exercise's real purpose, to ensure Roberts's defeat by splitting the vote. Smallwood lingered in the legislature for a year, almost never speaking, and finally resigned for the last time in June 1977. Roberts, who had every reason not to forgive him, praised him as "the colossus of public life" and observed that "the history of the country in these last thirty years can be written in terms of his life alone."

It was only now, in his late seventies, that Smallwood really began trying to learn some of the arts of statesmanship. He went on a cross-country speaking tour as a national unity ambassador, revelling in being introduced everywhere as the Only Living Father of Confederation. He travelled widely, most particularly to China. One trip there spanned five thousand miles. He emerged to pronounce China a "paradise" with "no unemployment, no crime, no prostitution, no addiction, no alcoholism."

In fact, he didn't do too badly as a retired-politician-turned-statesman. To the surprise of most who knew him, he made no comments at all on current Newfoundland affairs. No Maison du Egg Roll-type proclamations issued forth from his house on Roache's Line. The explanation for his self-imposed Coventry was straightforward. He had pursued power all his life, had won it finally in early middle age, and then had exercised it more absolutely for a full quarter-century than any modern Canadian leader except Maurice Duplessis. But once he no longer possessed absolute power, he lost all interest in power itself. He spurned the customary rewards of past power – an ambassadorship, a seat in the Senate. He made no attempt to pick up any of the customary perquisites of past power such as a seat on some royal commission or, like a tribal elder, being called upon to issue sage declarations pre-approved by the government of the day.

He even mellowed, a bit. He attended many performances of the play *Joey*, and although it portrayed him rather harshly, and, more jarringly, made him seem a bit of a tragi-comic figure, he stoutly declared that it was "good fun." He showed little interest in all the memoirs published about him by old friends and old enemies, if only after he'd safely retired. Of these, the best was Horwood's. It was an unexpectedly mellow book to come from so prickly a figure. Horwood dismissed as inconsequential the accusations that Smallwood had dipped deep into the public purse to provide for his retirement. (More exactly, some colleagues had done this, steering some cash to him as self-justification and self-protection.) Horwood recalled that Smallwood was "bothered greatly" by accusations that he was a dictator, and that while he ran a one-man show this was because "it was the only kind of show he knew how to run." (The harshest memoir, John Crosbie's *No Holds Barred*, appeared in 1997, after Smallwood's death. He denounced Smallwood as "a demagogue and a despot . . . venal and corrupt. . . . a colonial King Tut." Getting a bit carried away even by his own standards of partisanship, Crosbie described Smallwood as guilty of "the most blatant and crass venality and conflict of interest in the history of twentieth-century Canadian politics." Yet his closing comments were, "To this day, I am ambivalent in my feelings about Joey Smallwood because I knew him to be a great Newfoundland patriot and a great lover and booster of Newfoundland.")

Rather than occupying himself with what he might have done, or with what others might think about what he'd done, Smallwood focused all his energies on his first love – writing and publishing. His first effort, the autobiography *I Chose Canada*, published in 1973, was, as always, written too quickly; as a result, his chronicling of his years in office was embarrassingly self-serving. His recollections of his pre-power days, and especially of his youth, were quite different in style and tone, though. He made his own early life come alive for readers: "What a paradise of excitement for boys was St. John's. There were parrots and sugar-cane and conch shells that seamen brought from the West Indies, and great puncheons of molasses from Barbados and Jamaica laid out on the wharves, their bungs hanging out so the gases could escape – we would stick our fingers in the bung hole and lick the molasses off them, and on lucky days, we might get some sugar-molasses, the thick, sweet, congealed molasses that formed a deposit on the bottom on the puncheon."

Through to the end of his life, Smallwood's passion was the project to publish a five-volume, five-thousand-page *Encyclopedia of Newfoundland and Labrador*. It was magnificent, and extravagant and absurd. At one time, twenty people were working full time on the project. Time and tenure in office hadn't improved Smallwood's aptitude for accountancy. In October 1983 he announced that the project – the first volume had been published by then – had run out of money. The second volume appeared in 1984 – just. In a desperate attempt to raise money – so much for the presumption he'd retired into affluence – he arranged for the sale of the four most valuable books in his library, including a mint edition of a seventeenth-century work, William Vaughan's *Golden Fleece*, for $16,000. As he had in the 1930s with his first *Encyclopedia of Newfoundland*, he toured the outports in a van selling individual copies. Eventually, a charitable foundation, with the actor Gordon Pinsent as honorary chairman, raised enough money to allow the project to continue. The third volume appeared in 1991, shortly before his death, and the fourth and fifth volumes posthumously in 1993 and 1994. The reviews of the volumes were quite laudatory. With the solicitude of age, Horwood, his old opponent, wrote: "There was a terrible purity in this last public action, in his willingness, at the end, not to accept the comforts of honours and adulation but to extend himself to the limit, to sacrifice everything, not only his worldly wealth of which he had accumulated a modest bit, but even his dignity, such as it was, to this all-important task."

There were comforts in his old age. Old friends, whom once he'd smothered and overwhelmed and just plain exhausted, now found they could actually talk to him. The handshake back across the years that mattered by far the most to Smallwood was extended by Greg Power, the ablest and wittiest (and most cynical) of his old praetorian guard; after a rupture of a quarter-century, they again became the closest of friends, scoring verbal points off each other with mutual delight. He also began to discover his grandchildren, becoming especially close to his granddaughter Dale Russell Fitzpatrick, who managed the foundation for the encyclopedia.

Fate was not kind to him. On September 24, 1984, Smallwood, who had had only one operation in his entire life and who had missed work for only a handful of days for causes such as flu, suffered a cerebral hemorrhage. He lived for another seven years, but the stroke robbed him permanently of the ability to read or write or utter more than a few brief phrases. He spent his time watching television or listening to the radio, sometimes urging on the workers on the encyclopedia, and making the occasional, faltering public appearance to try to raise more funds. He was too frail, in December 1986, to travel to Ottawa for his induction as a Companion of the Order of Canada.

The end came, peacefully, in his sleep, on December 19, 1991. His funeral, three days later, following a lying in state in the porticoed Colonial Building, the old legislature where he had begun his campaign for Confederation, was the largest in Newfoundland's history. The crowd of mourners, twelve hundred of them in the church alone, was so large that the service had to be held in the Catholic Basilica of St. John the Baptist, once the seat of his anti-Confederation opponent, Archbishop

Roche. Prime Minister Brian Mulroney, who flew down with dozens of other dignitaries, called him "the greatest Newfoundlander in the world."

His journey was done. But as a white whale, he ploughed on.

Smallwood's persistence as a political force for so long after he'd retired, even after he'd fallen completely silent, and even after his death, is comparatively easy to explain.

It is partly circumstantial. Many of the members of the "Kiddies Corner" whom he had recruited into his government in the early 1960s, extravagantly young themselves then and impossibly young in relation to him, reached their political prime long after he had at last stepped aside for them. Well into the mid-1990s, opposition members in the legislature would regularly taunt the then premier, Clyde Wells, and Ed Roberts, returned to politics as minister of justice, for their old association with Smallwood. Outside the legislature, John Crosbie, the holder of a succession of senior portfolios in Ottawa, culminating in the poisoned chalice of the fisheries, seldom missed a chance to even verbal scores with his old opponent. The first entirely "Smallwood-free" government didn't take office until Brian Tobin's election victory in 1995. No political genealogist was required, however, to trace the source of Tobin's rhetorical rhythms or his instinct for the bold, fate-defying gesture, like the seizure of the Spanish trawler *Estai*.

The substantive cause is that most of the overarching issues that confront Newfoundlanders today are exactly the same ones Smallwood struggled with. First and most exigent is the collapse of the cod fishery. Once Smallwood had tried to drag Newfoundlanders away from the sea with his battle cry, "Burn Your Boats." Now the sea was taken away from them. The reasons were multiple – overfishing (local as well as foreign), governmental mismanagement (federal and provincial), the outpacing by technology of the conservation regulations, and even of the understanding of conservation. Some of the causes seemed to be unfathomable, and perhaps were: unusual coldness of the water, changes in currents and feeding patterns, or just a mysterious transformation of a once-abundant ocean into an underwater desert. Federal programs, like TAGS, softened the blow of the loss of jobs for some thirty thousand fishermen, for a time at least. Nothing could soften the psychic blow of the loss of the fishery itself. Next, resettlement, not a government-sponsored evacuation of selected outports this time, as with Smallwood in the early 1960s, but their random hollowing out from within as the young moved to distant jobs and the old moved to escape loneliness and the memory of defeat. As always there were the issues of the terms and conditions, and of the opportunities and temptations, for the development of the province's resources. This was most spectacularly so in the instance of the huge nickel deposit at Voisey's Bay in Labrador and – most intimately connected to Smallwood in the instance of the hydro-electric power of the Lower Churchill Falls – the leftover of the giant project that he had bluffed and bullied into existence, and then, right afterwards, had bartered away to Hydro-Québec.

Above all, there was the fact that Newfoundlanders should now be confronting, this time directly, the nightmarish threat that once prompted Smallwood to his near-hysterical "Let the welkin ring" attempts at instant industrialization back in the early 1950s. This is the challenge of depopulation, and thus the challenge of societal demoralization. In the 1996 census, Newfoundland's population dropped, for the first time in its history, to 565,000 from 580,000 in 1991. (The only Canadian precedent is Saskatchewan.) A plummeting birthrate, now the lowest in the country, is a secondary factor. The defining one is that with the cod fishery closed and with unemployment insurance reformed, and so closer to an actual insurance scheme, the outports can no longer absorb the society's perpetual surplus of labour (not far short of one in five perpetually unemployed, even in boom times). The outflow is self-reinforcing. As people – always the young – leave the outports, they both provide a kind of advance camp that makes it easier for others to join them, and, by going, they diminish the local tax base, diminishing more importantly each community's human resources and spirit, making it harder for others to hang on. A projection by the Atlantic Institute of Market Studies forecasts that by 2036, the province's population may contract to 430,000, one-fifth less than its level in the 1990s.

In his 1973 memoir, Smallwood seemed to harbour a premonition that this kind of trauma might face his people. Near the book's close, he wrote: "We are so far removed from the corridors of power, so far from the massed population and power of Canada, so far from the main Canadian market, so out of the minds of Canada's principal captains of industry and finance, that we can easily be wasted down the drain. Never say die. Never give in. Turn a deaf ear to the timid and faithless. And, if the very fates defeat us, go down not with a whimper but defiantly to the end." Contemporary political rhetoric is much more modulated and ironic. But there's not a Newfoundlander who wouldn't understand and cheer on his battle cry.

Had Smallwood spoken out while he still could, he wouldn't have had anything especially original and insightful to say about his people's contemporary problems. Indeed, on developing the Lower Churchill Falls his only advice could have been "Don't do as I did." But he had been there, had done all of it, or had tried to. He was like a ghostly presence at a feast, a feast that he himself had created. This felt, unexpressed contribution came through most strongly in the debate that broke out in Newfoundland in the 1980s, and continues today, about what might have happened differently at the time the society entered Confederation. This debate isn't about separation. It's about Newfoundland's proper place within Confederation.

The driving motive for the debate is the attempt to come to terms with the fact that Newfoundland, uniquely in the history of nation-states, gave up independence voluntarily after having first achieved it. Some historians, like John Fitzgerald, have dug into the archives in search of proof that Newfoundlanders didn't really do this, that instead Whitehall did it to them by rigging the votes, in favour of Confederation, in the second referendum. (This is also the theme of the film *The Secret Nation*.) Not a scrap of concrete evidence exists to justify this thesis. There's no doubt, though, that Britain did all it could to manoeuvre Newfoundlanders into the arms of Canada and out of its own impecunious hands. An argument often heard in St. John's these days is that before entering Confederation, Newfoundland should first have regained the self-government it gave up in 1933. This wouldn't necessarily have improved the terms of confederation, goes the argument, but it would have cancelled out the defeat that Newfoundlanders had inflicted upon them and also inflicted upon themselves when, in 1933, they become the only people in history to voluntarily give up self-government after having won it. This proposition isn't academic. It's an attempt to heal the psychic wound, a gnawing at self-esteem that lingers on in the collective memory of Newfoundlanders because of that act of national surrender. The counter-argument is essentially that the needs of individual Newfoundlanders mattered more, and still do, than those of the collectivity.

The best contemporary expression of this view was provided by Ed Roberts in a 1997 speech to the Newfoundland Historical Society: What Confederation did, said Roberts, was to relieve Newfoundlanders of "the awful burden of history," of poverty and isolation and backwardness. The best counter-argument of all was provided a half-century earlier by Smallwood himself. His "We Are Not a Nation" speech of October 27, 1946, in which he introduced the notion of Confederation to the National Convention, was the finest of his career: "We love this land. It has a charm, it warms our hearts, go where we will, a mystical tug on our emotions that never dies. . . . [But] we are so used to our ways that we do not even see their inadequacy, their backwardness. We take for granted our lower standards. We are not indignant about them, we save our indignation for those who publish such facts." The revisionists, proud and fiercely patriotic though they may be, can never escape the white whale.

Smallwood's role as a presence in Newfoundland's artistic imagination is much more equivocal; indeed, it is downright contradictory. When the first serious opposition to him began to be expressed in the mid-1960s, it was voiced most loudly by artists.

Nevertheless, it is in that decade that the connection begins. If there was any single catalyst for the extraordinary explosion of creativity in Newfoundland – "Flowers on the rock" in the phrase of its chronicler,

Newfoundland-born social historian Sandra Fraser Gwyn – it was the consequence of the rage and despair of that emerging new generation of the sixties at witnessing their heritage and their society's very reason for existing being destroyed, as they saw it, by Smallwood's program of forced resettlement. In fact, their anger was exaggerated. The great majority of those given subsidies to move were delighted to be brought within reach of hospitals, schools, power, paved roads. Moreover, the population of the outports actually *increased* during the 1970s and 1980s as ever-more-generous unemployment insurance payments ($1.60 in payments for each $1 actually earned in the fishery) and ever-larger government subsidies made it possible for more people to remain where they were and for others to join them.

Regardless, artists found in resettlement a cause that connected them to their society as a whole, and most especially – most artists and professionals were St. John's "townies" – connected them to outport Newfoundland. The irony in the connection is obvious. Resettlement *from* rural Newfoundland connected urban artists *to* rural Newfoundland, that is to Smallwood's Newfoundland. The quality that defines Newfoundland artists is their overpowering sense of place, which in turn gives them the particular self-confidence that comes from knowing that they and their audience are one. St. John's townies most certainly have a sense of place about that antic, effervescent city. But that Newfoundland artists should have a sense of place about their whole society and whole island they owe in part, in an almost absurd paradox, to their old enemy Smallwood.

There are two other reasons, more subtle and more potent, why Smallwood remains a force in the Newfoundland artistic imagination, even if seldom recognized and even more rarely admitted.

Smallwood was the first Newfoundlander to be noticed by the world outside. His external image was alternately shiny and dark: He was a visionary and a dictator, an orator and a clown, a hero and a villain. But he was noticed. For about three decades, so far as vast numbers of people outside the place were concerned, Smallwood *was* Newfoundland. He made people pay attention to Newfoundland, something no one had done for five hundred years. And he did this while himself living in Newfoundland.

That torch has now been taken over by Newfoundland's artists. To many people both within and outside the island, their songs and writings and paintings *are* Newfoundland. Most still live in Newfoundland, as Smallwood did, or, if in exile, remain attached to it as if by an umbilical cord. In the end, their sense of place is no different from his.

The principal connection between Smallwood and Newfoundland's artists, individual egos and abilities aside, is the mission they share: the survival of the unique, fragile society that is Newfoundland. To that task, Smallwood brought raw power and bluff and exaggeration and guileful raids upon the federal treasury. The contribution of the artists is to hold up a mirror to their society and to the outside world. Their intellectual and moral mentor, the late George Story, compiler of the epic 1982 *Dictionary of Newfoundland English*, once defined their mission: "It is our creative ability that ensures our survival as a recognizable people and culture and enables us to contribute to the enrichment of the nation of which we form a distinctive part."

When Smallwood began blazing the trail, the outlook ahead of him couldn't have been bleaker. Outside of perhaps Appalachia, Newfoundland was the only part of North America that was truly, remorselessly poor. As soon as it had made its bid to escape poverty by joining Canada it risked, as he put it, "being de-nuded of our population."

Today's outlook is almost as bleak. The closure of the cod fishery has struck deep at the society's psyche. While the fishery is no longer of great importance economically, it is, psychologically, the society's organizing principle, "Newfoundland's DNA" in Rex Murphy's memorable phrase. Even after the moratorium ends, some time past the millennium, the cod fishery will never come back in the same way. Some wonder if it will ever come back at all. In his 1997 study, *Lament for an Ocean*, Michael Harris quotes the remark of National Sea Products executive Henry Demone that the inshore, small boat fishermen, the *real* fishermen of Newfoundland, may be "the last of the buffalo hunters." Other events have magnified the bruises to the society's psyche: the disclosure of mass sexual abuse by Christian Brothers at Mount Cashel orphanage, a violation of the trust that knits together this small society; and the international campaign against the seal harvest that has depicted Newfoundlanders as coarse, blood-stained brutes. Then there's the trauma of the outflow of population.

It would be a gross exaggeration to describe the artists, literary and visual, print and electronic, as a kind of thin red line guarding Newfoundland's survival. Significant recuperative forces are at work – a sudden respect for education, a small but burgeoning high-tech industry, new types of value-added fishing (fresh sea urchins for Japan, for example) so that the fishery's export value is actually higher now than before the moratorium. The society's new mood was well expressed by inshore fishermen's leader Cabot Martin: "We have for far too long blamed the weather or location or others for our problems. It's about time we took a long, hard look at the mirror." That attitude is the culmination of the ethic of self-responsibility, and of an end to deference, that "Started in Burgeo" at the end of the 1960s, as described in Chapter 26 in the original edition. The specific contribution of Newfoundland's artists to this rebirth is that, as Smallwood once did, they are pursuing excellence, *there*.

The last paragraph of the original text ended this way: "He leaves to his successors a society that is vibrant and dynamic, full of problems still but full also of possibilities. His imperishable achievement was to give his people the self-confidence to 'seek human excellence.' The generation of Newfoundlanders that defeated him are the beneficiaries of his life's work. Their achievements will be his memorial." Just one addition needs to be made. A quarter-century on, Smallwood's memorial can be found in the astonishing productivity of Newfoundland's artists on paper, on canvas, on film, in videos, in song and play and novel, and in sculpture and painting and photography. Where once he stood, they stand.

Index

McLean, Neil, 92, 119

McLintock, A. H., 26, 78

McNair, John Babbitt, 225-26

McNair Commission, 225-27

McParland, Donald J., 331

Meighen, Arthur, 261

Memorial University, 155, 216, 229, 236, 238, 264, 269, 284, 336, 338, 353, 369, 373-78

Mercer, Rick, 435

Methodist College Literary Institute, 42, 85

Miag Machinenbau Gesellschaft, 176, 197-98, 200

Minto, Lord, 322

Miskins, Gregory, 173

Moaser and Sons, Hamburg, 188

Monitor, The, 130-32

Moore, T. Ross, 244

Moores, Dorothy, 422-23

Moores, Frank, 346, 350, 363-64, 394, 396, 397n, 404, 409-11, 413-14, 416-17, 422-27, 430, 438

Morell, E. D., 10

Morgan, Bernice, 435

Morgan, Major C. W. F., 17, 19

Morgan, M. O., 375

Morgan, Pam, 435

Morrison, Herbert, 374-75

Morse, Wayne, 123

Moss, Wilfrid, 257, 259

Mowat, Farley, 280, 390

Mullowney, Tony, 84, 86, 89, 91

Mulroney, Brian, 442

Munsinger, Gerda, 305

Murphy, Noel, 396, 397n

Murphy, Rex, 336, 435, 447

Musgrave, Sir Anthony, 77

N. M. Rothschild and Sons, 188

NAFEL, 139

National Film Board, 377

Neary, Peter, 368, 386

Neary, Steve, 368

Neue Technique Corporation, 182

Newfie Bullet, 91, 354, 359

Newfoundland and Labrador Corporation (NALCO), 185-87, 189-93, 293-94, 304

Newfoundland Brotherhood of Wood Workers, 249-50, 264-65

Newfoundland Commission of Government (1933-48), 56-57, 67, 70-71, 100, 102, 126, 136-37

Newfoundland Constabulary, 255-57

Newfoundland Co-operative Union, 157-59

Newfoundland Democratic Party, 266, 286

Newfoundland Department of Economic Development, 155, 167

Newfoundland Department of Fisheries and Co-operatives, 155, 157

Newfoundland Federation of Fishermen, 157-59, 369

Newfoundland Federation of Labour, 252, 267, 283

Newfoundland Fishermen, Food and Allied Workers, 370

Newfoundland Fishermen's Union, 366, 368-70, 417, 421

Newfoundland Housing Corporation, 155

Newfoundland Hydro-Electric Commission, 155

Newfoundland Labour Code, 156